Hegel's Idealism

Hegel's Idealism

The Satisfactions of Self-Consciousness

ROBERT B. PIPPIN
Department of Philosophy, University of California, San Diego

PUBLISHED BY THE PRESS SYNDICATE OF THE UNIVERSITY OF CAMBRIDGE
The Pitt Building, Trumpington Street, Cambridge, United Kingdom

CAMBRIDGE UNIVERSITY PRESS
The Edinburgh Building, Cambridge CB2 2RU, UK http://www.cup.cam.ac.uk
40 West 20th Street, New York, NY 10011-4211, USA http://www.cup.org
10 Stamford Road, Oakleigh, Melbourne 3166, Australia

First published 1989
Reprinted 1993, 1995, 1999

A catalogue record for this book is available from the British Library

Library of Congress Cataloguing-in-Publication data is available

ISBN 0 521 37923 7 paperback

Transferred to digital printing 2001

FOR JOAN

Contents

Acknowledgments

I would like to express my gratitude to the following institutions: to the National Endowment for the Humanities, for an Independent Study and Research Grant that freed me from teaching and administrative duties in 1984–5 and made possible much of the work on this book; to the Earhart Foundation for a summer grant in 1983 that greatly aided the writing of an early version of Chapter 7; to the University of California, San Diego, for a sabbatical; and to the UCSD Committee on Research for various word-processing and travel grants. An early version of part of Chapter 2 was presented at the Sixth International Kant Congress and will be published in its *Proceedings*, and a version of Chapter 3 has appeared in the recent "Fichte" issue of *The Philosophical Forum* (vol. XIX, nos. 2–3, 1988). I am grateful to the editors of both for their permission to reprint here. I am also much indebted to Jay Bernstein, who read with generosity and much insight the penultimate draft of the manuscript, and to a number of individuals who offered valuable suggestions about sections of the manuscript or my general interpretation of Hegel. I am particularly grateful to Henry Allison for comments on the first three chapters and for several years of conversation about the issues raised in these sections; to H.S. Harris for various acts of assistance and support; and to Jerry Doppelt and Andrew Feenberg for hearing me out on any number of Hegelian topics and for offering criticisms and suggestions. Finally, I owe more than can be expressed to my wife, Joan, for her help, understanding, and wit throughout the long period of this book's composition.

Primary texts abbreviations

FICHTE

SK = *The Science of Knowledge. With the First and Second Introductions*, trans. P. Heath and J. Lachs. Cambridge: Cambridge University Press, 1982.

Werke = *Gesamtausgabe der Bayerischen Akademie der Wissenschaften*, ed. R. Lauth and H. Jacob. Stuttgart: Frommann, 1965.

WL = *Grundlage der gesamten Wissenschaftslehre* (1794), in *Werke*, I, 4.

KANT

AA = *Gesammelte Schriften*, ed. Königlich Preussischen Akademie der Wissenschaften. Berlin and Leipzig: de Gruyter, 1922.

A/B = *Kritik der reinen Vernunft*, ed. R. Schmidt. Hamburg: Felix Meiner, 1954.

= *Critique of Pure Reason*, trans. N. Kemp Smith. New York: St. Martin's Press, 1929.

CJ = *Kant's Critique of Judgment*, trans. J. Meredith. Oxford: Clarendon Press, 1952.

HEGEL

B = *Briefe von und an Hegel*, ed. J. Hoffmeister and R. Flechsig, 4 vols., Hamburg: Felix Meiner, 1961.

BK = *Faith and Knowledge*, trans. W. Cerf and H.S. Harris. Albany, N.Y.: SUNY Press, 1977.

BPhG = *G.W.F. Hegel: The Berlin Phenomenology*, trans. M. Petry. Dordrecht: Riedel.

Diff = *The Difference Between Fichte's and Schelling's System of Philosophy*, trans. H. Harris and W. Cerf. Albany, N.Y.: SUNY Press, 1977.

DS = *Differenz des Fichte'schen und Schelling'schen Systems der Philosophie*. *GWe*, IV, 1–92.

E = *Enzyklopädie der philosophischen Wissenschaften im Grundrisse* (1830), ed. F. Nicolin and O. Pöggeler. Hamburg: Felix Meiner, 1969.

EGPh = *Einleitung in die Geschichte der Philosophie*, ed. J. Hoffmeister. Hamburg: Nicolin, 1959.

PRIMARY TEXTS ABBREVIATIONS

EL = *Die Wissenschaft der Logik. Erster Teil, Enzyklopädie der philosophischen Wissenschaften. SuW*, vol. 8.

EnL = *Hegel's Logic. Part One of the Encyclopedia of the Philosophical Sciences*, trans. W. Wallace. Oxford: Clarendon Press, 1975.

FPS = *First Philosophy of Spirit* in *G.W.F. Hegel, System of Ethical Life and First Philosophy of Spirit*, ed. and trans. H.S. Harris and T.M. Knox. Albany, N.Y.: SUNY Press, 1979.

GW = *Glauben und Wissen. GWe*, IV, 313–414.

GWe = *Gesammelte Werke*, ed. Rheinisch-Westfaelischen Akademie der Wissenschaften. Hamburg: Felix Meiner, 1968ff.

JA = *Sämtliche Werke. Jubiliäumausgabe in zwanzig Bänden*, ed. H. Glockner. Stuttgart: Frommann, 1968.

JS = 1804–5 *Jenaer Systementwürfe II. Logik, Metaphysik, Naturphilosophie. GWe*, vol. 7.

L = *Hegel: The Letters*, trans. C. Butler and C. Seiler. Bloomington: Indiana University Press, 1984.

LM = *G.W.F. Hegel. The Jena System, 1804–5. Logic and Metaphysics*, translation ed. by J.W. Burbidge and G. di Giovanni. Kingston and Montreal: McGill-Queen's University Press, 1986.

PG = 1803–4 *Philosophie des Geistes. GWe*, vol. 6, 265–326.

PGII = 1805–6 *Jenaer Systementwürfe III. Philosophie des Geistes. GWe*, vol. 8, 185–288.

PhG = *Phänomenologie des Geistes. GWe*, vol. IX.

PhR = *Hegel's Philosophy of Right*, trans. T. Knox. Oxford: Clarendon Press, 1952.

PM = *Hegel's Philosophy of Mind*, trans. W. Wallace and A. Miller. Oxford: Clarendon Press, 1971.

PN = *Hegel's Philosophy of Nature*, trans. A. Miller. Oxford: Clarendon Press, 1971.

PR = *Grundlinien der Philosophie des Rechts*. Hamburg: Felix Meiner, 1957.

PS = *Phenomenology of Spirit*, trans. A.V. Miller. Oxford: Clarendon Press, 1977.

RPS = "Relationship of Scepticism to Philosophy, Exposition of Its Different Modifications and Comparison to the Latest Form with the Ancient One," trans. H. Harris, in *Between Kant and Hegel*, trans. G. di-Giovanni and H. Harris. Albany, N.Y.: SUNY Press, 1985.

SL = *Hegel's Science of Logic*, trans. A.V. Miller. London: George Allen & Unwin.

SS = *System der Sittlichkeit*, ed. G. Lasson. Hamburg: Felix Meiner, 1967.

SuW = *Werke*, ed. E. Moldenhauer and K. Michel, 20 vols. Frankfurt, Suhrkamp, 1970–1. (Theorie Werkausgabe.)

Sys = *System of Ethical Life* in *G.W.F. Hegel, System of Ethical Life and First Philosophy of Spirit*, ed. and trans. H.S. Harris and T.M. Knox. Albany, N.Y.: SUNY Press, 1979.

TJ = *Theologische Jugendschriften*, ed. H. Nohl. Tübingen: Mohr, 1968.

TW = *Early Theological Writing*, trans. T.M. Knox. Philadelphia: University of Pennsylvania Press, 1971.

WL = *Wissenschaft der Logik*, Bds. I and II. Hamburg: Felix Meiner, 1969.

SCHELLING

STI = *System der transzendentalen Idealismus*. Hamburg: Felix Meiner, 1962.

SW = *Sämtliche Werke*, 14 vols. Stuttgart and Augsburg: J.G. Cotta'scher, 1856–61.

I
The idealist background

1
Introduction

The "Hegelian aftermath," as a recent book calls it,[1] involves a puzzling irony. Simply stated, Hegel seems to be in the impossible position of being both extraordinarily influential and almost completely inaccessible. On the one hand, there is Hegel's enormous philosophic and historical influence. Although an arguable claim, it is not unreasonable to assert that much of what current academic practice categorizes as "contemporary European philosophy" begins with and is largely determined by Hegel. For the most part, this influence has to do with Hegel's introduction of the problem of "historical subjectivity" into that tradition, and the way in which his account of that issue decisively altered the traditional understanding of a wide variety of philosophical issues. What before Hegel might have seemed, unproblematically, to be an empirical fact or a conceptual truth or a moral claim now seemed to many distinctly *historical* phenomena – products, in some way, of the activity of human "spirit" – and so to require a very untraditional account. Moreover, even when he was violently opposed, it was Hegel who seemed to set the agenda, and even when he was ignored or held in contempt, his shadow stretched across various debates in ways often not recognized. And, of course, the mere mention of the name of Marx is sufficient to summarize Hegel's most visible influence on world history.

And yet, on the other hand, Hegel seems to have convinced or enraged so many intellectual luminaries without the existence of anything remotely resembling a consensus about the basic position of Hegelian philosophy. Hegel is one of the most lionized and most vilified philosophers of history, at the same time that it is widely believed that no one really knows what he was talking about.[2]

To be sure, there are well-known textbook formulations of Hegel's basic position. It is clear enough that the thesis of Hegelian philosophy centrally involves some claim about what Hegel calls the "self-actualization of the Notion," a progression fully and finally "realized" in the "identity of Notion and reality," or in the "Absolute Idea," that Hegel believes "reality" *is* the Absolute Idea. But throughout the history of Hegelianism, such a claim has inspired a tradition of commentary often more opaque than the original texts, and there is so much controversy about what such claims mean that there is virtually no consensus about how they might be defended against objections or philosophically legitimated.

Such ambiguity and philosophical confusion are especially obvious in those commentators who treat Hegel as an idiosyncratic Christian, romantic metaphysician, a "world-soul," or a "cosmic spirit" theologian (some of the German literature refers to Hegel's "onto-theological metaphysics").[3] Such interpretations vary widely, depending on how traditional a romantic or Christian one finds Hegel, but the essential point of the "metaphysical" Hegel has always been that Hegel should be understood as a kind of inverted Spinozist, that is, a monist, who believed that finite objects did not "really" exist (only the Absolute Idea exists), that this One was not a "substance" but a "subject," or mental (hence the inversion of Spinoza), and that it was not a static, eternal, Parmenidean One, but developed in time, a development somehow responsible for the shape and direction of human political history, as well as the history of art, religion, and philosophy (all such shapes of Spirit express the unfolding of the Absolute Idea).[4] And such development was, supposedly, philosophically intelligible only by transcending the limitations of standard "reflective" logic and embracing a "dialectical" logic, a logic of Heraclitean flux, even of "contradiction." This is, roughly, the textbook version of Hegel's core position, the Hegel widely taught to undergraduates, and the one that usually comes to mind among philosophers, historians, Marxist theorists, literary critics, and so forth (and, often enough, Hegel specialists) when his name is mentioned.[5]

If, however, such a metaphysical monist or speculative, contradiction-embracing logician is the "real" Hegel, it is not the historically influential Hegel. Indeed, it was the profound obscurity of this standard view that drove so many to the more manageable "edges" of Hegel's vast system, and it is there, in many of Hegel's conclusions, rather than in the speculative arguments used to support those conclusions, that Hegel's real influence lies. Without any systematic attempt to rely on the incredibly opaque details of the *Science of Logic* to understand Hegel's full or "real" position, his claims about the historical character of human spirit, about the social nature of self-consciousness, about the alienation and fragmentation of modern society, about the limitations of the "moral point of view," about the modern nation state, or even some aspects of his general antifoundationalist holism, can all be discussed more manageably, in their own right, as independently valuable insights.

Usually the central text in such revisionist accounts is the 1807 *Phenomenology of Spirit*, and the position extracted is some form of philosophical anthropology and/or social theory, whether of a proto-existentialist, historicist, Marxist, or Heideggerean variety (or, in the case of Kojève, all of the above[6]). Hegel's *Lectures on Aesthetics* and *Philosophy of Right* are also leading candidates for a similar approach, one that gestures toward the official Hegelian claim about the indispensability of the speculative position but that attempts to make no real use of that position in its reconstruction of a more contemporary, accessible Hegel.[7]

Thus we have the wide array of current positions on Hegel resulting from this "reception" problem: For many, Hegel is a speculative metaphysician and a failure, either an interesting failure, representative of the failure of philosophy itself (a view started by Kierkegaard and still quite influential in France), or simply a dismal failure, representative only of Teutonic smoke, self-indulgent excess, and the ugliest prose style in the history of the German language. For others, he is a speculative metaphysician of great note, although one whose system is too unusual and radical to be presented in normal, discursive language, and so is resistant, even hostile, to the normal traditions of philosophic commentary. For still others (indeed, most contemporary commentators), he is an extraordinarily uneven philosopher whose analysis of the modern world, or whose ethical, political, or aesthetic philosophy, or whose imaginative, dialectical category analysis, or perhaps whose "method" is invaluable, but whose speculative core is hopeless.

As already indicated, the motivation for both approaches, particularly the latter, is obvious. Hegel's supposedly romantic, spirit monism and the self-moving, speculative logic that goes along with it are so philosophically obscure, and yet so much of what he has to say about the last moments of the Western rationalist tradition in philosophy, and about the unique kinds of problems faced by modern scientific, cultural, moral, and political institutions is so suggestive, that one would indeed want some way to discuss all the latter without the former. On the other hand, merely extracting a conclusion from Hegel, and then reconstructing a way of understanding it and arguing for it that bears little resemblance to Hegel, can easily be a pointless exercise – pointless, that is, if one expects to learn anything from Hegel, if one tries to think along with him. But *that* kind of admission just seems to readmit one to the World of Romantic Metaphysics, with its self-posing Divine Mind ejecting the moments of Spirit's history and the determinations of the natural world.

These alternatives, opting either for the "historical spirit" Hegel or the "systematic," metaphysical Hegel, are familiar ones by now, just as familiar as the problems inherent in each approach.[8] The metaphysical Hegel looks like some premodern anachronism (or totalitarian bogeyman in some versions), and accounts of Hegel's political and social theory cannot be said, finally, to be genuinely Hegelian without some reliance on the speculative system. Obviously, such an interpretive dilemma could be solved if it could be shown that Hegel's speculative position, basically his theory of the Absolute Idea, his claim that such an Idea alone is "what truly is," could be interpreted and defended in a way that is not committed to a philosophically problematic theological metaphysics. Such an interpretation would deny that the metaphysical position defended by the "right" or Christian Hegelians and scorned by the "left" or revisionist school represents the speculative position Hegel meant to defend, the position that his philosophical anthropology and political philosophy do indeed depend on. In recent years, there has been considerable interest in such a speculative but "nonmetaphysical" Hegel (where "metaphysics" is understood traditionally as a priori knowledge of substance). Some of that interest originates in so-called Hegelian Marxism or from those elements in such a critical theory that take seriously the dependence of Hegel's social analysis on his speculative logic but reject the "mystifying theologian" caricature of the speculative Hegel long prominent in the official Marxist tradition.[9] Much of that interest has been generated by commentators committed to showing that Hegel's speculative logic is a "category theory" with no substantive metaphysical commitments.[10] In this book, I also propose to defend a nonmetaphysical interpretation of Hegel, but one that does not see Hegel as primarily a philosopher of social change or as a category theorist. Put most simply, I want to understand Hegel's speculative philosophy as an "idealism."

At first glance, of course, such a suggestion seems obvious and quite unhelpful. Clearly, Hegel is an idealist (he called himself an "absolute idealist").[11] What else could his claims about the reality of the Absolute Idea, that all objects are "in truth" the Notion, that the traditional dualism of subject and object had been overcome, that Substance had been thought as "Subject," and so forth, mean? Moreover, to the extent that treating Hegel as an idealist does not just restate all the obscurities of his position, it gets us nowhere, since Hegel uses the term "idealism" so loosely that he characterizes *all* philosophy worthy of the name as idealism.[12]

But I have a much more specific sense of idealism in mind, although again it is a sense that appears initially unhelpful. Simply put, I propose to take Hegel at his word when he tells us, in an early work, that it was the argument of Kant's Transcendental Deduction that first came close to and made possible the speculative identity theory he ultimately created,[13] and, in a later work, that his own theory of the Notion, and indeed the relation between the Notion and reality, or the basic position of his entire philosophy, should be understood as a direct variation on a crucial Kantian theme, the "transcendental unity of apperception."[14] I shall claim that these and many other references to Kant's critical idealism are indispensable for a proper understanding of Hegel's position, and that they point to the basic Kantian issue that clarifies the important ways in which Hegel's position extends and deepens Kantian antiempiricist, antinaturalist, antirationalist strategies. That issue, as Hegel again tells us, is the apperception theme, Kant's claim about the "self-conscious," ultimately the "spontaneously" self-conscious, character of all possible human experience.

It might appear that adding "Kantian" to the idealist categorization of Hegel is again either unhelpful or misleading, unhelpful because it is obvious that Hegel relies everywhere on Kant's case for the "constitutive" role of the subject in experience, his denial of the possibility of a foundational "immediacy" in experience, and on Kant's demonstration of the "antinomial" results of traditional, reflective philosophy, but misleading because Hegel so obviously rejects, even scorns so much of Kant, ridiculing his "thing in itself" skepticism and in general his "merely finite" idealism, and transforms the Kantian transcendental subject into an Absolute Subject or Divine Mind, leaving Kantianism well behind. But such standard views of the much discussed Kant–Hegel relation do not, I shall argue, take into sufficient account the numerous details of Hegel's appropriation and do not follow through sufficiently on the issue of how Hegel's appropriation decisively influences his later formulations and so provides for a far different reading of these formulations (and of his frequent, odd use of the language of Christian theology) than is standard.[15]

Again, this is particularly true of the apperception or self-consciousness theme, the one Hegel points to as the key to his relation to Kant. Indeed, as I shall also try to show, it was not just Hegel who relied so heavily on what Kant called the "supreme" condition of human knowledge. The two other important German idealists, Fichte and Schelling, referred often and reverently to this Kantian origin and, in different ways than Hegel, tried to work out the implications of the claim that all human thought and action is "self-reflexive." Thus, to understand Hegel not just as a successor to Kant, but as a so-called German idealist, means to understand not only how he understood Kant, but how he agreed and disagreed with his contemporaries' reading of Kant on the issue that all of them believed defined their project, what they all took quickly to calling, in ways that sound very strange to contemporary ears, the "freedom" of consciousness itself.

To be sure, this whole complex of common issues—the Deduction, spontaneity, apperception, freedom—are not themselves easily appropriated in an attempt to interpret Hegel's idealism. They cannot at all be taken to mean what they seem to mean in a contemporary context and, indeed, as used by these figures, they can certainly be as obscure as any technical term of art in Hegel. To make use of them at all will require some explanation of their original meaning in Kant; some explanation of their extended meaning in Fichte, Schelling, and Hegel; and some assessment of whether those extensions are responsive to genuine deficiencies in Kant's position, all with the hope that there is some philosophically useful payoff in reading Hegel so intensely in the light of Kant's actual project.

More to the general and more obvious point, however, much of the standard view of how Hegel passes beyond Kant into speculative philosophy makes very puzzling, to the point of unintelligibility, how Hegel could have been the post-Kantian philosopher he understood himself to be; that is, how he could have accepted, as he did, Kant's revelations about the fundamental inadequacies of the metaphysical tradition, could have enthusiastically agreed with Kant that the metaphysics of the "beyond," of substance, and of traditional views of God and infinity were forever discredited, and then could have promptly created a systematic metaphysics as if he had never heard of Kant's critical epistemology. Just attributing moderate philosophic intelligence to Hegel should at least make one hesitate before construing him as a post-Kantian philosopher with a precritical metaphysics.

Although the results of reading Hegel as, to quote him, "completing" Kant[16] are, I shall try to show, quite complex, such a Kantian focus does immediately and straightforwardly isolate a complex of specific issues in Hegel as basic to his project. Most of Hegel's significant revisions of Kant involve his transformation of Kant's theory of *concepts*, his reinterpretation of Kant's account of the *objectivity* of concepts, and his different treatment of the notion of *subjectivity* relevant to an idealist version of such issues. To a large extent, their common theme involves the argument that any subject must be able to make certain basic discriminations in any experience in order for there to be experience at all. Accordingly, such basic conceptual discriminations cannot be derived from experience and, if it can be shown that such distinctions are constitutive of the possibility of experience, cannot be refuted by experience. They thus agree that, contrary to the rationalist tradition, human reason can attain nonempirical knowledge only *about itself*, about what has come to be called recently our "conceptual scheme," and the concepts required for a scheme to count as one at all. Hegel, to be sure, makes use of a far more expansive and dramatic language in describing Kant's "self-legislation by Reason." His talk is about thought's "infinite self-relation," its "freedom" or complete autonomy, but, as we shall see, Kant and Hegel continue to share a common problematic: a search for those aspects of a conceptual scheme without which there could not be a scheme, and so could not be objects discriminated by that scheme. More to the point of the topic previously introduced, they share a common rationale when defending this claim. They both rely heavily on the ineliminably reflexive or apperceptive nature of any possible experience in making the case for the necessity of such nonempirically based discriminatory capacities (concepts). It is this requirement that provides their common base in rejecting both empiricist and naturalist accounts of such a scheme. For Hegel and his idealist colleagues it is the issue that leads to their most important topic – "ground" – a natural enough topic to raise once the former two alternatives, and Kant's, are rejected. Once this is understood, their agreements and disagreements about the consequences of such an apperceptive principle, especially for their theory of concepts, will, I think, be easier to see.

Hegel's revisions of the Kantian account of the *objective validity* of such pure concepts involve the more notorious aspects of his speculative logic, since Hegel interprets the problem in terms of the Schellingean language of the "identity within difference of subject and object." But that position too can be best understood by trying to understand how it emerges from Hegel's concrete difficulties with Kant's position. For Kant believed that there were any number of "logically possible" ways to "unify a manifold synthetically" or to "conceptually determine" the given, that it was not self-contradictory to conceive of all possible objects as substances and attributes, causes and effects, minds and bodies, or in terms of an infinite being and finite beings. The only way of distinguishing between the logically possible and the a priori "really" possible, those discriminations objectively valid of the extraconceptual, was by reliance on intuition, in the case of a priori knowledge, "pure intuitions." This is a complex doctrine that will be considered in the next chapter, but the result was that Kant thought he could justify claims about the validity of pure concepts *only* with respect to possible objects of human (finite, spatiotemporal) intuition, that all human knowledge was only "of appearances" or phenomena. For a variety of reasons that will be considered, Hegel rejected this reliance on pure intuition, and so rejected Kant's phenomenality restriction. (He, of course, did not reject the role of sensible received information in much human knowledge. What he objected to was the use to which Kant put the supposedly strict distinction between intuitions and concepts.) And it is at this point that Hegel departs most radically and most controversially from Kant. For it is with the denial that a firm distinction can ever be usefully drawn between intuitional and conceptual elements in knowledge that distinctly Hegelian idealism begins, and Hegel begins to take his peculiar flight, with language about the complete autonomy, even freedom of "thought's self-determination" and "self-actualization." (Indeed, it is with Hegel's, or rather Hegel's use of Fichte's, attack on the Kantian doctrine of intuition, together with his continued acceptance of Kant's idealist rejection of empiricism, that much of later Continental philosophy, with its antiempiricist, antipositivist thrust, from Schopenhauer, Nietzsche, Heidegger, Merleau-Ponty, Sartre, to structuralism and postmodernism, began. Without the Kantian "anchor" in intuitions, the Kantian subject is either not restricted by its finite intuitional forms, and so should be considered an Absolute Subject, or, given the perceived collapse of the Hegelian system, it cannot be considered a self-*objectifying* subject and so is merely empirical, or historical, or individual, or creative, self-interpreting, or "groundless" or, finally, not a subject at all, since it is not opposed to or constrained by anything.) Such a denial leads to Hegel's account of the "content" of concepts as fixed by their possible relations to other concepts (and not by a "transcendental schematism," another Kantian use of pure intuitions), his rejection of the claim that we do not know things in themselves and his extensive replacement of Kant's deduction of the objectivity of these concepts by his *Phenomenology of Spirit*. Predictably, it is this aspect of his position that requires the most extensive explanation to the "echt Kantianer" who wants to know how Hegel pulls off such a deduction without resort to the precritical notion of intellectual intuition. (Thus the formula for getting Hegel from Kant would be: Keep the doctrine of pure concepts and the account of apperception that helps justify the necessary presupposition of pure concepts, keep the critical problem of a proof for the objectivity of these concepts, the question that began critical philosophy, but abandon the doctrine of "pure sensible intuition," and the very possibility of a clear distinction between concept and intuition, and what is left is much of Hegel's enterprise.)[17]

It is an enterprise with an apparently impossible task ahead of it. For the preceding summary attributes to Hegel three claims, each of which is difficult enough to establish but which, prima facie, simply cannot be true collectively. First, there is the claim about nonempirical constraints on what could be a possible experience, pure concepts, or Hegel's "autonomous thought." Second, there is Hegel's denial that these are only conceptual forms, that they must be connected with intuitions to be objective; or his claim that such concepts *themselves* determine "actuality" (*Wirklichkeit*) as it is *in itself*. Third, there is the fact that Hegel accepts much of Kant's criticism of the"dogmatic" tradition, and in particular rejects a reliance on the classical notion of intellectual intuition. (He has his own version of that idea, but it certainly is not classical.) Clearly, if (3) were dropped, you could at least consistently try to maintain (1) and (2); you could be a rationalist of some stripe. If (1) were dropped, you could try for (2) and (3) with some version of empiricism, or even naturalist realism, all depending on what counted as "knowing what there really is." Or (2) could be dropped, and with (1) and (3) one could pursue some version of the Kantian program. However, with a roughly Kantian program, but without the Kantian concept/intuition distinction, and without the rationalist option of justifying a priori knowledge, what is left?

This is an important way to think of Hegel's project, because, as I shall try to show, the Kantian program (speaking loosely) is quite a powerful one, the rationalist option is foreclosed by it, and yet Kant's use of intuition *fails* in the Transcendental Deduction. It was Hegel who, in the early 1800s at Jena, began to see, with much greater clarity and scope than his colleagues, what all this amounted to, and drew out its implications boldly, imaginatively, sometimes in an extreme and indefensible way, but always "critically," never, I hope to show, by sliding into precritical claims about cosmic mind.

All of this raises some understandable suspicions. For one thing, such an approach to Hegel might seem so narrow as to be at best anachronistic, at worst simply to miss the point. The framework just outlined appears destined to be incapable of connecting the idealist Hegel, as so defined, with the famous Encyclopedic Hegel. The latter Hegel, the much more well-known historical Hegel, is the one who argued that Western intellectual, religious, and political history had achieved a grand, final synthesis, an ultimate *Aufhebung* or sublation of its prior incompleteness, the suprarationalist Hegel who wanted to argue that Protestant Christianity, or Cartesian skepticism, or market capitalism were "necessary" developments in Spirit's collective attempt at self-consciousness, or who thought that everything from the distinction between plant and animal life to the division of faculties in human psychology was equally necessitated by the requirements of a progressing spirit. And, the objection would go on, the particular slant given to the Kant–Hegel relation previously mentioned simply ignores too much of the historical Hegel, the Hegel who spent most of his early adult intellectual life struggling with Kant's moral theory and philosophy of religion, not with his Transcendental Deduction. The suggestions just made, in other words, look as radically revisionist and fragmentary as any contemporary interpretation of Hegel. Here again we seem to be forced to choose between the presumably historical Hegel, the romantic "totalizing," absolutist monist or, in this case, that "post-Kantian idealist" *fragment* of Hegel, the Hegel who may have a few interesting objections to empiricism or naturalism, but who can hardly be said to represent Hegel's position as a whole.

Such complaints about the implications of reading Hegel's idealism in the way suggested are far too complicated and important to be addressed briefly here. Although I plan to deal with such doubts in the body of what follows, I should at least note that I do not regard the project of providing an interpretation of Hegel's speculative philosophy, even one that can suggest an appropriate way to connect such speculation with his "Realphilosophie," to be *thereby committed* to a wholesale reconstruction of his *Encyclopedia*, much less of the content of his many lecture courses. Partly, I simply do not have the space for such an extension. Partly, I do not think it is possible; that is, I do not think that many of Hegel's reformulations and applications of his speculative position are justified. Indeed, many of his claims in the philosophy of nature and spirit are as ludicrous as they are reputed to be (although many are not), and it does Hegel no disservice to admit that he could be as guilty of overstating what he could demonstrate philosophically as was, say, Kant on the completeness of the Table of Categories or the architectonic necessity of a system of pure reason derived from syllogistic forms of inference. Most importantly, however, I want to argue that there simply *is* a coherent, identifiable position in Hegel on the implications of post-Kantian idealism that runs through the basic argument of his two most important books, the *Phenomenology of Spirit* and the *Logic*, is argued for independently of what Hegel considers to be the implications of that position, to a great (although not decisive) extent alters the way such implications ought to be understood, and is far less obscurantist and far most interesting philosophically than has traditionally been understood. It is that position, Hegel's idealism, that I want to discuss. Once such an idealist position is developed, and, especially, the significance of Hegel's theory of historical self-consciousness for that position is defended, its determinate implications for his theory of "objective spirit" or art or religion can, I would argue, he made out much more successfully. Clearly, though, such an idealist reading of Hegel's systematic and practical works is a major task in itself and depends everywhere on the version of idealism one originally ascribes to Hegel.

The historical criticism raises separate problems. First, Hegel nowhere provides an adequate justification for his numerous critical remarks about Kant's *Critique of Pure Reason*.[18] Sometimes he hammers away at a point that almost everyone would agree is indefensible in Kant (especially the claim about the completeness of the Table of Categories) but that no one thinks is as devastating for the important features of Kant's theory as does Hegel. More often, Hegel tosses off a paragraph here or there, or a Remark in the *Logic*, and clearly assumes that the justification for his dismissal of Kant on some issue is obvious (when it obviously is not). The same kind of brevity occurs in those passages where Hegel reveals his enormous debt to Kant. Clearly, to argue that the Kant–Hegel–idealism theme is the central one in Hegel commits one to showing that Hegel's own position contains the resources to reconstruct the justification for both the critical and the affirmative remarks; that the details of Hegel's own account of subjectivity, concepts, objectivity, his own idealism, can fill in the enormous gaps in his official pronouncements; and that his own position can be better understood when it is reconstructed for that purpose. (Given the paucity of detailed Hegelian analysis of Kant, the approach suggested here also implies that the best way to introduce such a view of Hegel – say, as a postcritical thinker rather than a precritical metaphysician – would be to show that Hegel's central complaint about Kant's philosophy, his objection to its "formality," could be *internally* justified by an analysis of the *Critique*. I mean by this that Hegel's own project would be much more clearly philosophically motivated if an assessment of Kant's texts, made without Hegelian assumptions but with the formality criticism in mind, could show that the criticism is well founded, that Kant's position does not provide the resources to answer it. I have tried to provide such a prolegomena to this reading of Hegel in *Kant's Theory of Form*.)[19]

Moreover, it might also be fairly charged that, by proposing to wade through the jungle of the details of both Transcendental and Speculative Idealism, we are likely to lose sight quickly of the great historical impact of the German Idealist tradition. Everything of real significance in Kant's project (he himself would admit) comes down to Kant's attempt to "make room for" the moral life of human beings, to work out some way of defending the possibility of such a free life, while admitting the "objective reality" of the modern scientific, essentially determinist conception of all nature, including human nature. And everything of real significance in the work of the later idealists amounts to a rejection of what they regarded as an ultimately untenable dualism, at the same time as they retained the Kantian assumption that a genuinely moral life could not be understood if a determinist metaphysics were admitted. Their problem thus *must*, for many, be understood to involve a restoration of some kind of metaphysics, a "morally significant monism," and it does not appear that such an attempt will get a fair hearing if one concentrates so exclusively as here proposed on the theoretical issue of idealism.

Like the problem of the Encyclopedic Hegel, this issue – understanding the relation between the "anti-dualist, Absolute Freedom" Hegel and the post-Kantian Hegel I propose to look at – is too complicated to be addressed briefly. But it is important to note at the outset that the Hegelian claims about overcoming Kant's dualism between phenomena and noumena, or between "understanding" and "reason," are clearly intended by Hegel to be the *result* of his original argument with Kant about pure concepts, the nature of their objectivity, and the status of skeptical doubts about such objectivity. After all, the key move in Kant's argument for the possibility of morality involves his restriction of human knowledge to phenomena, objects of finite forms of human intuition. It is thus altogether appropriate to spend a great deal of space attempting to clarify exactly what might be wrong in such an account of intuition, and what Hegel thought a more adequate account, before jumping to any conclusions about Hegel's relation to Kant. It is Hegel's account of the nature of the requirement for such conceptuality in experience, and the way that requirement is tied to claims about the spontaneity and reflexivity of any intelligible experience of an object, that introduces his own rather idiosyncratic notions of freedom and actuality, and so his rejection of Kant's dualistic assessment of the results of critical philosophy. Put crudely, one cannot understand the Hegelian payoff, his holism and the moral theory that depends on it, unless, again, one understands the Hegelian investment, the original engagement with Kant's critical philosophy. As with many other issues, once that investment is properly understood, many traditional readings of the dualism issue, dependent as many are on a metaphysical reading of Hegel, might begin to look very different.[20]

Finally, it should also be noted that it is true and relatively trivial that, in many cases, the Kantian, nonmetaphysical language I make use of in this interpretation is not what the historical Hegel "would have said" or "really had in mind." Obviously Hegel did not put things as I suggest and felt free to use the language of Christian theology, Greek metaphysics, Hölderlin, Schelling, and his own many, many neologisms to express his speculative position. If Hegel had put things as suggested here, there would be little need for this kind of commentary. But there is, I want to show, more than ample evidence that this focus on the post-Kantian idealism theme does identify the issues most important for Hegel's project as a whole, helps reveal why many standard views of the metaphysical Hegel cannot be correct, and, most importantly, illuminates the Hegelian themes of greatest philosophical significance. As with all such claims, however, the proof must lie in the details of the interpretation itself.

A final word on the texts used and on the organization of the following chapters. Hegel wrote only two actual books in his lifetime. The first was the extraordinary 1807 *Phenomenology of Spirit*, written when Hegel was a still struggling, thirty-seven-year-old philosophy teacher and published, appropriately, in the chaos and the continuing revolutionary excitement of Napoleon's victories. The other, the work Hegel always referred to as his most important, was his *Science of Logic*, written, remarkably, while Hegel was extremely busy teaching high school students at Nürnberg and published in 1812–16. (A second edition was published in 1831.) Hegel published two other works, both outlines of his lecture courses, student handbooks of a sort. His *Encyclopedia of the Philosophic Sciences* first appeared in 1817, a year after Hegel finally found another philosophy job, at Heidelberg. It was republished in 1827, after Hegel had moved to Berlin and had become a celebrity (this edition nearly doubled the size of the previous one), and again in 1830 just before Hegel's death. In 1821 he also published another handbook called *Natural Law and Political Science in Outline; Elements of the Philosophy of Right*. Besides these works, there are some important articles written by Hegel when he was at Jena and published in a journal he coedited for a while with Schelling, and a variety of other less important articles and notes.

Hegel scholars are divided on many issues, but on no issue as much as on how to understand the relation among these various texts. The great issue concerns the relation between the *Phenomenology* and the *Logic*, although there is almost as much controversy about the status and function of the *Encyclopedia* and about the striking differences between the mature, post-Heidelberg (especially Berlin) Hegel and the earlier Hegel. In the interpretation I shall defend, both the *Phenomenology* and the *Logic* are indispensable in the articulation and defense of the philosophical center of Hegel's project. I do not think there is any credible evidence that the later Hegel abandoned the *Phenomenology* and reassigned its topics a minor role in the *Encyclopedia*'s account of Subjective Spirit. Nor do I think that the later Hegel, supposedly more theologically inclined and politically reconciliationist, represents a departure from the daring, unprecedented *Phenomenology* Hegel. Hegel tells us in the *Logic*, even after its late revisions, that the *Phenomenology* is indispensable for its justification, and he tells us in the *Phenomenology* that the whole point of that work is to justify the "absolute standpoint" from which the *Logic* can be understood. Accordingly, the major focus of the following chapters will be those two works, although throughout this volume, the case for linking them will be thematic rather than historical. That is, the argument for treating both of them together will depend primarily on what Hegel's position requires, and not on a systematic survey of his quite varied later remarks on the proper unity of his "system."

Further, although the *Encyclopedia* can be a difficult text to interpret, Hegel's attempt there to present his position to university students, while making far fewer concessions than one might expect, often expresses things in a somewhat more accessible and straightforward way. This is particularly true, with one great exception, of the *Encyclopedia* version of the *Logic*, and in my chapters on the *Logic* I have tried to make judicious use of such formulations.

Accordingly, my approach is as follows: Since I am claiming that so much in Hegel depends on a proper understanding of his appropriation of Kant, I begin with an examination of the particular Kantian issues Hegel is concerned with, and attempt to construct the details of Hegel's objections to Kant's strategy in the Deduction. This provides the basis for a broad overview of Hegel's objections to Kant's theoretical philosophy. Secondly, since Hegel got so much of his Kant through Fichte, I examine the relation between Fichte and Kant on the issue that, as emerges quickly in Chapter 2, determines so much of Hegel's idealism: the problem of "spontaneous" apperception. The issue here will be whether Fichte's version of this issue, the version that so influenced Hegel, was as committed to the wild, improbable psychological and metaphysical claims as it seemed to be. I argue that he is not so committed, that the issue is not a world-creating metaphysics, or a theory of self-awareness and identity, but a continuation of the properly critical theme of *transcendental* apperception in Kant. Finally, in Chapter 4, I examine those Jena texts of Hegel's wherein he first began to formulate his own version of idealism and try to read those texts in the light of the problems developed in Kant and Fichte. A major issue in such a reading involves Hegel's relation to Schelling, that "Prince of the Romantics" whose terminology Hegel often adopted but whose position (often the world soul metaphysics attributed to Hegel) he began carefully to distance himself from. My hope is that with the Kantian background thus established, the major interpretive work of the book, the chapters on the idealism "deduced" in the *Phenomenology* and presented in the *Science of Logic*, can be more adequately understood and appreciated.

2
Kantian and Hegelian idealism

1. Apperception

In a letter to Schelling in 1795, when Hegel was still a tutor in Bern and still preoccupied with theological, political, and pedagogical issues, he writes enthusiastically that "From the Kantian system and its highest completion, I expect a revolution in Germany." And "The consequences that will result from it will astonish many a gentleman. Heads will be reeling at this summit of all philosophy by which man is being so greatly exalted."[1] It will take Hegel almost a full decade (and a break with Schelling) before his published work begins to reveal how he construed this completion of Kant, and indeed, why Hegel thought Kant's philosophy needed to be completed. Even then, and throughout his career, this positive reaction to Kant is intertwined with deep theoretical disagreements, a distaste for what Kant's practical philosophy had become in the hands of unworthy epigones, and in some highly rhetorical passages what appears to be a personal contempt for Kant's timidity, his not having the courage of his own convictions. However, as indicated in the previous chapter, whatever difficulties might exist in untangling the issues involved in Hegel's complex and often elliptical relation to Kant, without some understanding of that issue, many of the items on Hegel's own idealist agenda cannot be properly understood, and the questions Hegel undertakes to answer will remain hidden. Indeed, I shall argue throughout this study for something stronger than the exegetical value of "keeping Kant always in mind" in reading Hegel; I shall claim that Hegel's completion of Kant's project involves far more continuity, particularly with respect to the transcendental break with the metaphysical tradition, than has been recognized.

Accordingly, I must first provide both a general overview of Hegel's relation to Kant's theoretical philosophy and a summary of the Kantian arguments that Hegel refers to and often (without much acknowledgment) relies on in presenting his own idealism. Although this will not provide a complete picture of Hegel's relation to Kant (too much of Hegel's long struggle with Kant's practical philosophy will be absent), it can, however briefly, set the context for evaluating whether Hegel's theoretical position completes Kant by regressing to a pretranscendental metaphysics or genuinely extends and even radicalizes Kant's Copernican revolution.[2]

It is relatively uncontroversial, although not very easily understood, that at the center of Kant's influence on his successors, particularly in the 1790s and early 1800s on Rheinhold, Fichte, Schelling, and Hegel, is the central argument in the *Critique of Pure Reason*, the Transcendental Deduction, Kant's attempt to deduce the objective validity of the pure concepts of the understanding.[3] It is clear that this argument became the basis for what came to be called the "identity" theory at the core of much German Idealism (i.e., the "identity within difference" of subject and object, of "subjective" constraints on our thought of objects, and objects themselves). And it is also clear that it was not only Kant's conclusion, and the general strategy of his argument, that was so influential. As noted in the previous chapter, in many cases, and certainly in Hegel's, what was primarily influential was Kant's understanding of what he called the "fundamental principle" of his entire theoretical philosophy, the "transcendental unity of apperception," and his use of that principle in justifying synthetic a priori knowledge.[4] What is not clear is whether Hegel (and Fichte) identified with sufficient sensitivity the foundational arguments in Kant's position, and if they did, whether they proposed a cure worse than the disease, whether, eventually, Hegel's speculative identity theory mystifies rather than resolves whatever genuine problems might exist in Kant.

To begin to answer this question, I turn first to the *loci classici*. If we limit ourselves to the theoretical philosophy, there are six major discussions of Kant in Hegel's corpus.[5] Many different issues are raised in these passages, ranging from rather strange-sounding accusations about the mere "finitude" of Kant's idealism, or his misunderstanding the principle of identity at work in his own Transcendental Deduction, to more accessible but no less controversial charges that Kant has failed to distinguish his position from mere psychology. However, for the purpose of understanding their respective positions on idealism, there is one extraordinary claim about Kant that Hegel makes at a point particularly acute in his own project, one that clearly indicates what issues in Kant Hegel is relying on and so what needs to be discussed here.

In the beginning of the third and final section of the *Science of Logic*, Hegel chooses to structure his entire discussion by constant reference to, and often reliance on, Kant. What is important about this reference, coming as it does in preparation for Hegel's most comprehensive statement of his own position, is not only that it clarifies the magnitude of Hegel's debt to Kant but that it unequivocally sets out the specific Kantian terms within which Hegel wants his own position to be understood, however superior he ultimately takes his to be. Thus, in presenting his difficult claim for an epistemic and even ontological priority for "the Notion" (*der Begriff*), Hegel begins by confronting the commonsense understanding of notions and concepts as what I "have" when I think: thoughts, *Gedankendinge*, universal entities, or propositions. In a typical passage, Hegel counters that the situation is rather that "the I *is* the pure Notion itself which, as Notion, has come into existence" and that neither the one nor the other can be truly comprehended unless the two indicated moments are grasped at the same time both in their abstraction and also in their perfect unity. (*WL*, II, 220; *SL*, 583)

When he then tries to explain what he means by this, he turns to Kant as the first thinker who freed us from our misleading, commonsense understanding of the "I" and its "thoughts," and the one who set us on the proper path. Here is the crucial remark:

It is one of the profoundest and truest insights to be found in the *Critique of Pure Reason* that the *unity* which constitutes the nature of the *Notion* is recognized as the *original synthetic* unity of *apperception*, as the unity of the *I think*, or of self-consciousness. (*WL*, II, 221; *SL*, 584)[6]

Now, attempting to understand the conclusion of Hegel's idealist logic, his claim about the progressive "self-determination" of the Notion, or the final "actualization of the Absolute Idea," by appeal to Kant's doctrine of apperception, raises several interpretive problems, several of which are potentially quite complex.[7] [Hegel himself warned that "Expressions like 'transcendental unity of self-consciousness' have an ugly look about them, and suggest a monster in the background" (*EL* 118; *EnL*, 70).] The preceding might begin to distinguish Hegel's own notion of a subject from a traditional substance theory of mind (or with aspects of Hegel's own Jena position),[8] and can point to Hegel's similarity to Kant on a functional theory of concepts, but what else this encomium to Kant might suggest is not immediately apparent. Moreover, the quotations just cited provide only introductory and fragmentary evidence of the importance of the self-consciousness theme in understanding Hegel's relation to Kant and his own idealism. To be sure, that evidence is already striking, but it will need to arise again and again before its full implications are apparent. Since the issue is a controversial and ambiguous one in Kant, it is important first to look at the Kantian position, at least at those aspects of it relevant to Hegel.

Of particular importance are two issues, neither of which lends itself to summary exposition. There is first the simple issue of just what Kant means by asserting that the transcendental unity of apperception is the "supreme"or "original" principle of all human experience. Then there is the issue of how such a claim functions as the principle of the argument of the Deduction, and so in what sense its role in the Deduction helps contribute to an idealist conclusion – in Kant's terms that the experience the categories make possible is restricted to appearances; in Hegel's quite different terms that "objects in their truth" *are* "their Notions."

In the first edition's version of the Deduction, Kant states his basic claim about apperception this way:

There can be in us no modes of knowledge, no connection of unity of one mode of knowledge with another, without that unity of consciousness that precedes all data of intuition, and by relation to which representation of objects is alone possible. This pure, original, unchangeable consciousness I shall name transcendental apperception. (A107)

In this and other passages, Kant compresses together a number of related claims about what a subject of experience must be in order to count as a subject that can be said to have "experiences." (In the following discussion, I shall follow Kant's usage and take the notion of "experience," *Erfahrung* to refer synonymously to "empirical consciousness of objects" or "representation of objects," where such representing is understood as a function of judgment. I also note that Kant is interested in the "conditions for the possibility" of all such representing, whether the object is an object of "inner" or "outer" sense.)

There are three such related claims, involving *identity, unity*, and *self-consciousness*. Such a subject must be an *identical* subject through time. For any "I" to have experiences of any kind, the experiences must belong to *that* I. Without such identity, the synthetic reproduction and reidentification that Kant has already argued are necessary for experience could not occur. But, he also maintains, this "belonging together" of representations in one subject does not occur unless it is effected *by* that subject. For there to be the relevant *unity* of representations in a single subject, that subject must actively (or "spontaneously") unify them. Or: "The transcendental unity of apperception forms out of all possible appearances, which can stand alongside one another in experience, a connection of these representations according to laws" (A108). Finally, and most controversially for our topic, Kant also argues that such elements could not be unified, and so there could not be this required same subject throughout experience, if such a subject "could not become conscious of the identity of function whereby it synthetically combines it [the manifold] in one knowledge" (A108). That is, as the word "apperception" already indicates, Kant is arguing that self-consciousness is, in some way that needs a great deal of clarification, a condition of experience. As we shall see in exploring the role of this principle in the Deduction's argument, Kant wants to maintain that if I could not "become conscious" of the rules I was applying in unifying my representations, in attempting to represent objects I would not *be* following rules or representing objects, but merely associatively producing subjective states, states that, since merely associated, could not count as being representative states, as having objects or being experiences. That is, in one of Kant's most influential claims, being *in* a subjective state, even a merely momentary subjective state, does not count as having an experience *of* and so being aware of that state unless I apply a certain determinate concept (a "this-state," not "that-state" concept, say) and judge that I am in such a state, something I must *do* and be able to know that I am doing.

It is this last component of the claim that looms so large as an influence over Fichte and Hegel (and even, as I shall show, over Schelling) and that requires the most comment. It is so influential in Hegel particularly because it is the clear origin of an entire Hegelian strategy in the *PhG*, the distinction between what consciousness is "in itself" and "for itself." ("In itself" consciousness is self-consciousness, although not "for itself.") It is a problematic influence because of the variety of ways in which Kant explains what he means by calling the transcendental unity of apperception the "supreme" principle or condition of all experience.

There are, first of all, formulations similar to the summary just given, where Kant is clearly referring to apperception as a logical condition, that it must be logically possible for me to ascribe my representations to myself, to "become" conscious, as the A108 passage puts it, of the "functions" whereby I unify the data of consciousness. The stress on what Allison calls the "necessity of a possibility" approach[9] is an important one because it helps distinguish what Kant is saying from a much stronger, "Cartesian" version. In the "logical condition" version of the apperception principle, the objects of empirical consciousness are straightforwardly objects of inner and outer sense; the objects are not the self or the mind's own states and activities. The mind's ability to attend to its own representing activity is a *distinct* ability, logically presupposed as a condition of experience. (We couldn't *be* representing objects unless, in all cases of such representing, we could *also* become conscious of our representing.) In what I am calling the Cartesian reading, all consciousness, including what Kant is calling experience, *is* a species of self-consciousness, representing objects is at the same time attending to the mind's activities and objects.

There is such a reading of the role of apperception in the Deduction, the so-called conflation interpretation, the claim that Kant is somehow arguing that consciousness *is* self-consciousness, that in any conscious intending, I am aware of my own activity of creating or imposing my order on the world (of the "a priori synthesis").[10] Surprisingly there are passages (e.g., A108, A116) that seem to support such a view, but almost all of them tend to drop out in the second edition, where there is a good deal more stress on the logical condition language and much less on some putative awareness of my identity and my constituting activity in every conscious representing. In that edition, instead, we find passages like the following:

> As *my* representations (even if I am not conscious of them as such) they must conform to the condition under which alone they *can* stand together in one universal self-consciousness, because otherwise they would not all without exception belong to me. (B131–3)

In terms of this passage, the phrase "even if I am not conscious of them *as such*" indicates that Kant takes himself to be avoiding the conflation thesis, and the claim that *all* my representations must be subject to the conditions of "universal self-consciousness" indicates that he is making a claim much stronger than one that relies merely on what is required *in any case* of self-consciousness or self-ascription.[11] Indeed, even at A116, where he says that "We are conscious a priori of the complete identity of the self in respect of all representations which can ever belong in our knowledge," he also adds "as being a necessary condition of the possibility of all representations," indicating that what we can be said to be aware of a priori is the existence of such a condition.

However, the logical condition approach is not the end of the story, for the simple reason that we must go on to explain just why it is that self-consciousness is a condition of experience. Being able to ascribe states to myself and to become conscious of the principles of unification by means of which I effect a unitary experience is not simply a distinct reflective ability I happen to possess. It is a *condition* of experience because, according to Kant, experience itself *is* "implicitly" reflexive. That is, if the claim is that consciousness of objects could not possess the unity necessary for it to be an experience of an identical subject unless that subject effected that unity, then although it need not follow that such a subject must always be attending to its own judging in experience, it is required that such a subject be making such judgments *in a way* that permits such an attending. It must make some difference in an account of representing objects that such a representing activity itself be "potentially self-conscious." Although Kant often wanders into some conflationist language when he tries to describe such implicit reflexivity, his considered view seems to be the one expressed in the quoted passage at B131.

That is, consciousness of objects is implicitly reflexive because, according to Kant, whenever I am conscious of any object, I can also be said to "apperceive" implicitly my being *thus* conscious. In any remembering, thinking or imagining, although the object of my intending is some state of affairs or other, I am also potentially aware *as* I intend that what I am doing *is* an act of remembering, thinking, or imagining. My asserting that *S is P* is not an assertion of mine unless I am implicitly aware as I assert that I am *asserting*, not entertaining the possibility that, *S is P*. And no such complex judgment, Kant thinks he can show, is possible unless there is one subject of experience continuing over time, potentially aware of its continuity in any conscious act. Again, this apperceptive characteristic does not mean that the fact that I am perceiving rather than imagining is itself directly attended to. It is not the case that the self-relation of apperception involves a representation of the self, whether of my self or of subjectivity itself. But it is the case for Kant that my implicitly "taking myself" to be perceiving, imagining, remembering, and so on is an inseparable component of *what it is* to perceive, imagine, remember, and so on.[12]

Or, to use some common examples to make the point, in trying to recollect the name of a friend who is approaching me, I am implicitly aware that I, the subject of all past instances of contact with the friend, am trying to recollect, without a second-order judgment, "I am recollecting," occurring. One could say that without the act of recollecting somehow being "held in mind," the pursuits undertaken *within* that context would be unintelligible. Or, I can consciously *follow* a rule without consciously *applying* a rule. This must be possible if any rule following that is not an explicit application is to be distinguished, as it should, from behavior completely accounted for by lawlike explanations. So, in the same way that we can say that someone playing baseball (1) must be able to articulate to himself the basic rules of the game he is playing for him to be playing the game and (2) is thereby playing the game and implicitly following the rules without it being the case that (3) we should understand (2) to mean that he keeps the rules in mind, attends to them directly, in any act of the game.

This is an important enough issue for me to risk belaboring the point with another example, one that will point more concretely to the complicated extensions of such claims about self-consciousness effected by Hegel. Suppose that someone, S, in accounting for an action, offered a *moral* justification of that action. We then ask, qua philosophers, what makes such a justification a *moral* one; in Kantian language, we are asking for its "conditions." Clearly, one condition is that there should actually *be* the institution of morality; otherwise, S would only think that he is offering a moral justification. In fact, he could not, if there were no such thing as morality. However, it is also the case that S cannot simply produce the words sanctioned by this institution as a moral justification, without any self-understanding that that *is* what the institution demands, and that fulfilling such a demand is what he is doing. If S is so thoroughly confused about such an institution that he merely mouths the words, or understands their literal meaning without any comprehension of why they have the force they do, we would claim that he only seems to be offering a moral justification. In the language I have developed thus far, we can say that S must take himself to be offering such a justification in order for it to count as one. But it is now a little clearer just how complex and potentially controversial such "implicit apperception" and "inherent reflexivity" are in this example. As Kant himself realized in developing his moral theory, the question cannot be limited to the "conditions" of moral or worthwhile action alone, to properties that actions or policies simply have (as in consequentialist theories). In Kant's "moral idealism," what a subject takes himself to be doing is equally criterial in determining whether the act is morally worthwhile. But much of the controversy stems from trying to decide exactly how to describe such moral self-consciousness. Just how much of a moral self-understanding must we claim to be implicit in what the subject takes himself to be doing, and just how implicit is it? How much must *he* be able to produce, if challenged, for us to be satisfied that he really, if implicitly, knows what he is doing? Clearly, however, there must be *some* connection between the formal conditions for an act counting as a moral act and the self-understanding of the agent. And we can easily imagine cases where S has presupposed the fundamental core of the moral point of view, and are satisfied that we, or some other philosopher, can account fully for all that such a core presupposes and implies.

If we think of such an issue in the epistemological context, we can begin to see how Hegel will appropriate and develop this Kantian insistence on self-consciousness as a condition required for acts or judgments *to be* acts or judgments of mine. In that context, I could say that when S claims to know P, S must be implicitly understanding himself to be participating in the practice of judgment and justification, and that S must contextually or implicitly understand enough of such a practice to count as participating in it. (Such a reflexive awareness might simply always be implicit and evinced only by what else S can and would do.) We can claim that there is such a connection between S's self-understanding and such a condition or set of conditions without attributing to S any mysterious subconscious awareness of the full conditions of such a practice. Of course, philosophically, there might be a great deal of controversy over what such a practice is, over what genuinely counts as participating in it. Hegel will alter Kant's approach to this issue quite drastically in the *PhG*, and will provide a reconstructed ideal "history" of what a subject would reasonably come to regard as the conditions of such an enterprise, a history determined by a phenomenology of what it would be like to participate in various candidate practices (empirical realism, phenomenalism, rationalist realism, transcendentalism, etc.). But the very general reliance on the apperception argument should, I think, be understood along the lines suggested here. (It will help, too, to keep such a view in mind in understanding the intimidating *SL*. There Hegel provides an extremely abstract, ideal account of the various Notions implicitly presupposed by any S self-consciously intending a claim about a *determinate* object, even though any actual S might have only the crudest sense of such presuppositions. He is still playing the logical game by self-consciously attempting a judgment about a determinate object, event, or state of affairs.)

And there are still other Kantian ways of explaining the nature of this apperception condition.[13] For example, Kant frequently characterizes human, discursive, apperceptive understanding as a "spontaneity," and in some passages seems even to tinker with the idea of drawing some metaphysical implications from this aspect of thought.[14] But for our purposes, what this synonym means, given that Kant uses it to mean an uncaused or perhaps self-caused cause, is that there is a feature of discursive thought that cannot be described as empirically grounded (i.e., caused). That feature is the apperceptive quality of human thought. As suggested previously, although it is true that when I, for example, perceive X, I also take myself to *be* perceiving, or apperceive, the latter is not only not an isolatable experience, it cannot be described in any way as an inference I draw or as a causal result of my perceiving.[15] One could perhaps imagine an unusual situation where I do not know, say, whether I am perceiving or hallucinating, and where I try to infer from the evidence what I am doing or undergoing, but even in that case, what I *originally* experience already includes my perception of the state I am in *and* my implicit apperception of being in an unfamiliar state, and no later judgment about the case could be said to "add" apperception to my experience. One way of stressing this would be to suggest that this apperceptive feature of experience is "adverbial," that when I perceive, think, imagine, and so on I *apperceptively* perceive, think, imagine, and so on.[16] This would be a way of explaining what it means to claim that Kant is denying the possibility of any form of direct realism about the objects of consciousness, that a Humean theory of such objects cannot account for the determinacy of such objects for consciousness. Or Kant's theory is meant to show that consciousness of objects can be said to involve the "subject's activity" without that activity being either an object of consciousness itself or somehow going on at a preconscious level, whatever that would mean.

Finally, and most importantly in this context, even though Hegel sometimes appears to take Kant to be a conflationist, in his more careful moments he does not say that consciousness is self-consciousness (again, whatever that would mean), but rather that self-consciousness is *the truth* of consciousness. As we shall see later, Hegel's full account of consciousness is complex and often baffling, but he frequently makes remarks about consciousness as both a self-relating and a relation to something *other* than consciousness. In many of these contexts, then, self-consciousness being the "truth" of consciousness is to be taken as a claim about what must be *true of* any cognitive, conscious intending even if, in Hegel's language, that self-consciousness is not attended to "for itself." So, in a summary passage from the *Berlin Phenomenology*, he stresses the fact that the direct intentional object of consciousness is an object, not the subject's activities or states, by writing, that "In consciousness I am *also* self-consciousness, but *only also*, since the object has a side in itself which is not mine" (*BPhG*, 56).

Naturally, all these issues are best discussed when they arise in Hegel's own text, but since I am placing such heavy weight on the theory of self-consciousness within Hegel's idealism, I want at least to suggest here that the preceding gloss on Kant's apperception theory is a plausible interpretation of Kant, and likely the one that Hegel advanced himself. The more difficult problem for the moment, however, is whether Hegel's stress on this theme in Kant does justice to the argument of the Deduction, and especially to Kant's case for idealism.

2. Hegel on Kant's idealism

One could already charge that following Hegel's emphasis on and beginning with the apperception issue as a way of understanding Kant's idealism clearly misses the much more complicated and extended argument for idealism in the first *Critique*. This attention to the self-consciousness theme in Kant, almost to the exclusion of all else, appears to ignore blatantly the very foundation of Kant's idealism, his account of the ideal forms of sensible intuition. For Kant, the whole difference between a merely formal, or general, logic and a transcendental logic depends on the use of pure intuitions to distinguish "real possibility" from merely logical possibility, to distinguish, that is, conditions necessary for the representation of an *object* from conditions necessary for a thought just to be a possible thought or representation. Kant did hold that we can prove that there must be pure concepts for there to be representations of objects or judgments, but he clearly also believed that we can succeed in such a proof only by reference to the unique forms of intuition we happen to have (especially by reference to the temporally successive nature of our apprehending). The very heart of Kant's answer to his own synthetic a priori knowledge question, the question of how thought can successfully determine a priori what is other than thought, is his claim that we can somehow represent a priori all possible intuited objects, things other than or given to thought, in a preconceptual way; that there are pure intuitions. That this notion is not a particularly clear or, I have argued elsewhere, successful notion[17] should not obscure its importance in Kant's understanding of his own idealism. Yet, as we shall see, apart from some brief passages in the Jena writings, Hegel never takes on this issue in the detail it deserves, a fact that would seem to undermine seriously any claim about the philosophical insight and significance of his appropriation of Kant.

At this point, though, well before we can make any such judgment, we should note that the issue at stake between Hegel and Kant on intuition should be divided into two. First, there is the question of why Hegel thought Kant could not successfully defend his notion of a nonconceptual form of sensible intuition and make use of it as a separate element in his idealism argument. Second, there is the question of whether, apart from reliance on the ideal status of intuited objects, Kant's argument about the forms of thought as "forms of apperception" itself can be said to result in idealist conclusions. As we shall see in the next chapter, the simple but initially unhelpful answer to the first question is: Fichte. It was Fichte and his animadversions to Kantian apperception and spontaneity that influenced Hegel on this point so much that he rarely acknowledges the issue or the influence, although the marks of Fichte's formulations remain everywhere in Hegel's mature reflections on Kant. Thus part of the answer to the first question will depend on a Hegelian reading of Fichte's idealism – in particular, Fichte's understanding of the priority of spontaneity in Kant, and why that makes a strict distinction between concepts and intuitions impossible. But part of the answer also depends on the details of the argument strategy in the Deduction, particularly, I think, the second edition version. There are indications that Hegel believes that that strategy broke down internally over the use of pure intuitions to establish the objective reality of the categories, and, from a philosophical point of view, a reconstruction of Hegel's position requires some account of why the Kantian reliance on pure intuitions *could* not have been satisfying to Hegel. Accordingly, I offer here a brief summary of that "Hegelian problem" with the Deduction, particularly with respect to the role of pure intuitions in Kant's claims about synthetic a priori knowledge. Then I present a discussion of the general idealist implications of the apperception claim.

There are, of course, scores of interpretations of the Deduction. But the issues relevant to Hegel can be extracted from a few passages, many in the second edition version, especially passages immediately surrounding the discussion of pure intuition and the imagination referred to explicitly by Hegel and central to his reformulation of Kant's strategy. However, the issues raised in these passages are among the most contentious in Kant interpretation. A rough approximation of the context within which they arise, though, will now be given. (I shall attempt to avoid the complicated issue of the relation between the two versions and a number of contested issues of interpretation in order to provide the summary of the argument relevant to Hegel and, I think, fair to Kant's case, given the limitations of space.)

Kant often asserts that the central notion at work in the Deduction's argument is that of the "possibility of experience." By "experience" he means empirical knowledge, and so he intends to investigate the conditions necessary for our ability to make possibly true or false claims about the world ("objective" claims). Central to that possibility is our ability to "represent objects" (in the second edition version, more frequently, our ability to judge). For Kant, experience of any kind involves such a cognitive ability, even if the kind of experience in question is a subject's experience of the "internal flow" of his own mental states. Even such a subject is judging *that* such states are "flowing" in that order.

He also argues that any such representational ability must involve the ability to unify a manifold, that the unity of a representation sufficient for it to count as a representation of an object is "synthetic." This claim, in turn, is tied to Kant's historically decisive argument that awareness of an object, even a mental state, cannot be understood simply in terms of having or directly inspecting a mental state. Our ability to recognize the internal complexity of the state *as* belonging together in one state, our ability to discriminate, in some manifold of intuitions, which belong together with which, our ability to represent just *these* elements as components of a representation of *that* object in the presence of that object and much else in the intuited manifold, all for Kant point to this necessary synthetic ability.

He then asks how this synthetic ability is constrained; what accounts for the normative limitations on collecting together and uniting that constitutes representing? His answer, after a dense account of why the object cannot function as such a constraint without all the questions being begged (A104), is that all unification that can count as representative must be "rule governed." According to Kant, unification of a manifold according to a rule *is* what constitutes the representation of an object. A mere series of associated representations would not be a representation *of* anything, according to Kant, and if a representation is of the sequence of events in my mental life, then *that* is the rule that constrains my synthesis. But although unification according to rules might thus be a necessary condition of our representing ability, it leaves wide open the question of which rules can apply in this objectivity-conferring function. Surely not any rule.

Here is where Kant introduces his supreme condition: the transcendental unity of apperception. What he wants to show is that any such putative rule must conform to conditions under which a unified, potentially self-conscious subject of experience is possible. It is this claim that, when properly analyzed, Kant thinks allows him to claim that there must be "pure" rules that, prior to any experience, already determine what could count in general as an object of experience. If there were not these "meta-rules" determining which empirical rules could be formed, there would be only associative unities, and so no unity of experience and no possible experience at all. These pure rules are the "categories" (referred to generically and without much specification in the Deduction), and so this argument establishes that the categories (or some pure concepts) are necessary conditions for the possibility of experience. In *that* sense, they can be said to be objectively valid, that is, in the sense that there could not be objects encountered in experience that did not conform to the categories. If the categories did not predetermine what could be an object, there could not be experience.

All the problems for the post-Kantian reading of this argument, and, interestingly enough, for Kant himself in the period between the two editions, can now be seen to stem from this last claim about the objective validity of the categories. What exactly does it mean? It could quite fairly be claimed that the foregoing argument proceeds by an analysis of the conditions necessary for any subject to be able to represent objects. Such constraints, however, need have nothing to do with objects in the world or, in Kant's language (lest it appear that we are talking about things in themselves), with objects as they are just given in intuition. The preceding concluding claim about the objective validity of the categories could then only properly assert that the categories are valid for all representable objects, for all objects considered in terms of the intellectual conditions of their representability. And this restriction would mean that the Deduction's argument is confined to an analytic claim about the subjective conditions of representability. If we stress heavily the necessity of these constraints, we might be tempted to believe that that alone *is* what establishing objective validity means (subjective indispensability). Alternatively, if we adopt a phenomenalist reading of Kant and "reduce" objects to representations, then the argument establishes objective validity, since what there is – objects – consists of just thoughts.

Kant's version of this problem and his solution to it involve some of the densest passages in the whole *Critique*, but there is little doubt that he sees the problem and wants a resolution. At B138, he insists that the synthetic unity of consciousness (together with the categories as conditions for such a unity) "is not merely a condition that I myself require in knowing an object, but is a condition under which every intuition must stand in order *to become an object for me.*" And again, the problem is how he can show that, or, most generally, how he can advance a genuinely synthetic a priori claim, a claim about objects. The same insistence on this "extension" of the Deduction is made in the famous "Highest Principle of Synthetic Judgments" cited by Hegel in explaining his own identity theory. There Kant asserts that the "conditions of the possibility of experience in general are likewise conditions of the possibility of objects of experience" (B197–A158). In many versions of Kant, establishing the conditions referred to in the first half of this claim is all he can really pretend to do. Kant means, though, to establish a synthetic claim here, as his title for the assertion indicates. And central to his attempt to do so is the two-part strategy of the second edition Deduction[18] and the problem of pure intuition.

The same duality we have been discussing (conditions necessary for representing an object versus the claim that objects, as given, conform to such conditions) is visible at section 20 of the B edition, where Kant summarizes his results thus far, and in section 21, where he asserts that, even though he had claimed in section 20 that "the manifold in a given intuition is necessarily subject to the categories," only "a beginning" of the Deduction had thereby been made. His statements about how he means to extend the Deduction all confirm the preceding interpretation and make clearer why, given their own projects, Fichte and Hegel were most drawn to these sections of the Deduction.[19] For it is in this argument that Kant both attempts to justify the "Highest Principle" claim cited earlier (what would begin speculative identity theory) and where, for his later critics, he begins to misunderstand his own results; where his attempt to rely on pure intuition to establish such synthetic claims about objects fails and can be shown to undercut his own separation between intuition and concept; and where Kant thus incorrectly restricts his results to "phenomena." This issue, the account of intuition in the second half of the B Deduction, is thus not only important, but potentially confusing, since it brings to a very fine point Fichte's and Hegel's appropriation of Kant, their agreement with him, in a way very tightly interwoven with their disagreement, their rejection of elements that Kant regarded as essential to his project. So it is worthwhile to consider the issue carefully.

In section 21, Kant claims:

> Thus in the above proposition a beginning is made of the deduction of the pure concepts of understanding; and in this deduction, since the categories have their source in the understanding alone, independently of sensibility, I must abstract from the mode in which the manifold of intuition is given, and must direct attention solely to the unity which, in terms of the category, and by means of the understanding, enters into the intuition. In what follows (cf. #26) it will be shown, *from the mode in which the empirical intuition is given in sensibility, that its unity is no other than that which the category (according to #20) prescribes to the manifold of a given intuition in general.* Only thus, by demonstration of the a priori validity of the categories in respect of all objects of our sense, will the purpose of the deduction be fully attained. (B144–5; my emphasis)

As he does put it in section 26, unless we can do this – explain the possibility of claiming to know something about "whatever may present themselves to the senses" (and not just whatever may conform to our conditions of representability) – then "there could be no explaining why everything that can be presented to our senses must be subject to laws which have their origin a priori in the understanding alone" (B160).

The key phrase in Kant's attempt to effect this extension is the claim that the understanding can "determine sensibility inwardly," a claim that already suggests the philosophic direction of Fichte and Hegel, rather than Kant's strict separation between sensibility and understanding and his insistence on the constraints exercised *by* sensibility on the understanding. Basically, what he tries to argue, by means of an analysis of the relation between apperception and inner sense, the role of the imagination, and the synthesis of apprehension, is that it is incorrect to think of an intuited manifold as simply "presented to" the understanding for a determination of which concepts to apply. If we did think of it this way, we might think of the categories only as rules for our representation of objects, independently of the manner in which the objects are given, that pure concepts are mere subjective determinations of the given, "whatever" is given. And again, the key issue in the Deduction is Kant's dissatisfaction with such a result, his attempt to establish a synthetic link between conceptual conditions and the "given," sensible objects.

Thus Kant explains that in the first part of the Deduction he had "abstracted" from the problem of a manifold of intuition and now wants to show that nothing can be an *intuited* object unless it also conforms to categorical conditions. (There thus *could not be* a "lack of fit" between intuited objects and pure concepts; anyone who entertained such a possibility would not have understood the full conditions under which an object can be said to be an intuited object.) So, in two separate arguments, he claims that, given what we know about the pure forms of sensibility from the Aesthetic, we also know that nothing could count as an object of *inner sense*, and so in time, unless "apperceived" or subject to the understanding's unification (this is his account of the "paradox" of self-knowledge, at B152–7), and nothing could count as an object in space unless a quantity (this is his account of the "apprehension of the manifold of a house" at B162–5). Thus the categories are not just subjective conditions of representability; we can also show that nothing given *in* intuition can fail to be subject to the categories.

There is a great deal of controversy in Kant commentary about how the two arguments previously mentioned work, and indeed about the whole strategy in the second half of the Deduction. But with respect to the later idealists, we can concentrate on one supreme problem. Kant had argued that some pure concepts were necessary conditions of the possibility of experience, since without such pure concepts, if all unification rules were derived from experience, there could not be a unity of apperception. He also wants to prove that such conditions determine the possibility of an intuited manifold; said negatively, there is no possibility that an intuited manifold could fail to conform to the categories. To the later idealists, it is this claim that must have looked like a serious blurring of the distinction between concept and intuition. In this B Deduction extension, Kant does not appear to be merely offering further grounds (based on more detail about human forms of intuition) for the claim that experience would not be possible if restricted to intuitions alone. That would only further support the first, "analytic" half of the Deduction, the claim that we must conceive the data of experience in certain ways. He appears to be trying to argue that objects "in their very givenness" conform to the categories. But if he is successful in doing this, then he has shown that what counts as given in experience is also determined by conceptual conditions, by the "spontaneity" of the subject. And this would render problematic the whole distinction between spontaneity and receptivity; it would set us on a path where it would then be possible to speak of the "nicht Ich" itself as a "posit" of the "Ich," and where a "speculative" identity between Concept and intuited Particular looms on the horizon.

And again, what makes this controversy between Kant and his successors so difficult to assess – aside from the fact that it concerns what may be the most difficult interpretive issue in the first *Critique* – is that it is extremely difficult to distinguish between what Hegel in particular seemed to see as a *problem* in Kant and what Kant would state as the successful result of his Deduction. Alternatively, the issue between Kant and his successors could be put simply as follows: How should one understand the claim that "intuitions must conform to the categories for experience to be possible"? Is that a genuinely synthetic claim, the result of demonstrating something universal about all possible intuitions, and so a demonstration of the objective reality of pure concepts? Or does Kant's own case rely on undercutting his own understanding of syntheticity and objective reality? Does such a claim amount to the assertion that we can know a priori that intuitions conform to categories because there is no real independent "giveness" in experience, and thus that an "identity" between concept and intuition has been established, that "thought" has successfully determined its "other"?

The issue in Kant's account comes to a head in a footnote to the second edition Deduction. In a note to a claim at B160 that space and time are not just forms of intuition but are themselves "pure intuitions," he admits that the issue for him is not only, speaking roughly, how intuitions, as given, are conceptualized; he also wants to claim that conforming to the *intuitional* constraints of sensibility itself requires a minimal conceptualization. The claim is important enough to quote at length:

> Space, represented as object (as we are required to do in geometry) contains more than mere form of intuition; it also contains combination of the manifold, given according to the form of sensibility, in an intuitive representation, so that the form of intuition gives only a manifold, the formal intuition gives unity of representation. In the Aesthetic I have treated this unity as belonging merely to sensibility, simply in order to emphasize that it precedes any concept, although as a matter of fact it presupposes a synthesis which does not belong to the senses but through which all concepts of space and time first become possible.

I have argued that this claim must be viewed in the light of Kant's attempt to "complete" the Deduction with an argument about all possible intuited objects, a way of claiming that there can be no intuitions not subject to the categories. Viewed in this way, there is some Hegelian irony in the fact that, as Kant tries to make his argument, he takes back, in a sense, his strict distinction between intuition and understanding and here argues that all *intuited* unity "presupposes a synthesis," that nothing in experience can conform to intuitive conditions unless already subject to the categorical rules of synthesis. He goes on:

For since by its means (*in that the understanding determines the sensibility*) space and time are first given as intuitions, the unity of this a priori intuition belongs to space and time and not to the concept of the understanding (cf. #24). (My emphasis)

The last claim might appear to take back everything else Kant had said in the note, but it is again consistent with the "synthetic" extension of the Deduction he is attempting. By claiming that the "unity of this a priori intuition belongs to space and time and not to the understanding," Kant is arguing that he is not only asserting that any manifold of space and time must be "thought" subject to the categories to count as an object of experience (that its unity does not merely "belong" to the concepts of the understanding, in the language of the note), but that the content of any intuited manifold must be subject to the categories just to *be* an element of a spatiotemporal manifold in the first place. (I think that the reference to section 24, otherwise obscure, confirms this reading, since it directs us to Kant's account of this distinctive conceptual determination of the given "figurative" synthesis.)[20] As argued earlier, Kant must make such a claim if he is to follow the strategy he sets for himself and defend the possibility of synthetic a priori knowledge.

All of which still leaves open a number of Kantian responses. In particular, a Kantian might still object that there is all the difference in the world between "blurring" the contributions of intuition and understanding in experience and demonstrating their necessary cooperation in any possible experience, and that all of the later idealists simply failed to understand this distinction. However, what is at stake at this juncture of Kant's argument is the supposedly distinct roles of pure intuition and pure concepts in synthetic a priori knowledge, the demonstration of the objective reality of the categories, and the passages around B160 do not, I think, show Kant establishing a "synthetic link" with pure intuitions, as much as they show him extending, or trying to extend, his account of conceptual conditions "into" the manifold of intuition itself. Moreover, this is only the beginning of the problems that surround Kant's doctrine of "pure intuition." If there can be such an intuitional constraint on thought, a constraint that can be made out a priori, then much of Kant's philosophy of mathematics and his "transition" to a philosophy of science would have to be defended. It is, I think, fair to claim at the very least that the prospects for such a defense look dim.[21]

At any rate, I hope that enough has been said to help motivate important elements of the Hegelian enterprise. For we can now see somewhat more clearly what it means, in Hegelian language, to claim that we are here shifting from an account of thought's relation to the pure manifold of intuition to thought's "self-determination." As we shall see, this does not at all eliminate the role of the given in knowledge, but it will radically relativize to "thought" the ways in which the given can be taken to be given, will introduce a very different notion of objectivity and a different strategy for dealing with the obvious problem of realist skeptical doubts about the work of thought's self-determination. These issues will be considered as they emerge in Hegel's texts. What I argue here is that it is the kinds of problems (genuine problems) found in the second half of Kant's Deduction that generate such a desired "completion" of Kant, problems that lie behind Hegel's use of the Deduction rather than Kant's doctrine of intuition as a source of his own idealism.[22]

3. Apperception and idealism

This brings us to the second issue noted earlier: the charge that Hegel incorrectly assumed that the argument of the Deduction *itself*, whatever its internal complications, can be said to entail an idealist conclusion. So the issue is: What in the Transcendental Deduction and, in particular, what use of some claim about apperception involves a commitment to idealism?

In the first place, although it has been denied recently,[23] it is not at all hard to substantiate Hegel's interpretation that Kant believed that the success of the Deduction required some commitment to idealism, and that this commitment is made out by reflection on the requirements for apperceptive consciousness. When Kant sums up the second edition Deduction as a whole, in a section entitled "Outcome of This Deduction of the Concepts of Understanding," he states explicitly, "Consequently, there can be no a priori knowledge, *except* of objects of possible experience" (B166; my emphasis). And in giving what he calls a "Brief Outline of This Deduction," he writes:

> The deduction is the exposition of the pure concepts of the understanding and therewith of all theoretical a priori knowledge, as principles of the possibility of experience – the principle being here taken as the determination of appearances in space and time in general, and this determination, in turn, as ultimately following from the original synthetic unity of apperception, as the form of the understanding in its relation to space and time, the original forms of sensibility.

It might be thought that the simple reference to objects of possible experience or even appearances does not yet have a strong idealistic commitment, that is, unless one sees Kant contrasting the terms with "things in themselves," which he rarely does at this stage of the argument. (Otherwise, Kant might be taken to have left open the possibility that the objects of our sensible experience *are* things in themselves.) But Kant does not conclude that categories apply to possible objects of experience, and just leave it open until the Antinomies to argue that such objects cannot be things in themselves. The preceding passages make clear that Kant sees an intimate connection between his proof that the categories are valid for all possible objects of experience and his restriction that they are valid *only* for possible objects of human experience, or "determinations" of "appearances." This means that because the categories could be established only for our possible experience (for creatures with a sensible intuition and discursive, or apperceptive, understanding), no claim about their being conditions for the possibility of some other experiencer (e.g., God), or about these categories being *also* true of objects considered apart from their sensory and conceptual conditions, can be made. And what figures crucially in showing that the categories are required for experience turns on the conditions for the possibility of a unity of apperception. At B145 Kant writes that the understanding "can produce a priori unity of apperception solely by means of the categories" and states that this is a "peculiarity" of *our* understanding. (At B148 Kant points to the way in which the Deduction "limits" the applicability of categories, just as the Aesthetic "limits" the employment of pure intuition. There is no way to interpret these claims if we assume that Kant argues for his "restriction" thesis only in the *Transcendental Dialectic*.)

Such a dependence on what is required for a unified apperception is what Hegel is referring to when he says, as he frequently does, that Kant and Fichte both try to "deduce" the categories "*from* the 'I' alone" or "ground" them in the "I." Such phrases, if taken out of context, can make it sound as if Hegel's reworking of this position in his Absolute Idealism will have some divine mind *creating* "Notions." Taken in context, though, such passages reveal that Hegel simply understands the idealistic consequences of Kant's use of the apperception thesis – the strongly antiempirical argument for the a priori status and necessity of such conditions, and the claim that no proof of the validity of such concepts can depend on experience, because the categories are constitutive of what could be apperceptive experiencing in the first place. Stated more simply, Kant's argument about the validity of the categories and the possibility of knowledge itself is everywhere oriented to the requirements of an apperceptive subjectivity and achieves idealistic results, results relativized to such a subject.

Moreover, in the first edition, there are equally explicit Kantian formulations about the idealism involved in the Deduction. For example, after writing that "objects, as appearances, constitute an object that is merely in us," Kant goes on at A129 to explain what he means by this Berkeleyean-sounding phrase:

> Now what this notion expresses, the notion that all these appearances and consequently all objects with which we can occupy ourselves, are one and all in me, that is, are determinations of my identical self, is that there must be a complete unity of them in one and the same apperception.

In this passage, the crucial idealizing phrase "in me" asserts a different kind of dependence on the subject than it first appears to express. "In me" seems to mean that "anything I represent must be capable of being represented by an identical self-conscious subject and so subject to the conditions for the possibility of such a unitary 'I.' " Whatever modes of unification are necessary for the very possibility of a unitary subject of experience determine what could count as a possible object of experience, and so provide the "ideal" unity of experience. Or, again, in Kant's famous claim, "The conditions for the possibility of experience in general are likewise the conditions for the possibility of the objects of experience" (B197–A158).

So when Hegel, particularly in his early writings, praises the Deduction's idealism because of the way it initially reveals the "speculative principle of identity," he need not be construed either of badly missing where Kant argues for his idealism or of importing some metaphysical-theological theory about the identity between God's mind and its thoughts. He is simply praising Kant for realizing that what counts as "object" can only be determined by a "subject," that all an object *is* is "that in the concept of which the manifold is united" (all this without taking into account the obvious fact that Hegel also severely criticizes the idealism as "finite" and "psychologistic").

Thus, besides the fact that these nonempirical conditions of unity are themselves ideal because linked to the requirements of *our* apprehension, it can also be said that Kant's position is idealistic because it asserts that what we experience is always subject to those conditions. To claim that we "only know appearances" would then be to claim that, even though we can come to know a variety of things about externally existing, spatiotemporal objects, such judgments are themselves always subject to specific and categorical conditions. The fact that the categories can *only* be proven to be objectively valid for our apprehension of the world renders their status ideal; and the fact that they *can* be established as necessary conditions for any experience, in that sense and that sense alone, renders our experience itself ideal.

As we have now seen, although Kant himself believed that there was an important further connection between these claims for an ideal unity to experience and the ideality that results from the argument in the Transcendental Aesthetic (cf. B145), it is the idealism required by the apperceptive character of all experience that is the focus both of Hegel's explicit discussion of Kant and, as the earlier quotation concerning the Notion revealed, of his own reworking of this characteristic of thinking. This is nowhere more obvious than in an *Encyclopedia* passage that, I hope, can now be understood in its proper Kantian context:

> The word "I" expresses the abstract relation-to-self; and whatever is placed in this unit or focus is affected by it and transformed into it. The "I" is as it were the crucible and the fire which consumes the loose plurality of sense and reduces it to unity.... The tendency of all man's endeavors is to understand the world, to appropriate and subdue it to himself: and to this end the positive reality of the world must be as it were crushed and pounded [*zerquetscht*], in other words, idealized.
>
> (*EL*, 118; *EnL*, 69)

Unfortunately, there are not many other passages that clarify *how* Hegel thought Kant advanced from some claim about the apperceptive nature of experience to some claim about the specific nature of the ideal or subject-determined unity of experience. However, it is at least clear that he is accepting, in a general way, a highly plausible and well-known version of Kant's strategy. Since his very term for consciousness is "being-for-self," it is clear that he accepts completely that there must be a unity of apperception in *any* conscious subject–object relation. It is also clear from such passages as the following:

> There can be no consciousness without self-consciousness. I know something, and that about which I know something I have in the certainty of myself [*das wovon*

ich weiss habe ich in der Gewissheit meiner selbst] otherwise I would know nothing of it; the object is my object, it is other and at the same time mine, and in this latter respect I am self-relating. (*BPhG*, 55)

And, although Hegel will radically alter Kant's procedure for deducing the objective validity of categories, he goes on in this passage to indicate that he too will try to discover in the requirement for a unity of apperception the specific a priori constraints that must be taken to be involved in all experience. To be sure, Hegel uses so much of his own terminology to make this point that the relation of his procedure to the Transcendental Deduction is often hard to make out. But it is still discernible in such claims as the following:

As this self-certainty with regard to the object [the implicit self-relation wherein I take myself to be intending *this* in *such* a way] abstract self-consciousness therefore constitutes the drive to posit what it is implicitly [*an sich*]; i.e., to give content and objectivity to the abstract knowledge of itself, and conversely, to free itself from its sensuousness, to sublate the given objectivity, and to posit the identity of this objectivity with itself. [That is, to understand none of the fundamental ways in which I take myself to experience the world as empirical or "sensuous," and yet still to understand their objectivity, that they are not just "my" way or my species's way of taking things to be.] (*BPhG*, 59)

Moreover, they would both deny "realist" theories of consciousness, particularly rationalist claims about sensation being a direct, immediate, though "unclear" apprehension of objects. They agree, that is, on a basic consequence of the apperception thesis: that all apprehension is mediated by the subject's *taking itself* to be apprehending in a specific way, so that a necessary component of any relation to objects is a self-relation. And they agree that this does not mean that this self-relation should be taken to imply that the subject is aware of its own mental states, as in dogmatic idealism or phenomenalism.[24]

In general, then, this is what I take to be the broad context of agreement between Kant and Hegel about the apperceptive element of experience, and at least some of the idealistic implications both drew from such a feature. To be sure, such an agreement by no means exhausts the topic of Kantian idealism, and it construes such idealistic implications in a broad way. That is, I have been following Hegel in calling idealistic claims like the following: The unity of apperception is possible only if nonempirical concepts apply to all objects of experience, and experience itself is intelligible only as "conditioned" by such requirements of thought. Since I have undertaken this discussion as a way of introducing the main problems of Hegel's idealism, I now turn to a general account of Hegel's chief criticism of Kant's fundamental premise.[25]

4. Kantian formality

One of the most important of their differences, the one most apparent in Hegel's best-known text, the *PhG*, is that the Kantian account of human subjectivity restricts itself to the point of view of "consciousness" alone, and so does not understand subjectivity as it should be, as "spirit," *Geist*. To make good such a charge, Hegel attempts to reformulate the notion of subjectivity itself, attacking virtually all of the post-Cartesian assumptions, denying that consciousness is "private," "inner," or a "spectator" of itself and world, and asserting that it is, in a special sense of the term, "communal," "public," and even socially interactive. But, as I have been trying to show throughout this introduction, one can again begin to see what Hegel is trying to do in such a project by noticing how he proposes to alter the aspect of Kant's *idealism* that he found so otherwise attractive: Kant on the apperceptive nature of experience. In that context, the problem is easy to state, but fully understanding it will finally lead us, along the Fichtean road, to Hegel's own texts.

The criticism, which I only introduce here, is that Kant's account of the unity of apperception is excessively *formal*. For example, throughout the section of the *Berlin Phenomenology* that deals with Kant ("Consciousness"), Hegel repeats frequently charges identical to ones made in his earliest Jena writings, that, for Kant "the I is for-itself *only (nur)* as formal identity"; that "the Kantian philosophy can most accurately be considered as having grasped spirit as consciousness," and so cannot understand a full "philosophy of spirit"; that this (consciousness's) identity with itself is, again, "only formal"; and that because of this restriction, "Since the I is construed not as the Notion, but as formal identity, the dialectical movement of consciousness in it is not construed as its own activity, but as in itself; that is, for the I, this movement is construed as a change in the object of consciousness" (*BPhG*, 11).[26]

These passages, together with many others, pose the problems of accounting for the significance of this constant reference to Kantian formality as "mere" or "only" formality, and of explaining Hegel's positive alternative, his claim that the various fundamental modes of self-understanding required for conscious experience and knowledge are not various because of new discoveries about objects and are not (or at least are not wholly) "empty" forms, the entire "content" of which must be supplied exogenously. Such passages also introduce Hegel's idiosyncratic view about the "a priori" status of the Notion, here described as the "dialectical movement of consciousness." "A priori" must be put in quotation marks because even though, as this and other passages make clear, Hegel clearly believes that there is a level of "conceptual discrimination," pure concepts, that is unrevisable by the "objects of consciousness," by any experience, come what may, he does not subscribe to the standard view, we might call it, according to which what is a priori (and "necessary for any intelligible, determinate discrimination of objects," for that matter) is unrevisable, full stop.[27] As the peculiar language of the preceding quotation indicates, the Notion "moves." This idea will require considerable explanation, but Hegel has in mind a demonstration that any attempt to make use of a certain, determinate pure concept in discriminating objects fails or is inadequate in a way that leads to a certain kind of "revision" of such a Notion, particularly a revision of its exclusiveness or independence, an understanding of its relation to other concepts necessary for its own application, concepts that might originally have appeared "other," or the contrary of the original. This highly idealized account of "how thought would move, revise itself" in its attempt to overcome the various internal difficulties it can be said to encounter in making use of a Notion, is, of course, the story of Hegel's controversial "dialectical logic" and will be encountered in great detail later.

But again, all such Hegelian completions of Kant depend on a plausible construal of the formality criticism, and that, it should also be noted, is somewhat ironic, since Kant constantly insisted that one of the great *values* of his approach was its formality; that not only had he arrived at a defense of the conditions required for the possibility of "any possible knower" (i.e., one that is "formally" indifferent to any "material" – contingent, empirical, or metaphysical – property of subjects), but he had done so in a way that revealed precisely the mistakes of any account of the possibility of knowledge that tried to say something "noumenal" about that which thinks. That which thinks is only *that which* thinks, and so the "unity of apperception" can be accounted for "formally" as what any experiencer must minimally be able to "do" to be conscious. So, what Hegel is denying is Kant's frequent claim that the implicit "I think," the transcendental unity of apperception, is only, as Kant claims at A341, the "vehicle of concepts," the mere form of any thinking, and not itself a thought. However, Hegel does not argue thereby for a return to a "pre-Paralogism" position – that, for example, in *my* thinking, I must be aware of the specific referent of the personal pronoun (my "identity") or of some Cartesian mental substance or mental state. His counterposition on the self's relation to itself in experience, while extremely abstract and loaded with the unique terminology of Hegelian "negation," nevertheless involves no such claims – as when he writes,

> The I is now this subjectivity, this infinite relation to itself, but therein, namely in this subjectivity, lies its negative relation to itself, diremption, differentiation, judgment. The I judges, and this constitutes it as consciousness [*Ich urtheilt, diess macht dasselbe zum Bewusstsein*]; it repels itself from itself; this is a logical determination. (*BPhG*, 2)

This counterposed "logical determination," thought's "negative relation to itself," represents the core of Hegel's idealism and will require extensive commentary throughout the rest of this study. But it is apparent, even at this initial stage, *why* Hegel regards such a topic as his central problem. If, in other words, Hegel is right that Kant's own case for the apperceptive condition of any possible experience undercuts his strict separation between concept and intuition, and in particular renders impossible the use of some extraconceptual representation, a pure intuition, to account for categorical determinacy, then Hegel's project, as hinted at in the preceding quotation, is clearly on the horizon. It is, that is, if one still accepts the basic Kantian case against empiricism and the necessity for independently constitutive, conceptual conditions for experience, but can no longer answer the question of *which* conditions by an argument based on the requirements of a "pure manifold of intuition." Or, as I attempt to show in the next two chapters, Hegel realized more deeply and thoroughly than his contemporaries how *much* was involved in giving up a Kantian reliance on pure intuition, how one *had* to develop a theory of "thought's *self*-determination" if one was to retain Kant's central idealist insights. At least, so it appears if one accepts that the earlier suggested reconstruction of Hegel's views on the insufficiencies of Kant's Deduction is on the right track. If it is, then little of Kant's transcendental turn can be preserved unless we can come up with an alternative account of the *determinacy* of the supposedly necessary categorial determinations of objects (there can be no "schematism" on this account) and an alternative account of the objectivity of such purported determinations (there can be no "second half" of the B Deduction on this account).

Indeed, such a point of departure opens the door to a number of related issues that Hegel must address. He would agree that it is not enough just to explicate the "moments" of a conceptual scheme, even if it could be shown that the use of pure concepts involves an unusual dialectical relation among such concepts. It is obvious that the discriminations specified by such a scheme could be, to use the relevant Kantian term, "empty"; it could be that there are no relevant instances of such dialectically determined concepts.[28] And the obvious Kantian question, once Hegel has revised the basic Kantian maxim that "concepts without *intuitions* are empty," is how Hegel will prove the contrary. That is, he must establish that there are empirically nonrevisable concepts necessarily presupposed for a subject to be able to make use of any concepts at all. He must *also* show that these concepts have "objective validity," although, as understood by Hegel, this Kantian term has a number of variations. It can mean something weaker, a proof that there can be no experience that is uncategorizable, that could conflict with the required conceptual distinctions, or something stronger, that objects do exhibit the distinctions we demand. And Hegel does try to prove both the stronger and weaker versions, in one case by showing (1) what a subject's "experience" would be like in any possible "relation to objects," as defined by some possible Notion, and (2) how there could not be such a relation at all in the absence of such a Notion, and yet how the experience is ultimately incoherent unless the Notion is "dialectically revised." And in another case, Hegel tries to show how thought does "determine itself" in its relation to objects in a way that exhausts the "purely conceptual" possibility of determinate, "thinkable" objects. The former refers to the *PhG* as the "deduction" of the *Logic*, the latter as what Hegel calls the "immanent deduction" present in the *Logic* itself.

Obviously, however, there still seem to be serious problems in such projected alterations of and disagreements with Kant in the first place. Why go through all this if the end point whose argument we are trying to reconstruct appears so implausible? If one denies that there are "formal" conditions for the possibility of any apperceptive experience, what else can one counterpose except an empirical or psychological or conventional or pragmatic account of how we come to acquire "what we find the hardest notions to give up" in the self-construals that make up our experience? How could such a development ever be successfully construed as a rational, internally negating, self-determination by "shapes" of "historical spirit," until finally, absolute subjectivity is attained? And, assuming that such an "absolute standpoint" could be reached, what would it mean to claim that a "logic" of "thought's pure self-determinations" could not only be given, as the "logic" of "objects in their truth," but that it could be *completely* given? Not only, would such an initial complaint go, are there never any detailed anti-Kantian arguments in Hegel, but what he proposes as a competing account is so hopelessly and endlessly vague, and yet so important in Hegel's project, as to warrant a wholesale rejection of that project. To paraphrase a well-known historical remark: Without the idea of the Notion's self-determination, one cannot enter the Hegelian system; but with that idea, one cannot remain within it.

The purpose of the rest of this book is to address these questions. However, even now, if we keep in mind the Kantian context Hegel himself sets for his discussion of the Notion (the passage quoted earlier that claims to adopt the Kantian insight that the unity of the Notion is the *unity of self-consciousness*), it should at least be clear that Hegel is not heading toward any neo-Platonic theory of conceptual emanation, with some "cosmic spirit" ejecting the world in its becoming self-conscious. The point of the Hegelian proposal so far presented seems rather to begin with, and take its bearings from, a certain theory of *self-conscious subjectivity* and the relation between such a subject and any possible account of the conditions of knowledge. Accordingly, what Hegel is committing himself to in this criticism of formality and "mere" subjectivity in Kant is not a deduction of the content of the actual universe or of world history. He is committing himself to the necessity of nonempirically derived and so (for Hegel) "self-determined" conditions for the intelligible experience of any object; to an eventual claim that these conditions can be derived by showing how even the most general conceptual function (e.g., the notion, "being") requires a much more complicated conceptual structure just for its own application; and to a strategy that can show why this idealist program is not subject to the standard realist attack – that even if *our* best criteria for "knowledge of X" are fulfilled, we still have no way of knowing whether such fulfillment does tell us anything about X. To be sure, although such a reading does not commit Hegel to a metaphysical, Absolute Spirit or to a divine intellectual intuition, creating the instances it intuits, it nevertheless does commit him to a radical and extremely complex view of "any possible subjectivity" only parts of which, I shall try to show, can be adequately defended.

Ominous as potential problems loom, though, their origin in the particular way that Hegel is appropriating Kant should not be lost sight of. Since Hegel says explicitly that the "unity" of the "concept" can be understood, at least in part, as what Kant meant by the "unity of apperception," and that the doctrine of "negativity" at the heart of his dialectical logic can be understood in terms of the way any *subject* both unifies experience and "negates" this unity by realizing (in a nonempirical way) its internal deficiencies, then it can at least be claimed that Hegel should be interrogated in terms of this kind of project and not some other. There are no doubt difficult and perhaps insoluble problems in Hegel's sweeping attempt to explain basic conceptual change through attention to the dynamic of presupposition and practical self-refutation internal to any conceptual position, and to his simultaneous attempt to hold on to and radically extend Kant's Deduction argument that pure concepts are not merely subjective impositions, but determine the nature of objectivity itself in ways that, progressively articulated, eliminate the possibility of skeptical or realist objections. There may be no such preempirical categorial level; whatever it is, the way it changes and interprets itself may not at all be rationally progressive; and a basic aspect of the "practical" self-determining aspects of self-relation might be wholly individual or "groundless," rooted neither in the logic of self-relation nor in its historical manifestation.

But what Hegel's critics and Hegel ought to be arguing about in such disputes can be made much more concrete if the preceding suggestions about his debt to Kant are correct.[29] Such disputes should ultimately be about such claims as whether any possible experience *is* inherently reflexive or not; whether a necessary condition of such unitary reflexivity *is* an interdefined, historically progressive, complex of pure or nonempirically derived concepts; whether some nonmetaphorical sense can be given to the notion that any subject attempting to unify experience coherently by means of some such candidate concept would be involved in some sort of "self-negation," would require some specific successor concept in order to resolve, if only provisionally, such a negation; and finally, whether, by understanding the logic of such determination and self-negation, one could finally understand how such a systematic relating of pure concepts could be *completed*, resulting in a "science" of intelligibility itself, an account of all possible account giving, or a "science of logic."

Admittedly, this is only an introductory sketch of how the self-relation or apperception problem survives and remains central in Hegel's project. But Hegel's criticisms of Kant do help raise the crucial issues of his own idealism, what one might call the radically "internalist" tendencies of Hegel's argument. That is, by rejecting the notion that a firm distinction can be drawn between Kantian form and matter, or between nonderived subjective conditions and sensible matter, whether that metaphor is used to illuminate all knowledge or the specific issue of formal apperception and material self-knowledge, Hegel has committed himself to what appears to be an extremely eccentric and implausible theory. Hegel seems to believe that the specification of a wide range of conceptual determinations, from philosophical theories to scientific principles, can be shown to develop "internal" to any subject's *self*-understanding, without reliance on empirical "matter" and without an exogenous foray into the table of judgments. And he believes that it can still be shown that such internally derived "forms of experience" are *not*, finally, only forms of experience, or subjective impositions, cutting us off from things in themselves, but constitute "all that objectivity could be." But before such interpretations can be stated, the initial implausibility of Hegel's idea of the "notion determining itself" should be confronted more determinately. I believe that can be done by examining Fichte from a Hegelian point of view, since Fichte is a philosopher who, it seems, *does* try to "deduce" what he called the material "not-I" from the formal "I." Examining this attempt should help, then, to introduce and to focus the idealism problem that Hegel's own major texts will attempt to solve.

3
Fichte's contribution

The importance of Fichte for a proper understanding of Hegel's idealism goes beyond the fact that Hegel's all-important appropriation of Kant was everywhere influenced by Fichte's reading of the central issues and unresolved problems in Kant. However much Hegel vigorously dissociated himself from Fichte, from some of his earliest philosophical work in Jena to what may be the most important discussion in the *Science of Logic* (the rejection of both "external" and "positing" reflection),[1] the Fichtean account of subjectivity would nevertheless remain recognizable in Hegel's later system, as would Fichte's speculative understanding of "thought" as a "self-determining activity."[2]

Hegel's debt to Fichte is, then, quite real and quite complex.[3] The important interpretive issues raised by it are, in the context of this study and the problem noted previously, twofold. First, what is the status of Fichte's interpretation of Kant? More specifically, does Fichte's interpretation of Kant's idealism contribute anything of significance to the issues raised by Kant? Indeed, one must ask, as one must with Hegel, does Fichte even identify such issues properly, in a way relevant to Kant's argument? Not surprisingly, it turns out that Fichte marks the path for Hegel's later interests by insisting on the centrality of Kant's account of apperception for idealism and, having done so, suggests a bold, radical revision of the principle. As we shall see more clearly in the next chapter, it was with these revisions that Hegel began to see how Kant's theoretical idealism might be interpreted in such a way as to be of relevance to the practical issues of social disharmony, religous positivity, and Kantian moralism or asceticism so important to him prior to his move to Jena and throughout his life. Assessment of the philosophical significance of this Fichtean turn in the idealist tradition has already been partly prepared for by the preceding discussion of Kant, and can now be completed by attending to the central statements of Fichte's early idealism.

Second, it is important to discuss the details of the failure of Fichte's contribution, for all its value and suggestiveness. Understanding that failure, at least as Hegel saw it (correctly, I believe), is one good, initial way to understand Hegel's early statements of his position. That is, understanding in detail why Hegel thought Fichte failed is an obvious way to avoid confusing Hegel's position with Fichte's, however misleading some of Hegel's own formulations are.

3. FICHTE'S CONTRIBUTION

1. The spirit of Kantianism

There is, first of all, little doubt that, as a matter of historical fact, Fichte believed that his early (pre-1804)[4] versions of idealism were firmly based on Kant's transcendental idealism; that, despite such indebtedness, he had identified a serious problem in Kant's account; and that he believed that his own "Doctrine of Knowledge" (*Wissenschaftslehre*) had made great progress toward solving that problem. However, identifying in Fichte such a contribution to the post-Kantian problem of idealism is notoriously difficult, given Fichte's hermetic style, clumsy neologisms, and often wildly speculative, unsupported claims. Indeed, Fichte's references to Kant can be quite subtle, as when, without mentioning Kant, he begins his first *Introduction* by borrowing Kant's borrowing of a passage from Bacon's *Instauratio Magna* as the epigram of the *Critique of Pure Reason*.[5] The borrowing from Kant is ironic because Fichte alters what Kant uses from Bacon, leaving out a phrase Kant had included: "De nobis ipsis silemus" ("We are silent about ourselves"). Not only does Fichte decline to repeat what had already been a slightly ironic Baconian humility, he is also silently pointing to his great difference with Kant about an issue at the center of their relationship. As we shall see, for Fichte, Kant was indeed too silent about the subject, about ourselves, and that is the deficiency Fichte aims to correct.

Such an intention comes out more clearly in Fichte's explicit remarks about Kant (especially in the 1797 *Introductions*) and in the opening moves of his 1794 *Wissenschaftslehre*. In the former, he proclaims proudly:

> I have long asserted and repeat once more, that my system is nothing other than the Kantian; this means that it contains the same view of things but is in method quite independent of the Kantian presentation.[6]

The spirit of Kantianism that Fichte purports to be extending does indeed include a number of recognizable features of the Kantian project; the object "is posited and determined by means of the faculty of knowledge (*durch das Erkenntnisvermögen*), and not the faculty of knowledge by means of the object"[7]; and the "object of philosophy, as the ground of the explanation of experience, must lie outside experience."[8] But it is when he launches into his own "presentation" of this "ground" that Fichte stakes out a claim that appears to transcend both Kant and philosophic respectability. For, Fichte argues, what Kant had presupposed as a necessary condition of experience, the "I that thinks," or an apperceptive subject, had remained unclarified and incompletely presented in Kant. It was not enough, for Fichte, to tell us that "the 'I think' must accompany all my representations" or that human understanding was necessarily apperceptive, without telling us how *that* condition was itself possible or what was fully entailed by a self being "in relation to itself" in all its experiences. All of this means that for Fichte, the basic problematic of transcendental philosophy cannot be either the refutation of Humean skepticism about synthetic a priori knowledge or the exposure of rationalist/realist transgressions of the subject-determined, ideal limits of experience. Both such claims depend on an explanation and a systematic expansion of the single issue Fichte praises Kant for discovering but criticizes him for "forgetting" to pursue further, the issue Fichte himself expresses as: "how is the I for itself?"[9]

All of this introduces the first problem in assessing Fichte's transformation of Kant. Clearly, these and many other related remarks involve a claim to have given a more adequate account of transcendental subjectivity than Kant did, and then to show, again more adequately, how the "I's" relation to itself in all experience can be shown to be in some sense "responsible" for the ideal structure of experience and its possible objects.

This is already an unusual, elusive issue, but it gets more complicated when we summarize simply the two other major elements of Fichte's Kantian animadversions. First, in characterizing the *Intelligenz* or subjectivity that is the ground of the possibility of experience, Fichte stresses, or, more accurately, exaggerates the Kantian claim about thought stressed in the previous chapter – it is an "activity,"not a "passivity." For Fichte this appears to mean a kind of *complete* autonomy for the intellect; it depends on nothing but itself and "has no being proper, no subsistence."[10] That is:

> The intellect, for idealism, is an act, and absolutely nothing more; we should not even call it an active something, for this expression refers to something subsistent in which activity inheres.[11]

And this unusual claim about the self-determined nature of intellect and its radical priority means, in Fichte's idealism, that it is only "out of the activity of this intellect [that] we must deduce specific presentations: of a world, of a material, spatially located world existing without our aid, etc., which notoriously occur in consciousness."[12] Hence the most controversial Fichtean thesis: the so-called deduction of the not-I from the I and its "activities."

Second, and in many ways more prominently, Fichte draws immediate practical consequences from his account of this "self-active intellect," namely, that from "the philosophic point of view," such a subjective activity must be seen as *free*, and that therefore there can be a systematic connection between Kant's theoretical and moral philosophy. And as noted earlier, this introduces the central theme of post-Kantian German Idealism: the reconciliation, in a higher systematic unity, of Kant's fundamental dualism of nature and freedom. According to Fichte, a proper understanding of "how the I is for itself" will accomplish this goal.

If, then, the question is whether Fichte's revisions of Kant, revisions that were so important in Hegel's even formulating the problem of idealism, represent any philosophically significant extensions of genuine problems in Kant, the issues in terms of which that question will have to be decided are these three claims by the early Fichte: (1) that Kant's account of apperception was incomplete, (2) that it must be completed in a theory of an autonomous, self-positing subjectivity upon which our experience of objects can be shown to depend (my discussion will concentrate on these two claims), and (3) that this activity can be shown to be relevant to the moral issue of practical freedom. (This issue introduces a book-length set of issues and can better be discussed independently. I have already tried to indicate why I think it depends on a resolution of the first two.)

At issue in such a summary is the precise Kantian origin for such claims by Fichte as the following:

> Without self-consciousness there is no consciousness whatever; but self-consciousness is possible only in the manner indicated: I am simply active.[13]

As we have already seen, it is not hard to detect a general Kantian origin for such remarks. Kant does indeed insist that consciousness, construed as a representing activity, must be inherently reflexive in order to be representative, genuinely to have objects. As I have interpreted this claim to self-consciousness, it does not involve a commitment to some mysterious, secondary, *intentional* self-regarding, but rather defines certain cognitive abilities as conditional on other cognitive abilities; in the most obvious case, that a genuinely judgmental ability presupposes one's understanding that one *is* judging, making a claim subject to the rules of "redemption" and legitimation appropriate to such claims. Or, stated in representational terms, this means that there is no internal property of a mental state's occurring in me, and no property of that state's real relation with other states, that makes it a representation *of X*. For such a state to represent *I* must "take it up," unite it with other (or other possible) representations, and thereby self-consciously represent X.

Further, again as noted in detail in the previous chapter, Fichte is on solid ground both in stressing that apperceptive consciousness (or what he has called the "intellect") is an activity and that it is some sort of "unconditioned" (at least empirically unconditioned) activity. For, defining "the mind's power of producing representations from itself," Kant does indeed (at B75–A51) introduce that frequently used "Fichtean" synonym for the "understanding": "the spontaneity of knowledge." And "spontaneity" is the term Kant also uses in describing the "unconditioned causality of freedom" (B561–A533) or indeed any "self-causing" activity, such as God's intellectual intuition. Indeed, given these other associations, and the way Kant uses the term throughout the first *Critique*, such a characterization of the understanding as spontaneous seems to be, from his point of view, a puzzlingly strong one. Prima facie, it appears to commit Kant to the claim that an apperceptive understanding cannot be construed as a matter-of-fact or empirical relation among mental states or as a formally described faculty that might (for all we know) be instantiated in a causal system of some kind. It certainly looks like a flat-out claim that the intellect must *be* a self-causing activity, and that appears to be a much stronger claim that Kant's own transcendental formalism will allow. However strong, though, it is quite an important one, as is evident by its role in *the* fundamental Kantian duality – between receptivity and spontaneity. That the intellect's synthesizing activity is not, even in some highly complex, indirect way, a result of sensible receptivity, but a separate, autonomous condition of experience, is an indispensable component in Kant's idealism; although, as Fichte often points out, Kant does not say enough about it, or draw out its full implications.

However, trying to decide what Kant did mean by such a term, or what he thought he was and was not committed to by claiming that apperception was spontaneous, would require its own lengthy discussion.[14] At this point, in this Fichtean summary of Kant, we shall just note that Kant did indeed leave open a number of possible interpretations of his claim that experience of objects was necessarily apperceptive (in Fichtean terms, that experience of objects depends on, even could be deduced from the self's relation to itself), and that he frequently intimated without fully explaining a characteristic of such apperception that Fichte will seize upon and expand dramatically – the "spontaneity" characteristic.

2. Fichtean apperception

As this brief summary indicates, much of Fichte's early project depends on an extremely compressed interpretation of Kant's transcendentalism. As noted, for Fichte, Kant's theory of apperception is the idealist fulcrum because of its function as a necessary condition for all experience; any representation of X involves, as a necessary condition, my taking myself to be representing X, and this condition cannot be the result of other representations if it is also a condition of *their* possibility. Hence such a self-relating must be "spontaneous," a self-determined activity. Although he does not explore the matter in any detail, this alone, for Fichte, forecloses the possibility of realist and empiricist epistemologies, and in a more attenuated way, materialist or determinist metaphysics, and so establishes the project of a practically relevant transcendental idealism – *if*, that is, the concept of such an epistemic self-determination can be explained. However, in looking for such an explanation, we encounter a variety of controversies.

First, some of Fichte's formulations occasionally appear to claim that the apperception condition *does* mean that there are two separate "moments" of all intentional consciousness, or he seems simply to conflate consciousness and self-consciousness. His position sometimes seems to claim that in "thinking a thought," *two* mental events occur, or two two-place relations, between my thinking and its thought, and between me and my thinking a thought. Thus, although he admits that he is speaking figuratively (*bildlich*), he does say that there is always a "double series" (*doppelte Reihe*) in experience, of "being" (*Sein*), by which Fichte denotes the content of consciousness, and of "looking on" (*Zusehen*), not just an object apprehended by a subject, but by a subject that "looks on" at its own apprehending.[15]

If this is what he really means, then all sorts of problems are obvious. The most damaging is the iteration problem. If consciousness and self-consciousness are treated as separate aspects of any consciousness, then the arguments that showed why consciousness of X must be accompanied by consciousness of consciousness of X would all apply to the latter too, since self-consciousness, at least as suggested by this version of Fichte, would also be an instance of consciousness and so subject to its conditions. Yet there are strong indications that this conflationist tone in Fichte arises more through sloppiness than through intent, and he often makes clear in the same passage, sometimes in the same sentence, a countervailing and somewhat more Kantian tendency. For example, the "intelligence" (*Intelligenz*), he writes,

> observes itself, and this self-seeing pertains to everything that is; and in this immediate unity of being and seeing consists the nature of the intelligence. What is in it, and what it in general is, is for itself (*für sich selbst*).[16]

In this passage, the image of an intelligence "observing itself" suggests that an explicit self-consciousness accompanies all acts of consciousness, an interpretation that seems confirmed in this passage when Fichte, using imagining an object as his example, claims that I am conscious of, or observe (*zusehen*), the act of bringing forth the object (*hervorbringen*) and the object (*Sein*). However, the indication that this is not the full statement of Fichte's theory is signaled by his use of the adverb "immediately" in describing this self-seeing, and by the phrase the "immediate unity" of being and seeing (*unmittlebare Vereinigung*). If the self-observing in question is "immediate," or, as we shall see, an "intuition," then Fichte must be talking about a component of experience, not an accompanying experience. If indeed there is such an immediate unity, then there *cannot be* a "thinking of X" that is in some way subsequently or separately "observed" by a transcendental self. Transcendental self-consciousness could not be an inference I draw about myself, or my observing myself doing or undergoing something; it must be "immediately" part of what it is to do or undergo something consciously.

But such a qualification, important as it is, is still a piece of scene setting. Fichte's own contribution is apparent only when he advances quite a radical claim in the body of the 1794 *Wissenschaftslehre* that this transcendental apperception should be understood as a "pure" self-positing – his version of what we have seen as Kant's spontaneity thesis – and when he develops an idealist system based on this basic condition. So, to come finally to the heart of the matter, what *does* it mean, in the Kantian context developed earlier, to claim that apperception is a spontaneous self-positing?

At this point, one way of understanding what he might mean is to consider an extremely important and widely influential interpretation of this issue, that argued by Dieter Henrich in his article "Fichtes ursprüngliche Einsicht." So many of the more philosophic reconstructions of Fichte in recent years have been influenced by Henrich that a consideration of his approach might provide a useful entreé to the problem.[17] Henrich's treatment is, by design, limited. The insight that he is exclusively interested in is Fichte's demonstration of the impossibility of any "reflective theory of self-consciousness." Henrich's suggestion is that we can see what Fichte means by apperception by understanding the power of his critique of all conventional, reflective theories.

I. THE IDEALIST BACKGROUND

According to Henrich, any theory that claims that self-consciousness involves some kind of bipolar reflective awareness of a self must founder on two objections. First, the account must be circular. I am supposed to become aware of myself by virtue of directing attention to "me" as an object of consciousness. But if *I* do that, then, insofar as I know I'm doing it, I am already self-conscious. So the "act" of self-consciousness presupposes itself, and I can become self-conscious only if I already am. Second, the reflective theory suggests that I identify an object of my awareness *as* me, as if I have criterion of recognition that I apply in becoming aware of myself. But this begs the question of *how* I can be said to identify some intentional object as myself in the first place. It assumes (by the postulation of this criterion) that I have already so identified myself and *that* self-consciousness requires its own explanation. Henrich does not mention other well-known problems with the self-as-object-of-awareness view of self-consciousness, such as Hume's phenomenological difficulty (there is no such object to be found in my experience) or Ryle's temporal problem (the self I observe would not be me as observ*ing*, and so would not be *self*-consciousness), but the problems he states are certainly enough to cast doubt on what appears to be a commonsense interpretation of self-consciousness.[18]

These, then, Henrich claims, were the considerations that led Fichte to his first (1794) statement of his own self-relation theory, summarized in Henrich's phrase as "The I unqualifiedly (or absolutely, without mediation) posits itself" ("*Das Ich setzt schlechthin sich selbst*"). The *schlechthin* in that formula is supposed to prevent us from thinking that there *is* an *I* prior to its self-positing, as the grammatical structure of the phrase suggests. The notion of a "self-creating" *I* is, of course, very hard to understand, much less to state without this grammatical structure. Fichte tries to find a way of doing so, but succeeds only in adding to the confusion:

> Self-positing and being (with respect to the I) are completely the same. The proposition: I am, because I have posited myself, can accordingly also be expressed: I am just because [*schlechthin weil*] I am.[19]

To be sure, for all his obscurity, Fichte is nevertheless struggling with an important issue. The idea that one's self cannot be said to exist except as the thought one has of oneself, and that this "thinking of oneself" is not a reflective grasp of a self, but a kind of activity that constitutes the self, is an idea that reaches far beyond Fichte, back to its romantic motivation and forward to Nietzsche, Sartre, and other twentieth-century thinkers. But Fichte's original formulation of the issue is itself, Henrich claims, subject to fatal deficiencies. Simply put, although, in Henrich's version, Fichte is clearly indicating by his notion of positing his desire to free himself from the reflective metaphors of self-observation, or "turning around" to see the self, he does not succeed in doing so, or "elements of the reflective theory are now insinuating themselves into Fichte's counter-proposal."[20] That is, this version of Fichte's fundamental or first principle still implies a distinction between the self as positing, and, as a result of that positing, as posited; in that case, we have no true self-consciousness *in* self-positing. The fact that Fichte must claim that the *I* as *subject* of such activity posits *itself* clearly reveals how much Fichte is still wedded to the bipolarity of the reflective model. Even though that relation is now one of activity and result, rather than of subject and object, there is still such a relation. Fichte tried to deny this result by claiming that the I does not exist prior to or as a result of this positing, that it just *is* such self-positing, but he gave us no clear way to see how that could be described.

This is the first and most important move in Henrich's reconstruction, his attempt to praise Fichte for an incomplete but important insight that Henrich claims philosophers have never noticed in him: his powerful case against reflective models of self-consciousness. According to Henrich, what makes Fichte's insight so powerful is the fact that the entire modern tradition can be shown to assume the reflective theory of self-awareness dealt a devastating blow by Fichte. In this regard, Henrich briefly cites Descartes, Leibniz, Locke, Rousseau, and especially Kant.

However, at this point it begins to become clear that there are two distinct issues involved in Henrich's reconstruction of Fichte, and that his discussion is concentrating on only one of them. There is, first, the strictly transcendental issue: *how* the "I think" should be said to accompany *all* my representations of objects. Then, given what one might discover about Fichte's reasons for claiming that this self-relation cannot be a reflective one, there might be very good reasons indeed for going on to argue that the kinds of self-consciousness important to other philosophers in a nontranscendental context *also* cannot be based on a reflective model. But it would not then be correct, for that reason alone, to lump together such theories, many of which try to explain the experience of self-consciousness, with Fichte's apperception problem. Although, as indicated earlier, Fichte is not totally consistent on this score, in the First and Second *Introductions*, the 1797 *Versuch einer neuren Darstellung der Wissenschaftslehre*, and other works of this period, he is quite clear that his account of "self-positing" is *not* to be taken as a theory of the experience of self-consciousness.[21] He insists that this original self-relation "is not a conceiving" but a "mere intuition" and that "It is also, accordingly, no consciousness, not even a consciousness of self."[22] And in his fullest statement:

> By the act described, the self is merely endowed with the possibility of self-consciousness, and therewith of all other consciousness; but no true consciousness comes into being as yet. The act in question is merely a part, and a part not originally separated but only to be distinguished by the philosopher, of that entire enterprise of the intellect, whereby it brings its consciousness into being.[23]

In the *Versuch*, he writes:

> Now the discussion here concerns no other being of the I [*Sein des Ich*] than that in the described self-intuition; or put still more strongly, than the being of this

intuition itself. I am this intuition and simply nothing more, and this intuition itself is I. It is not the case that through this self positing, something like the existence of the I, as a thing existing independently of consciousness, is brought about.[24]

Even in contexts where Fichte is trying to make use of his account of apperception to build a theory of explicit self-determination, as in the 1798 *Sittenlehre (Doctrine of Ethics)*, he is careful to point out that the self's original self-positing is not "for itself" an act of self-creation, and that this activity must be distinguished from what happens when you make yourself the object of a conscious intention.[25] And, in summarizing his earlier 1794 *Science of Knowledge*, he writes

This self-consciousness comes about, but not as a fact (*Faktum*), for as such it is immediate, but in connection with all other consciousness as reciprocally conditioning that consciousness, as it is conditioned by it, as proved in the *Foundations of the Entire Science of Knowledge*.[26]

Thus, what Fichte is trying to explain in the 1794 version cannot be a form of self-identification but, as with Kant, the possibility of self-conscious judgments about objects. To be sure, Henrich is right; he is quite clearly denying that this condition of self-consciousness should be construed as requiring some supervening "looking on" by the self of itself (I do not judge in every judgment *that* I am judging). Unfortunately, the way Fichte decided to stress the *immediacy* of this aspect of experience, the fact that my taking myself to be perceiving, judging, imagining, and so on is not an inference or observation, was to use this *causa sui* language of positing. In trying to claim that the subject could not be "determined" to represent X if the representation was to count as a representation, Fichte's terminology created the impression that an intentional relation other than observing was necessary to explain the condition of self-consciousness, a productive, self-causing intentionality. But, as we have seen, Fichte is denying that this self-relation, as a transcendental condition, is an intentional relation at all. So his theory of self-positing cannot be a theory about the self's positing itself as an object, and therefore the self-creating terminology must be read quite carefully. (In Hegelian language, Fichte continues to be interested in the self as subject, not as experienced or intentional object. Even with respect to itself, it is its own subject, not an object.)[27]

According to Henrich, Fichte tries to correct some of the deficiencies created by this language when, in 1797, he states, "The I posits itself, absolutely as self-positing" ("*Das Ich setzt sich schlechthin als sich setzend*").[28] On Henrich's reading, Fichte realized with this formulation a continuing problem with his whole enterprise: that in any act of self-identification construed as positing or self-determining, such positing does not simply occur, but even such an originary *causa sui* is (and here all the problems return) itself a *self-conscious* activity. Now the "I" has to *be* self-positing and to *know* itself as self-positing, which seems to mean positing itself as a self-positing, ad infinitum. Said another way, Fichte has no way to unite the intuitive and conceptual components of his position: the intuitive immediacy of the self's positing and the conceptual reflexivity of a subject's consciousness of that activity.

As already indicated, however, although this reformulation does suggest a difficulty in Fichte, it should not be construed as a difficulty in a theory of self-identity or self-consciousness. I suggest that in this case, at the properly transcendental level of discussion, what Fichte is calling attention to is not merely the immediacy and nonisolatability of apperception in experience but the fact that such apperception, construed as an activity, introduces an implicit recognition of defeasibility into all empirical experience. That is, the "self-positing" of apperception "carries with it" necessarily a recognition that experience *is being* construed or judged in a certain way; the positing occurs *qua positing*, rather than qua caused, or in some other way, unknown to the subject.[29] And although I am certain that I am positing, I am not certain, just because I know I am responsible for such positing, that my positing "hits the mark." And it is only in *this* transcendental context that Henrich is correct in noting how the problem of the ground of such activity forces Fichte back to some account of the origin of determinate experience, prior to this unstable mixture of immediate positing and reflective realization. Although that ground problem is not, I have argued, related directly to the problem of self-identification, it is indeed a problem for Fichte to explain such obvious problems as *why* I take myself to be perceiving X when I am, or, to phrase the issue in a question Fichte would try to reject but cannot escape: What does the I rely on when it posits itself as such a particular *kind* of self-positing? Fichte's answer is as obvious as its unsatisfactoriness is immediate: The self relies on . . . the self!

And it is dissatisfaction with this obviously deficient answer that led, according to Henrich, to Fichte's major "turn," with the introduction in 1801 of a different set of metaphors. Self-consciousness is now "an activity in which an eye is inserted."[30] From this point on, Fichte will talk about the self's activity without reliance on any "product" of that activity, and will continue to expand the seemingly un-Fichtean images of an "eye" that sees itself, and of its being "inserted" in the I's activity.[31]

3. Idealism in the *Wissenschaftslehre*

But for our purposes, the course of Fichte's later development is not as important as what the preceding discussion can reveal about Fichte's idealism. That is, it has been argued thus far that if Fichte has an important contribution to make, it resides in his claim to have noticed the undeveloped nature of Kant's central claim about transcendental apperception, and especially to have developed, to have drawn the right consequences from, the claim that such apperception must be spontaneous or self-positing. As just noted, this means that Fichte's problematic cannot begin with the issue of an individual subject's knowledge of itself as an intentional object, or with the contents of its mind as belonging to that subject. Rather, the problem at stake is how to state coherently the self-positing apperception inherent in all representation of objects.

And the chief reason for noting this, for stressing that Fichte's problem – "how is the I for itself?" – cannot be isolated as a problem about the experience of self-consciousness, but concerns the self-mediated character of all conscious experience of objects, is that it helps make clearer an issue introduced in the last chapter: the largely implicit post-Kantian rejection of the Kantian doctrine of intuition. I suggested earlier that part of that rejection had to do with problems inherent in Kant's project that the Sage of Königsberg himself realized, and part had to do with the influence of Fichte's reading of Kant. We can see now that Fichte largely ignores the Kantian use of the doctrine of intuition in defending his idealism because he sees a much more sweeping, supervening idealist principle at work in Kant. Fichte essentially combines the explicit Kantian thesis about the centrality of judgment in experience (that objects can be considered possible objects of experience only as conforming to the conditions for the possibility of judgment) with the more implicit and undeveloped Kantian claims that such judgments are apperceptive and spontaneous. For Fichte, these two conditions can only mean, first, that the basic structure and coherence of our experience must be seen as a *result*, a result of an original "act" whereby any subject posits itself to be in relation to objects in certain fundamental ways. (This is why the true opponent of idealism for Fichte is always naturalism – the form of "dogmatism" he mentions most often – the claim that such a relation is determined or caused to be what it is by the object.) Thus, even a more developed Kantian transcendental argument designed to show why a subject must judge that all objects of its experience are in, say, a causal relation to others is still an argument about how a subject construes or determines itself. Second, such a stress on the apperception problem helps explain *why* Fichte was so infamously unwilling to preserve the fundamental Kantian distinction between receptivity and spontaneity. As we shall see in more detail in this section, Fichte thought it a necessary consequence of his own account of transcendental apperception that what Kant would regard as the manifold of intuitions given in experience should indeed be understood as a limitation on the subject's activity, but a limitation again taken or posited *to be* such a limitation *by* a subject.[32]

But in order to see the connections between this "supreme condition" (spontaneous apperception) and Fichte's version of idealism, we can now turn to a brief review of the argument of the 1794 *WL*. That work has three principal parts. Part One concerns the "fundamental principles" (*Grundsätze*) of the *WL*; Part Two is an account of the "foundations" (*Grundlage*) of theoretical knowledge; and Part Three discusses the foundations of the science of the practical. This organization suggests that there is a level of philosophic generality that includes, or can be shown to be presupposed by, both theoretical knowledge of objects and intentional activity, such that this transcendental level can account for the conditions of the possibility of such activities. This is indeed what Fichte proposes to do. Part One presents what, in Kantian terms, would be called a "regressive" transcendental argument intended to establish three such fundamental principles.[33] Then the possibilities of theoretical knowledge and practical activity are discussed in terms of these principles. In his own summation of the task of the *WL*, Fichte at one point describes it as demonstrating that the characteristics of "pure" activity itself, its "absolutely posited" and "self-grounded" characteristics, are the "ground" of *all human activity*, and everything in Fichte's early idealism turns on this use of "ground." From the earlier discussion we might expect that the obvious candidates for such foundational principles would be the self's "positing of itself" (or the Fichtean characterization of apperception) and the crucial epistemological issue – the relation between such positing and the "not-self" (or the Fichtean equivalent of Kant's transcendental deduction).

This is what is eventually introduced, but Fichte presents his case in a way very different from Kant's. For one thing, Kant's specific concentration on the possibility of synthetic a priori judgments in philosophy, science, and mathematics is abandoned in favor of a much broader, more ambitious goal:

> Our task is to discover the primordial, absolutely unconditioned first principle of all human knowledge. This can be neither proved nor defined, if it is to be an absolutely primary principle.[34]

With this ambition, Fichte quickly comes up with a good candidate for the most general presupposition of any "thought" in any context: the law of identity, A = A. Whatever our eventual ontology, epistemology, or morality, we can assert that, in any context, everything is, at least, what it is. Just as quickly, he notes that considering such a claim as a claim or a judgment reveals immediately its differences from "There is an A," or "A exists," or even "A." That is, for A to be identified with itself, it must in some way be putatively "divided" from itself; less metaphorically, A, for example, must be said to retain its identity *over time*.[35] At this point, we might expect a discussion of A's various properties and an argument designed to show the possibility of A = A by appeal to some essential property or properties that A cannot lose and still be A. But Fichte wants to keep his discussion as general or as primordial as possible, and this means explaining the possibility of the *knowledge* of identity without a commitment to essentialism or any specific criteria of identification. The issue is supposed to be the *possibility* of identification itself, considered independently of the metaphysics of identity. Hence, Fichte just calls this connection between A and itself "X."[36] *Whatever* A is, he then argues, its identification (the transcendental issue of identity) would necessarily presuppose a unity of consciousness sufficient for A to be posited, "carried along" as A, and reidentified. If there could not be some such consciousness within which A is identified with A, the possibility of this principle as involved in any thought of anything could not be established. Thus, we have quickly reached an even "higher" principle: the principle of the identity of the self in all its experiences, or I = I. However we end up accounting for the minimum conditions of stability of reference, conditions necessary for there to be thought (or language) at all, we shall still always presuppose in such accounts a selfsame subject within the experience of which such monadic units, whatever they may be, can be identified over time and reidentified by indexicals, names, or descriptions. For reasons already discussed, Fichte cannot regard *this* self-identity as a result of another act of identification, and so he claims that it must be considered an original positing. So, "standing at the forefront of a Doctrine of Knowledge" is *the* principle, "the self begins by an absolute positing of its own existence." And given what we have argued about the transcendental nature of such self-positing, we know that Fichte is not talking about the self's "second-level" experience of itself as posited or created, but is referring to the apperceptive nature of all judging about anything. The Fichtean "I = I," I am claiming, refers to *my* taking *my*self to be experiencing this or that in doing so. And thus, so far at least, all of this can be seen as what Fichte says it is, an analog to the Kantian principle that judging (even here in its minimal, least complex manifestation – identity judgments)[37] can only be the self-conscious activity of a subject (if it is to count as judging) and cannot be "ascribed to sensibility" or to any sensible cause.

This all seems, admittedly, quite a long way around the barn, and we still do not seem to be closer to a genuinely idealist conclusion. But it does raise the issue of how such an activity *constrains* itself, and so raises the idealist issue of "objectivity." If the self is not determined causally by its interaction with A, or by anything else, to identify A with A, what accounts for the obvious constraint on not being able to identify A with – A? This problem is the subject of Fichte's much more difficult second principle. Fichte calls the second principle the "principle of opposition" and argues, or asserts, that it cannot be deduced from the identity principle. The new principle is expressed as A ≠ – A. However, he also, as in the first case, draws a conclusion here about the way in which this claim presupposes a condition of consciousness, and that inference is much more compressed and confusing. He argues:

> As surely as the absolute certainty of the proposition – A is not equal to A is unconditionally admitted among the facts of empirical consciousness, *so surely is a not-self opposed absolutely to the self.*[38] (My emphasis)

In one explanation of this inference, Fichte appears to reason that the earlier argued necessity for I = I as a condition of A = A already implied a capacity on the part of any I to distinguish itself from the content of its representations. Such a self not only takes A to be identical with A, and not only implicitly takes *itself*, as a continuous subject of experience, to be identifying A with itself, but also differentiates itself from A, it posits itself as other than A, and so posits a not-self. Given that Fichte provides very little explanation, much less defense of this claim, it is hard to see why there should be this transcendental connection between the logical difference principle (A≠−A) and the epistemological issue of the subject's being distinct from (and being able to distinguish itself and what is due to its activities from) an object, or I≠−I. The latter might be said to be an instance of the former, but that is clearly not how Fichte intends to argue, since the latter, as in the first principle, is supposed to be a condition for the possibility of the former's being knowable.

Although the use of this second principle is by far the most complicated and obscure aspect of the *WL*, Fichte's intention is clear enough. The second principle becomes necessary when we cease treating A as a representation of "anything at all," in our consideration of the necessity of its self-identity, but treat it as some determinate thing, in Kantian language, as a possible *object* of a conscious representation. Since I do not identify "anything at all" with itself, but *this* or *that* thing, we have clearly left out a consideration of the conditions for my being able to recognize this or that *as this* or *that* in the first place. Fichte maintains that such determinate identification requires an ability to differentiate A from what it isn't, or A≠−A, and he suggests that it is *this* ability that presupposes that I≠−I. He had claimed that in considering any A or representation, say a cube representation, I can be certain that whatever A refers to, or *whatever a cube* is, is identical with itself, and can thereby also recognize the necessity for the self to be posed as identical with itself (i.e., as a condition for the recognition of such a continuous identity). When, however, I determine a *cube*, and just a cube, to be identical with itself, I can do so only by relying on some criterion that distinguishes a cube from, say, a sphere. A can be determined and identified *as A* only if it can be distinguished from −A. And it is the next step in Fichte's reconstruction that, finally, can be identified as his most important problem. In order to be able to distinguish a cube from a sphere, he reasons that I must be able to distinguish whatever is true of the cube I am attending to by virtue only of *my* perceiving or imagining it in a certain way from what it is about *a cube* that *limits* or restrains whatever I can think of it and still be thinking of a cube. This is what I take him to mean when he argues that the possibility of differentiation depends on the self's ability to distinguish itself and *its* "determinations" from the not-self and its limits on my "determinations." Fichte has then reinterpreted the Kantian notion of sensible intuition so that it does not simply mean what is immediately given to a subject and what immediately constrains the subject's synthetic activity, but is a constraining component of knowledge intelligible only *within* the context of such an original activity and so as a *self*-limitation.

The problems with this view (aside from the fact that its status as a separate principle is questionable, i.e., that the move from A to some specific A does not establish any separate issue but just further specifies what could be an A) clearly involve Fichte's "idealist" commitment to the priority of the self's originary self-positing activity.[39] To anticipate Hegel's point of view, Fichte now has no way of thinking together, as *co-original*, the self's identifying and differentiating positings. Consequently, he *must* end up interpreting the not-self not only as a kind of *result* of the self's self-construings, but as only and exclusively that. Or, in the language used earlier, the self *is* not simply restricted by the not-self, but simply takes itself to be restricted, raising the possibility of Hegel's favorite charge against Fichte: that he is a "subjective" idealist. One way of seeing what this means is to use the problem now apparent: that there is a non-sequitur in Fichte's account. He constantly reasons from the fact that apperceptive representing cannot be "determined" by the object (that would be dogmatism, an ignoring of the conditions under which an object could be an object for the subject) to the claim that, therefore, the subject's representing activity is wholly *un*determined. This renders it virtually impossible for the determinacy of representing to be coherently explained and ignores the Hegelian option of reconstruing the notion of "determination" (i.e., in terms of the *development* of any subject's fundamental forms of apperceptive representing).

Said another way, Fichte's idealism centrally involves a claim about the "derivative" status of the not-self. I have been arguing that the best way to understand this claim is in a transcendental context, and so as a claim about what Kant would call the phenomenal status of objects of experience – they can be such objects only as subject to certain conditions. This is an idealist position not because the I somehow produces its own representations or knows its own thoughts. Rather, Fichte is explaining the consequences of the claim that *representing* an object is something that I reflexively *do*, that it is a relation I must *establish*, and he is impressed by the fact that such an activity must be spontaneous, ultimately determined by the subject, if the representing is an epistemic and not a matter-of-fact relation. Accordingly, Fichte's famous claim about positing amounts to the claim that we can never know the not-self except *as* determined by the self. It is thus not simply the necessity of its being represented that makes the not-self ideal (the mistake Rheinhold constantly made),[40] but the fact that the representation is necessarily reflexive, a result of what the *subject* takes to be a representation of an object. (By itself, of course, this line of thought does not establish that the results of such activity do not and cannot coincide with what the not-self is in itself; it only claims that we cannot be said to *know* whether that is so or not.)

Fichte's own treatment of that problem can be seen in his third principle and his use of this principle to account for the possibility of theoretical knowledge and free activity. The third principle, the "grounding" principle, is clearly intended to resolve the problem of how such a not-self can be anything other than a *merely posited* not-self. And Fichte is fully aware of the problem throughout the rest of the *WL*, aware that a posited not-self is not a *not*-self, and that if the not-self is not posited as such by the self, it cannot count as a not-*self*; it is just whatever it is, and does not, of itself, "oppose" anything. His way of asking this question is, "How can A and – A, being and non-being, reality and negation, be thought together without mutual elimination and destruction?"[41] And Fichte's answer is reasonable, though it remains far too programmatic to be of much help: "they will mutually limit each other."[42] This principle is later called the principle of "interdetermination" (*Wechselbestimmung*) and is said to be applicable in two ways. Either the self posits the not-self as limited by the self (where limited means limited in part and in part not limited), or the self posits itself as limited by the not-self. The first is the foundation of practical activity, the latter the foundation of theoretical knowledge. In each case, the interdetermination is supposed to be represented by the notion of "limit," what Fichte will later call, in discussing theoretical knowledge, a "check" or "shock" to the self's positing (*Anstoss*). However, in each case, Fichte continues to claim that such a limit is *posited* as a limit, as he must if he is to retain his version of the apperception thesis (self-positing) as the most comprehensive condition of all knowledge and action.

As one might expect, trying to maintain both claims at once presents some problems. One can frequently see Fichte trying to maintain both, although one never finds a successful resolution to what Fichte himself admits looks like a contradiction. Thus:

> The self posits itself as determined by the not-self. Hence the self is not to determine, but to be determined, while the not-self is to determine, to set limits to the reality of the self.[43]

But only four brief sentences later:

> But to say that the self determines itself as determined obviously amounts to saying the the self determines itself.[44]

And, having pushed the problem this far, Fichte, at least from Hegel's point of view, gives up.[45] In trying to determine a "common ground," where self and not-self can be thought together without canceling each other, Fichte admits:

> such a ground is incomprehensible, since it is not included under the basic principle thereof, viz, that the self posits itself as determined by the not-self; on the contrary it is presupposed by that principle. Hence a ground of that kind, if it is to be identified at all, would have to lie outside the boundaries of the theoretical Doctrine of Knowledge.[46]

As the last phrase indicates, Fichte does believe that such a ground can be discussed, but only in the context of the practical and so admittedly derivative part of the *WL*. That is, since Fichte regards any instance of a self's positing itself, or taking itself to make some claim or other about the not-self, that is, any claim of empirical knowledge, to be some kind of "limitation" of the self's activity, it is also an instance of the self's "alienation from itself." It *is* an instance of self-determination, but one in which the self cannot be said to determine itself completely (or "infinitely"), however the limitation by the not-self is understood.[47] Thus the origin of this limitation cannot be fully accounted for; said another way, a radical skepticism about the tenability of such a limitation by the not-self is always possible, and so the ground by virtue of which I limit myself might not be what I assumed or wanted it to be. Hence the rather loosely applied notion of alienation. The possibility of achieving such a complete self-determination is clearer in the moral sphere, where Fichte, despite many revisions, adopts much of the Kantian notion of freedom as autonomy or self-legislation, where freedom not only means acting self-consciously on my own motives, but where those motives themselves are not determined by the not-self (or nature, as in the Kantian account of heteronomy), where the motive is freedom itself, and where acting for the sake of freedom is acting in conformity with the moral law. As in Kant, such a full self-determination can never be achieved, and Fichte again exaggerates a strain in Kant when he describes morality itself as an "infinite striving" (*Sollen*) for an ideal of complete self-positing that includes knowledge as well as action.

All of this obviously leaves Fichte with a much longer story to tell. For one thing, for all of his revision of Kant, and, as Henrich points out, for all of his strong challenges to modern assumptions about self-consciousness, Fichte continues without resolving perhaps *the* Kantian and modern problem – skepticism. To be sure, Fichte states that problem so much in his own terminology that it can barely be recognized. In his terms, since the I's establishing its relation to the not-I is always a spontaneous activity, and can never be said to be the result of its interaction with the not-I, the establishment of that relation is forever subject to potentially radical (not just empirical) revision. The I's fundamental (or categorial) *self*-limitation ensures that its satisfaction with this limitation, its closing the idealist gap between being and merely taking myself to be so limited, must forever remain a *Sollen*, or ought.[48]

However, to return again to Fichte's contribution, his unique formulation of the problem also suggests a way of seeing how this limitation might be *overcome*, at least in principle (something not possible in Kant's noumenal skepticism). In Kant, the limitation of knowledge to a specifically conditioned kind of experience is ultimately a kind of species limitation, a given transcendental fact, if you will. And, as we have seen, a great problem in the post-Kantian tradition has always been the problem of understanding the nature of this "fact" and our a priori knowledge of it. At times, as in neo-Kantianism, this notion of the limitations of knowledge simply turns into positivism of a generally scientific or, more specifically, psychological or sociological kind.[49] At times, such limits have been expanded and made cultural or historical conditions, as in Cassirer, or simplistic interpretations of Hegel. But always the problem of "fixing" such limits, and of understanding how we could, has remained.[50]

Fichte's contribution to the problem was to point out that all knowledge, including transcendental knowledge – the I's taking itself to be limited by the not-I – is a self-determined self-limitation, not one simply encountered as given or discovered as fact. In that context, any noumenal doubts about the general or categorial ways in which the I so posits itself, doubts about whether the not-I *is* as it is posited to be, are concrete doubts that can arise only within the I's experience of itself and the results of its activity. There is no general point of view from which the results of the I's positing and the not-self in itself can be compared. Like Kant, this ensures a kind of permanent dissatisfaction with phenomenal knowledge, but unlike Kant, it denies that the terms of that dissatisfaction can be discovered and fixed. They too must be potential subjects of dissatisfaction if the I is originally spontaneous or undetermined.[51]

In this sense, Fichte's emphasis on the self-relatedness inherent in knowledge suggests a profound reconstrual of the project of knowledge itself in a dramatically un-Kantian way, an account of knowledge as a kind of self-satisfaction rather than as primarily based on or directed by intuition. Fichte does not provide us with this extension of his project. For a variety of reasons, he believed that neither he nor anyone else could do so. But looking at his enterprise this way might supply the proper context for understanding the attempt by his famous colleague to do just that, and so might suggest a broader way of understanding the difference between so-called subjective and Absolute idealism, or complete *self*-satisfaction.[52]

4
The Jena formulations

1. Schelling and the Jena writings

Although there has always been a good deal of scholarly interest in Hegel's early historical, theological, and political essays, most commentators agree that Hegel began to develop his own philosophical position after his move to Jena in January 1801.[1] To be sure, throughout the work of the Jena years (1801–7), Hegel continued to develop his sociopolitical philosophy and the reflections on art and religion central to his approach to society, but what makes such essays as the "Natural Law," "System of Ethical Life," and "Philosophy of Spirit" particularly interesting is that they reveal the way in which Hegel's developing position on speculative philosophy altered the approach, terminology, and content of his "Realphilosophie."[2]

These developments in Hegel's speculative position first became visible in two articles written for the journal that Hegel briefly coedited with Schelling, *Critical Journal of Philosophy* – the so-called "Difference" essay, "The Difference between Fichte's and Schelling's System of Philosophy" (1801) and "Faith and Knowledge: Or the Reflective Philosophy of Subjectivity in the Complete Range of Its Forms as Kantian, Jacobian, and Fichtean Philosophy" (1802) – and in a variety of lectures, particularly those written after 1804–5, on logic, metaphysics, philosophy of nature, and philosophy of spirit. What makes these works important, particularly for the approach taken here, is that they set out what will be central aspects of Hegel's final position in ways that are directly connected with those of his predecessors. In beginning to outline his own position by contrast especially with Kant and Fichte, and by beginning early on to distance himself from Schelling, Hegel reveals more clearly than elsewhere how to understand his position in terms of those of his predecessors, how his contrasts make sense only within a certain continuity, and how that continuity is often more important than the contrasts, more important even than Hegel lets on. Not surprisingly, I shall argue that this is particularly true with respect to the self-consciousness theme and the relevance of that theme to the issue of idealism.[3]

All of this is not to deny that these are, however important, very difficult texts to read properly, at least with intentions such as those sketched earlier. For they are, after all, early works; they express a position in transition (particularly with respect to issues like intuition), predate monumental changes in that position (especially on the centrality of history or the need for a phenomenological introduction to the system), and may have been written so much under the pressure of Schelling, or in the expectation that Hegel would follow the Schellingean line, that they are not completely trustworthy records of Hegel's own views.[4] But there is more than enough in these works clearly connecting Hegel's position with the issues discussed in the preceding chapters, and with the idealism defended in his mature works, to make them indispensable in this account of that idealism.

This is particularly true of two large themes, themes I have used to organize the major divisions of this chapter. There is, first, the contrast mentioned previously that reappears throughout Hegel's work and is used by him frequently to explain the distinctiveness of his position: that between "reflection" and "speculation." Of great early importance in such a contrast is the role of "intuition" and the connection between that notion and issues already developed here in Kant and Fichte. Also, in these works, Hegel's own account of the speculative principle of "identity" is on view for the first time, and this will be especially important for us since, even in Hegel's early formulations, it will be apparent that Hegel is rapidly moving away from Schelling's use of the notion in his philosophy of nature and toward a "logical" interpretation of the issue that will associate Hegel much more closely with Kant and a transcendental logic, even more than the criticism in *DS* and *GW* might lead one to suspect.[5]

However, as is already clear, any analysis and assessment of Hegel's first attempt at a speculative or Absolute idealism must begin with the obvious fact that such attempts are heavily influenced by the final member of the triumvirate of important post-Kantian idealists, Schelling. In many of the early works, Hegel adopts freely (often for his own purposes) Schelling's language of infinite and finite, the Absolute, the identity of subject and object, the identity of identity and nonidentity, the indifference point of subjective subject–object and objective subject–object, or the whole apparatus of what Hegel would finally treat as an "objective idealism," what would be popularly known as a romantic, world-soul, "living nature" metaphysics. Given this obvious influence, my earlier suggestions about the inherently critical idealism and transcendental subjectivity retained by Hegel, and the clear inconsistency of the former with the latter, something preliminary needs to be said here about the complex "Schelling problem."

After all, as Düsing, among others, has shown, the fact that Hegel clearly construes the issues of recent German philosophy as a contrast between the subjectivism of Kant and Fichte on reflection, and a nonsubjective, speculative science certainly suggests the possibility of a special sort of *substance* as the goal of a new metaphysical program, the "Absolute," itself representable as neither subject nor object.[6] And such commitments do appear prominent in the early philosophical essays (although more so in *DS* than in *GW*), and so appear to commit Hegel not to a new *subject matter* for philosophic speculation – roughly, the self-conscious "activity" that is, strictly speaking, neither subject nor object because prior to, a condition of, the self-determinations of any concrete subjectivity and the self-limitations of objectivity – but to a new "divine" substance, the object, in an attenuated sense, of an "intellectual intuition."

Moreover, the first pages of *DS* are full of what might be termed Schellingean or romantic motivations for believing in such a substance. Hegel uses such phrases as the "urge toward totality" (*Trieb zur Vollständigkeit*), or "living participation" (*lebendige Anteil*), or that the very "need" (*Bedürfnis*) of philosophy itself is the pervasive and distinctly modern "fragmentation" or "disunity" (*Entzweiung*) of daily life (*DS*, 9; *Diff*, 85). He even goes so far as to claim that there is a "Need for a philosophy that will recompense (*versöhnt*) nature for the mishandling it suffered at the hands of Kant and Fichte," and he promises a "reason in harmony with nature" that will result from a reason that "constitutes (*gestalt*) itself *into* nature" (*DS*, 8; *Diff*, 83).

All such claims call to mind the early works of Schelling,[7] that is, the works published before and just after the *System of Transcendental Idealism* (1800) or before the uneasy balance between Schelling's speculative "identity theory" and his emphasis on freedom came unbalanced, destroyed the possibility of a transcendental idealism, and led him (as it did Fichte, for different reasons) into a much more clearly theological conception of the Absolute.[8] Hegel's language in the *DS* clearly echoes the romantic, "objective" idealist Schelling, the Schelling who, in works such as the 1795 *Philosophical Letters*, had announced "My determination in criticism is, namely: Strive towards intransient selfhood, unconditioned freedom, unlimited activity," all as a way of "overcoming" the "terrors of the objective world."[9] In the 1797 *Ideas Concerning a Philosophy of Nature*, he announced that philosophy succeeds or fails with the attempt "to derive the necessity of the succession of representations from the nature of our spirit, thus of finite spirit in general."[10] And it was Schelling who tried to carry out such a derivation by developing a philosophy of nature in which "physics" or "dynamics" could show, contra all mechanism, that nature's "activity" was itself a manifestation of the Absolute's intuition of itself, all as a way of showing that there was a "common origin" for nature's *objective* subject–object relation and finite spirit's *subjective* subject–object relation.[11] Schelling argued in a number of different ways that the notion of an "object" confirming a subject's judgments or dependent on a subject's transcendental conditions was as derivative and conditioned a notion as that of a "subject" whose judgments or conditions required external confirmation or transcendental deduction. It is always a mistake to begin by accepting such distinctions as absolute. The task instead is to try to think without the metacategories of subject and object.

Even though Schelling never succeeded in presenting and consistently defending such an origin (called variously the "indifference point," the "identity of identity and nonidentity," or finally, even an "Ungrund"), the spirit of his enterprise appears to be carried on in Hegel's criticism of Fichte's subjective idealism, in the reconciliationist goal of his own philosophy, and in the search for an Absolute within which subject and object, freedom and nature could be identified while still differentiated.

Or, at least, so it would appear. The exact nature of the relation between Hegel's and Schelling's positions during these years has long been a confusing and much debated issue. Recently, some outstanding work by many different scholars, especially Kimmerle, Pöggeler, Harris, Görland, Siep, Düsing, and Horstmann, has been able to put many of the issues in a clearer light (and has helped especially to establish the relation among the various Jena texts and to confirm Hegel's relatively early divergence from Schelling).[12] But there remain several oddities in Hegel's use of Schellingean language in these essays, some of which will be discussed in the next section. For the moment, I want to note two things: First, it is indeed true that when Hegel entered the post-Kantian idealist discussion, he did so as at least a partial supporter of Schelling. As noted, this meant that instead of the Kantian language of apperception, synthesis, and phenomenality or the Fichtean language of self-positing and infinite striving, he first takes up the topic we are pursuing, idealism, in the Schellingean terms of subject–object identity, transcendental intuition, "the" Absolute, and freedom. And such language would seem to commit him as well to the radically expanded "romantic" version of the idealist project, as it was just described, all contrary to much of the approach suggested here.

Second, however, it should also be noted that *Schelling's* idealism, however romantic, metaphysical, or even theological its goals, still originates in the basic problematic and retains much of the approach of post-Kantian idealism, the search for an adequate explanation for the self-conscious character of human experience, and the transcendental connection between such a self-relating and objective knowledge. Schelling is simply the philosopher who pushed the problem of Kant's "fundamental condition" to its speculative limits; but it is still the same problem at issue. That is, speaking roughly, if Kant is right and knowledge cannot (ultimately or totally) be a matter of empirical determination and association, or a matter of the mind's rational grasp of its own ideas, morality not a matter of sentiment, passion, or self-interest, nor a matter of an intuition of the good, all *because* the human subject must be in some sense self-determining, somehow responsible for what it takes to be a unity within its experience or for what it takes to be a passion that will serve as a motive, then the proper account of such an activity, and especially what quickly became the problem of its "ground," are indeed the fundamental problems of philosophy. Since the very terms of the problem foreclose any attempt to ground such an activity in empirical antecedents or metaphysical substance, and since the issue remains a transcendental one for Schelling (i.e., not a problem of individual psychology or mental events, but of the logical requirements that any such self-relating must conform to if it is to count as constitutive of knowledge or free activity), the problem quickly becomes the "German" version – self-grounding subjectivity. In that context, it is easy to see why the options developed by Fichte and Schelling should have developed so quickly: If Kant's reliance on the pure forms of intuition and the fixed, logical requirements of judgment will not ground such an activity, then we have either a theory of a self-creating subject (terminating in Fichte's *Sollen*) or Schelling's self-*intuiting* subject.

That is, the way Schelling took up the Kantian self-consciousness problem naturally led him to such a view of subjectivity. If the determinacy of the subject's objectifying activity cannot be understood as grounded in "pure sensible intuition," and if Schelling, like Hegel, rejects Fichte's notion of a subjective self-positing, then, roughly, a subject's self-limitation, its determination of what could be an object for it (or a motive in action) should, it would seem (given the premises already accepted in this account), be understood as a subject's intuitive determination of itself, that thought is somehow *given* to itself in its very activity. A subject intuits its own self-constraining activity in the activities of thought and action themselves, and since this intuiting is to reveal the Absolute origin of all possible thought and action, it must also be understood as a manifestation, a moment, of the self-posing process, the "life-pulse" of "*the* Absolute." (Here the famous Schellingean paradigm for a self-producing "identical" with the Absolute's activity: the "knowledge" achieved by artistic geniuses, superior to philosophy even if not articulable.)

In other words, Schelling continued to ask the questions Fichte also raised: how Kant's original condition was itself possible, how it could be known, what the claim was about, and so on, and, to answer these questions and avoid Kant's (for him untenable) skepticism, Schelling formulated his theory of a truly "original" ground, the Absolute that would account for what Kant left unexplained. (As we shall see in a moment, one way of putting Schelling's claim is to note that he claimed that the true model of original "subjectivity" was not Kant's first *Critique*'s account of transcendental, finite subjectivity, but the third *Critique*'s account of "divine" subjectivity, manifested in the beauty and purposiveness of nature, and since unlimited, infinite, not properly a "subject" at all, but divine nature itself.)[13]

So, in noting Schelling's influence on the early Hegel, it is also important to note that in *STI* at least, Schelling clearly commits himself to an idealist transcendental philosophy by committing himself to the "highest principle" of knowledge, according to such an idealism: "self-consciousness."[14] And he just as clearly indicates that he is interested in the Kantian version of the principle, not the Cartesian, that is, that he regards all knowledge *of objects* as inherently reflective or apperceptive, not that he wants to begin with the subject's knowledge *of its own "thoughts"* and then to try to construe knowledge of objects as some version of self-knowledge (cf. his general "Remark on Matter and Spirit").[15]

As just noted, what Schelling distinctively adds to this project is precisely what appears so unusual and confusing in Hegel's first attempts at formulating an absolute idealism. "Our entire philosophy," he writes, "rests on the standpoint of intuition, not reflection."[16] Earlier, Schelling had defined the I, qua subject, *as nothing but* a "self-intuiting activity."[17] In line with his more metaphysical approach to this "source" ("*Quelle*"[18]), Schelling describes "pure self-consciousness" as "an act that lies outside of time and that first constitutes all time," and as a "freedom" that "proves itself only through itself."[19] As we have seen, Fichte also stressed to some extent the *immediate* and so intuitive character of this primordial self-relation, but laid no great emphasis on the methodological problems of giving a transcendental account of this necessarily presupposed self-positing activity. Schelling, however, *so* stresses the originary quality of such an act that he thereby raises as a difficulty how philosophy could analyze such an act without presupposing it. And he finally admits that this self-intuiting identity of self with self cannot be isolated and known, that it is "eternally unconscious" or only an "eternal presupposition."[20] Although Schelling does have an account of how the self "strives" to intuit itself explicitly, and even produces a "history" of self-consciousness (i.e., a history of how the self comes to realize its origin "in itself"), he denies that this process can ever be completed in systematic knowledge – all *because* such an originary intuiting activity must always lie at the ground of *any* conceiving and, perforce, any conceiving of *it*. Only occasionally artistic geniuses can, in their creations, embody the identity of free activity and a product of such freedom that nevertheless also objectively constrains what can be made of it. Thus, all of Schelling's romantic elements: as a first principle, an ultimately inarticulable self-intuiting (finally, the self-intuiting of the Absolute manifesting itself as subject and object) rather than self-understanding; a commitment both to absolute freedom and to an ultimate identity of human nature and nature; and, most important for Hegel, a belief that philosophy can articulate these principles only by rejecting the "reflective" procedures of standard modern philosophy[21] and making the intellectual intuition it investigates *its own principle*, although even at that, such philosophy will still be inferior to the revelatory power of art.[22]

I do not pretend that any of this begins to deal with how Schelling justified (or at least tried to justify) any of these claims. I note here the way the apperception problematic survives in Schelling's version: to wit, as a principle of self-intuition in experience and activity *so* originary as to be inaccessible to philosophical analysis and available, if at all, only in great art (free self-consciousness restraining itself); and that this sets up the most important context for Hegel as he begins to sort out these issues – the contrast of "reflection" and "speculation" as rival attempts to deal with such an origin.

Finally, a more general qualification of Hegel's romanticism should be noted. Although Hegel is, from the opening of the *DS* on, relatively sympathetic to such romantic concerns, he never identifies himself with them. In reporting on the alienated and fragmented character of modern existence and modern philosophy, he treats the romantic impulse always as a symptom, not a solution.[23] In his own voice, he points to the inability of the dominant versions of Kantian and post-Kantian philosophies to resolve the dichotomies, antinomies, and paradoxes they have themselves created as a cause of such a situation. More significantly, particularly with regard to Schelling, Hegel does not treat such disunity as itself necessarily a problem. He recognizes that "The sole interest of reason is to suspend [*aufheben*] such rigid antitheses," but he immediately adds that this does not mean that "reason is opposed to position and limitation." It cannot be so opposed because such opposition is "necessary" within the totality of "life" (*DS*, 13–14; *Diff*, 90–1). Such an emphasis on "difference," opposition, negativity, and other such abstract characterizations of what presents itself as "opposed" to the idealizing activity of any, even Absolute, subjectivity already indicates, just by its prominence in Hegel's two essays, the beginning of his split with Schelling.[24] And, even when explicitly comparing Schelling's system with Fichte's, Hegel concentrates on the basic idealist issues and usually stays far away from Schelling's romantic philosophy of nature.[25]

All of these considerations should, I think, give anyone pause who might take the romantic terminology in the two essays ("harmony of reason with nature," "absoluteness" of human freedom, etc.) to be unequivocal evidence of a Schellingean romantic *metaphysics*, especially one taken to form the core of Hegel's mature philosophy of Absolute Spirit. The apparently metaphysical terminology used in Hegel's early works cannot be straightforwardly, without further ado, taken as evidence that Hegel has rejected critical idealism in favor of an indefensible metaphysics of an Absolute Subject or a God within which all finite beings are pantheistically related. But to make this claim, one must be able to demonstrate the continuity I have been claiming exists both between the Kantian and Fichtean positions and the one Hegel now begins to develop, frequently with Schellingean language. That is what I propose to do in this chapter.

2. Reflection and speculation

Both of Hegel's early essays are built around an opposition, what might today be called a "metatheoretical," two-sided dispute about philosophy. In *DS*, the dispute is pictured as almost a kind of war between proponents of reflective and speculative philosophies. In *GW*, the terms of the dispute are "belief," or what stands outside the possibility of knowledge, what cannot be known but must still, for some practical reason or other, be believed, and knowledge proper. Since, according to Hegel, those philosophers who mistakenly draw the line between belief and knowledge by much too narrowly restricting what they will count as knowledge, are, with the exception of Jacobi, much the same group as the reflective philosophers criticized in *DS*, it is clear that both essays concern roughly the same problems, namely, the *limitations* of reflection and the question of whether nonreflective theory should be counted as speculative knowledge or consigned to the philosophical Hades of "mere belief" (or what we today call "mere speculation").

As indicated earlier, Hegel borrows this speculation–reflection contrast from Schelling,[26] and although both tend to mention Kant when they want to illustrate what they mean by reflective philosophy, the term "reflection" is also used in a wide variety of ways. First, both use the term to refer to the enterprise of modern philosophy itself, Descartes as well as Locke, Leibniz as well as Hume, Fichte and Reinhold and Schulze as well as Kant. Although, for example, Locke's definition of reflection is psychological, it paradigmatically points to the issue Hegel and Schelling want to use to unite the various strands of the modern tradition. In the *Essay*, Locke writes that reflection is "that notice which the mind takes of its own operations."[27] Post-Cartesian philosophy in general, motivated by the philosophic problems created by modern science (its conflict with Aristotelean assumptions, the discrepancy between commonsense and scientific accounts of the real), insisted that philosophy must begin with such a notice by the mind of its own activities, that the possibility of any knowledge depends on such a reflection. As the term itself indicates, modern philosophy is thus animated by a certain foundational dualism or even "alienation" between the subject and itself, its own thoughts, beliefs, and desires. In the intellectual crisis provoked by modern science, the task of philosophy had to be a "reflection," a "turning around" by the mind to examine itself, particularly in an attempt to determine which of its unreflectively held beliefs could stand the test of its own skeptical reflection, even such natural beliefs as belief in an external world or in the persistence of objects when unperceived. And it is this familiar reflective turn in philosophy, the "priority of epistemology," or what Kant's contemporaries called the "critical" spirit in philosophy, or what Hegel called the philosophy of "self-limitation," that is being referred to by the general notion of "reflection."[28]

Second, Hegel sometimes uses the notion of reflection in an even more sweeping way, to refer to philosophy itself, when it is understood as reflection "on" some originally given or independently constituted domain. He means, that is, to refer to philosophy that accepts or simply begins from such divisions or oppositions as science, art, ethics, religion, or politics, and sees itself either as a clarification of the concepts of each domain, or as an account of the kind of justification appropriate to the claims made in each, or as an interpretation of the kind of meaning conditioned by each, and so forth. Reflection thus proposes no theory about the origin of such divisions and so cannot ultimately account for the underlying "unity" among them, the unity that can, supposedly, be understood speculatively.

For the most part, it is modern reflection, in the former sense, that Hegel especially wants to oppose in these early texts. As we shall see, he wants to deny that a philosophic reflection on the mind's own "reflecting" powers can succeed without an account of the mind's *possible* relation to any *object*, including itself (echoing again here the Kantian beginning, contra Locke and Hume), but that this activity and relation cannot be understood unless they are treated "speculatively." Initially this will mean something primarily negative: understanding such activity neither as empirical nor as metaphysical objects, nor as Kantian formal conditions. Much more obscure is the positive dimension: understanding such activity as, to state his position all at once, freely self-determined moments of Absolute Subjectivity. It is this speculative turn that will require abandoning the reflective restrictions on knowledge evident in the numerous versions of modern skepticism. Or, stated more simply, the most advanced forms of philosophic reflection, accounts of the possibility of the mind "reflecting" or knowing objects, were Kant's and Fichte's transcendentalisms, and the task now is to show how their enterprises are not possible unless their subject matter (the subject's self-relation) is reconstrued speculatively (as Reason's absolute self-knowledge), rather than formally or subjectively or psychologically, and unless the results of that reflection are reconstrued in the same way, speculatively rather than skeptically, in absolute rather than finite reflection.[29]

As already noted, in both works the contrast between reflection and speculation is built around an essentially Kantian distinction, what had been in Kant the distinction between the "conditioned" activity of "the understanding" (*Verstand*), the faculty conditioned by the sensible manifold, conceptualizing it according to "subjective" but logically required categories, and the unconditioned "ascent" of "Reason" (*Vernunft*), taking the results of the understanding's work as its object, and attempting to think the unconditioned totality of those results. Indeed, in these relatively familiar Kantian terms, the easiest preliminary way to understand Hegelian speculation is to note that once the distinction between concept and intuition is thought to be problematic (as discussed in Chapter 2), the distinction between a conditioned understanding and Reason's self-"projections" is also rendered questionable. In that case, the speculative integrations of Reason, "ungrounded" and not confirmed by empirical intuition, cannot be viewed as, for that reason, a distinct, secondary, "merely regulative" intellectual activity. The apprehension of any determinate cognitive object is dependent on (in Hegelian language, "is" a moment of) the "free" self-articulations of reason. Alternatively, reason's "self-legislation," as Kant called it, can be viewed as constitutive of the possibility of objects if Kant's requirement that objects must be intuited (or made possible by pure intuition) is abandoned, if it can be shown that what Kant thought was an independent intuitive condition was itself a moment of Reason's self-determination. (And a further reason that this is an especially good way to introduce the Hegelian problem of speculation, and its "objectivity," is that Kant himself seemed to admit, in several passages, the very same thing – though not without some damage to the coherence of his overall position.)[30]

According to Hegel's frequently repeated charges, Kant's official position on the abstract opposition of these faculties ensures the limitations of reflection and, because of these limitations, its antinomial dualisms. In particular, the contemporary reflective dualisms of intuition/concept and, in the practical domain, heteronomous desire/self-legislated will are of most interest to Hegel, even though he extends the meaning of the notion throughout all prior philosophy, criticizing the incompleteness and ultimate inconsistency of basic reflective oppositions between form and matter, subject and predicate, supersensible and sensible, universal and particular. But, again, he is particularly concerned, in his remarks on Kant and Fichte, with tracing the origins of such dualisms to reflection's self-limitation in the modern period; to determine how the mind's "attention to itself" has resulted in the mind's restriction to its own impressions, thoughts, syntheses, positings, or self-legislations. Ultimately, he claims that this form of reflective self-denial has led to a notion of Reason that is "nothing but the dead and death-dealing rule of formal unity" (*DS*, 53–4; *Diff*, 142) and, correspondingly, to a notion of Nature that is "something essentially determined and lifeless" (*DS*, 50; *Diff*, 139).

By contrast, speculative philosophy is the philosophy of Reason, totality, the whole, and, everywhere throughout the early writings, the philosophy of identity. In his preliminary characterizations of such an enterprise, Hegel regularly suggests that the main issue in such a fundamental contrast concerns what has become a familiar theme in this study:

> For Reason, finding consciousness caught in particularities, only becomes philosophical speculation by raising itself to itself, putting its trust only in itself and the Absolute which at *that* moment becomes its object. (*DS*, 11; *Diff*, 88; my emphasis)

And in another passage, one that attempts to extract the speculative project in Fichte, Hegel states very clearly what will, I am arguing, always remain the goal of his speculative project:

> Philosophy must describe the totality of empirical consciousness as the objective totality of self-consciousness. . . . To mere reflection this deduction appears as the contradictory enterprise of deducing the manifold from unity, duality from pure identity. But the identity of the Ego = Ego is no pure identity, that is, it does not arise through reflective abstraction. (*DS*, 36; *Diff*, 122)

Fichte, of course, does not succeed in describing the "objective totality of self-consciousness," but it is a fine Hegelian catch phrase with which to pose the question of whether *he* succeeds in such a description, particularly since it indicates that Hegel does not envisage any "deduction" of the manifold from such a unity. (That characterization is what "mere reflection" would assume.) So, it should be initially clear from the terms in which the issue is posed that Hegel still conceives of at least the fundamental problem in what we can call "nonmetaphysical" terms; that the issue is what Kant would call Reason's "projection" of itself as the order and structure of what there is, all in a way not empirically determined or metaphysically grounded; and that this problem, which constitutes the content of speculative philosophy, is *some* sort of special reflexivity, a self-relation the results of which will not simply fix the limits of a subjective faculty but will determine, "absolutely," *what there is* (if, that is, the results of speculation do conform to the speculative principle, or identity of subject and *object*). "Speculation," Hegel always insists throughout these works, "is the activity of the one universal reason directed upon itself" (*DS*, 12; *Diff*, 88).[31]

It is this issue – how we are to understand what Kant called the "subjective" demands by Reason for coherence, structure, and order as not merely subjective demands, but as Reason's "raising itself to itself" *in* its identity with objects, "the *objective* totality of self-consciousness" – that Hegel is referring to when he introduces his own understanding of "the Absolute." As with Kant, Fichte, and Schelling, the possibility of a "transcendental logic" of such activities is accepted; the question is not what sorts of projecting activities ("theorizings," "needs" for coherence and unity, speculative "intuitions," etc.) have been common in the intellectual tradition, or have been empirically useful, or seem to be required by our species in its interchanges with nature and others, but what forms of the many possible "conceptual legislations" can be said to count as an "objective" (or "absolute") totality. ["When, where and in what forms such self-reproductions occur as philosophies is contingent. This contingency must be comprehended on the basis of *the Absolute positing itself as an objective totality*" (*DS* 14; *Diff*, 91; my emphasis).] "The" Absolute is thus Reason's final epistemic self-legitimation, the understanding, in a philosophical system, by reason of its own activity, not as determined by the nature of a subjective faculty, an infinite striving for an identity with the non-ego, and not as an inarticulable, transcendentally conceived "point," the mere result of a theory that stipulates that "there must be" a subject–object "indifference point."[32]

In the texts at issue, Hegel's own account of how we should understand such a holistic, integrative, ultimately complete, Absolute self-reproduction of Reason makes heavy and often confusing use of the Schellingean notion of "intuition" to explain this self-relation.[33] Indeed, it is one of the great virtues of the texts after the early Jena period that Hegel replaces the intuition language with his position on thought's "determinate" self-negation, its developing self-correction in its free, logical self-determination. But the intuition language is quite important in these texts, and some elements of what Hegel is after in these discussions do survive and so ought to be discussed.

There is little doubt that in the early Jena works Hegel strongly associated himself with the altered language of post-Kantian idealism, with Schelling's early suggestion to Fichte that Kant's language of spontaneity and apperception be discussed as a problem of intellectual intuition.

> It is of the profoundest significance that it has been affirmed with so much seriousness that one cannot philosophize without transcendental intuition. For what would this be, philosophizing without intuition? One would disperse oneself endlessly in absolute finitudes. (*DS*, 28; *Diff*, 110)

Without reliance on such a "transcendental intuition," reflection is caught up in dualisms and oppositions whose origins it cannot understand and, especially, cannot free itself from its own self-limitations, cannot account for any connection between its own conceptual clarifications and objective reality. It regards any "transition from being to concept or concept to being" as "an unjustifiable leap" (*DS*, 28; *Diff*, 111). But it is with intuition that the "self-production of reason" can "shape itself into an objective totality" (*DS*, 30; *Diff*, 113), that the "conscious" articulations of reason can also be said to be the "non-conscious" positings of the Absolute, and so objective.[34]

Toward the conclusion of *DS*, Hegel again enthusiastically asserts that

"Intellectual intuition is the absolute principle of philosophy" (*DS*, 76; *Diff*, 173) and suggests that not only is speculation *about* such an intuiting (reason's self-determining of itself as objective) but that speculation *is* an intuiting:

> In science, intellectual intuition becomes the object of reflection, and for this reason philosophical reflection is itself transcendental intuition. (*DS*, 77; *Diff*, 173)

He restates this position in a passage where he reveals his greatest deference for Schelling's formulations:

> In order to grasp transcendental intuition in its purity, philosophical reflection must further abstract from this subjective aspect so that transcendental intuition, as the foundation of philosophy, may be neither subjective nor objective for it, neither self-consciousness as opposed to matter, nor matter as opposed to self-consciousness, but pure transcendental intuition, absolute identity, that is neither subjective nor objective. (*DS*, 77; *Diff*, 173)

Compare Schelling's similar claim:

> Intellectual intuition is the Organ of all transcendental thinking. For transcendental thinking proceeds in making for itself through freedom something as object that would otherwise not be an object; it presupposes a faculty of producing and at the same time intuiting certain activities of spirit, so that the producing of the object and the intuiting itself is an absolute unity; but just this faculty is the faculty of intellectual intuition.[35]

And, as noted previously, for Schelling, it is very rare to find this kind of identity of concept and intuition, of determinate articulation of content, and unconscious identification, in such activity, with Nature's objective process. Only some great artists achieve this identity and non-identity of subjectivity and objectivity. All of which makes it even more remarkable that Hegel, in this supposedly fundamental contrast of Fichte and Schelling, lays so very little stress on the latter's use of artistic activity. One can only surmise that Hegel is already quite uncomfortable with this intuitional "objectifying" of thought's activity, and, for all his polemic, is more inclined toward a Kantian–Fichtean approach, one that could not regard such an intuitional self-representation as determinately what it is unless it could be self-consciously *understood as* what it is. With such an approach, we still confront the problem of how to understand the ground or constraints on such a fundamental self-construing, but, as Hegel just begins to work out his own response to that issue, it already seems a more promising approach than Schelling's intuitionally expressed Absolute.

In these texts, Hegel's own Kantian language about the tasks of Reason and what appears already as his sense of the *conceptual* task of Reason's "self-reproduction" stand in some tension with his obvious borrowings from Schelling and hint that he regards the intuitional approach to speculation as a dead end. Moreover, that intuitional position on speculation ultimately so denigrates the accomplishments of reflection that its role in Absolute Knowledge amounts to mere "self-destruction," and if that is so, the general intelligibility of the speculative position, in language, for consciousness, seems impossible to defend. Further, since we know that Hegel will soon, in effect, radicalize Fichte's position on self-consciousness – arguing that the I's self-posing is in no sense an original principle, but a *developing* self-relation that is not originally identical with the not-I – it is not surprising that he is so ambiguous about his relation to a position that insists on an original, "eternal," ineffable identity of subject and object. Moreover, and most importantly in any reconstruction of Hegel, Schelling's "resolution" of the unresolved self-relation problem of Kantian idealism has all the virtues of theft over hard work, and Hegel would very soon come to see that and write about Schellingean intuition with almost the same scorn he here heaps on Jacobi and romanticism in general.

Such an incipient dissatisfaction with Schelling might explain why, in *GW*, Hegel addresses this same problem in Kant by staying much more within Kant's own terminology. Now Hegel picks up a characterization of this spontaneity that Kant provides at A118ff:

> The transcendental unity of apperception thus relates to the pure synthesis of the imagination, as an a priori condition of the possibility of all combination of the manifold in one knowledge. But only the *productive* imagination can take place a priori; the reproductive rests upon empirical conditions. Thus the principle of the necessary unity of pure (productive) synthesis of imagination, prior to apperception, is the ground of the possibility of all knowledge, especially of experience.

Although this passage contains its own puzzles (productive imagination is said to be "prior" to apperception, and a paragraph later, is identified with the unity of apperception or the understanding), it introduces the notion of a productive imagination that *replaces*, in *GW*, the earlier talk of intuition. Hegel thereby is able to distinguish in yet another way speculation from reflection, and although his account still remains extremely programmatic and sketchy, at least this version does not toss the blanket of intellectual intuition over all the problems. In adopting the Fichtean-sounding "principle" of all experience, the pure, *productive* imagination, Hegel still distinguishes himself from Kant by cautioning us not to do what he did, to understand that faculty as "the middle term that gets inserted between an existing absolute subject and an absolute existing world." Instead:

> The productive imagination must rather be recognized as what is primary and original, as that out of which the subjective ego and objective world first sunder themselves into the necessarily bi-partite appearance and product, and as the sole In-itself. (*GW*, 329; *BK*, 73)

Or, reflective philosophy simply posits a dualism originally mediated by the productive imagination, a dualism of conceiving subject and object-determined intuitions. The speculative task would be to understand *why* reason begins from such an opposition, and thereby to show that this duality is itself produced by a more original, "absolute" activity, an activity that would complete the idealist search for a self-constituting ground that began with Kant, an "absolute" in the sense of not being conditioned by an initial assumption of any understanding–intuition duality; and, finally one that can be understood as neither a subjective condition nor an empirical result.

To be sure, such a shift to Kantian terminology doesn't help all that much. The way is now open to ask a variety of questions about this apperceptive, productive imagination, about the rules for its activity, and the status of its results, that would be much harder to ask about some original intuition. But Hegel does not ask such questions and leaves most of the serious issues still unresolved. He has, though, made it quite clear that getting the nature of this original transcendental activity right is the key to a speculative project, and he uses one more Kantian theme to explain such an activity. This theme will reverberate far more deeply in his mature system than Schellingean intuition.

3. Reflective and speculative judgments

Although the technical task of the third *Critique* appears to be yet another extension of the critical enterprise into yet another area – this time an account of the conditions for the possibility of objective aesthetic and teleological judgments – it is much more than an account of the special kind of claim such judgments might have on others. It is at once the most speculative and synthetic of Kant's works. In the "Introduction" it is announced as "a means of combining the two parts of philosophy into a whole," and it works toward that end by discussing judgments about the "supersensible" *in* nature, of how we are led to postulate a dimension to nature beyond that captured by the understanding's categories and modern natural science. The experiences of beauty and sublimity, and the subjective necessity for assuming a teleological order in and an intelligent author for nature, reveal that the practically necessary assumption of moral autonomy also has a kind of "warrant" beyond subjective, practical necessity. The distinctive objectivity of aesthetic and teleological judgments provides that warrant and so helps to legitimate a way of thinking about our moral and natural natures that points to a common unity in the supersensible realm. As we have already seen, this should make the text fertile ground for speculative commentary.

For Kant, this enterprise will depend on making out the unique characteristics of such judgments. They are "reflective," not "determinant," judgments. This means that such judgments involve a (relatively) indeterminate attempt to find the appropriate "universal," once a "particular" is presented in intuition, the experience of which somehow involves more than can be expressed in a determinant judgment, the application of a universal to a particular. Thus the experience of beauty involves an intuition so incompletely determined by a concept that it involves a "free play" of the faculties, an indication of a purposiveness without a (specific, or conceptual) purpose.

It should be clear by now how much of such a project would appeal to Hegel. The experience of beauty and sublimity, and the ascription of an intelligent cause to nature, threaten at once the rigidity of Kant's reflective categories of concept and intuition, and the intelligible–noumenal and the natural–phenomenal. And Hegel's objection to Kant's treatment of the issue can be summarized just as quickly: He vigorously objects to Kant's assigning such judgments to the realm of merely regulative or subjective, and not constitutive, or possibly objective, concepts. For Kant, the ground of the possible objectivity of aesthetic and teleological judgments lies in a claim about the similarity of *subjective* responses to beautiful and ordered objects, and not in the apprehension of any property objectively ascribable to an object. "Hence, the concept of purposiveness of nature in its products is necessary for human judgment in respect of nature, but has not to do with the determination of objects."[36]

In the closing sections of his account of Kant in *GW*, Hegel argues that Kant (1) gives us no reason, other than vague empirical observations, to believe that our faculties are structured as he says they are, so that it is *they* that produce the "need" or requirement he says they do, and (2) Kant himself neglects to consider that his own account of beauty does not claim that, say, the subject's "idea" of beauty requires reason to think of nature as if supersensible, but that the *intuition of beauty* prompts this reflective determination:

> [Kant] does not recognize that as beauty, it is positive, it is intuited, or to use his own language, it is given in experience. Nor does he see that the supersensuous, the intelligible substratum of nature without and within us, the thing in itself, as Kant defines the supersensuous, it is at least superficially cognized when the principle of beauty is given a [conceptual] exposition as the identity of the concepts of nature and freedom. (*GW*, 340; *BK*, 87–8)

If this is true, then, according to Hegel, Kant ought to have pursued more vigorously a genuine integration of the rational, moral, and subjective dimensions of human life with what appears as the causally necessary realm of nature; in epistemological terms, the original unity of concept and intuition; in speculative terms, of subject and object. (If the conceptualization *of the intuited object* really *is* incomplete in cases of beauty and sublimity and teleology, then that "completion" in reason's self-legislation is required for the *object* to be properly understood as *it* is, and not just to satisfy a subjective need.)

There are various Kantian responses to such charges, but by far the most important issue in this context is *why* Kant thinks he has no option other than this subjectively necessary, regulative status for this postulation of the "identity" of the intelligible and the natural. That reason returns us to the issue that has emerged as the most complex and crucial in this look at Hegel's early idealism, not to mention the most misunderstood – the problem of intellectual intuition.

The Kantian argument is that the contrast between reflection and some putative "speculation" is critically or epistemologically unsound. For Kant, it would come as no surprise at all that the epistemology of such speculation made so much of an intellectual (or, in general, non-sensible) intuition. It is precisely *because* we have no such intuition, no such immediate access to our own activity, and certainly no access to an "identity" between such activity and being, that the thought of natural purposiveness or of the ground of the objectivity of aesthetic judgments *must* rely on what Kant calls the "contingency" of our subjective faculties being as they are. Such judgments of purposiveness and natural beauty can have some *claim* on others only by reference to their being similar sentient and intellectual beings. That is, for Kant it is the problem of the objectivity of certain kinds of judgments that requires such a subjective ground, although, of course, the world in itself may be really beautiful or purposefully ordered. As we have seen, according to Kant's theory, the only way the results of reason's self-determinations (nonempirically based, speculative theorizing) could be said to be genuinely objective is if reason produced or created its object in knowing it. Otherwise there will always be the Kantian gap between the speculatively possible and either the noumenally or phenomenally actual.

In section 76 of the *Critique of Judgment*, Kant lays the ground for his attack on the possibility of a nonsensible intuition by noting this very fact: that "things can be possible without being actual, and that consequently no conclusion can be drawn as to actuality from mere possibility." And, as he understands it, for an intuitive intellect (or a being with "intellectual intuition" or a "spontaneity of intuition") there would be no such distinction. Throughout his philosophical career, this is always what Kant meant by arguing against the possibility of an intuitive intellect; all he could see that possibility amounting to was the idea of a being for whom no "critique" of reason would be possible, whose thoughts could not be of possible objects, but must be of necessarily actual ones *because* such a being's intellect was intuitive, in "immediate" contact with the reality of what was thought. And, Kant further claims, the only possible representation of such a being we could have would have to be of one who could *create* the objects of his thoughts, as they are thought, an *intellectus archetypus*, or God, whose "causality" is different from any we could concretely imagine. So:

> Here the maxim always holds that all objects whose cognition surpasses the faculty of understanding are thought by us according to the *subjective* conditions of the exercise of that faculty which necessarily attach to our (human) nature. (My emphasis)[37]

And in section 77:

> Our understanding has then this peculiarity as concerns the judgment, that in cognition by it, the particular is not determined by the universal and cannot therefore be derived from it; but at the same time this particular in the manifold of nature must accord with the universal by means of concepts and laws, that it may be capable of being subsumed under it. This accordance under such circumstances must be very contingent and without definite principle as concerns the judgment.[38]

Now, as already noted, or at least promised, we shall see in the next chapter that Hegel's understanding of this issue begins to change somewhat when he discards the Schellingean language of intuiting and develops his notion of the dialectical development of the Notion. But he never fundamentally changes his rejection of these paradigmatically Kantian passages in sections 76 and 77 of the third *Critique*. The mature Hegel (of, say, the *Encyclopedia Logic*) would continue to suggest that even Kant's problematic and hesitant representation of an "intuitive understanding," with its suggestion of a "universal which is at the same time apprehended as essentially a concrete unity," is among the only "ideas" in which "the Kantian philosophy reveals itself to be speculative" (*EL*, 140; *EnL*, 88). And Hegel would continue to define much of his own project in the very terms Kant rejected, claiming that Kant's project "instead of the actual realization of the ultimate end" (which Hegel, of course, claims to have achieved), "clings hard to the disjunction of the Notion from reality" (*EL*, 140; *EnL*, 88). Thus, besides Hegel's negative attack on Kant's understanding of the status of reflective judgments (merely subjective, regulative), he appears to want to defend such judgments by defending the possibility of such an *intellectus archetypus*, both denying Kant's claim that such a being is precisely what we are not and affirming again the existence of such a divine intellect and our Schellingean identity with it.

These and similar criticisms of Kant in *GW* suggest again that any interpretation of Hegel that wants to take seriously his central claim about the "Notion's self-determination" must now assume the added baggage of what this rejection of Kant on reflective judgment would seem to imply. It would seem clearly to imply that Hegel believed that the "particular" *could* be "determined by the universal" and thereby be "derived" from it, or that there was, and we could know there to be (or could even be ourselves), a "divine" intuitive intellect.

However, the context in which Hegel introduces his reaction to Kant's views on intuition, and the more general context that I have been arguing is required to understand Hegel's idealism, reveal that what Hegel wants to *affirm* with respect to intellectual intuition is *not* what Kant is *denying*. Hegel is here again his own worst enemy in that he often uses language that clearly suggests that he means simply to resurrect rationalist metaphysics, as if the critical objections to it had never been raised. Moreover, by making use of Kant's notion of a divine intellect, Hegel appears to make the matter worse by promising to defend the necessity of a being whose reason does *create* and so intuit its own objects, in whose activity we somehow participate. But nothing is more important, I believe, for the correct understanding of Hegel's project than noticing, first, how radical and unmotivated such a resurrected rationalism would be in the context of the problematic of German Idealism – the *transcendental* problem of self-consciousness – and, second, that for all his vagueness and abstraction, Hegel does indeed indicate that such a traditional project is not what he intends, and that he means to be understood in the context of Kant's transcendental idealism. Consider this passage from the concluding paragraphs of Hegel's discussion of Kant in *GW*:

> The Idea of this archetypal intuitive intellect is at bottom nothing else but the same Idea of the transcendental imagination that we considered above. For it is intuitive activity, and yet its inner unity is no other than the unity of the intellect itself, the category still immersed in extension, and becoming intellect and category only as it separates itself out of extension. Thus *transcendental imagination is itself intuitive intellect*. (*GW*, 341; *BK*, 89; my emphasis)

Several things make this passage very difficult to understand. For one thing, with respect to Kant's idealism, the claim that the "unity" produced by the transcendental imagination "is no other than the unity of the intellect itself" would provoke a vigorous denial by Kant. As we have discussed, Hegel was fond of a passage in the second edition Deduction where Kant makes it sound as if the unity produced by formal intuition in experience is really the unity of "intellect" or understanding (B160n), but the predominant Kantian position is clearly that the intellect *cannot* produce unity within experience "on its own," that the form and matter of intuition are required. For another, as we have seen, calling the activity of the "imagination" "intuitive" requires a clarification and defense. For still another, Hegel's use of Schelling's terminology [of "intuition" and "extension" (*Ausdehnung*)] to reach back through the idealist tradition to Kant's first *Critique* severely compresses in a few sentences the story of the transformation of "apperception" into "self-positing" into "self-intuiting" into, now, the intuitive activity of what Kant called, in another of his names for the understanding, "productive imagination." Finally, and most importantly, Hegel does not even mention the fact that Kant, in the passages of the third *Critique* that Hegel is referring to, is concerned *only* with the grounds for assuming a purposeful author of nature (the special character of the objectivity of teleological judgments), and shows no inclination anywhere to transfer his speculations about the intuitive activity of *this* being to the domain of *human* knowledge. I submit that the only explanation possible of why Hegel feels entitled to claim that Kant's *own* doctrine of our transcendental, productive imagination commits *him* to an intuitive intellect is that Hegel means to refer to the post-Kantian problem of trying to account for, to find a clearer ground for, the spontaneous self-relating involved in all experience. It is *that necessarily spontaneous apperceiving* that Hegel is calling an intellectual intuiting.

And this reference to *our* productive imagination as what Kant should have been talking about when discussing the intuitive intellect of *God* is no mere slip by Hegel. It informs the rest of his discussion of Kant in *GW*. Thus, he will, a few pages later, after discussing Kant on *God's* purposiveness, move without transition or explanation to Kant on *our* capacity to intuit the beautiful. In both cases, Kant is held to be wrong in saying that we "must absolutely not go beyond finite cognition," and, equally in both, Hegel's so "going beyond" is tied to showing that Kant's own account of *our* finitude (our restricted understanding and wholly passive intuition) can be shown itself to involve the "infinite" dimensions of an intuitive intellect.

These terms give Hegel what he regards as the resources to define what transcendental knowledge itself should have been and what it became in Kant's version. He again refers to the deduction and its central premise in contrasting a view of the transcendental unity of apperception as either an "organic Idea of productive imagination" or, as in Kant, "the mechanical relation of a unity of self-consciousness which stands in antithesis to the empirical manifold, either determining it or reflecting on it" (*GW*, 343; *BK*, 92). The fact that these are mere promissory notes (especially with respect to the objectivity of such an activity), not worked out counterproposals, is not as important here as noting the connection between an intuitive intellect and *our* ("organic" rather than "mechanical") self-consciousness. We still do not know enough about what Hegel thinks a truly productive imagination involves for us to be able to understand what his identification of our organic apperceptive capacity with the Kantian paradigm of divinity amounts to, but at least it is clear that he is not simply claiming that Kant's subjective necessity (God) was an objective fact, and that Hegel's affirmation of Kant's "self-determining" universal can be read as a straightforward approval of what Kant was denying.[39]

Of course, it does not help matters much to note that Hegel, by rejecting Kant's denial of the possibility of a human intuitive intellect, could not have been proposing some version of a creative, divine intellect; that he was instead introducing his own idea of a progressively developing, collectively self-conscious subject, purposively active, in some epistemological sense "identical" with Nature, and one whose own activity is not regarded as merely subjective or regulative. It does not help much because we know so little about what the latter descriptions amount to. But at least, I would hope, the possibility of the kind of idealism I am attributing to Hegel has not only been held open by this consideration of the Jena writings but in many ways suggested by them. The task will be to understand in what sense Hegel thinks reason's self-determination is organic, that is, purposeful and integrative, and how to understand the objectivity of the results of such a self-posing.

However, continuing such an interpretation with the Jena texts alone, beyond the preceding general remarks, is not possible. Understanding the "transcendental" version of the Absolute in Absolute Idealism must obviously wait for a further treatment of Hegel's later texts. This is especially so since the notion is not only the most important one "inside" Hegel's project, it is the issue that most separates him from all of his successors in the European tradition. His earlier allies, Fichte and Schelling, gave up rather quickly on the idea of the "absolute reflection" Hegel thought he had accomplished. In doing so, they gave up on the perennial philosophic problem Hegel believed he had solved, what one might call the "*self*-legitimation of reason." For them, giving up on that problem meant realizing the unsolvability of all the reflective paradoxes associated with the problem of the origins of reason, the attempt by reason to understand and justify itself, its role in human conduct, in empirical research, in mathematics, and in theological speculation, all without the vicious circularity endemic, so they believed, to reflection. Hegel, of course, did not give up, and thought he had discovered a way in which reason's self-understanding and self-legitimation could be given an absolute form, one not in principle susceptible to skeptical attack. Such an ambition in Hegel, and its centrality in everything he talks about, is always the deepest issue when Hegel's project is compared with other attempts to account for the origin and meaning of "being rational" or, more broadly, being a self-determining subject, whether they be the theological abysses or existential presentiments of the late Fichte and Schelling, or the naturalisms, instrumentalisms, pragmatisms, or historical materialisms of the post-Hegelian age. At any rate, this is the issue at stake, I want eventually to argue, when we can survey all the important evidence concerning "absolute knowledge."[40]

For the moment, there is one final topic introduced in these works and in Hegel's lecture courses that should be considered, although it too is better discussed in full in the *Logic*. That is Hegel's idiosyncratic use of the language of "identity and difference."

4. Identity theory

"The principle of speculation is the identity of subject and object," Hegel announces early in *DS*, referring again to Kant's Deduction as the *point d'appui* for later speculative maneuvers (*DS*, 6; *Diff*, 80). He thereby contributes another defining mark of speculation in his many-sided attempt to distinguish it from reflection. Rather than a negative criterion (speculation's denial of reflective dualisms), an epistemological criterion (speculation's pursuit of absolute knowledge, not the finite knowledge of reflection, relativized to our species or a foundational axiom), or a methodological criterion (speculation's reliance on transcendental or intellectual intuition), this use of "identity theory" is at once the most sweeping and the least explained in the Jena critical writings. It is also one of the most continuous and extensive of Hegel's themes, clearly visible in his prephilosophical work, a major issue at all stages of his political and social philosophy, and a central topic in all his mature theoretical work. Indeed, as commentators like Görland and Harris have pointed out, it is this attention to identity *theory* that, more than anything else, marks the transition in Hegel's development to the philosophical phase.[41] The theological and social writings are frequently occupied with the identity issue as the existential issue of "life," a form of human existence wherein an individual's experience of his individuality would not preclude, but be experienced as identical with, the "living totality" of a community:

> The concept of individuality comprises an opposition to an infinite manifold (consciousness) and a connection with that same manifold in himself (self-consciousness); a person is an individual life, insofar as he is something other than all elements, and other than the infinity of individual lives outside him, he is only an individual life insofar as he is one with all elements.[42]

Frequently, it is the experience of "love" that, in the early writings, plays this differentiating and identifying role. In a fragment from the same period, this "unity" of subject and object is also said to be the "Ideal," the "object of every religion."[43] Thus, to paraphrase Görland, it was when Hegel replaced the search for a way to overcome existentially this alienation or difference from God and the religious community with an analysis of the implications of Kant's transcendental unity of apperception that Hegel began a distinctly philosophical quest for, essentially, the same kind of goal.[44]

This connection between Hegel's existential and social concerns and Kantian epistemology was hinted at in material cited earlier – for example, in Hegel's championing an "organic" understanding of self-awareness instead of Kant's "mechanical" view – but the conjunction of these two issues still seems anachronistic even at that very abstract level.[45] When the topic is formally introduced in *DS*, such a suspicion is not helped much by the sketchiness of Hegel's discussion and the unsystematic and often bewildering introduction of the items that are said to be identical with each other in speculative theory. In Chapter 2, it was reasonably clear, I think, that Hegel's discussion of Kant's "Highest Principle of Synthetic Judgments" in terms of an identity of subject and object was a genuine restatement of Kant's goal. The "are" in "the conditions for the possibility of experience are at the same time the conditions for the possibility of objects of experience" could be read as an identity claim, as could the "is" in the definition of "object," in "an object is that in the concept of which the manifold is united." But Hegel also goes on to say that a Kantian synthesis should be said to effect further identities, between "the free and the necessary . . . the conscious and the unconscious . . . the infinite and the finite, the intelligible and the sensuous," and, later in the text, between the universal and the particular. *All* of these identities are said to occur in any successful instance of "knowledge," although they are fully understood only in speculative theory.

In *GW* also, Hegel again reconstitutes Kant's synthetic a priori judgments as identity claims:

> How are synthetic judgments a priori possible? This problem expresses nothing else but the idea that subject and predicate of the synthetic judgment are identical in the a priori way. (*GW*, 327; *BK*, 69)[46]

Indeed, it even appears that Hegel thinks that all true, affirmative, synthetic judgments express an identity (and difference) between subject and predicate (*GW*, 329–30; *BK*, 73).[47]

In the context of this interpretation, such claims must be capable of a more successful exposition than Hegel gives them here, since Hegel also explicitly says that the central achievement of his idealism is his speculative account of identity theory. So, I offer here a provisional account of Hegel's identity theory as it figures in his idealism, and return to it again where it arises in *SL*.

The transformation of Kant's language of a "necessary synthetic unity in experience" into the speculative claim about an "identity of oppositions" (which retain their difference within such an identity) is a little easier to see if we begin with Hegel's discussion in *GW* of synthetic a priori judgments. If Kant were to read the previously quoted passage about these judgments, he would obviously object that if, say, the Second Analogy were read as an identity between subject and predicate, the judgment would have been reinterpreted as an analytic judgment, incorrectly construed as an analytic *identity* claim at that, and the critical project ended before it started. But the context of Hegel's discussion makes it clear that he does not think synthetic a priori judgments are *analytic* identities. He admits freely the logical characteristic of such judgments that, in the Kantian context, makes them "synthetic": The logical elements (subject and predicate) *are* "heterogeneous" (*ungleichartiges*), even though *also* "absolutely identical" (*GW*, 327; *BK*, 69). Indeed, what characterizes genuinely speculative identity claims is just this identity within difference. Whatever that is, it does not involve a reduction of Kantian syntheticity to analyticity.

But this problem – how to *identify* a priori subject and predicate in synthetic a priori judgments while also admitting their heterogeneity – raises other Kantian problems. For one thing, according to Kant, the logical form of the most important synthetic a priori judgment is not subject–predicate but hypothetical, and in that form, no question of identity of antecedent and consequent, and no transformation of the hypothetical, or ground–consequent relation into the "is" of identity, would seem relevant. But one hint of what Hegel is getting at is given when he notes that this identity of subject and predicate would be an identity of "particular," designated by the subject term, and "universal," designated by the predicate term (*GW*, 328; *BK*, 72). To see what this means, one needs to note that in Kant's treatment, the synthetic a priori judgment at issue is the *transcendental* claim that all alterations (or events), possible objects of a spatio-temporal, sensible intuition, take place in conformity with the law of cause and effect. And that can be claimed to attribute a universal predicate ("is an event which presupposes something upon which it follows according to a rule") to a subject ("any event") that designates all possible particular events. Hence the "synthetic identity" as understood by Hegel: All events *are* events that presuppose something upon which they follow according to a rule. Such a formulation does not involve an analytic identity of meaning – for Kant and for Hegel, there is no analytic necessity in a temporal occurrence being (or being qualitatively identical with) a causally ordered temporal occurrence – and it is formulated in what seems to be an identity claim.

It should also be noted that this way of talking already transforms Kant's terminology and alters, to some extent, the problem Kant was trying to solve. For one thing, Kant's best statements of the problem of synthetic a priori judgments make use of the "intuition/concept" terminology, not "particular/universal." As we have already seen, although his definitions vary somewhat, the best definition of the Kantian problem of synthetic a priori judgments involves the question of how some pure representation of all possible particular objects of experience can be subsumed under a pure concept, a possibility that obviously cannot be explained by reliance on some limited empirical experience of even a great many particular objects. The Kantian term for this "pure representation of all possible particular objects" is "pure intuition," and the issue can then be stated as the problem of justifying the subsumption of pure intuitions under pure concepts. In Kant's general explanation of the problem of judgment, however, he is careful to avoid the confusions Hegel sometimes invites. Since Hegel frequently treats all synthetic subject/predicate judgments as particular-under-universal types of judgment, he creates the impression that particulars qua particulars are the *logical* subjects of such judgments. And obviously, in almost all synthetic judgments, the logical subject is a concept, or universal, a fact that Kant often points out. Hegel is not terribly careful about distinguishing logical form from the "real" content of a judgment type, but for the moment, it suffices to note that nothing in his discussion in these essays would prevent him from availing himself of a Kantian response to this problem. To wit: that in synthetic judgments the concept qua logical subject is being *used* to *refer* to a particular or class of particulars *about* which a universal claim is being made. Or, in stricter Kantian terms, a synthetic judgment is a "representation of a representation" in which some component of the subject term's representative "marks" must designate or represent the particulars about which the claim is being made.

But, one must still ask, why an *identity* claim, as opposed to a claim about "necessary conditions" of all alterations? Or why not the "is" of predication (here a case of necessarily true predication) rather than the "is" of identity? (Why not "All events are caused events" rather than "All events are identical to caused events"?) The answer, although difficult to discern in these works and ultimately presented only in the mature *Logic*, is that Hegel does not think there *is* any distinction between the ascription of necessary – indeed, constitutive – properties (or what he will call "essence judgments") and identity statements.[48] The short answer for why he doesn't involves recalling, first, that Hegel obviously does not regard identity statements as limited to analytic statements of identity of *meaning*. Second, when we arrive (through the yet to be explained speculative "self-realization" of the Notion) at a "determination" without which an object (particular, or kind of particular) could not be such an object, we have *essentially identified* the object. And for a variety of reasons, Hegel thinks it is important to state that claim as a claim about the identity between such objects and object(s) that . . . (some speculatively determined category). For the moment, the most important reason for stating it this way is that it reveals *both* that a synthetic discovery has been made (in the process of thought's progressive realization of self-consciousness, a determination originally not known to be a speculatively necessary determination of objects is subsequently known to be) and that, once we know that it is true, we know that the particulars are, could not be other than, are essentially, particulars that. . . . (Another reason for this stress on identity is, it might be said, rhetorical. Hegel is trying to make a point as strongly as he can, inviting the air of oddness it creates; he is trying to say that the "thought determinations of the real" – whatever they will turn out to be – *are* what it is to be real. Emphasizing such an identity is a way of rejecting Kant's principle of nonidentity, as Hegel understands it: that Kantian categories are objectively valid only for possible objects of experience that are "not" things in themselves.)

But, an objector might still complain, since Hegel says that in synthetic a priori judgments, the *particular* is identical with the *universal*, he seems to say that, for example, "*Water* is identical to 'H_2O'," an obvious use/mention mistake. I have already indicated that there is nothing in Hegel's *GW* discussion to lead one to think that he believes that particular things are identical with universal *terms* and that he obviously means to identify "essentially" all the relevant particulars with "*the* universal" designated by the predicate/universal term, a problematic enough position, but not an obvious howler. There is little reason to believe that Hegel means by such an identity that what we first thought were particular things – tables, dogs, molecules, and so on – turn out really to *be* universals like Tableness or Dogness. To be sure, it is a confusing way of putting things, but the most important Hegelian twist to keep in mind in this talk of subject–predicate and particular–universal identity is the supervening, supreme speculative identity Hegel is after – the identity of object and subject. That is, Hegel is not a realist about such universals, but an idealist. They are not objects or kinds of things at all, but ultimately (i.e., as explained in the *Logic*) the self-determinations of pure subjectivity, of pure thought thinking itself.

The indication of this idealist identity in the texts we are considering is simply that frequently Hegel explicitly calls the identity between particular and universal, represented by subject and predicate, an identity between objective and subjective. As in Kant, where concepts are subjective forms of unification, in Hegel concepts are also (in a different sense) "subjective determinations," although in his case that is tied to an unusual theory about the relation among all concepts, *the* Concept or Notion, and the Absolute Subject's self-understanding. For now, all we need note is that the "identity" in question is meant to express the claim that what, prior to a full speculative understanding, might have seemed the merely *subjective* specification of the ways in which the world is divided up, *is* the way the world is divided up.[49] That is, a synthetic claim is a truth claim, and what is being asserted is that some characterization *of ours* about things *is* (is identical with) a characterization of things.[50] So, although admitting that Hegel has a great deal more to explain concerning his theory of concepts, and especially how this objectivity claim might be supported with respect to what kinds of "thoughts," for now I simply claim that there is nothing logically incoherent about his transformation of the problem of synthetic a priori judgments into the problem of identifying particulars considered just qua particulars with particulars qua qualified conceptually (universally) in some determinate way.[51]

Of course, aside from all the outstanding ambiguities to be cleared up, this kind of position faces a much more famous problem. Since Hegel's theory of the Notion is a developmental theory, and since his account of the role of such Notions in the possible intelligibility of any particular is so strong (as indicated by the "identity" language of essential predication), it would seem to follow that we ought to say that at some stage of the Notion's development, any object qua object *is* C, is identical with some conceptual identification in the sense of identity suggested earlier, but also *is not* C, since C is not the full self-realization of the Notion. And, although giving up bivalence is something most antirealists are used to doing, Hegel bites the bullet on this one so enthusiastically, so celebrates the "living contradiction" of the speculative proposition, that the intelligibility of his position seems threatened. He simply seems to take the preceding statement of the apparent consequences of his position not as a problem but as a kind of confirmation of its adequacy. And this shall be a large problem for future discussion. I mention it here because I think this is the way it ought to be understood: as one of the long series of consequences for Hegel's *Logic* that follow, I am arguing, from his acceptance of Kant's basic position on apperception and idealism, and from his rejection of the concept/intuition distinction.[52]

This can all be confirmed if we notice how Hegel contrasts his speculative understanding of identity with Kant's in the Deduction. In exploring the Kantian answer to the problem of synthetic a priori judgments, Hegel again notes that Kant solved this problem by establishing only a "relative" or formal identity between subjectivity (or "thought") and objectivity (or "being") (*GW*, 331; *BK*, 76). By this he means that Kant succeeded in establishing this identity only by relativizing what he counted as possible objects, relativizing them to "possible objects of our experience." He could thereby establish his identity claim by showing that, since the objects could be objects only as subject to our conditions for knowability, since their very "objecthood" depended on the conditions for a unity of apperception, "pure" subjective principles (categorial properties) could be said to be identical with the properties of any object *qua object of possible experience*. This is the Kantian "we get out of experience only what we put into it" strategy, and opens the door to Hegel's charge of a merely subjective idealism, with its merely (subjectively) relativized identity.

As with so many of such charges, this one can appear to suggest that Hegel intends to resurrect a classical, rationalist position on the identity between thought and being in knowledge, as in Spinoza's famous claim in the *Ethics* that the order and connection of thoughts "is the same" as the order and connection of things.[53] [This is just what he does suggest in *GW* contra Kant: the "absolute identity of thought and being" (*GW*, 345; *BK*, 94).] But, as I have been suggesting all along, that would be far too hasty an inference to draw, and, by noting Hegel's continual allegiance to Kantian principles, one can show that he does not mean to invoke a noncritical metaphysics, but rather to deal with critical skepticism about whether objects considered as objects of our possible experience *are* objects as they are in themselves, all in a non-Kantian way. In this context, that continual allegiance is apparent in Hegel's use of the transcendental unity of apperception premise from the Deduction.

For example, in the discussion of Kantian philosophy in *GW*, Hegel not only does not reject Kant's use of the unity of apperception thesis to "idealize" objects of experience, he radically *extends* what he takes to be the implications of the apperceptive nature of experience. Hegel denies that the "unity" of the unity of apperception, my "making" all objects of experience part of my experience by "taking" them up and "holding" them together, should be understood as a unification of elements (received intuitions and spontaneous concepts) presupposed as an "absolute" opposition, where the "identity might look as if it was by nature posterior to the opposition." He goes on to claim:

> But in Kant, the synthetic unity is undeniably the absolute and original identity of self-consciousness, which of itself posits the judgment absolutely and a priori.
> (*GW*, 328; *BK*, 71)

and

> The absolute synthesis is absolute insofar as it is not an aggregate of manifolds which are first picked up and then the synthesis supervenes on them afterwards.
> (*GW*, 328; *BK*, 71)

Such a claim about how the "absolute" unity of self-consciousness is invoked to justify a claim about the synthetic identity between concepts and objects had been prepared for by an earlier claim that this original, necessary, constitutive activity in experience should not be conceived as operating on the results of our receptive, sensible contact with the world (given that this consideration is occurring at a transcendental level, where a formal characterization of the constituents of all possible received data could be given). Instead, what counts as such general features of receptivity is said to be *itself* a product of apperceptive activity, or the productive imagination, a fact that, as we have seen in looking at Fichte, greatly alters the *nature* of our consideration of conceptual objectivity. Here is the passage from *GW* mentioned in Chapter 2 in which Hegel most clearly states his reading of how Kant's own position is leading him in this speculative direction:

> Here, the original synthetic unity of apperception is recognized also as the principle of the figurative synthesis, i.e., of the forms of intuition; space and time are themselves conceived as synthetic unities, and spontaneity, the absolute synthetic activity of the productive imagination, is conceived as the principle of the very sensibility which was previously characterized only as receptivity. (*GW*, 327; *BK*, 69–70)

What, then, would *not* abstractly isolating receptive sensibility mean? At the very least, it would mean that, in any particular case of "my taking *this* to be *P*," or in a general claim about "my taking any *this* necessarily to be *P*," we must admit that there is no way in which the intuited particular, or formally characterized domain of intuited particulars, can play a cognitively significant role except as already minimally conceptualized particulars. Always involved in such judgments is my having taken *this* to be this-such, even in a quite minimal or highly abstract way ("this thing here, now"). This does not mean that Hegel is thereby denying the possibility of, or the role of, actual interchanges with the world in empirical knowledge. What he is denying is that either the interchange itself, or some supposedly "immediately" presented mental state produced by that interchange, can function "independently of the productive imagination," either as the nonconceptual item to which concepts are applied or as some epistemic "validator," some foundational *non plus ultra* for empirical certainty.

If this claim can be demonstrated (and Hegel does not attempt to do so in either *DS* or *GW*, though, I shall argue, he does in the first three chapters of the *Phenomenology*), some of the more ambitious Hegelian claims can be understood: that an "absolute" subject "divides itself into subject and object, and then identifies itself with itself"; that there is a dialectical relationship between what a subject takes to be its possibly true or false characterization of an object and what it takes to confirm or disconfirm that characterization; that the dialectical inseparability of these elements means that we shall have to rethink "confirmation" both empirically and philosophically. Hegel does not spell out these consequences, but it is clearly where he is headed, as for example, when he rebukes those who think that this talk of the productive imagination opens the door to "unlawfulness, whim and fiction" (or one might add, in our own age, to epistemological anarchism), and that it is they above all who must grasp the basic point, that

> the in-itself of the empirical consciousness is Reason itself; that productive imagination as intuition, and productive imagination as experience are not particular factors quite sundered from Reason. (*GW*, 329; *BK*, 73)

In this context, though, rather than spelling out what he means by Reason and its internal development, he stays close to his critical intent, mostly by trying, in a variety of ways, to come up with a way of stating this thesis about the "totality" of "Reason" within experience that will not sound as if we simply make up what we think about and how we think about it. [His most unusual statement is one that tries to express the fact that the "conceptualization of an intuition" is a conceptualization of what one takes to be intuitively given. So, the intuited content cannot simply be "A" but must be A determined as such in some way, say, A = B. And the thought of it is thus a kind of "double" determination by a subject of its own determination of itself, or a claim like $A^2 = (A = B)$. Or perhaps, I take (what I take to be this) to be *B* (*GW*, 328; *BK*, 70–1).]

Consider, then, in conclusion, where this overview of Hegel's predecessors and of his early work has left us. Kant's excessively formal understanding of apperception left inexplicable the origin and nature of the specific, fundamental modes of apperception argued to be necessary conditions of experience. This was traced to a general problem (visible in Kant's practical, aesthetic, and teleological theory as well) in Kant's overly abstract isolation of the spontaneous and receptive or passively determined aspects of experience. Thus the obvious problem: How *could* this radical critique of Kant's idealistically qualified empiricism, with Hegel's assertion that receptivity must be considered as somehow a moment in a subject's progressive self-understanding, do justice to the purported "materiality" of such a "moment," its being a genuinely objective determination? And this was just the problem that Fichte, whose criticisms of Kant (or extensions of the "spirit" of Kant) Hegel approved of, could not escape. Construed in the language of subjective idealism, Fichte's second principle, the I's positing of the not-I, was either not a genuinely different principle from the first (the not-I, as the I's positing, could not genuinely be a not-I), or it was a second principle, but unmotivated and inexplicable. And, finally, Hegel rejects (ultimately, but visibly even in these works) Schelling's nonsolution, his various attempts to argue just *that there must be* some "indifference point" principle that is neither subject nor object (and so also inarticulable).

Where did all this leave Hegel? In his defense of speculation in *DS* and *GW*, it appears to leave him with a sketch of a position that could be subjected to *all* of the previous criticisms. If anything, it still resembles, most of all, Schelling's programmatic indication of what an "Absolute" principle of speculation *would be* like. It would be nice not to have a position saddled with the skeptical doubts of modern reflective theories and not burdened with the dogmatism of modern rationalist realism, but this does not mean that there is such a position. Hegel has not yet been able to offer any clear, positive position on the speculative and idealist possibility of reconciling the "self-constituted" and the "objective." We just have that Schellingean insistence that there must be such a position.

Stated more generally, the larger problems awaiting solution can be summarized in terms of two issues. First, Hegel cannot rest content with programmatic statements about how the subject's self-relation in experience can be said to involve already a "production" of specific forms of such relations. What will soon become Hegel's theory of the Notion's self-determination needs to be filled out in much more detail if it is to be made plausible. The other, larger problem is even more fundamental. One of the most prominent characteristics of Hegel's early philosophical work is also one of the most typical of German philosophy in this period. It was full of "system sketches," rapidly produced programs, outlines, introductions, revisions, proposals. Somewhat ironically, a tradition animated largely by the "metacritical" problem of how Kant *could* have known what he claimed to know about the subject did not itself evince much concern for the critical problem. So much attention was focused on what a speculatively successful system would be *like* that the questions of *how* we could be said to *know* that this was such a system or that it was successful were too often overlooked.

Both of these problems became more and more prominent in Hegel's work. The first is apparent in Hegel's lecture courses on logic and his so-called real philosophy, his understanding of the relation between logic (fulfilling now a more positive, less "self-destructive" role) and the "material" issues of politics, nature, and "spirit." Hegel's struggle with the second problem, what Rosenkranz long ago identified as the "crisis" in Hegel's early philosophy, resulted in what is still the most controversial and exciting of Hegel's works.[54] Somewhat ironically (given Hegel's famous attack on critical philosophy and skepticism in its Introduction), only a serious engagement with the problem of *skepticism* about the possibility of speculative philosophy would produce a work that could begin to make good some of Hegel's speculative promises, the 1807 *Phenomenology of Spirit*. Or so I now argue.

II
The phenomenology of idealism

5
Skepticism, knowledge, and truth in the Jena Phenomenology

1. Idealism and skepticism

Whatever else Hegel intends by asserting an "Absolute Idealism," it is clear by now that such a claim at the very least involves Hegel in a theory about pure concepts, and about the role of such concepts in human experience, particularly in any possible knowledge of objects, but also in various kinds of self-conscious, intentional activities. Moreover, his account of this role is clearly committed to the priority of such a conceptual element. Throughout his mature system, his general term of art for such a nonempirical and supposedly "spontaneously self-moving" condition is "the Notion" (*der Begriff*) and, simply put, his claim is that the Notion originally determines the possibility and character of human experience. And it is also uncontroversial that Hegel does not want to be committed to any claim that would construe such a relativization of objects of experience or norms of action to our conceptual structure as a *limitation*, one that leaves us, to use his highly speculative language, with the finitude of subjective idealism rather than the infinity of Absolute Knowledge. There is, in Hegel's final position, no possible *contrast* between our conceptual framework and "the world," and hence no such limitation.[1] Finally, in much of the Jena material, Hegel had begun to connect the possibility of such a fully developed or "Absolute" Notion with a theory of subjectivity, an account of what it was to be a self-conscious subject in such a "Notional" relation with objects, an account, that is, of what he will call "Spirit."

In the 1807 *PhG* we are introduced to the terminology with which Hegel will attempt to articulate and defend such idealism. The position that the *PhG* will "introduce" us to, "educate" us about, and "deduce" is called simply "science" (*Wissenschaft*), knowledge of "the Absolute." Hegel appears to have a number of things in mind with each of these versions of the *PhG*'s task, and he characterizes such a science in many different ways, but in the Preface it is at least clear that "the proper exposition" of such a science "belongs to Logic, or rather it is Logic" (*PhG* 35; *PS*, 28).[2] In further describing what will be the 1812–16 *Science of Logic*, the "standpoint of which" the *PhG* will in some sense justify or "lead us to," and that *SL* will present, Hegel bluntly summarizes the basic claim of such a Science as "truth has only the Notion as its element of existence" (*PhG*, 12; *PS*, 4), and he later says that "Science dare only organize itself by the life of the Notion itself," a "Notional life" Hegel constantly describes as "self-determining" (*PhG*, 38ff.; *PS*, 31ff.). Indeed, in describing the subject matter of science, "the Absolute," Hegel goes so far as to say:

Of the Absolute it must be said that it is essentially a result, that only in the end is it what it truly is; and that precisely in this consists its nature, viz., to be *actual, subject, the becoming of itself.* (*PhG*, 19; *PS*, 11; my emphasis)[3]

These claims that "the Absolute" – variously also called "the truth," "actuality," "what there is, in truth," and "objects, in truth" – *is* "the Notion," and that such Notionality must be understood as the "logic" of a "self-determining" subjectivity are summed up in the most famous claim of the *PhG*: that "everything turns on grasping the True, not only as Substance, but equally as Subject" (*PhG*, 18; *PS*, 10). In fact, Hegel will quickly alter the "equally as" (*eben so sehr als*) language of this claim and state more directly that the true "living substance" or "what is in truth actual" "*is* in truth Subject" (*PhG*, 18; *PS*, 10; my emphasis), that "Substance is essentially Subject" (*PhG*, 22; *PS*, 14), that "substance is in itself or implicitly subject," and that "all content is its own reflection into itself" (*PhG*, 39; *PS*, 33).[4]

These are the claims that, I have argued, are best understood in terms of both Hegel's debt to Kant and Fichte, and his rejection of the Kantian account of pure intuition. The question now is simply whether he can make clear what such claims about "absolute" subjectivity amount to, and especially whether he can defend his assertions, particularly that the "results" of such a self-determining subjectivity are objective, indeed, incredibly, that such results comprise "absolute truth."

As we have seen, the defense of such an objectivity claim involves Hegel's highly abstract formulations about the "identity within difference" of "subject and object." Understandably (given a straightforward interpretation of "identity"), this is the claim that is at the basis of most metaphysical, or Spirit-monism, interpretations of Hegel. And so, with the preceding discussion of Hegel's idealist predecessors as a starting point for a potentially nonmetaphysical account of Hegel's idealism, we might also put the question to be pursued as follows: Is there a way of understanding the "subject–object identity" formulations of Hegel's absolute idealism as what he says they are, *extensions* of Kant's project, rather than a complete rejection, or a transformation so radical that Kant is no longer recognizable in it? If there is, then there is one problem more than any other that ought to be the focus of such an interpretation.

Simply put, the issue that radically differentiates Hegel from Kant and Fichte is expressed in the charge that Kant and Fichte, despite their achievements, are *skeptics*, philosophers who finally undercut their own results by admitting that they have no way of establishing that the conditions for a possibly self-conscious experience of objects are genuinely objective. The results of their respective "deductions" either relativize claims about objects to mere phenomena or create an infinite and infinitely futile task, a "striving" for a reconciliation that can never occur. Kant and Fichte reenact a Christian, religious tragedy of human finitude; they insist on a fundamental, eternal difference between the human and divine perspectives, and ascribe to the latter the only genuine, absolute knowledge of things in themselves.

Thus, to all the other questions Hegel needs to be asked, we must ask the most pressing: How has he avoided the "transcendental skepticism" of Kant and Fichte? And, faced with such a question, there are two reasons to think that Hegel will have a difficult time answering it. The first stems from the results found in Chapter 2. Given Hegel's Fichtean rejection of Kant's reliance on pure sensible intuition in the Deduction, it seems far *more* likely that it will be Hegel, not Kant, who will be restricted to a mere finite or subjective idealism. In the second half of the Deduction, Kant at least tried to establish a priori that *phenomenal objects* (objects of intuition) must conform to the categories. Without such a strategy, it seems prima facie that the best Hegel can hope for is some case for the subjective indispensability of pure concepts, some way of describing our fundamental "like-mindedness." The *PhG* could then be read as an imaginative, original account of how and why various "shapes of Spirit," or Notions, came to be "experienced" as fundamental, unrevisable by experience since somehow *thought* to be constitutive of its possibility. But there now seems even less reason to think that whatever we can establish as a Notional condition of experience, necessary for experience to be a self-conscious unity, will have anything to do with "objects" of experience, much less be "identical" with "what there is, in truth."[5]

Second, Hegel's extraordinary Fichtean emphasis on the autonomy and self-determining character of this Notional level seems clearly vulnerable to empirical or material objections, broadly construed. Even if it can be shown that the possibility of determinate experience requires an empirically independent or in some way "self-determined" condition of some kind, it is unclear why we should think, even initially, that the best way to understand what such conditions are, and how they might change, is in the wholly "internalist" way Hegel has already begun to suggest: that accounts of some such Notional transformation should rely only on other Notions, that this Notional level has, if you will, a life of its own. A philosopher who might be inclined to travel with Hegel away from realism, to accept the transcendental objections to empiricism, and to be sympathetic to Hegel's criticisms of Kant's transcendentalism, might indeed find Hegel's systematic pretension to a "self-developing" Notion to be the greatest barrier to any further travel.

This interpretation – that the achievement of Absolute Knowledge claimed at the end of the *PhG* primarily involves a "deduction" of the absolute objectivity of the Notion (*both* the deduction of its basic structure and the deduction of its objectivity), without the transcendental-skeptical remainder of things in themselves – will obviously require a great deal of elaboration.[6] And finally, all of this will depend on some general interpretation of the *PhG* itself, an account of what kind of book it is that could claim to establish such a goal, and of its status within Hegel's mature system (as an "Introduction," whether scientific or historical, as the "First Part" of the system, as finally transformed into a component of the "science" of subjective spirit, or as some kind of "propadeutic" for the system).

I shall begin to address the last question in Section 4 of this chapter. But since my interpretation of the *PhG* depends heavily on a claim about the engagement with skepticism I shall try to show is at the heart of the work, I continue to motivate that approach by reference to Hegel's own remarks about such a deduction and what it must show.

2. Phenomenological deduction

It is not difficult to find passages where Hegel clearly attributes a "deductive" intention to the *PhG*, and where he explains how that deduction succeeds by means of a particular kind of encounter with *skepticism*. By far the clearest of the former passages occurs in the Introduction to the *SL*. There Hegel says that the *PhG* had treated "*all* forms of the relation of consciousness to the object," and that by doing so had provided a "justification" (*Rechtfertigung*) of the Notion; indeed, he says that this procedure was the *only* justification the Notion could have received (*WL*, I, 29; *SL*, 48). And on the next page, he states directly that the *PhG* is "nothing other than the deduction" of the notion of pure science, and that it accomplishes this by having "eliminated" the "separation of the object from the certainty of itself" (*WL*, I, 30; *SL*, 49).[7]

This possible separation between the "object," or what Hegel also calls "truth," and the "self-certainty" of the subject, as well as his use of the term made so important by Kant, a "deduction," which will accomplish the elimination of this separation, suggests clearly that the confrontation with a "realist skepticism" about our conceptual scheme is the self-appointed task of the *PhG*, and the best indication of how we should understand, at least initially, the notion of absolute knowledge.[8] By this I mean that even if Hegel can show that we cannot make knowledge claims about any particular matter of fact unless such claims are subject to pure conceptual conditions, such a demonstration would still leave open the "separation" mentioned earlier, the possibility that we are describing a transcendental subject's criteria only for self-certainty, not for "genuine knowledge." The latter can, on such an account, only be what the robust realist insists it is: The world is as it is, independently of any activity of ours; knowledge worthy of the name must accurately represent the nature of things; and we must be able to give some account of how we know which of the claims or beliefs we make about that nature are the true ones. Hegel has set himself the task of rejecting such realist doubts, even while defending the objectivity of the results of what he calls "Spirit's experience of itself." Indeed, he thinks he can establish that such results, despite such skeptical suspicions, constitute "absolute knowledge."[9]

This is suggested even more directly in the Introduction to the *PhG*. There the realization of the continual "untruth" of "appearing knowledge" is called explicitly a "thoroughgoing skepticism" (*sich vollbringende Skepticismus*) and is immediately distinguished from a merely or incidentally skeptical or interrogative attitude (*PhG*, 56; *PS*, 50). And, as claimed in the *SL*, this overcoming of skepticism, a skepticism said to be "directed against the *whole* range of phenomenal consciousness," is what "renders spirit for the first time competent to examine what truth is" (*PhG*, 56; *PS*, 50).

So much for Hegel's statements of intention. The questions they generate include, among others: What does he mean by "skepticism," and what does he mean by overcoming skepticism and establishing Absolute Knowledge? From what we have seen thus far, Hegel is apparently restricting himself to the question of skeptical doubts about his own version of a priori knowledge, doubts that there *are* a priori conditions (Notions) for the possibility of experience, that such predetermining subjective constraints on what could be an object of experience ought to be understood as a result of "Spirit's developing knowledge of itself," and that such Notions simply "are what there is, in truth," that they do not merely represent how it is that Substance is *thought* as Subject.

All of which means that Hegel's relation to the modern skepticism problem is complex, that many of the problems Hegel poses for himself in the *PhG* presuppose a point of view on a great many other issues. Hegel may write that the *PhG* is the "pathway of doubt," even of "despair," but it is only a particular *kind* of doubt and despair at issue, and it is not initially clear what kind. That is, like Kant, Hegel is, from the start, interested in the conditions of the possibility of knowledge, and nowhere seems interested in the modern post-Cartesian problem – Is there ever any good reason to believe that we know *anything*? – or with what is often a kind of test case for the radical problem – Is there any good reason to believe that there is an external world? Also, like Kant (who, though, finally did feel compelled to address such problems), Hegel offers little systematic discussion of why he has posed the problem of knowledge in the way he does, and why he generally ignores all sorts of other skeptical problems in epistemology.

What little discussion there is, coupled with a little getting-ahead-of-ourselves, suggest the following. What we can call the "Cartesian," as opposed to the "Kantian," skepticism problem originates in a problem about inference. On the supposition that one is with certainty, incorrigibly, and so foundationally, having a certain experience, or is in a certain state, the problem is: How can one justify an inference about anything other than such a state, either the causal origin of that experience or the objects presented as such and such in that state/experience? This is a problem because it can be shown that there are no good (non-question-begging) reasons for preferring the commonsense or "natural" inference over other, more fanciful ones. So, the "sensations" naturally compatible with my inferring that I am in fact seated in front of the fire I seem to be seated in front of are equally compatible with my dreaming that I am so seated, or even with the existence of an evil demon who deceives me when I think I am in fact so seated. If I claim to know, in other words, that the evidence I have supports conclusion p, it must be possible to show that such evidence *could* not be compatible with −p, and the skeptical challenge is that I cannot, in many apparently obvious cases, fulfill this latter condition.

Understanding Hegel's reaction to and rejection of such a problem is important, not only as a clarification of the skepticism issue he *is* interested in, but because it introduces us, through the problem of skepticism, to his own usual theory of "thought's negative relation to *itself*," and so to what he might mean by "overcoming" such self-negation. One early discussion brings his own Kantian skepticism problem into focus sharply and shows why he rejects, like Kant, the entire "inferential" apparatus presupposed by the Cartesian problem.

In the 1802 review of a work of the romantic skeptic G.E. Schulze (Aenesidemus) entitled "The Relation of Skepticism to Philosophy, a Presentation of Its Different Modifications, and a Comparison of Modern with Ancient Skepticism," in the course of arguing that the ancient skepticism was superior to the modern, he asserts that the latter involves a *dogmatic* confinement to the "facts" of common sense and sense experience. Modern skeptics like Schulze, Hegel asserts again and again, profess to restrict themselves to the "facts of consciousness" alone; they claim that there is no possible inference "beyond" or "behind' such immediate experience; and they conclude that if there is, such an "act" or projection is itself just another immediate experience. Schulze thus qualifies as the Cartesian skeptic described previously.[10]

As is apparent in Hegel's very characterization of the position, and as is more explicit in his ironic comparisons with ancient skepticism, the problem with the whole approach, as Hegel sees it, is that it is not skeptical enough, not as skeptical as ancient attacks on the integrity of commonsense experience, and it is dogmatic about its own point of orientation. It is not at all clear, he asserts, that there can be an immediate, "self-explanatory" fact of consciousness from which inferences are to be made. Such a position is dogmatic because it assumes that the mind simply perceives directly that it is in a certain state, and that the state is this-such a state.[11] Such a beginning is not self-explanatory at all; an account of the "conditions of *its* possibility" is necessary, and since it is necessary, we must reject wholesale any problem that is generated by assuming some original "fact of consciousness." Knowledge is not a matter of inference from noninferentially warranted states. There are no such states. And ultimately, such a claim will mean that the philosophical "problem of knowledge" will shift to the question of the "conditions under which" judgments about objects (even objects of "inner sense") could be true or false ("objective").

Although in this essay Hegel is mostly concerned with the superiority of ancient doubts about such supposedly indubitable foundations in consciousness, it is clear from the other essays written around this time that he has been quite influenced by Kant's similar attacks on the "dogmatic realism" of even the skeptical philosophers of the "new way of ideas," and in particular by Kant's claims about the "self-consciousness" condition and so the necessary "mediation" of any conscious experience. Such an orientation naturally leads him to view the skepticism problem, as Kant did, in transcendental terms. If there are original conditions necessarily presupposed even for the possibility of the skeptic's generation of his counterpossibilities, then the original task is to discover these pure conditions. Such an orientation already undercuts the skeptical contrast between the certainty of immediate experience and the dubitability of inferences about objects, and it raises the transcendental problem of the "conditions" under which self-awareness and a distinction between self- and other-awareness is possible.

It thus also raises the skepticism problem in a different way. Even if it could be established that there are "pure conditions" for the possibility of any experience, and that such conditions ensure that a distinction between inner and outer experience is possible (even if, say, empirically difficult to demonstrate), it is not clear what the "dependence" of experience on such conditions finally says about the possibility of *knowledge*. Our robust realist might claim: All right, so you do not maintain that knowledge is a matter of inference from the occurrence of mental states; you do not maintain that we have some direct access to such states, and so are not subject to my attack on the rationality of any such inference. But I do not see the value of shifting the issue to the problem of "transcendental conditions." Now you are maintaining that the possibility of making true judgments about objects (even inner objects) is always relativized to subjective conditions for the possibility of judgments, and I maintain now that there are no good, non-question-begging reasons for assuming that such conditioned judgments have anything to do with knowledge of the world as it is.[12]

From Hegel's point of view, this is precisely the argument that Kant fell victim to in his admission that we do not know things in themselves. Accordingly, although Kant himself is not a "vulgar Kantian" like Schulze, he is still a "psychological idealist," subject to the skeptic's attack. What this suggests is that Hegel thinks his own idealism can accept the Kantian rejection of the Cartesian problematic and not inherit the Kantian skepticism that the transcendental approach seems necessarily heir to. Yet another tall order.

However, it is already becoming clear that Hegel will not, in some directly "realist" way, simply try to establish the identity of Spirit's self-determinations and "being as it in itself." Indeed, if the skepticism problem is posed as it is earlier, and if Hegel were to try to solve it by meeting the realist's objections directly, his project would look hopeless. What becomes apparent at this point, particularly when one briefly surveys the vast range of topics discussed in the *PhG* (all presumably having some connection with the programmatic goals summarized earlier), is that Hegel is just as radically *altering the terms within which* the problem of the "objectivity" of "Spirit's self-moving Notion" ought to be understood as he is defending such an objectivity claim. It will take considerable effort to explain the nature of this alteration, and to assess whether Hegel has begged the relevant question, but it is in the context of such an alteration, such an idealist project, and such a "deductive" goal that, I shall argue, the *PhG*'s otherwise bewildering array of topics, from Perception to Master/Slave, from physiognomy to the Christian religion, must be understood.[13]

The general intent of such an alteration is clear enough; it is in the way Hegel proposes to justify such a strategy that some of his original and most influential contributions to philosophy become manifest. That is, the only strategy Hegel can use, consistent with his own idealism, will be to *undercut* the presuppositions involved in standard realist assumptions about "being as it is in itself." That is, Hegel will try to undermine and exclude the *relevance* of such doubts, progressively and systematically, rather than answer them directly. He will try to show, determinately, why, given some putative Notional determination of objects, doubts about whether objects must or even can be so Notionally specified, are the relevant, determinate doubts they are, only as a *consequence* of that Notion's own incompleteness. This in turn means, for Hegel (summarizing everything at once), that such an "opposition" between "subject" and "object" is itself a "determination of the Notion," and so such an incompleteness can itself be made out only on the assumption of a developing Notion *of* objectivity. There is no *point*, Hegel constantly remarks, in abstractly asking whether the world "really" is as we take it to be, whether, "for all we know," this or that bizarre scenario might actually be occurring. Doubts about the adequacy of our conceptual scheme must have some basis, a concrete *ratio dubitandi*, for them to be serious doubts, and Hegel thinks he can show that the only legitimate basis for such doubts is what he calls "Spirit's experience of itself," an experience always determined *by* the "developing Notion." If this is true, then, roughly, what Hegel is after is a way of demonstrating the "ultimate" or absolute objectivity of the Notion not by some demonstration that being as it is in itself can be known to be as we conceive it to be, but that a Notionally conditional actuality is all that "being" could intelligibly be, even for the most committed realist skeptic. Or, if you like, Hegel's skeptic is co-opted into the idealist program, not simply "refuted." (Although such a project is not yet clear, some aspect of what Hegel proposes is apparent in the passages where he attacks Kant's "thing in itself" doctrine and, like Fichte, does not simply claim that we *can* know the world as it is, independent of our transcendental conditions, but that the subject's knowledge of itself, finally, properly understood, *counts* as the knowledge of the thing in itself that Kant paradoxically denied.) We know this, if we do, by in effect systematically overcoming any objections based on realist assumptions, objections that Hegel thinks he can show arise within an "experience" putatively determined by some Notion. This is the way the *PhG* must overcome skepticism. And it brings us to the issue that must be explained in much more detail if the preceding compressed, still admittedly quite vague summary of Hegel's methodology is to be assessed – what Hegel means by such an appeal to "Spirit's experience of itself."[14]

Before doing so, however, we should briefly note the extent to which, already, this post-Kantian statement of Hegel's project conflicts with a widely held view of Hegel. After all, it could be asserted, Hegel is known as a prototypical *realist*; whatever he means by the claim, he does assert that we know "reality" (Absolute Spirit) as it is in itself (what else could the denial of Kant's "thing in itself" remainder amount to?). Yet, as we have just seen, Hegel also states that reality *is* the developing Notion, and this certainly suggests a kind of contemporary antirealism, a relativization of truth claims to the Hegelian (Notional) equivalent of something like warranted assertability, or provability, or membership in an ideal theory. And as the project of the *PhG* has been stated so far, it does indeed seem that Hegel is making both such claims, or stating a fundamentally antirealist, idealist position, as if it *could have no realist competitor*, and so can be construed as itself constitutive of "reality as it is (could be) in itself." As noted, this will involve his elimination of the possibility of realist-skeptical attacks on the internally developing Notionality of various possible "shapes of Spirit" and the development of a technical sense of "actuality" (*Wirklichkeit*), one that can make plausible the counterintuitive consequence of his position: that actuality must be said to "change" if constituted by an internally "self-determining" Notion.[15]

3. The science of the experience of consciousness

There is in the Preface and Introduction of the *PhG* an abstract, often very confusing summary of what such a "self-examination by Spirit" is supposed to consist in. I discuss the specific terms of that explanation in this section. But we should also briefly remind ourselves why, given the intellectual ancestry of Hegel's idealism, his position on the "problem of objectivity" itself should indeed be as distinctive as his proposed absolutist solution.

Consider first that when Hegel is describing the conclusion or termination of the case made by the *PhG*, he is just as likely to describe such Absolute Knowledge in the terms used earlier (the overcoming of skepticism, the identity of subject and object, the comprehension of Truth as the Notion) as he is to state such things as the following:

> The Spirit that, so developed, knows itself as Spirit, is Science; Science is its actuality and the realm which it builds for itself in its own element. (*PhG*, 22; *PS*, 14)

And, "finally, when consciousness itself grasps this its own essence, it will signify the nature of absolute knowledge itself" (*PhG*, 62; *PS*, 57). Such passages testify even more directly to the point made earlier: that Hegel's resolution of the objectivity and skepticism problems raised by his idealism must involve a way of arguing *that* such a self-knowledge by Spirit, although not "metaphysically identical" with "what there is, in truth," nevertheless in some way defines or transcendentally constitutes the possibility of "objects."

Posing the problem this way should make clear why so many commentators have concluded either that the metaphysical interpretation is correct (the Spirit-monism view) or that what is "living" in Hegel is simply his theory of Spirit's experience of itself, that he has an independently powerful "philosophical anthropology," a theory of "culture" that ought to be disconnected from the view of "the Absolute," or Science. Prima facie, any other view would seem unable to do justice either to the Absolute Knowledge claim or to the "Spirit's knowledge of itself is Science" claim. I have already indicated some reasons why the former view cannot account for Hegel's central idealist project, and shall present others as his case unfolds. Hegel himself would object strongly to the latter "disconnection" move. He claims often that we cannot understand what he means by Spirit "having itself for its object just as it is" unless we realize that *thereby* "the separation of knowing and truth is overcome" (*PhG*, 30; *PS*, 21) and that, in such self-knowledge, we have attained the "simple oneness of knowing, the True in the form of the True" (*PhG*, 30; *PS*, 22).

Yet such a connection between complete "self-consciousness" and Absolute Knowledge should not, by now, sound so strange or require the choices suggested earlier. First, as we have seen in some detail, the foundations of the general connection between self-consciousness and the original possibility of a subject making judgments about *objects* were laid in Kant's apperception doctrine and Fichte's and Hegel's appropriation of Kant. If (and, of course, it is a big "if") Hegel's version of a "Deduction" can be defended, there will be nothing unusual about claiming that Spirit's full knowledge of itself is a kind of Absolute Knowledge. For it is a self-knowledge on which the very possibility of knowledge of objects depends. Second, although Hegel's disagreement with Kant about the availability of some pure representation of givenness, about pure intuitions, has greatly altered the issue of the objectivity of the various ways a subject might, a priori, bring its experiences to a unity, it has not eliminated the problem of objectivity. It is still a critical problem that Hegel fully accepts. Third, this latter should suggest the Fichtean legacy in Hegel's project, that the *problem* of such objectivity, when and if it arises as a problem, does not involve the pure synthesis of a "merely material manifold," but can only be understood as the subject's experience of some kind of "*self*-opposition," some way for a subject's projection of a possible experience to be "internally deficient" and "internally correctable." ("Internal" because, at such a level, empirical correction is not possible.) And this is where all the murkiest problems begin. The latter ought at least to mean, roughly, that (1) a subject's cognitive relation to an object can be shown to be possible only by that subject's reliance on some Notion of objects in general; (2) that such a reliance, although often deeply implicit, nonetheless reflects that subject's spontaneous apperception, an empirically undetermined Notion that reflects the subject "taking" the objects of its experience to be such objects; and (3) that in any such putative experience of objects, if such a Notional determination is inadequate as a condition for a self-conscious experience of objects, that inadequacy can be determined internally, just by a description of what such an experience would be like. With such a Notion of objects, a cognitive relation to objects could not be coherently established. In *this* sense, a subject or a projected "candidate" subject could be said to be "opposed to" or "dissatisfied with" *itself*.

The problem is how all this "opposition" and "overcoming" is supposed to be *described*, indeed, presumably, to be described as some sort of idealized "history" of Spirit's self-education. Moreover, not only is this the kind of connection between apperceptive subjectivity and objectivity that must be accounted for if Hegel is to have any criteria for the adequacy of his own claims; the issue, posed this way, also helps to explain the generality and breadth of this issue of a "subject's experience of opposition" in the *PhG* as a whole. As noted previously, Hegel is attempting both to alter the way in which the objectivity of the results of "Spirit's experience to itself" are assessed and to defend such a newly defined objectivity. In fulfilling the former goal, he takes it upon himself to provide an account of how and why an idealized subject (any possible subject) would experience an "opposition" between its self-determining activity and what it is trying to determine – in our earlier language, why a subject would doubt that the way it takes things to be is the way things are. If such an account is to have a chance of providing a general enough description of such experienced opposition to be used in the kind of deductive strategy described earlier, the one that results from the rejection of pure intuition and that will fulfill the latter goal, it must be very general indeed, comprehensive enough to explain the *nature* of such "opposition" and so the skeptical doubts that originate from it. And, true to form, Hegel charges ahead and tries to provide such an extraordinarily general account. He tries to account for such things as how and why a subject would find its views of *another subject* "opposed" by such a subject; how social subjects, groups, or classes find their desires, and especially their view of their own desires, opposed and negated by other social subjects, groups, or classes; how political subjects with certain Notions about political life would (and did) find themselves in sometimes "tragic" opposition; in what way laboring or even worshipping subjects find their experience of their own activity "in opposition with itself"; and so forth.

Here, aside from this general, still quite programmatic, account of how Hegel will solve the enormous objectivity problem he has created for himself, we can also summarize the rather more technical discussion presented in the Preface and especially in the Introduction, and see if that is any help with the problem.

Having only loosely and provisionally defined Science (*Wissenschaft*) as knowledge of the Absolute, or "the truth," Hegel notes the obvious: that any specific such Notion of objects is initially just that, a Notion like any other, only initially what he calls an "appearance" (*PhG*, 55, *PS*, 48). This is so because such a putative Science "comes on the scene alongside another mode of knowledge," and so, without further ado, is as suspect as these others of just being a "bare assertion." In this context, the problem Hegel sets for himself is to show how such manifestations of absolute claims "free themselves" from this situation of "merely seeming to be absolute" (*von diesem Scheine*) (*PhG*, 55; *PS*, 48).

Hegel realizes that this immediately sounds like a simple survey of arguments used to justify claims about the "absolute objectivity" of various Notions, and he quickly moves to correct the impression that his own "exposition" (*Darstellung*) in the *PhG* "seems not to be Science, free and self-moving in its own most shape." And, in beginning to defend the scientific nature of his own "exposition" of such an objectivity problem, he states all at once the most controversial and intriguing aspects of the *PhG*. The presentation

> can be regarded as the path of natural consciousness that presses forward to true knowledge; or as the way of the soul, which journeys through the series of its own configurations as though they were the stations appointed for it by its own nature, so that it may purify itself for the life of Spirit in that through the complete experience of itself, it attains knowledge of what it is in itself. (*PhG*, 55; *PS*, 49)

Later, this "detailed history of the education of consciousness itself up to Science" is said to involve a "necessary progression" and a final "completion" of the attempt by "natural consciousness" to rid itself of doubts about its own phenomenal status.

Throughout the Introduction, Hegel characterizes such "natural consciousness" much as he did in his earlier works when referring to "reflection" or the reflective point of view. This means that all points of view other than what he had called the "speculative" (now "scientific") are characterized by an internal dualism, a separation of subject and object. In his language, this means that the very possibility of consciousness presupposes that a subject can "distinguish itself from something" while it "at the same time relates itself to it" (*PhG*, 55; *PS*, 52). This is his way of formulating the issue of how a subject can be said to intend its objects determinately, if merely being in a state or having an experience cannot count as such an intention. The problem is then how to *account for* this "natural" or constitutive characteristic of consciousness, how a conscious subject comes to judge as it does about the objects taken to be the objects of awareness. He calls this point of view "natural" in the *PhG* to emphasize the power of its hold on the way we think; it is indeed natural to think of "subjects" who can, for example, wonder if their moral claims have objective justifiability or their epistemic claims objective warrant. This is especially the case, of course, given a conception of subjectivity in which there are such moral claims, or possible knowledge at all, only as a "result" in some sense of a subject's self-determining activity. No form of knowledge or claim to an objective authority of any kind seems immune from the possibility of such a "separation."

In sum, then, by referring to the self-examination of natural consciousness as the "coming on the scene of Science," Hegel is presupposing that there are various fundamental ways in which an experiencer can understand its relation to objects, that such Notions, or presuppositions about the Absolute, are conditions for the possibility of experience, at least in the sense that they are not revisable in the face of experience. (He must now successfully identify such Notions, and defend their fundamentality and the nature of the transformation he will claim that any experiencer making such a presupposition or another must undergo.) And he believes that a deduction of Absolute Idealism can be effected by such a self-transformation because (1) such a deduction, a demonstration that natural consciousness ultimately presupposes the truth of Idealism, is the only way that the standpoint of Science can avoid begging the question against objections and because (2) identifying such presuppositions of natural consciousness identifies presuppositions so deep and fundamental that they constitute the only alternative to Science. So, if *all* "basic" positions that assume the nonidentity of Notion and Object can be shown to presuppose the identity of the fully developed Notion and Object, that identity will be established. That is why establishing Science *for* natural consciousness *is* the final overcoming of the possibility of skepticism about Absolute Knowledge.[16]

This all takes us back to the deepest issue raised by the Introduction's claims: Hegel's original characterization of the nature of consciousness, such that it can be said to experience itself as Hegel says it does and to transform itself in a "scientific" direction. That characterization can be summed up in one brief sentence, although, I have been arguing throughout, there is no way that it can be understood or justified without keeping in mind Hegel's appropriation of Kant and Fichte:

> Consciousness is, however, for itself its own Notion; thereby it is immediately a going-beyond the limited [*das Beschrankte*] and, because the limited belongs to it, a going-beyond itself. (*PhG*, 57; *PS*, 51)

The Kantian roots of this claim are even more visible in a later characterization of consciousness:

> For consciousness is on the one hand, consciousness of the object; on the other hand, consciousness of itself; consciousness of what is for it the truth, and consciousness of its own knowledge of that truth. (*PhG*, 59; *PS*, 54)

Both passages represent Hegel's appropriation of Kant's claim about the necessarily apperceptive nature of experience and Fichte's emphasis on the spontaneous, active nature of such cognitive activity. As we shall see in more detail, they express as well his proposed correction of Kant (such self-consciousness "depends" on the *experienced development of the Notion*, not on a Table of Categories) and his different answer to Fichte's question, "How is the I for itself?" (not as an original source of ground but as, at least partially, a *result* of previous self-interpretive activity).

That is, Hegel has simply assumed what we described earlier as the Kantian thesis about the inherent and ineliminable reflexivity of "consciousness" or empirical knowledge, although he is already expressing in his own terms that Kantian theory of apperceptive judging and what Fichte called the "double series" (*doppelte Reihe*) character of experience. Those terms also indicate, however, that as with Kant, Fichte, and Schelling, this self-relational component of experience is not being treated as some species of self-awareness or some kind of attending to one's mental states. Hegel does *not* say that consciousness, in knowing an object, is also (or even "really") aware of its mental states and activities. Although he does not clearly argue for the claim here, the passages just quoted at least indicate that he holds that consciousness is indeed "of the *object*," as well as "of itself." Moreover, he parses "of itself" as "consciousness of its own knowledge *of that truth*," not "consciousness of its mental states, or subjective, constituting activity," and so on. This is Hegel's way of making what is by now a familiar point: that in, say, assertoric judgments, *we* self-consciously assert; the act of asserting is complex, since it involves not only the representation of what we assert but our fulfilling a criterion for asserting, a component of experience that cannot be isolated from *what* it is we are asserting. Both what we take to be "the truth" (in this example, the propositional content) and *our taking* it to be "the truth" are involved.

Keeping these Kantian categories in mind makes it, I think, much easier to see what Hegel means when he claims that

> consciousness simultaneously distinguishes itself from something and at the same time relates itself to it, or, as this is expressed, it is something for that consciousness. (*PhG*, 58; *PS*, 52)

As Hegel proceeds, again appropriating a good deal from Kant, it is clear that he can make this claim because he regards consciousness as judgmental, as having a "relation to objects" by *establishing* one through its active judging. Consciousness *relates itself* to objects. And, I am claiming, it is because Hegel assumes that it does this apperceptively that he can also claim that consciousness distinguishes itself from its objects; it has established this relation, and so must hold in mind the object's possibly being other than it has been construed to be for consciousness.

A good deal of this orientation, and its relation to Hegel's own speculative language, is made much clearer in the Preface to the *PhG*. Although transformed within Hegel's new terminology, the idealist presuppositions noted previously are, as we have said, prominent in that famous passage from the Preface where Hegel claims that "everything turns on grasping and expressing the True, not as Substance, but just as much as Subject" (*PhG*, 18; *PS*, 10). In discussing this substance as subject, Hegel claims that a substance can only be "actual" (*wirklich*) as subject, that is, as the "movement of the self-positing" of this subjectivity, or the "mediating of its becoming other with itself" (*PhG*, 18; *PS*, 10). I suggest that the reference to self-positing is Hegel's way of expressing the necessary role of apperceptive judging in the possibility of experience, and the reference to a "becoming other" that finally becomes reconciled "with itself" expresses the skeptical worries that result from such insistence on the role of subjectivity in experience and their eventual resolution.

If, that is, we keep in mind the fate of the doctrine of apperception in Fichte's account of the self-posited nature of experience and so the "alienation" from the not-I that thereby resulted, and in Schelling's account of an intellectual intuition of self "out of which" subject–object opposition could be understood, then the following bit of Hegelese will seem very much like a continuation of the same theme:

> It [substance] is, as subject, pure simple negativity, and thereby the dissolution of the simple, or the opposing doubling (or any simple), which is again the negating of this indifferent diversity and its opposition; only this self-restoring sameness [*Gleichheit*] or reflection in otherness within itself – not the original or immediate unity as such – is the True. (*PhG*, 18; *PS*, 10)

The original "negation" there referred to is Kant's idealistic denial of the possibility of immediacy, whether in phenomenal givenness or the intellectual intuition of the rationalist tradition, a denial tied to his insistence on the self-mediated or apperceptive requirements for the possibility of experience. It is this necessary, subjective "negative activity" that results in the antinomies and dualisms of reflection, that cannot be overcome from within the Kantian or Fichtean point of view, that requires a final "second negation," or, as interpreted here, a way of resolving the basic "opposition" of reflection itself, between objects as appropriated (and so "negated") by us and as they are in themselves; or, a resolution of transcendental skepticism.

Indeed, at one point in the Preface, Hegel, when explaining the nature of "mediation" in "Absolute Knowledge," notes that this mediation is

> nothing other than self-moving self-sameness, or it is reflection in itself, the moment of the being-for-itself I, pure negativity or simple becoming. (*PhG*, 19; *PS*, 11)

This string of appositives is quite revealing, since one of the synonyms for *pure negativity itself* is the "being-for-itself I" (*fürsichseyenden Ich*), a clear reference to Kant's apperceptive I.[17]

With this at least provisionally established, one can next ask what Hegel means by saying not merely that consciousness is "of itself" in experience, but that it is implicitly the "Notion of itself." [In the Preface, Hegel's terms change somewhat, and he refers to the Notional element of consciousness as "self-moving or form" (*PhG*, 19; *PS*, 10), which must be reconciled with "essence," though the point he makes is identical to the Introduction's use of Notion and Object.] This claim obviously ties the possibility of reflexive judgments to modes or kinds of describing, classifying, categorizing, and so on, but, frustratingly, Hegel has almost nothing to say about the level of generality, or other logical characteristics, that define this issue of "the" Notion's priority in experience. Clearly, he cannot be talking about *any* concept used in knowledge claims when he refers to the necessary inherence of *the* Notion in consciousness. The enterprise of the *PhG* cannot be to show that our doubts about the objectivity of any concept can be overcome. Although Hegel will rightly claim that his full account of conceptuality as such, and so of the Notions that do articulate the "Absolute" nature of things, must await the third book of his *Logic*, we ought to have some indication of what he is referring to when he talks about the "realization of the Notion" in consciousness's self-examination.

There are some indications of what he means in the passages where Hegel identifies the experience of natural consciousness with the appearance of Science itself. This implies that a condition of conscious experience is some (usually implicit) Notional presupposition. Given the passages just cited, what this now appears to mean is that the possibility of consciousness establishing a "relation to objects" depends on consciousness implicitly taking itself to be in some kind of relation to objects in general, that its judgments about objects are governed by some normative assumption about what there is for it to establish a relation to. Since concepts of particular kinds of objects would have already had to be formed by interaction with objects, and so the coming into play of such a prior criterion, this Notion cannot be empirically established or disconfirmed. Such a "criterial" level of generality is indicated in this passage:

> Therefore, in that which consciousness declares from within itself the in-itself, or the true, we have the criterion [*Masstab*] which consciousness itself sets up, by which to measure its knowledge [*sein Wissen daran zu messen*]. (*PhG*, 59; *PS*, 53)

This passage, and the course of the *PhG* itself, indicate that what is at issue for Hegel is whether consciousness's "Notion of itself," its presupposition both about what there really is to know ("essence" in the language of the Preface) and the way in which it, consciousness, could know such a reality ("form" according to the Preface) are what, at some moment or other, it takes them to be. His interest is in whether a certain conception of experience, a self-understanding about the conditions under which a judgmental relation to objects could be established, can in fact succeed in accounting for such a judgmental relation.

For present purposes, such a discussion as a whole can be taken to confirm that "the Notion inherent in any consciousness of objects," or what Hegel also calls the "essentiality" presupposed in consciousness of "existence," or what he again calls the "knowledge of itself" in any knowledge of existence (*PhG*, 35; *PS*, 28), is a criterion (*Masstab*) determining the possibility of objects. And what makes Hegel's proposal about this theoretical dimension so unusual is that he wants to show that this criterial presupposition is as "deep" as it can get – it involves a Notion of objecthood itself, a criterion for what there is. Moreover, he has proposed that such Notions be understood within a reconstructed account of possible Notions, a reconstruction that would show how and why some particular Notion of the possibility of objects could function as such a Notion only if expanded or transformed in ways that Hegel thinks are systematically connected with other Notions.[18]

Hegel calls this experience the "dialectical movement which consciousness exercises on itself," and he claims that its results affect "both knowledge and its object" (*PhG*, 50; *PS*, 55). Obviously a very great deal, perhaps everything in Hegel's idealism, will come down to his ability to demonstrate that the way in which our Notions change within a progressively more inclusive system can also be understood as a progressively more adequate articulation of the Absolute, the "determinations" of "anything at all," the ontological constituents anything must have in order to have any specific contingent properties. How we *know* that this is so, or what I have been calling the *PhG*'s problem of transcendental skepticism, is the problem it must solve.

And again, as noted previously, it is the generality of this issue of objectivity that, in the interpretation I am presenting, introduces the "existential" and "historical" themes other readers find so important in the *PhG*. That is, consider the results of the earlier sections of this chapter, the results, that is, of attributing a deductive intention to the *PhG*, of locating the problem of such a deduction in a realist skepticism, and of the preceding brief sketch of Hegel's "internalist" (or, to use a more well-known word, "dialectical") procedure in fulfilling these goals. On Hegel's view, a fully thought-out skepticism (i.e., not the empirically based skepticism of modernity) is potentially a source of "despair," not merely a "skeptical attitude." This is so because in any critical examination of a claim to know, we discover that it is possible to doubt both the legitimacy of any given claim and the implicit Notion of an object presupposed for there to be any such determinate claim. Since Hegel also thinks he can show that it is impossible to claim that there is no self-conscious experience of objects (there can be no mere sense- or self-certainty), and can show the futility of appeals to a metaphysical or naturalist foundation of knowledge (they too would have to be taken to be such foundations by a subject in order to be foundations of *knowledge*), then the question of the adequacy of any potential Notion in the face of such skepticism can only be understood relative to other possible Notions. Such a Notion is necessary for there to be experience; there *is* experience, and the question of legitimacy thus can only arise relative to other possible Notions. However, this means that the sense of this relative adequacy of legitimacy is still, as it were, up in the air. There is no independent criterion to help us decide what an adequate, full, constitutive Notion of objects should be. And it is thus in the context of this problematic that Hegel's *PhG* can be said to transform radically the traditional notion of epistemology. For, with the issue set up this way, Hegel is committed to showing that the issue of the deductive legitimacy of any potential Notion (naive realism, empiricism, atomist metaphysics, post-Newtonian science, Kantian idealism, etc.) involves, first, an account of why, in what sense, such a Notion would have *appeared* or would have been "experienced" as[19] adequate to Spirit at some time or other (given that there is no other ground for such adequacy) and why, in what sense, it would come to be *experienced* as inadequate. Both of these components must ultimately involve reference to a variety of practices, institutions, and "self-understandings" not traditionally included in epistemological or critical theory.

All of which is still pretty vague (especially the idea of something being "experienced as inadequate" in some wholesale, culturally relevant way). But before moving on to Hegel's more technical (not necessarily more precise) version of such claims, I need to make an important qualification. For, the question of a historically relative or developmental assessment of the very basic principles by which a "knowledge community" comes to understand itself and the world raises the great Hegelian bugbear of "dialectic" again. I shall not try to add to the vast literature on this topic here, but the following distinction is important for understanding Hegel's idealism argument in the *PhG*. To consider some Notional criterion, B, justifiable not in some absolute or realist sense, but because B improves on A, the best hitherto available option, can be taken in one of two ways. One way, by far the stronger, is to argue that, given the internal difficulties of A, B is the only possible resolution of those difficulties, and so represents a "necessary" correction of A. The weaker argument is that B *does* resolve the inadequacies of A in the appropriate way, and issues a challenge to any potential objector to provide a better resolution. Since the first looks like an attempt to prove the truth of a negative existential, it seems hopelessly ambitious, even though some of what Hegel says indicates that it is his view of this developmental or relative deduction. But, I shall try to show, a good deal of what is important about his idealism (both important in itself and for historical reasons) can be defended with the latter, weaker account. I shall only be interested in such a demonstration in what follows, and so in the plausibility rather than the necessity of Hegel's various claims. This will raise a question about Absolute Knowledge to which I shall return at the end of this consideration of the *PhG*.[20]

In summary, since Hegel regularly describes his idealist goal as, for example, the demonstration of "pure self-knowing in absolute otherness" (*PhG*, 22; *PS*, 14), this cannot be achieved by demonstrating that "otherness" (*Anderseyn*) is not really "otherness"; indeed, it is to remain "absolute otherness." Hegel's proposal throughout the Preface and Introduction has been rather to extend the Kantian and Fichtean notion of a necessarily apperceptive consciousness into a search for the Notional conditions of such "otherness" in experience. This commits him to a defense of Notionality itself, what logical properties a Notion must have to count as such (or, in this book, as a *fundamental* "shape of consciousness"), a demonstration that, prior to a fully self-conscious Science, the "experience" by a subject within any shape must be incomplete and self-negating, and, finally and most importantly, a deduction of the objectivity of such a completed system, *the* Notion. In the *PhG* this amounts, then, to an extended reductio ad absurdum of any skepticism about Notion–object "identity" once the full development of that relation has been explicated and developed. The identity in question, then, amounts to a systematic rejection of the *skeptical* claim of nonidentity between even the *necessary* conditions of our experience of the world and the world in itself.

4. Objections

Such an approach to the *PhG* raises several possible textual and thematic objections, most of which are best answered by attending to the details of the text. It is in those details that one can determine whether the previous suggestions best describe what Hegel thought he was doing and whether he has even a plausible chance of defending his ambitious claims. But there are some general issues that can be addressed briefly here.

There is first, the textual controversy. The title of Section 3 of this chapter was the original title of the *PhG*, and it already indicates the initial problem. The issue particularly concerns the role of the *PhG* as both an introduction to and a deduction of Hegel's *Science of Logic* and the system that depends on that *Logic*. The approach I have described, although it appears to be clearly supported by what Hegel says in the *PhG* and the greater *Logic*, has not been a popular one in much of the influential commentary. As Fulda has noted, those who take very seriously the systematic and in that sense "scientific" nature of Hegel's project find the *PhG* a piece of dispensable juvenilia.[21] They take quite strictly other of Hegel's claims about his project: that his system cannot have an introduction, that the standpoint of Absolute Science can depend on nothing outside that standpoint for its own legitimation (or: there cannot be any way for the standpoint of Absolute Science to be made intelligible or justifiable to "natural consciousness," and Hegel finally realized his mistake in trying). On the other hand, those who regard the *PhG* as Hegel's most successful, exciting, and even revolutionary book often tend to find the approach of the *PhG* superior to any systematic project it is meant to justify. For many of these commentators, Hegel's great breakthrough in the *PhG* was in being able to show that even the most abstract or supposedly "pure" philosophic positions can be, indeed must be, understood within the context of "Spirit's concrete self-consciousness," or even as existential achievements of "spirit"; that this approach allowed us to see the relations among history, social practices, religion, and philosophy for the first time; and that this insight is lost, or at least unfairly denigrated, if it is treated as merely a preliminary to reestablishing some mystified domain of Notional Reality as the locus of philosophic interest.[22] On either approach, the role of the *PhG* as a deduction of the validity of Absolute Idealism is denied, either because of a much more exalted sense of such Idealism (it does not need and cannot have an Introduction and Deduction) or because of a much more suspicious view of such Idealism (the move to an Absolute Science represents a religious or metaphysical repudiation of the accomplishment of the *PhG*, not its extension). Since I am arguing against the view of Absolute Idealism presupposed by *both* approaches, I think it is possible to understand the *PhG* as a component of Hegel's systematic project without either sacrificing its insights or rendering that systematic project incoherent.[23]

But this "programmatic" problem is only the beginning of the many controversies that surround the *PhG*. To claim that the *PhG* as a whole manages to establish an idealist position not subject to skeptical negation clearly implies that one takes the work as a whole to have this result, that there is an interconnected argument to this effect throughout the text. And that too has not been a popular position. Hegel himself contributed the most to the controversy by remaining silent about many of the most important architectonic issues, by scrambling the structure of his Table of Contents to produce a virtually unfathomable overview of the relations among all the parts, and by lopping off much of the 1807 *PhG* when the later *Encyclopedia Phenomenology* was repeated as a subsection of subjective Spirit. Scholars have had a difficult time trying to justify a unified picture of the work that could explain especially why the account of literature, politics, history, morality, and religion (Chapters 6 and 7) is "added on" (so it seems) to what appears to be the triadic unity of the work, the consciousness–self-consciousness–reason argument. For a long while, Haering's insistence that these three main sections constituted the most important "introductory" work of the *PhG* was widely influential, even among those who hoped that some more unifying interpretation could be found. Recently, Otto Pöggeler has effectively destroyed the philological evidence used by Haering to establish his claims, but Pöggeler has added to the controversy with his own interpretation of the composition of the work.[24] (He argues that Hegel originally intended a "science of the experience of consciousness" that would have at its center the development from self-consciousness to absolute self-consciousness, and so to absolute knowledge, but that in the summer of 1806, Hegel began to change his mind about the work, shifting a good deal of the weight for the book's claims to the sections on "spirit" and altering many of the key concepts in the work. The final product, for Pöggeler, represents the relatively disunified historical traces of both projects, a palimpsest, and so cannot be read as a coherently planned, well-worked-out argument.)

Both of these problems – the status of the *PhG* within the system and the coherence or incoherence of the parts of the book itself – are worthy of and have produced book-length studies in themselves.[25] My intention has been to stay clear, for the most part, of the mass of evidence concerning Hegel's real intentions and supposed development, changes of mind, and so on. As indicated in the previous section, there is, at least with respect to the problem of idealism, both a clear context for the central problem Hegel addresses in the *PhG* (completely overcoming a skepticism about the "Notion–object" gap) and at least an initially clear statement of the relation between that task and the science of the Notion, or of "Logic." There should, then, be a *thematic* question that can be pursued throughout the book, one that can be understood in terms of the idealist context developed in Part I, and that can be used to interrogate at least the general architectonic of the work, the success of the work as a whole in establishing its goal. (That is, *does* Hegel succeed in appropriating the idealist point of view he found in Kant and Fichte, and in solving its greatest problem – transcendental skepticism – without reverting to a precritical or romantic or Schellingean metaphysics?) It may be occasionally difficult to follow that thematic thread, some arguments in support of the theme may fail, and it may be impossible, on its basis, to construct an interpretation of the entire work, but I hope to show that pursuing this idealist problematic can shed more light on these two interpretive issues and can help reveal the power, if not the final success, of Hegel's approach to it.

There is, though, another plausible objection to this whole approach. Casting the *PhG* in the role of a deductive justification of the standpoint of Science, attributing to it a concern with skepticism and an investigation of "the problem of knowledge," can all seem to violate the spirit and the letter of Hegel's famous opening remarks in the Introduction. There he had appeared to deny the very possibility of what we would call epistemology, or any sort of prior investigation of the possibility of knowledge, contrary to the preceding suggestions about an epistemological intention in the *PhG*. He seems to ridicule the assumption that we first have to ensure that our "instrument" or medium is adequate to the object it wishes to apprehend, that we ought to begin by "distrusting" our distrust in our ability to know "scientifically," charges that the problematic of skepticism itself already dogmatically assumes a relation between knowledge and object (and so a possible gap between them) that it has no right to assume, and that this whole preparatory zeal is just an excuse for not getting down to the hard work of "providing the Notion" itself. In the *EL*, he repeated this with his famous accusation that critical philosophy reminds him of the resolution of Scholasticus not to venture into the water before he knew how to swim (*EL*, 43; *EnL*, 14).[26]

However, none of these claims undermine the attribution of a critical function to the *PhG*. Those who think they do, and who therefore stress Hegel's original, title page assertion that the *PhG* is the "first part" of the system, cannot, I think, successfully reconcile their view of these opening remarks with the rest of what is said in the Introduction. (Indeed, on some readings of Hegel, one gets the impression that the proper response to the ridiculed prudence of Scholasticus would simply be to jump straightaway into the "ocean," without first knowing anything about swimming.) In the first place, the assumption that generates a critical skepticism – a possible gap between our "Notions of objects" and objects in themselves (particularly our a priori Notions or categories) – is precisely the assumption that Hegel attributes to natural consciousness, the subject of the *PhG*. This may mean that although "we" (the investigators of natural consciousness) should not simply assume that this natural view of knowledge is true, Hegel clearly suggests that we must observe the problems its assumption causes in the "experience" of natural consciousness. Indeed, immediately after he entertains the suggestion that we ought to give up all critical, preparatory posturing, he *rejects* that suggestion and insists that Science cannot simply assure us that it has overcome the subject–object dualism. In that case, "one bare assurance is worth as much as another" (*PhG*, 55; *PS*, 49). Later he calls the *PhG* "an investigation and testing of the reality of cognition" (*Prüffung der Realität des Erkennens*) (*PhG*, 58; *PS*, 52), indicating that his antipathy to the critical examination of the possibility of knowledge has to do more with the assumed *absoluteness* of its initial assumptions than with a fundamental objection to critical philosophy. In the Preface he again clearly states that, in the *PhG*, "The goal is Spirit's insight into what knowing is" (*PhG*, 25; *PS*, 17). Thus, however uniquely Hegel will raise his "critical questions," his epistemological concern with the objectivity problem is not abandoned or disparaged in the Introduction and Preface. If anything, it is emphasized throughout.[27]

Finally, one might object directly to the terms within which the problem itself is posed. According to this criticism, the problem Hegel is trying to solve is, in itself, incoherent. Such an objection is based on the following line of reasoning. If we loosely summarize the goal of the *PhG*, it can be expressed as the attempt to show that the forms of the subject–object, or Notion–Truth opposition inherent in natural consciousness (or reflection, or all nonspeculative accounts of knowledge) themselves presuppose the speculative understanding of a subject–object or Notion–Truth identity, an enterprise that would thereby indirectly establish this identity by effectively disarming the only possible skeptical opposition to it. The identity is established by showing that it cannot be effectively denied. However, taking these terms at reasonable face value, this whole project can be charged with making a number of seriously confused assumptions. In the first place, one might claim, Hegel has not at all successfully identified what "truth" and "knowledge" *mean* in natural consciousness; in the second place, his own speculative view of what they mean, and of their final identity, is unintelligible.

On the first point, one might question Hegel's apparent identification of "the true" with "being in itself" what is "posited as existing outside" the subject. The "in itself" at whatever level, though, is not a "truth." Chairs and tables and even monads and souls are, if they exist, just objects in themselves, and although we might take some claim about them to *be* true, there is no reason to call *them* "truth." Only propositions are true, and any kind of inquiry into which propositions, even those of an extremely general and unusual sort, are true ought to be an inquiry into the evidence adduced to support a claim that a proposition is true, and not a search for an "object" that *makes* it true.

On the second point, since Hegel so often understands knowledge as a "subject–object" relation, it ought to be pointed out to him that this general logical relation defines *all* intentionality, and does not by itself distinguish the properties of epistemic intentionality. Believing, hoping, imagining, and so on all involve a relation between a subject and the "object" of consciousness, even, in some theories, a "real" state of affairs distinct from consciousness, without being a case of knowledge. And this inadequacy could be taken to reveal a deep one in Hegel's treatment, his treatment of knowledge as strictly a bipolar relation between subject and object, particularly in his own speculative claims about Absolute Knowledge as the final identity of subject and object. In contrast, one might reasonably point out, knowledge is multipolar; it involves a *belief*, a "holding to be true" by a subject, the objects or state of affairs in question, *and* the "good reasons" the subject must provide in order to confirm the claim made. It is easy to imagine a "subject" whose assertions about objects *are* true; states of affairs are as he says they are, but who cannot be said to *know* that they are true because, say, all his beliefs are merely lucky guesses, or produced by behavioral conditioning, and so on. Knowledge does not involve a "relation" between a subject and an object, but the attempt to confirm beliefs (propositions), and since that is what it is, the announced goal of an identity of any kind between subject and object *could* not be knowledge, and, so the criticism goes, introduces a dangerous dogmatism into metaphysical and eventually political speculation.

If these characterizations of Hegel's project were true (and, for example, Hegel did need to have it pointed out to him that tables and chairs are objects, not truths), then these would be decisive objections. One could even say, about Hegel's assertion concerning knowledge in natural consciousness, that

> one can only characterize this assertion, which the always sympathetic Hegel interpreters pass over with the greatest self-evidence, as a monstrosity. Here one can detect with what carelessness the philosophy of German Idealism descriptively introduces the concepts which it later feeds into the dialectical machinery.[28]

But the criticisms attack a straw man. However confusing Hegel's terminology may be, he does not propose any of the theses Tugendhat and others attribute to him and then easily criticize.

In the first place, he does not identify "truth" itself with external objects. In defining "das Wahre," he says:

> Thus in what consciousness affirms from *within itself* as being in itself or the True we have the *standard* which consciousness itself sets up by which to measure what it knows. (*PhG*, 59; *PS*, 53)

and later that

> these two moments, "Notion," and "object," "being for another" and "being in itself," both fall *within* that knowledge we are investigating.

In other words, the Truth refers in these passages to the criterion of objectivity that consciousness must fulfill *if* what it claims to know is to count *as* knowledge of objects. The criterion is affirmed "from within itself," and does not refer to any supervening "true" *claim about all objects*, and certainly does not refer *to* all objects existing outside of consciousness. As we have seen, it is precisely because, according to Hegel, consciousness must "establish" its relation to objects that it also "distinguishes" itself from objects. There is little doubt in the text that by "Wissen" Hegel means knowledge *claims*, and by "das Wahre" he means the *criterion* that must be satisfied (the "good reasons" in the modern context, the ground in his language), for such a claim to be successful.[29]

More importantly for Hegel's idealism in general, his appropriation of a post-Kantian account of apperceptive consciousness makes it impossible that he could conceive of the subject–object relation, in either a transcendental or an empirical context, as some sort of bipolar relation.[30] Since, according to Hegel, consciousness is "of what is *for it* the True, and consciousness of its knowledge of the truth" (*PhG*, 59; *PS*, 54), this ensures that consciousness can be said to be in a "relation to an object" only in the sense that it *takes itself* to be. Hegel is clear throughout that he does not think that objects simply appear within consciousness to be compared with the subject's Notions. From his denial of the relevance of Kant's concept–intuition distinction, Hegel has been claiming that any relation to objects must be understood as a moment within the self-conscious activity of a subject. In this context, that means that experienced objects are always objects of judgments for Hegel, and although in successful knowledge such objects turn out to be "in themselves" as they are characterized "for consciousness," they are still taken to be so identical, in a mediated sense, as a *result* of the subject's establishing that this is so. Thus, there is no indication that Hegel has obscured the difference between intentional relations in general and knowledge. Only, on his account, *by* consciousness attempting to fulfill a criterion of truth can an epistemic relation to an object be established. In other words, nothing about Hegel's project can be as quickly identified as Tugendhat does with what he calls the "object" rather than the "proposition" orientation of traditional philosophy, and so all the Eleatic paradoxes such a tradition produces.[31] Nothing about the Introduction's description of the inherent skepticism that results from the "Notion-mediated" (or apperceptive) nature of natural consciousness would make sense unless Hegel had rejected the traditional ontology and the "noetic" intellectual intuition that was its epistemology.

Admittedly, again, when the abstract goal of speculative idealism is stated only as "achieving an identity of subject and object," Hegel's position always seems committed to the precritical, metaphysical, Schellingean monism often attributed to him. The idea of subjects somehow "grasping" (*begreifen*) *objects* is pre-Kantian enough, but a claim about the identity of the two must be beyond the Kantian pale. But everything we have seen so far should caution us to be extremely careful about this supposedly speculative goal. From early in the Jena period, Hegel was already interpreting the subject as a self-conscious, self-relating, self-determining subject, always mediately, never directly in relation to objects. And as the Introduction has made clear, the relation to objects he is interested in involves a relation to a criterion of objecthood, the possibility of objects, *and* that this criterion is "affirmed" by consciousness "from within itself" as *its* subjective condition. Accordingly, a speculative science cannot be a knowledge of objects in the first-order, nonreflective sense, as if philosophical science is a competitor with natural science, say, and will eventually replace such sciences with a speculative knowledge of reality. Neither can it be a "first philosophy" of the traditional sort, finally discovering the truth about being in itself (understood in the traditional sense). The way the *PhG* is set up, the speculative goal can only be a knowledge by reflective subjectivity *of its own* criteria of knowledge, and hence of objectivity. Or, to sum up again the theme of this interpretation, Hegel's idealism does assign to philosophy the task of a radical self-reflection and self-understanding, and of examining and evaluating the *subject's* relation to what is "other than itself" *in* any such self-relating, but there is little reason (yet) to take this project to involve any monistic, metaphysical, or theological intention.

6
Overcoming consciousness

1. Demonstratives, descriptions, and theories

Hegel begins the *PhG* proper with a three-part section called "Consciousness." Despite his long, highly metaphorical, and expansive Preface and his short, abstract Introduction, he launches into the first part of this section without much explanation about why we begin as we do and with no explicit discussion of what exactly this first chapter is about. From his introductory remarks, we know that this section should begin the phenomenological justification of the standpoint of Absolute Knowledge, and although we do not begin with any clear picture of what the goal of Absolute Knowledge is supposed to be, from our look at Hegel's predecessors and at his transformations of those predecessors, we know that it somehow involves an ideal subject's knowledge of itself, or its own fundamental Notions, a self-knowledge that has managed to overcome the deep assumption of natural consciousness that any such reflection of self-consciousness must be *only* a form of self-knowledge, forever incapable of establishing any identity between such a subject and objects as they really are.

So the question becomes: How does this first chapter, apparently focused on a highly specific epistemological position,"Sense Certainty, or the This and Opining," begin to deal with this concept? We know from Hegel's organization that this is the first moment of an analysis of "Consciousness," and that, at least, tells us something. Hegel has already made it clear, in the Introduction, that consciousness for him always involves both a "relation to" and a "distinguishing from" an object, that this relation to and distinguishing from is something consciousness does. So, Hegel assumes a certain object-referring capacity as criterial for any possible cognitive experience (as a necessary, not sufficient, condition for a cognitive claim). To experience is, minimally, to be conscious *of* a determinate object, and not merely to be simply capable of receiving stimuli or of being in a certain mental state. However we ultimately account for this object-relating capacity, cognitive consciousness is clearly a kind of intentionality for Hegel, and that intentionality is always a result of a subject's activity.[1] To be in a conscious relation to this object is somehow to *establish* a reference to this and only this object. And so, the initial issue in the *PhG* is an account of the conditions of the possibility of such a capacity. An explanation of this capacity is the sine qua non of any ultimately successful epistemology (no more complex account of our cognitive activity makes much sense unless it can be explained). So it would seem useful to begin an account of the possibility of knowledge, ultimately the possibility of Absolute Knowledge, with this issue, with the possibility of a direct, nontheoretical, sensory intending.[2]

However, Hegel does *not* begin by directly exploring the implications of such a claim. In a way very typical of his mature philosophy, he begins by assuming the contrary of his own ultimate position, and so by proposing what amounts to a Hegelian reductio argument. He begins by entertaining the view that conscious experience is not the result of the activity just insisted on, that it is rather a direct, immediate apprehending. We begin, that is, with an initial emphasis on sense *certainty*, mere "apprehending" (not "comprehending"),[3] and especially on the supposed immediacy of our sensory attention. On the minimalist assumption Hegel considers first, we just are, in sensory contacts, directed to particular objects. Sensory contact with a particular is assumed, all by itself, immediately (without what Hegel calls the "complex process of mediation" (*PhG*, 63; *PS*, 58)) to account for the relating of consciousness to *this* object. It is, supposedly, the immediate sensory event itself, not what I do and not any complex property of the object, that establishes what is sought, the relation to the object.

Hegel begins this way for reasons that are again typical of his style of argumentation in his mature philosophy. In this case, since the question at issue throughout the *PhG* involves the precise status of the self-mediated character of experience, the role of conceptual determinations, and the role of "activity" in general, and so the problem of skepticism, Hegel begins by assuming that there is no self-mediated, conceptual component required for experience, that the component minimally necessary for experience to be experience (relating to and distinguishing from its objects) can be accounted for without any such self-mediation. Since such a position, if defensible, would provide the best foundation for a skeptical attack on Hegel's account of the Notionality of all experience, the clear intention is to demonstrate that even such a minimal apprehension presupposes, for its own possibility, a good deal more Notionality than is admitted by any proponent of sense certainty. The specific insufficiency of this model of experience will provide indirect, initial support, supposedly, for Hegel's eventual position. In "Consciousness" the goal is obviously to demonstrate that even the simplest form of demonstrative reference would not be possible without some describing capacity, a capacity that requires descriptive terms or predicates (and an internal complexity in the object), not merely deictic expressions and atomic objects, and then to show that such property talk must be embedded in *theory* of property relations, that without such a use of "laws" of the understanding, the justifiable use of properties in descriptions, and so the use of descriptions to effect reference, could not be explained.[4]

Hegel's subject in this opening move is, thus, quite broad. The minimalization described earlier included any characterization of experience that attempts to understand consciousness's referential or object-directed capacity in terms of some direct relation between consciousness and object, and all those accounts of the immediate *objects* of awareness committed to some atomicity or simplicity thesis. [Hegel's stroke is so broad here that commentators have identified many different historical objects of attack here (or potential objects), ranging from Parmenides's claim that the true object of knowledge can only be an undifferentiated "being" to Protagorean relativism, to Jacobi and the romantics on intuition, to sense-data phenomenalism (most clearly of a Humean variety), and even, for contemporary commentators, to Russell on acquaintance.][5]

Hegel himself stays away from any specific historical reference and tries to describe the position he is interested in undermining in as abstract a way as possible, a way that could potentially include all such partisans of "immediacy." So, in the general terms in which the position is postulated,

> the "I" does not have the significance of a manifold representing or thinking, nor does the thing signify a thing of various qualities. (*PhG*, 63; *PS*, 58)

This is a natural duality, obviously, since any complex characterization of the object apprehended would presuppose a mediating capacity for discrimination, memory, and unification, and insisting on the indispensability of such discursive capacities in any referential cognition would require the object of cognition to be complex.

Thus, with the criterion of knowledge simplified to this extent – one knows that there is an object of awareness by virtue of nothing other than apprehending that object – and with the content of knowledge simplified so radically – there is a "this-now" to which I am attending – the *PhG* can be said to begin its work by demonstrating the presuppositions of such a position.

The arguments used by Hegel to attack the internal coherence of purely "sense-certain" experience, and so to establish its perceptual and ultimately conceptual presuppositions, have understandably occasioned a good deal of confusion. Hegel in fact considers three rather different kinds of proponents of sense certainty, all more interested in the issue of certainty than in any particular problems of sensation. In the first example, the immediate object of apprehension is assumed to be real, spatiotemporal object, a "this." By assuming such a relation, though, a proponent of sense certainty must assume an ability to intend *just* this, and not that, and that is where all the problems with the position start. It is this contrastive, discriminatory ability that must be clarified if the initial, simple realist claim is itself to make sense. Indeed, as we shall see again and again, particularly in his *Logic*, this problem of determinacy, often called the problem of negation (of an object's "notbeing" some other), is at the center of virtually all of Hegel's theoretical work from Jena on.[6] To be an apprehensible, determinate this, such an object must be at least a this-*here*, this-*now*. What Hegel then wants to investigate is the status of these supposedly minimal, immediate determinations, "here," "now," in such a direct intending.

In doing so, he appears to claim, in quite a confusing way, that just by the use of these abstract spatial and temporal indicators, sense certainty has revealed its "reliance on universals," the dependence of its apprehension of a particular this on what, Hegel notes, is not-this, a Notion that covers many thises. "Now" is night, but then day; "here" shifts as the perceiver shifts; it is this-here *and* that-there. *If* experience is taken to be of an object specifiable only as "here-now," it cannot be said to be specifiable at all; such immediate determinations "vanish" as they determine. So, what a sense-certain experience would actually look like, on its own assumptions, would be the most indeterminate of experiences, even an ineffable experience, just the experience "it is" or "Being in general" (*PhG*, 65; *PS*, 61). Consciousness, Hegel says, here *means* or intends an experience of a particular this, but when it says what it means, "language . . . is the more truthful" and "it is just not possible for us ever to say, or express in words, a sensuous being that we mean" (*PhG*, 65; *PS*, 61).

This initial argument has raised the following questions. First, to some commentators, it seems as if Hegel is assuming that all experience somehow depends on language for its possibility – in this case, that conscious sensory experience depends on a linguistic capacity of some sort. And it certainly does initially seem that Hegel presupposes that a form of consciousness "must be able to say what it means" for it to be able to mean (*meinen*) at all. But if that were true, and some general (potentially quite controversial) thesis about the relation between language and experience were here introduced, we would, I think, certainly expect Hegel to make more of it than he does, and we would especially expect that in succeeding chapters this kind of language test would reappear as criterial in the *PhG*'s account of reflection. Neither is the case, however. It does not seem that the fact that consciousness cannot express in words the determinate character of its object is itself proof that it cannot immediately intend such an object. Rather, the impossibility of a direct apprehension of a determinate object is shown to be a consequence of the restrictions inherent in such a putative experience, a consequence of the absence of any determining capacity, whether linguistic or not. All that sense certainty could experience would be such an indeterminate presence; that means that no determinate relation to an object has been established, and that means that the possibility of "experience" has not been established. The difficulty of expressing a sense-certain experience in language is the difficulty it is *because* a sense-certainty–defined experience is necessarily indeterminate. The reference to language, in other words, plays an explanatory, not a justificatory, role.[7]

Second, Hegel does not pause to explain just what sense of universality he intends when he says that what we really "utter" in sense certainty, "here, now" are "universals." "Here" and "now" are obviously not class concepts under which fall numerically distinct particulars. Without more explanation, they can no more be said to be "universals" than, say, the proper name sense certainty might choose to indicate its object. As indexicals, it should simply be obvious that the terms themselves pick out nothing in the world (certainly not some class of objects) and, when used, refer only because of the *context* of use.[8] However, Hegel's point is made, even if somewhat confusedly, when we note that even in an appropriate context, assuming a directly intending relation and these referring expressions alone, *what results* from such an intending can only be said to be an indeterminate universality, not a particular object. The universality sense certainty ends up intending by trying to designate so directly is the result of its inability to "hold on to" any object of reference, once it restricts itself exclusively to deictic expressions. Hegel is not, in other words, celebrating the discovery of a reliance on "universals" in sense certainty as some initial confirmation of his own theory of the Notion. He is rather pointing to the unacceptable abstractness of *sense certainty's* "universal" object of apprehension, the mere "this-here."

Moreover, all of this means that great care must be exercised in understanding what Hegel means when he claims that the "universal" has thus been revealed to be "the true" (*das Wahre*) of sense certainty (*PhG*, 65; *PS*, 61). Independent of the preceding problem – the meaning of the "universal" here discussed – to some this seems like the beginning of Hegel's grand ontological denial of particularity, as if language reveals that what sense certainty truly does experience *is* "the universal," supposedly the true object of all knowledge. But, again, as with the former issue, Hegel is very clear that this result, that the object of sense certainty turns out "truly" to be an indeterminate universal, is an aspect of sense certainty's *failure*, not an intimation of its partial success. It is because Hegel holds fast to the natural consciousness assumption that consciousness of *determinate* objects is possible, that such discrimination must be possible if there is to be experience at all, that he maintains that this position of sense certainty, as now revealed in its "experience," must be *overcome*. Or later, at the close of the chapter, when he notes that language "cannot reach" the sensuous this, he means the sensuous this *as* defined by sense certainty, an atomic or simple unit directly apprehended. It is not that language or some conceptually determined experience cannot "reach" a determinate object at all, but it cannot reach it if that reaching and that object are defined as sense certainty defines them.[9]

I note also that Hegel's procedure here already betrays an important Kantian assumption about the apperceptive nature of consciousness. Hegel is not here claiming that in an immediate sense experience, for it to be true that such an experiencer intend a determinate object, *that experiencer* must be able to present and defend the logical conditions and semantic indicators by which that particular is intended. But he is assuming that *there must be* such conditions implicit in a possible sense experience, and that some explicit "for us" account can be given. Without such an explanation of how a conscious subject takes the "this" of its intending to be a determinate this, although we might be able to account for how an organism might be directed to a particular this in a particular context, we would not have an account of the experience of such a this. As an experience, the this must be for consciousness this determinate object, and so we must be able to explain how a conscious subject could effect this discrimination for itself, even if such a subject is not in all cases applying a theory of discrimination self-consciously.[10]

Put this way, it begins to appear that there is a kind of forced artificiality about Hegel's argument here, that he is merely drawing out analytically the implications of a position that he, Hegel, has set up to have the implications he produces. Put most crudely, the argument seems to be that a subject that cannot make discriminations among its perceptual objects cannot make discriminations among its perceptual objects. And to a certain extent, this suspicion about Hegel's procedure is true. But it is only the first step in a long march, or Hegelian "pathway," and it is important for Hegel to establish such a step for his own case. Thus he is not begging any significant questions by making the Kantian assumption described earlier; he is trying to motivate the unavoidability of the assumption by describing a putative experience in which there are no implicit conceptual conditions, and so no dependence on a subject's empirically undetermined activity. Moreover, although it would be ridiculous to try to characterize the results of Hegel's arguments as decisive against empiricism, say, it is true that the problem he develops is a significant one for some empirical philosophers, most notably Hume on the determinacy of impressions, and so should not be considered an analysis wholly internal to Hegel's self-generated project.[11]

Next, in order to make clear the generality of this claim about the internal incoherence of positions committed to incorrigible, immediate apprehendings, Hegel next shifts ground, or allows sense certainty to shift ground. In the first position, it might be thought that the great difficulty of explaining, within the limits sense certainty sets for itself, how a specific object was specified, was due to the realist assumptions of that position, and not to any general problem with the "immediate apprehending" model. That is, sense certainty could reflect that the dilemma posed for it – that every "here" or "now" was only *its* here and now, continually changing, or that the Here and Now were indeterminately universal and unable to specify any object – could be solved if it simply admitted one side of the dilemma. Perhaps the immediately apprehended object of experience should be taken to be a subjective state, a "determination" of me. The object now "is, because *I* know it" (*PhG*, 66; *PS*, 61). The here and now of the object apprehended are now admitted to be subject dependent, so there is no longer the earlier problem – the incapacity to specify the object by reference to these elusive predicates. What I experience just are "my experiences."

It is puzzling that Hegel does not here raise similar objections against this version of sense certainty. He does not challenge the position to explain how, even in reference to my experience as itself the object, I can "reach" *it* and just it, as a determinate object. It certainly seems quite possible to raise the issue again. The experience I am having "now" is, as I say it, not now, but then; the seeming to me to be here (from my position, etc.) does not seem to be "here" if that position changes, and cannot be said to be the same here if I seem to have a similar experience. Hegel instead points out another defect in this, let us say, Berkeley-inspired picture. He asks how, if the experiences are to count as unique, distinct objects of experience *by* all being mine, I understand *myself* as an immediately apprehended object, apprehended with, somehow, or as a horizon for, my experiences. Without such a determination, this experience cannot be said to be uniquely this now for *me*. However, sense certainty has no resources with which to account for such a specific "for me" quality. Again, all I can be said to apprehend immediately about my states is just that they are *an* "I's." And this leaves unexplained what was to be explained. Just as, on the first assumption, all I can be said to experience is being itself, a seamless and so unintelligible presence, so now I can only be said to experience states of awareness in an undiscriminated and unspecific way. Attempts to pick out such states, even as mine and only as mine, require more than a model of direct apprehension can provide.

Finally, Hegel outlines a possible position wherein sense certainty attempts to avoid such problems by avoiding any reliance on being able to distinguish this object as this experience of mine from any other. There is only this now, as I say or think it, this here as I experience it. If there is immediately a new now and here, so be it; at least there is immediate apprehension, even if of a now admittedly ineffable, barely momentary "object." Indeed, in this model intentionality should be understood as a kind of internal and external "pointing." But with this attempt, all the original problems do return explicitly in Hegel's account. The experience I am "now" having can easily be imagined to be of a complex enough duration to make it ambiguous which aspect of "this now experience" I am referring to (ambiguous even to myself), and "the this" I point to is obviously spatially complex enough to raise any number of questions about the exact object of my intending, no matter how precise my language or specific my pointing.

> The "Now," and the pointing out the "Now," are thus so constituted that neither the one nor the other is something immediate and simple, but a movement which contains various movements.

And the point at issue will clearly be to establish what admitting the existence of these "movements within various movements," Hegel's expression of conceptual determination, amounts to.

With this new problem suggested, our original questions now return: What has Hegel taken himself to have shown, and what significance has it for Hegel's idealism. At the very least, we are supposed to have shown, in this rather tour de force demonstration, that experience, construed in a particularly narrow way, cannot directly or immediately "mean" its objects, and thus we should next investigate what capacities a conscious subject must be assumed to have in order to experience successfully.[12] The mere capacity to receive momentary sense impressions will not do. With the postulation of that receptive capacity alone, an experience could not be said to *be* a distinct experience, even of those immediate objects.

But there are also indications throughout this discussion that Hegel thinks there are far bigger stakes involved here than the elimination of a putative model of direct cognition. For one thing, in discussing the real presuppositions of sense certainty, he construes those presuppositions in a highly unusual way. What is important for Hegel is what sense certainty must presuppose, not simply about its own experience but about "what there is," about "sense objects," as Hegel says, the "absolute truth for consciousness" (*PhG*, 69; *PS*, 65). Such an attempt to establish a necessary link between a putative form of experience and possible objects of such an experience is our first example of the unusual account of objectivity presented throughout the *PhG*. That is, Hegel begins here to try to show the dependence of any claim about objects on the specification of the conditions for its apprehension, and the vacuity of claims about objects, or what objects might be like, that do not include a reference to such conditions. This is, in a way, the flip side of his attempt to demonstrate how any account of knowledge is the account it is only because of a reliance on certain Notions of objects.[13]

Thus the propositions of sense certainty are construed as if a proponent of sense certainty were literally committed to the claim that what there is *is* always just the "here-now." When Hegel tries to state his own version of this connection between epistemic criteria and metaphysical commitments, he does so in a particularly insistent, even exaggerated, way. That is, "here" and "now" are made to serve as *subject terms* in our first examples of "speculative sentences," sentences to which sense certainty must be committed if its position is to be viable. Sense certainty is said to be implicitly committed to such weird claims as "Here is a tree, Now is noon." (The judgments reverse the order of generality standard in subject-predicate judgments; the subject term has a wider universality than the predicate, rather than vice versa.) Since, as Hegel thinks he has shown, sense certainty is committed to the apprehension of the most indeterminately "wide" universal, any attempt to specify what is determinately meant must make use of a predicate with a lower order of generality. "Now" is all there is for sense certainty, but since it must be discriminated to be experienced, it must be determined in this unusual way, "Now is noon," somewhat on the order of "Man is Socrates." But in that case, any such assertion "negates itself" (is an impossible claim, inconsistent with its equally true contrary), since "here" is *not* just this tree but also "that house," "Now" is not just "noon" but also "noon + 1," and so on. So sense certainty not only presupposes an inadequate notion of a subject's object-referring capacity, it also, largely because of that deficiency in its account of "knowledge," presupposes a contradictory account of "Truth" or of a possible object.[14]

This is no doubt an arcane way of putting the points Hegel is trying to make. The absence of any clear philosophic precedent for this way of talking, the lack of a clear context for this "position" or "shape of Spirit," and Hegel's eagerness to make use of some his logical theory to explain this analysis, all greatly confuse his attempt. But for our purposes, what is important is how his account does what the Introduction said the *PhG* was going to do: demonstrate and justify the Notional nature of experience. In the Introduction,

Hegel had claimed that the discovery, by reflection, of some deficiency in a criterion of epistemic adequacy should not be viewed as discovering merely a deficiency in the criterion, that it has to be adjusted or expanded in order to achieve a more adequate relation to objects of knowledge.

> it would seem that consciousness must alter its knowledge to make it conform to the object. But, in fact, in the alteration of the knowledge, the object itself alters for it too, for the knowledge that was present was essentially a knowledge of the object: as the knowledge changes, so too does the object, for it essentially belonged to this knowledge. (*PhG*, 60; *PS*, 54)

In the case of sense certainty's "alteration," then, we have an example of this extremely idealistic-sounding notion of the "object changing too" as a more mediated notion of intending is called for, and so we should have an instance of how Hegel's case for a progressively more adequate Notional determination of reality is being made. That is, we presumably have here an instance of the "internal negation" of some putative experience, the first step on the "pathway of doubt" that is supposed to establish Absolute Knowledge and overcome skepticism. The preceding quotation from the Introduction indicates that Hegel believes that, as more adequate accounts of the conditions of apprehension and comprehension unfold, it will continue to be the case that the nature of possible *objects* of experience will also be progressively better illuminated. This means that Hegel thinks himself entitled to claim, as a result of his analysis, that there cannot *be* indeterminate Being or mere presence (as an object of experience), and later that there cannot be just "things with properties" there to be apprehended, there cannot be only "forces" as conceived by a reflective understanding, and so on.

Given the issues discussed in the last chapter, and throughout our consideration of Hegel's relation to Kant, when stated this way, such a procedure might appear to beg the most important questions of idealism. Why can we not claim that Hegel has only shown that *we* could not attend to what there is if what there is is indeterminate being as it is in itself? Or simply that *we* cannot make certain distinctions that we need to make unless we can make other distinctions? Or that Hegel, by means of the highly artificial and strained methodology of dialectical progression, is engaged in the very account of subjective faculties, or "mere psychology," that he criticized Kant for? His answer to such a charge is mostly implicit in the procedure he employs throughout these opening arguments. It consists in the straightforward post-Cartesian assumption that a subject's various claim-making practices must be capable of some general assessment if they are to count as claims, judgments. Second, he accepts the Kantian assumption that it is fruitless to attempt such an assessment by attempting to consider the adequacy of such practices in the light of being as it is in itself. Such a consideration would depend on claims about being, and so we are always forced back to "Spirit's experience" as the context of any such investigation. Accordingly, the only possible assessment of such activities is an internal one, an assessment of whether the object intended or "meant" by the subject can be that object, given the Notion attributed to such a subject.

So, in this case, the object to be intended *must* turn out to be a more internally complex particular, a "thing," not a mere "this," if it is also true, as it is, that the required intentional capacity must itself be of a more mediated sort, as Hegel says, a taking to be true (*Wahr-nehmen*) rather than a direct intending. This is, to be sure, a designation of a possible object of intending that makes reference to what *we* could intend, but Hegel tries in his own way to prevent our interpreting this as a claim that, in a nondialectical way, simply *identifies* the categorial structure of objects with the subjective requirements of experience. The claim is that an object must *itself* be capable of exhibiting a property complexity in experience in order for there to be the mediated taking-to-be-true necessary for any perceptual intending. Although it is logically possible that no object exhibits such complexity, ever, in any experience, to entertain that possibility would also be to claim that consciousness cannot ever relate itself to and distinguish itself from an object at all. And Hegel clearly believes that he has established that there is no good reason for taking such a possibility as a serious skeptical threat. To the extent that such a possibility could be conceived as an experience, Hegel has already shown its self-refuting difficulties.

To be sure, there are already larger issues at play here. The issue sketched previously is the heart of the tremendously influential Heideggerean criticism of Hegel, one that continues to resonate with great effect in much post-modern criticism of Hegel's logo-centrism, subjectivism, and so forth.[15] For the moment, such concerns are best set aside until a further analysis of Hegel's account of objectivity as Spirit's self-satisfaction, the basis of all such criticism, can be presented.[16]

2. Taking to be true

From what has just been said, it should be clear that Hegel is not trying to deny that there is in empirical knowledge direct sensible contact with objects other than consciousness. The question that emerges concerns the subjective conditions relevant to the discrimination of the determinate objects taken to be the objects of such sensory experience. So, in the chapter on "Perception," Hegel maintains that "the sensuous" element of sense certainty (*das Sinnliche*) is *preserved* in this more complex position, but, as he begins to explain his crucial term of art, "sublated," *aufgehoben.* The characteristic of immediacy *as defined* by sense certainty, immediate presence in experience whose presence alone accounts for our attending to it, has been negated, even though the presentational character of objects of experience, the assumption that there are external objects present to consciousness, has been preserved. Thus we are still talking about what characteristics objects of experience must be able "on their own" to present immediately if they are to be intended objects; all this, even if our account of these characteristics begins to take its bearings, "for us," from the requirements of our intentional capacities.

So, the position in question postulates that a subject immediately apprehends qualitatively distinct sense impressions, qualities accessible through our fivefold sensory access to the world. We do not just apprehend a sensible this, but a white, sweet, so-dense, so-heavy, smooth this, for example. Hegel then proposes to assess whether a subject considered to be directly apprehending such objects (sense qualities) *could* in fact apprehend such objects. And the general direction of this argument is clear enough, although, again, the details get rather murky. The focus of Hegel's consideration is the issue of how such a perceiver could be said to experience such qualities as properties *of a thing*. Within the restrictions of the principle under consideration, the natural explanation for the mutual inherence of many properties in one object is associationist. I directly and immediately perceive a mere series of sense properties, but on the basis of repeated experiences of such series, I associate the properties as belonging together, as all properties of the same object. (In a strictly associationist account, of course, it is the repeated occurrence alone of such a series that simply produces the thought of their inherence.) Hegel will deny, in a variety of ways, that there is any way of maintaining that associationism of any kind can account for the mutual inherence of different properties. His most important claim involves an attempt to show that the *original* apprehension of the determinate properties *already* involves their being apprehended as properties of a particular thing. If this can be shown, then, since such an inherence cannot be immediately perceived, even though it is a condition of the possibility of determinate perception, the whole model of immediate sense experience must be seriously revised.

Stated another way, this account begins a decisive shift in the *PhG*, a shift in the understanding of a possible experience away from considering experience as essentially or foundationally the apprehension of objects and qualities toward a view of experience as originally the application of concepts and the mediation of theories. (It is not, as we shall see, a complete shift, since the "Understanding" still regards the universal understood to be the true object of experience as an external object, rather than a Notion, but the shift to what Hegel calls an "unconditioned universal," one of the most important in the *PhG*, begins here.) That is, if Hegel can show that the required condition for the apprehension of sense qualities, their all being qualities of this thing, cannot be accounted for by the model of Perception, then he will take himself to have established that that thing cannot be "apprehended" at all unless it is also "comprehended" in a certain way, originally, that the conception of objects, the use of a nonsensible characteristic in an original apprehension, is a condition of sensible apprehension. In his full case, this will mean that he is claiming that objects are apprehended by virtue of some concept by which various properties can be grounded in one object, that they are originally conceived as inhering together, and so are understood as a result of the object's various "forces." [So, for future reference, Hegel must show two things: (1) that it is true that a condition for the apprehension of a determinate property is that it be apprehended as a property of a particular thing, and (2) that "perceiving" alone, with its associationist principles, cannot account for such inherence.]

This is the overall intent of Hegel's case, and before examining it, we should note that Hegel is not only trying to undermine the possibility of classical empirical (Locke and Berkeley, for the most part) and rational (Leibniz, although there are obvious allusions to Plato and Aristotle as well) accounts of "thing–property" relations.[17] Although in the next chapter a variety of Kantian themes become much more prominent, it is important to note that the strategy Hegel pursues here also begins to undermine the Kantian picture of the understanding "working" on some supposed "given" manifold, a set of sensibly received elements. The analysis of Perception is one of the most direct attacks by Hegel on the possibility of understanding the relation between sensible intuition and the understanding in that way, and so is an important way station in Hegel's attempt to show that any aspect of sense experience, or any putative immediacy, is originally determined by "Spirit's relation to itself," and cannot be considered apart from that relation.[18]

But the details of this important transitional section are elusive. The heart of Hegel's case is a two-paragraph description of how such a perceiving consciousness would land in a certain dilemma, able to account for the *diversity* of sense properties necessary for the thing to be a determinate thing only by undercutting the possibility of understanding the *unity* of those various properties in that one thing. To develop that dilemma, he makes the following introductory points.

First, Hegel stresses that these sense qualities play a decisive role in the *differentiation* of objects of experience. "Here" and "now" could not play such a role, and so we now consider whether the sensible complexity of experience can function in such required differentiation.

> The wealth of sense knowledge belongs to perception, not to immediate certainty, for which it was only the source of instances; for only perception contains negation, difference or manifoldness, within its own essence. (*PhG*, 71; *PS*, 67)

Second, Hegel points out that to perform such a function, such qualities must be universals. The apprehension of an object as a white, smooth, sweet object would not pick out that object if such properties were themselves radically individual perceptual episodes. The sense certainty problem would start all over again. It is only because the aspect of the object attended to in this episode is like aspects of other episodes that it can be discriminated, attended to as distinct. The object's being apprehended as of a sense kind is what makes possible apprehending the object more determinately than as an ineffable, absolutely unique "this." Hegel puts this point in a highly abstract way when he says:

The This is therefore established as *not* this, as something sublated; and hence not as Nothing, but as a determinate Nothing, the Nothing of a content, viz. of the This. (*PhG*, 72; *PS*, 68)

This is a curious way to talk about the universality of sense qualities, but Hegel is trying to stress that such qualities are not particular sensory episodes but qualities of a particular; so each is not itself a "this," but a "not this" (that is, "not *just* the quality of this," but a universal property) attributed to a "this." They are thus "not things" (no-things) but reidentifiable properties, instanced in particulars ("the Nothing of a content," of "the This"). As we shall see, he is stressing this point, even to exaggeration, because it will play such a large role in the central argument of the chapter.

Third, since the universal property, whiteness, may be succeeded in my experience by the experience of hardness, or sweetness, or any number of distinct properties, the experience of such properties does not discriminate an object *just* by their successive occurrence. As they occur "they are indifferent to one another; each is on its own and free from the others" (*PhG* 72; *PS*, 68). This means that Perception construes the particular as a "medium," a "simple unity" in which properties "interpenetrate but without coming into contact with one another."

This sets up the alternatives Hegel now considers. We could put his point by saying that he considers what might happen if the experience of the mutual inheritance of a variety of properties in one thing were considered to *follow* from a succession of such properties (as in an associationist model), and he considers what experience might look like if such a unity were somehow prior to the experience of a variety of different properties, if the very possibility of that determinate variety were dependent on such a prior unity. The first case he calls thinghood as an "Also," the second, thinghood as "One." Simply put, what he will try to show is that the perceptual model of experience lands in a dilemma. A thing cannot be an "Also" unless it is already apprehended as a "One," and a thing cannot be apprehended as a determinate "One" unless it is already discriminated by reference to its several properties, as an "Also." He first tries to show that the "Also model" is insufficient.

if the many determinate properties were strictly indifferent to one another, if they were simply and solely self-related, *they would not be determinate*; for they are only determinate in so far as they differentiate themselves from one another, and relate themselves to others as their opposites. (*PhG*, 73; *PS*, 68; my emphasis)

One great problem with this chapter is that, although Hegel will rely on this claim to develop the various strategies open to Perception to solve the problem identified in this passage, he does not *argue* that there is a problem. He just states that in the "Also" model (say Berkeley's view), the properties "would not be determinate."

In a second version of this same claim, Hegel points out that, in a commonsense way, I first take myself to be perceiving the object, the One thing that has properties. But in apprehending the object's property I only apprehend a universal, a white quality that other objects could also share. So, I do not perceive the object merely by perceiving its properties, and I am led to consider the object as a "community" of properties. The object's determinacy is a function of its having this group of universal properties. But this creates the same problem, more briefly stated here as follows:

> I now further perceive the property to be determinate, opposed to another and excluding it. Thus I did not in fact apprehend the objective essence correctly when I defined it as a community with others, or as a continuity; *on account of the determinateness of the property*, I must break up the continuity and posit the objective essence as a One that excludes. (*PhG*, 74; *PS*, 71; my emphasis)

There is one brief indication of why Hegel believes that the "determinacy" of the property could not be accounted for by the model of a mere apprehension of a series of sense properties. (He certainly owes us at least such an indication. It seems prima facie plausible to claim that, for example, what distinguishes each property is its qualitative *intensity*, rather than its being the property of *this* thing.)[19] Right after the passage just quoted, in considering the "Also" alternative (what Hegel calls a "broken-up One"), he notes that on those assumptions, I would be perceiving just "the single property by itself which however, as such, is neither a property nor a determinate being; for now it is neither in a One nor connected with others" (*PhG*, 74; *PS*, 71). *This* means, he goes on to say, that such a sensory episode "remains merely sensuous being in general, since it no longer possesses the character of negativity."

Hegel thus returns to and relies heavily on the assumption of this chapter: that a particular can be discriminated only by the apprehension of a *property*, a quality sufficiently like other such qualities to be an instance of a kind, to be capable of being discriminated as this-white, this-sweet, this-dense, this-shaped thing. The property is a determinate property only if such "thisness" can be accounted for. And, Hegel assumes, this can be done only if the property is already apprehended as a property of this particular. If the property is "determined" by its qualitative intensity alone, and if this-*white* is contrasted with other "white-perceiving episodes" by its intensity, particular hue, and so on, then the problem is simply iterated. We have a new One (this episode) discriminated by a new "Also" (these second-order properties). And, of course, the problem is iterated again: We create a new One–Also dilemma if we try to account for the determinacy of any one of those second–order properties. Or, the only other alternative would be that the properties are just considered immediate sensory episodes, not instances of universals, and we are back at the problems of sense certainty all over again.

This leads Hegel to consider viewing the unity of properties as a "One," "a unity which excludes an other." But in that case, a perceiver only "means" or intends that there be such a substratum for properties, and although it must be committed to such a substratum, it has no way to allow it to play an epistemological role. I do not *perceive* such a unity, and as soon as I try to say what it is, to explicate its determinacy, it dissolves into the "Also," a mere community of specific properties. The unknowable substratum is perceivable only as a diversity of properties; but a diversity of properties is a diversity of determinate properties only if already apprehended as the properties of some particular thing.[20]

Hegel goes on to discuss two other strategies for perceptual consciousness to use in trying to account for determinacy of properties, but he already announces here, right after beginning, the upshot of this dilemma for consciousness. Consciousness is said to experience "that the outcome and the truth of perception is its dissolution, or is reflection out of the true and into itself." This "reflection," which will become the central term of art in Hegel's *Logic*, is explained this way:

> Thus it becomes quite definite for consciousness how its perceiving is essentially constituted, that it is not a simple pure apprehension, but in its apprehension is at the same time reflected out of the true and into itself. This return of consciousness into itself which directly mingled (*einmischt*) with pure apprehension . . . alters the truth. (*PhG*, 75; *PS*, 71–2)

We know very little at this point about what this reflection into itself entails. Hegel simply suddenly claims here that it "begins to dawn" on consciousness as it were, in this idealized "education process," that the only way to understand the relation between thing and properties adequately is to ascribe to consciousness a role in that relating, that without that role the thing turns into the propertyless bearer of properties, and so vanishes, and properties become indeterminate perceptual episodes and so not properties. At this point, consciousness "no longer perceives, but is also conscious of its reflection into itself, and separates this from simple apprehension proper" (*PhG*, 75; *PS*, 72). The key issue, the one on which most of the rest of the *PhG* will turn, is what is involved in this now admitted "reflection into itself."

What it first means for Perception is predictable. Since Perception takes itself to be constrained *by* the perceived determinacy of the object and its properties, it looks for ways to admit the role of conscious activity in perception while construing it as secondary to that primacy. In fact, this point of view regards all activities on the part of the subject as sources of deception (*Täuschung*), and involved in Perception at all only as elements to be bracketed as an unacceptable distortion (*PhG*, 73–4; *PS*, 70).

This brings us to the two strategies mentioned previously. First, the "unity–diversity" dilemma is dealt with by claiming either that the object is just that-which-possesses-a-diversity-of-properties and a perceiving subject is the source of unity; or the object is in itself a unity, and the perceptual diversity is due to the perceiver and the perceiver's contingently diversified sensible apparatus. Hegel then quickly shows how on the first alternative, on perception's own assumptions, the unification in question is a "deception," a falsification of what there is, even though required, as already shown, to account for the determinacy of properties. On the second alternative, perception is committed to a *je ne sais quoi* substratum that, given perceiving's epistemology, it has no right to claim but that, again, it requires for the coherence of its own position.

Next, Hegel considers a variety of ways in which the true unity of the object as the bearer of properties might be understood not as the association of all the object's properties, but that the object should be considered as those properties the object must be said to possess independently of its relation to others. These constitute the object as One; its various relational properties are the Also dimension. Again repeating in his own terms some classic arguments in the history of epistemology, Hegel shows that this distinction between essential and unessential, or primary and secondary, cannot be consistently maintained, that the secondary or inessential, if genuine properties *of the object*, are as much due to the nature of the object as any other class of properties, and that any so-called self-subsistent property must be able to do some contrastive work if it is to distinguish the thing. He suggests (with allusions to his logical position on this issue) that such contrastive possibilities could not be made out without some reference to relations or possible relations.

All of which sets the stage for the introduction of the Understanding. Given that the problematic issues for Perception have become accounting for the unity of diverse sensory elements and accounting for the universality of those elements, the necessity, in any discrimination, of picking out an individual instance, individual or sensory quality, as of a kind, it is not surprising that Hegel moves to consider the role of the Understanding, the role of the *thought*, simply speaking, of a nonsensible source of such universality, in any possible apprehension of determinate objects. For us, what is particularly important is the way in which Hegel's account of the Understanding's mediation in experience contributes to his idealist argument in the *PhG* – that is, his rejection of skeptical doubts about such mediation – and especially how the central dilemma of the chapter, the sensible/supersensible inverted world problem, moves the *PhG* to that wholly different conception of the problem of objectivity and knowledge promised in this account since our first look at Fichte.

3. The inverted world

It would be hard to overestimate the importance of Chapter 3 of the *PhG* for the idealism theme that forms the subject of this study. It completes Hegel's attempt to undermine various realist alternatives in epistemology, and so completes what Hegel regards as the first and most significant stage in his phenomenological justification of idealism. At the same time, the specific course of the argument begins his demonstration that the problems of pure concepts and subjectivity central to all post-Kantian idealism must be understood in a radically different way, that such subjectivity is "Spirit" and such concepts originate in Spirit's historical experience of itself. This crucial transition point, away from realism and toward a "historical" idealism different from that espoused by Kant and Fichte, occurs in Hegel's account of the "inverted world."

Since that section, as I shall interpret it, gathers together, brings to completion, and transforms many of Hegel's reflections on Kant's theoretical philosophy, I shall begin here with a brief review of the way in which the course of the *PhG* thus far reproduces much of Kant's first *Critique* problematic.

In Kant's account, the basic explicandum in experience or empirical knowledge was the possibility of a subject's representing an object. The "supreme condition" for such a possibility was the transcendental unity of apperception. Kant, as we saw, argued that for anything to count as a representation of mine, I must be self-consciously representing such an object, implicitly taking myself to be representing thusly. What I am doing in such representing, he went on to claim, is unifying a diversity of elements, and the basic question then became whether a strictly empirical account of the ground or basis of such a unity is possible. Since, he argued, on such an empiricist assumption, the possibility of an identical subject throughout its experiences could not be accounted for, there must be a nonempirical basis for such a unity, or pure concepts, understood by Kant as *subjective* conditions for the possibility of experience. Hegel, in a similar way, has tried to show that, for an object to count as an object of my experience, *I* must be able to attend to *it*, differentiate it as *that* object. The force of his "I must be able to say what I mean" condition in sense certainty repeats the Kantian insistence on the apperception condition. (They both assume, that is, that the results of any natural or causal relation between an object and a sensory episode in me could not count as *my* representing the object unless I take myself to be representing that object, unless the object is "for me" the object of my representing activity, and this self-conscious activity requires an account of its conditions.) Likewise, the key issue for Hegel in such a discrimination is the unity/diversity problem, an issue he approaches in the same terms as Kant, the unity of a sensory manifold. And, as noted, it is at this point in the argument that Kant then tries to show why this required unity, a unity necessary for there to be an identical subject representing anything, presupposes pure concepts of the understanding as conditions for the possibility of experience.

But Hegel's account wanders through a number of different issues before it picks up a similar theme. For Hegel also tries to show that the unity of diversity required for experience cannot be understood as the mere result of the occurrence of those diverse sensory episodes. Such a unity, he also claims, requires a reliance on a nonsensible ground, or, in his terms, an "unconditioned universal." But, partly as a way of motivating the claim that such concepts must be understood as somehow due to the subject, as having their origin in the conditions of full self-consciousness, Hegel explores, in a particularly meandering and confusing way, various *nonideal* candidates for the nonsensible unity of experience. As noted earlier, Hegel in this chapter initially considers various rationalist (and so realist) accounts of such a required nonsensible unity. In much of the chapter the idea is that the intellect can make use of its unclear sensory representations, clarify them, and so "see through" to the "inner" source of an object's "outer" manifestations. Or, again:

> This unconditioned universal, which is now the true object of consciousness, is still just an object for it; consciousness has not yet grasped the Notion of the unconditioned as Notion. (*PhG*, 82; *PS*, 79)

Or, later in the same paragraph, "consciousness is not yet for itself the Notion, and consequently does not recognize itself in that reflected object." Accordingly, his discussion takes him first through various themes in Aristotle, Leibniz, Newton, and, finally, Kant before he tries to summarize the common problem all of them (including Kant) face – that the nonsensible/sensible duality we now find is required for there to be experience at all results in an "inverted world," a paradox that cannot be resolved unless the origin of such conditions for unity is reinterpreted in a distinctly Hegelian way.

Such a theme will also return us to the "deduction of objectivity" problem. For Hegel's attempt to show that consciousness, in its necessary use of nonsensible concepts in effecting a discrimination of objects, is not relying on what transcends consciousness, in either an empirical or a metaphysical sense, but is "occupied only with itself" (*PhG*, 101; *PS*, 101), will certainly raise the issue of by what right certain concepts rather than others are relied on and in what sense they can be considered objective, more than merely subjective, requirements. This problem has loomed as a serious one since Hegel first indicated that he followed Fichte's attack on the Kantian intuition doctrine, and it will now come to a head as Hegel begins to present his own account of the connection between self-consciousness, concepts, and objects.

That is, Kant had gone to great lengths to show that the conceptual conditions for the unity required for any apprehension of an empirical manifold, the pure rules for synthetic connection, could be shown to be such conditions only as conditions for the necessary transcendental unity of apperception. But the requirement that there be *some* nonderived principles of unity that are prior to and condition the possibility of the apprehension of any empirical unity does not get us very far unless we know how to specify which principles are required for such a self-conscious experience, an experience I can have and know that I am having. As we have seen, Kant relies here on his account of pure intuitions, both to establish that the pure concepts he is interested in can be shown to be required for the self-conscious experience of *objects*, and not just required as subjective conditions alone, and, in the Principles argument, to establish why, given the particular form of our intuitive contact with objects, a self-conscious, unified experience of intuited objects would not be possible without this or that pure concept.

As we have also seen, now in great detail, Hegel rejects the possibility of such reliance on pure intuitions, the possibility of considering the characteristics of a purely intuited manifold. Since he also accepts, and will try to establish in this chapter, that there must be nonempirical principles for the unification and so discrimination of objects of experience, *and* that such rule-governed unification is effected by a subject spontaneously, that these principles are the results neither of empirical experience nor of intellectually intuiting what is "behind" such experience, he will have to provide some alternative account of the basis for a subjective determination of a possible experience. What Hegel suggests, in the most famous section of the *PhG*, is that to understand any such self-legislated condition, we must understand the requirements for a self-conscious subjectivity, and the issue of the objectivity of those requirements, in a much broader way, a way that takes account of the impossibility of grounding a subject's spontaneous, transcendentally required constitution of experience in pure intuition. We must understand what a subject *desires* in its interchange with the world, and the way in which its satisfaction with its desires and strategies for satisfying them are mediated by its experience of other subjects. That is, the questions of what, specifically, experience cannot force a subject to give up, a principle that is originally constitutive of experience, and why it counts as such a principle, are questions that for Hegel can be fully answered only by taking into account, in some transcendentally appropriate way, the issues of desire, satisfaction, and other. Such a broader consideration of subjectivity is the only possible way to answer such questions if this chapter establishes its Kantian conclusions about nonsensible conditions, without the Kantian theory of pure intuitions.

Does it establish such conclusions? The attempt can be divided into three main components. In the first two, Hegel discusses alternative ways of characterizing the role of the understanding in the experience of objects, and in the last, he presents his account of the inverted world paradox and begins to try to justify his attention to the problems of self-determination. In the first section, he presents an abstract discussion of a wide variety of metaphysical, or what I shall call "realist," ways of understanding the nonsensible ground of the sensible. The center of this discussion is the issue of "force," a term that seems intended mainly to call Newton to mind but that, as the account proceeds, clearly also refers to Aristotle on *energeia* and Leibniz on *entelechies*. This discussion is then generalized as the issue of "appearances" and something beyond or behind appearances. In the second section, Hegel considers more nomological conceptions of the "supersensible," or "law," the way in which necessary *relations* among appearances, inaccessible to mere observation but formulable by the understanding, count as the truth of appearances. In most of this discussion, the option in question can be labeled an "empiricist" or perhaps "logical-empiricist" one. The failure of each conception is then generalized as the problem of the inverted world.

The first two topics, and the problems shown to be inherent in each, call to mind alternatives on "giving an account" of nature still dominant in the Western tradition, alternatives that develop, on the one hand, from the Platonic-Aristotelian, Newtonian, or rationalist tradition and, on the other hand, from the Humean and eventually positivist (Mach-Duhem) tradition.[21] As Hegel has already shown, the possibility of any determinate empirical apprehension requires an ability to "think" or conceive certain events, episodes, properties together, as a unity. The issue at stake is now the status of such a principle of unification or ordering, or what exactly is involved in fully "comprehending" (*objectively*) the wide diversity of perceptual information any subject must confront. On one account, in thinking the occurrence of certain properties together, or in understanding the succession of certain events in a specific series, what we are ultimately aiming for and partially doing is comprehending the *reason* for the order, or unity, or determinacy of some phenomena. In doing so, we try to understand *why* the world of appearances is as it is by reference to some general structural features of nature. Nature is as it is because of the existence of natural kinds, or because of an infinity of atomic substances, or because of the existence of basic "forces," forces whose "expression" determines that the world is as it is. On an alternative account, comprehending *that* the order or regularity of appearances is as it is simply *is* "explaining" it. To know that B regularly follows A is to know why B occurred (because A occurred), if it is an empirically confirmable law of nature, consistent with other laws and more general covering laws that B follows A. On the first account, understanding the "basic structure of reality," to speak loosely, is required for a true understanding of the order and determinacy of appearances; on the second account, the possibility of prediction, or of successfully ordering our experiences, counts as such an understanding.

Each of these alternatives raises familiar problems, problems Hegel fully exploits in presenting his phenomenology of such experiences of the world. The first, relying on Ideas as *aitiai*, or on causal powers, or monadic representations, or basic forces, has always given rise to serious epistemological doubts. Skeptics have long insisted that, when pressed, such positions are wholly dogmatic and so incapable of distinguishing themselves from other inconsistent and even absurd appeals to occult forces or powers, or that, when pressed about the postulation of some such power or structure, it turns out that all that was meant was that some observable phenomena occurred in a regular way. On the other hand, the second alternative has often seemed no explanation at all, that the laws made so much of merely redescribe what happens and do not at all account for what happens.

To be sure, Hegel's versions of these difficulties make much use of his own terminology, and he sometimes constructs possible variations on these two basic themes that are very hard to understand and seem irrelevant to any serious proponent of either theme. But the basic positions and the basic dilemma are clearly present nonetheless. The epistemological problem inherent in, let us say, realist theories of account giving is discussed by attention to the relation between force, as the origin or ground of perceptual diversity, and the appearances themselves, what is supposed to be the expression of such a force. Since, Hegel believes he has already shown, an object's manifest properties, the characteristics that qualify it determinately, are properties that specify its relations or possible relations to other objects (including a perceiver), the explicanda for force, the explicans, will include such relations. This means that the determinacy of some force or other is specified by the relation with other forces made possible or excluded by the nature of that original force. Hegel discusses this whole issue in the obscure language of "soliciting" and "solicited" forces. But the point he tries to make is that such an account of the force in question, if it is to be a determinate appeal, rapidly turns into a reduction of forces into sets of possible interactions, so that the appeal to force becomes vacuous. The attempt to determine, to specify, the force in question ends up treating force as a mere "that which." An object with force F is simply an object that interacts with others this way rather than that way, simply has these appearances rather than those. In the specification of a force by appeal to "what happens when solicited by other forces," then, with respect to both forces, in Hegel's language,

> their being has really the significance of a mere vanishing. They do not exist as extremes which retain for themselves something fixed and substantial, transmitting to one another in their middle term and in their contact a merely external property; on the contrary, what they are, they are only in this middle term and in this contact. (*PhG*, 87; *PS*, 85)

Hegel then discusses the attempt to make such an appeal to force genuinely independent of an appeal to a set of appearances, the attempt to "look through this mediating play of forces into the true background of things" (*PhG*, 88; *PS*, 86). But, predictably, all this results in is that such an "inner world" is "empty, for it is merely the nothingness of appearance" (ibid.).

So, given the problem thus developed, Hegel naturally turns to a consideration of what he calls treating the "supersensible," that which must be "thought" in the apprehension of the sensible for there to be a sensible world, not as something "beyond" the phenomenal, but, as he says, "appearance qua appearance" (*PhG*, 90; *PS*, 89). He means by this a notion of account giving as the formulation of and subsumption under "law," "a stable image of unstable appearances" (*PhG*, 91; *PS*, 90), or the lawlike relations among appearances. Here Hegel suggests that there are two problems. First, such laws, if they are to be laws, must express natural necessities and must cohere together in a system of laws. For such a system to be a genuine system, the variety of different laws must be reducible to ever more general laws. "Explaining" nature has got to mean something more than redescribing empirical regularities, and on the "law" notion of account giving, such an explanatory function is fulfilled by such systematic pretension to ever more comprehensive and simple laws. Here Hegel suggests quite briefly, and without much detail, that such systematizing is bound to result in laws of such generality that they cannot possibly be said to explain anything. Sooner or later, he suggests, we shall get only the "mere Notion of law itself" (*PhG*, 92; *PS*, 91) or lawlike regularity in general.

This aspect of Hegel's case is not very effective as stated, mostly because his accounts of systematization, simplicity, and generality are too abstract to be of much use in identifying real philosophic options as targets. The more important point he is after, however, has to do with an issue prominent in the former, realist alternative. In this case, the issues of systematization and higher-order generality raise to prominence the nonempirical foundation of such required systematization, and so again the general issue of how laws, which depend for their general form on such second-order, nonempirical principles of order and simplicity, are to count as explanations of empirical phenomena. (To cite briefly an instance of this problem, one might mention the ambiguity in Kant's philosophy of science over just this point. When stressing the subjective origins or such systematic principles, Kant calls them merely regulative and seems to avoid claiming for them any genuinely explanatory role, but when stressing the indispensability of such a system of reason in any account of nature, he comes perilously close to calling them not only explanatory but constitutive of nature as such.)[22]

Such a problem is revealed much more clearly in Hegel's second line of attack, where he claims that laws that make no reference to basic structures of nature or fundamental forces [or where "force is constituted exactly the same as law" (*PhG*, 95; *PS*, 95)] formulate regularities into general laws that achieve epistemological safety at the price of vacuity. Such a view of the understanding "sticks to the inert unity of its object," and "not only explains nothing" but "really says nothing at all" (ibid.), and this point simply repeats, in a general way, one side of the age-old problem noted earlier as an introduction to this section. Hegel's point in both parts of his consideration of law is, thus, to pose a dilemma: Either some transcendence of the manifold of appearances occurs and laws of genuine universality and necessity are achieved, in which case the explanatory connection between such laws and the empirically apprehended manifold is hard to make out; or there is no such transcendence and so no real explanation of appearances.

It is at this point that Hegel summarizes both the realist and empiricist theories of account giving by saying that both of them generate the problem of an inverted world. The worlds in question are the "supersensible" and "sensible" worlds, or what we might more generally call the "empirically independent realities of force" and the "empirically undetermined legislation of law," versus the manifold of sensible appearances. To the extent that such realities and such legislation are empirically independent, they simply invert the sensible world into something else and do not explain it (the classic case being Plato's forms and Aristotle's objections)[23]; to the extent that they are not independent, to the extent that the empirical manifold is the sole criterion of knowledge, the sensible world "inverts itself," is unintelligible without the supersensible world (itself already caught on the first horn of the dilemma).

Now, to claim that the "true" world, whether supersensuous or sensuous, turns out to be an inverted world, "really" sensuous or supersensuous, respectively, is quite an unusual way of framing the dilemma described at the start of this section. But despite Hegel's extreme formulations of the point (the sweet is sour, punishment is revenge, etc.), I think that *that* dilemma is what Hegel is talking about, and the inverted world section simply generalizes and restates that dilemma in as paradoxical a way as Hegel can devise. But what the reader is totally unprepared for is Hegel's quite baffling, extremely compressed account of the origin of such a problem and his sudden, equally baffling, shift of topics.

First, he tells us that, given such an inversion, we must

> eliminate the idea of fixing the differences in a different sustaining element; and this absolute Notion of the difference must be represented and understood purely as inner difference, a repulsion of the selfsame, as selfsame, from itself, and likeness of the unlike as unlike. (*PhG*, 98; *PS*, 99)

Such language alone should tell us that we are suddenly deep in Hegel's speculative waters, a fact confirmed by the next sentence: "We have to think pure change, or think antithesis within the antithesis itself, or contradiction." From here, somehow in the next three pages, Hegel introduces the notions of infinity, life, and the dependence of consciousness on self-consciousness that will dominate much of the rest of the book. In short, this is as important a transition as any in Hegel, and it is unfortunately as opaque as, if not more so than, any other.

I suggest that we interpret Hegel's analysis of the "understanding dilemma" and its initial resolution this way: First, we should note that Hegel's presentation of these alternatives calls to mind a familiar version of prior philosophic history. Rationalist, realist accounts of the supersensible world are dogmatic, empty, or only count in explanations of the world as inversions, as reformulations of the sensible world. Empirical accounts are inherently skeptical, incapable of genuine explanation but, given the results of Perception, now also incapable of relying merely on the sensory manifold as true knowledge. Such a sensory world is inverted if known at all; an appeal to the nonsensible is required for its very apprehension. And this all begins to sound quite familiar.

Things become more familiar if we look ahead a bit in the chapter, at one of Hegel's clearer formulations of what is really involved in the relation between understanding and the sensible:

> The reason why explaining affords so much self-satisfaction is just because in it consciousness is, so to speak, communing directly with itself; enjoying only itself; although it seems to be busy with something else, it is in fact occupied only with itself. (*PhG*, 101; *PS*, 101)

On Hegel's account, the origin of the paradoxical inversion stems from not realizing the extent to which consciousness relies "on itself" in accounting for the nature of things. Quite obviously, then, Chapter 3 presents us with a Kantian statement of the basic epistemological problem and a Kantian suggestion about its resolution (a mere suggestion, given the extraordinary vagueness of "communing with itself" earlier). The required link between the nonsensible and the sensible, or, put another way, between pure concepts and the sensory manifold, is supplied by the understanding itself. And this is the problem and solution that defined Kant's critical period and that generally repeats his solution. The essence of appearances, the origin of the unity and order of appearances, is not some beyond, or some law like generalization, but the self-conscious activity of the understanding itself.

And this brings us back to Hegel's unusual formulations of this point and to the question of *why* they must be, from his point of view, so unusual, so different from Kant's. First, there is the introduction of the issue of change, even "contradiction." As with similar passages in the Jena material, understanding such claims must await a consideration of Book 2 of the *Logic*, but from the passage itself, we can already anticipate some of what Hegel is after here. Consider, first, that what Hegel has tried to show is that the basic work of the understanding cannot be understood as abstractive, reflective, or intellectually intuitive. All such versions, which presuppose the dependence of the understanding on some perceived "differences," generate the inverted world paradox, create another "alienated" world, rather than explain the appearing world. His summary conclusion from this result, expressed in his own language in the passage quoted earlier, is that we now know that we must "eliminate the sensuous idea of fixing the differences in a different sustaining element" (*PhG*, 98; *PS*, 99). Throughout, Hegel has been trying to undermine any reliance on directly apprehended differences for which the understanding is to supply the nonsensible ground. This attempt has amounted to a demonstration, he now tries to conclude, that there are no possible differences, no possible determinacy in any manifold of appearances, unless already thought in certain nonsensible ways. This means, in turn, that any such nonsensible condition already "differentiates" the manifold without reliance on any empirically or intellectually apprehended ground. And this means that the only possible ground for that required prior differentiation by the understanding (i.e., the avoidance of "fixing" differences in a "sustaining element") is "thought itself." And Hegel introduces that issue in two ways, both peculiar to his own systematic language.

He first notes that such a notion of the nonsensible involves understanding differences, possible differentiations of any sensed manifold, as "inner" differences, or even a "repulsion of the selfsame, as selfsame, from itself" (*PhG*, 98; *PS*, 99). Calling such basic differences (or, in Kantian language, categorial distinctions) "inner" stresses again that the ground of any such differentiation (i.e., why these rather than those distinctions) is independent of any "outer" differences, any sensibly or intellectually apprehended differences, and so begins to introduce the Hegelian idea of subjective conditions. Telling us that they represent the "repulsion of the selfsame, as selfsame, from itself" introduces the most distinctly Hegelian issue into the *PhG* thus far. For the phrase introduces Hegel's claim that the origin of such distinctions, such categorial prescriptions, is "thought itself," that thought can "differentiate itself," that in its unifying function, thought also differentiates the modes of its unifying functions. This is Hegel's way of saying that he can provide an a priori account of various possible different unifying functions, the relations among them, and why and in what sense such functions are required for there to be possible experience or, in the *Logic*, the intelligible thought of anything at all. As I have already tried to indicate and will discuss more fully in Chapter 8, such a claim for "thought's self-determination" introduces the problem of contradiction because it will turn out that thought determines itself in what appear to be equally indispensable yet logically exclusive ways. (Or: without a ground in experience or pure intuition, various apparently inconsistent concepts can be shown a priori to be intellectual conditions of any experience of an object.)

Here Hegel stresses the autonomous character of such self-determinations by first formulating the *constitutive* character of these conditions in language used throughout this chapter (i.e., he stresses that such subjective principles do not merely "regulate" the unification of appearances, but determine the possibility of a "world" of appearances):

> Thus the supersensible world, which is the inverted world, has at the same time overarched the other world and *has it within it*; it is for itself the inverted world, i.e., the inversion of itself; it is itself and its opposite in one unity.
>
> (*PhG*, 99; *PS*, 99; my emphasis)

He then, having developed this context, introduces another central term of his mature idealism. "Only thus [i.e., in the way described earlier] is it difference as inner difference, or difference in its own self, or difference as an infinity" (*PhG*, 99; *PS*, 99). It is this term that will serve as a focal point for Hegel's account of thought's autonomous self-determination from now on.

In this context, Hegel introduces the idea very generally, full of romantic flourishes. Such a "simple infinity" (or he notes, "the absolute Notion") is called the "simple essence of life," the "soul of the world," the "universal blood" "pulsating" through all differences. Aside from the flourishes, though, the issue thus introduced is whether Hegel can make good on his initially very vague suggestions about how the "life" of subjectivity itself can be said to *result* in determinate moments of the *absolute* Notion, whether such an incredibly abstract formulation of the origin of basic "differences" in the "repulsion of the selfsame from itself" can be rendered more concrete, and whether the claim for the absolute status of such results (their objective status, in the speculative sense) can be defended. Hegel begins to address these issues only at the conclusion of Chapter 3, but his beginning already indicates a good deal of how he thinks that case must go.

First, he makes things easier by beginning to use a simpler terminology to describe the issue of the "selfsame's repulsion from itself." Since the issue is consciousness's reliance on itself in distinguishing the manifold, the problem of consciousness has become simply the problem of self-consciousness. (He repeats the language of "self-repulsion" in introducing the self-consciousness issue at *PhG*, 101; *PS*, 102.) However, it is clear from the context of the discussion that Hegel is not claiming that, in any experience of an object, a subject "really" experiences its own thoughts of an object. As the line of argument developed throughout the first three chapters, the issue has become the one I have used throughout as a focal issue for German Idealism – implicitly apperceptive subjective activity required for the discrimination of a sensible manifold, for the "unity" of any diversity. And the transcendental dimension of that problem does not change now. Hegel does not, then, simply shift topics here and suggest that we examine how human beings have come to understand their own natures (self-knowledge, say). The issue is still framed in terms of this kind of problem:

> It is true that consciousness of an "other," of an object in general, is necessarily self-consciousness, a reflectedness-into-self, consciousness of itself in its otherness. (*PhG*, 102; *PS*, 102)

This and other passages continue to pose the problem as the issue of "self-consciousness" *in* the consciousness of an "otherness" or object, rather than to reduce the latter to a species of the former, and so cannot mean to interpret self-consciousness as a direct self-intending.

Further, this move to an exploration of the empirically undetermined, subjective constraints on any possibly self-conscious experience also alters the issue of objectivity. That is, the question is still whether any such putative constraint can be said to be sufficiently grounded; in this context, whether it can be called objective. But, as Hegel has suggested in the Introduction, there is always in such critical reflection a parallel critical problem: What *counts* as sufficiently grounded? We raise the question of objectivity with certain specific assumptions always in mind, particularly assumptions about a "criterion" (*Masstab*) that experience must meet to be considered objective. Hegel considers himself to have shown that the assessment of such objectivity cannot proceed by measuring possible knowledge claims against the standard of a noninferentially warranted given, the apprehension of universals, sense properties, the intellection of a nonsensible ground, or the reliance on law. Thus the possibility of Spirit's autonomous self-determination can now be measured, he concludes, only "against itself," in some way, not by comparison with any direct apprehension of a transcendent object. There is, Hegel thinks he has now shown, no *point* in formulating such a skeptical counterpossibility. These very possibilities depend on the active self-consciousness now being considered.

All of which means that the broad issue of objectivity, whether thought in its self-determination truly determines its "other," must refer to a criterion of otherness not subject to the limitations of consciousness. To accomplish this advance, Hegel's next move involves a consideration of the various ways in which a subject could be said to be self-conscious in its experience of objects, beginning with a putative pure, "undisturbed" self-certainty and advancing through ways in which such self-certainty might be challenged, the ways in which any such experience of self in the experience of other would give rise to a self-dissatisfaction, all within the assumptions about experience developed thus far in the *PhG*. It is, Hegel thinks, already established that what counts as the sufficient ground of a subject's thoughts, objectivity, is itself the product of the self-reflection of subjectivity, and this seems to return us to the Fichtean situation described in Chapter 3, although Hegel has argued for his case in a phenomenological, not "scientific," way. We are thus again at the point where "explaining," as Hegel says, is a kind of "self-satisfaction" (*Selbtsbefriedigung*), and we again confront the potential relativism, even anarchy, of various possible such satisfactions. As Hegel begins to explore how and why such self-satisfaction might be "absolute," at some level no longer subject to even an internal skepticism, he relies now on another central Fichtean notion to help him explore the potential dimensions of such a criterion of objectivity. He introduces the notion of such self-determination as mediated by "recognition" in an "other self-consciousness."

7
Satisfying self-consciousness

1. Hegel's turning point

In a dramatic passage at the beginning of Chapter 4, Hegel sums up the importance of the discussion that follows for the rest of the *PhG*, and especially for the idealism theme we have been pursuing:

> It is in self-consciousness, in the Notion of Spirit, that consciousness first finds its turning-point, where it leaves behind it the colorful show of the sensuous here-and-now and the empty night of the supersensible beyond and steps out into the spiritual day of the present. (*PhG*, 108–9; *PS*, 110–11)

What might have seemed the determinacy and solidity of empirical knowledge has turned out to be a mere "colorful *Schein*"; what might have seemed the purely rational determination of the "inner essence" or true ground of the sensible world has turned out to be an "empty night." And with the problem formulated in these obviously Kantian terms (empirical skepticism versus dogmatic rationalism), Hegel now refers again, as we have seen him do in so many other contexts, to the supreme Kantian condition of experience, self-consciousness, as "the answer," the "spiritual day" (*geistigen Tag*), or, earlier, the "native realm of truth" (*PhG*, 103; *PS*, 104), a way of understanding how the "self's relation to itself" will supposedly avoid such dead ends in consciousness's examination of itself and its possible knowledge. Moreover, with his suggestion that, in understanding the relation between the issue of self-consciousness and these prior epistemological problems, "we already have before us the Notion of Spirit," he implies that a decisive closure in the PhG's basic argument has occurred, that the problem of knowledge has now, with this chapter, become the problem of "Spirit's knowledge of itself."[1] If that is so, we should be able to identify such an important step in Hegel's phenomenological justification of Absolute idealism.

But identifying such a "turning point" is much easier promised than delivered. For one thing, at first glance there appears to be little connection between the topics of Chapter 4 and the theoretical issues addressed in the first three chapters, much less between those topics and Kantian idealism. Suddenly we are talking about desire, life, struggles to death, masters and slaves. To be sure, we soon return to recognizable philosophical topics (Notional determinations of the real, in Hegel's terms), with discussions of Stoicism, Skepticism and that magnificently concise characterization of virtually all Western history preceding Hegel, the Unhappy Consciousness. But, to say the least, Hegel's phenomenology of such moments seems very different from his earlier approach. For another thing, the relationship among the parts of this chapter is often as baffling as the relationship between the chapter as a whole and what precedes and follows it. The introductory section alone (the paragraphs preceding the master/slave discussion) ranks among the most opaque, even bizarre, in Hegel, and the point of many of the individual topics is often hard to make out.

There are two preliminary problems that must be addressed before we can understand the connections between this chapter and the idealism theme as it has been presented here. First, there is Hegel's obscure introductory discussion of "life." Second, there is his introduction of the practical issue of desire, and what that turn in his account reveals about his own view of the overall case for idealism made in the *PhG*.

The earliest passages suggest that the turning point we are looking for involves more a sudden lurch than a simple turn, away from the critical problem of ground altogether and an embrace of a pre- or post- or a least noncritical metaphysics. In his early remarks, Hegel discusses the problem of self-consciousness as the problem of "life," a topic that appears throughout his early and mature work, sometimes in the oddest ways. Here it appears that the introduction of the notion of life is meant to solve earlier problems in a sweeping way. Since the central problem in the positions Hegel summarizes as "consciousness" had been the determinate unity of what was other to consciousness, the unity of diverse sense properties, or the inability of a reflective, analytic understanding to comprehend the genuine wholeness or unity of objects in any way, Hegel seems initially here to be suggesting the beginning of his infamous spirit monism, the suppression of all apparent differences in a single organic, living whole (all on the apparent assumption that the only genuine unity or wholeness is organic). Hegel may be introducing here his own version of the romantic program we have discussed before, the Greek notion of a living, incarnated (but now self-conscious) Nature that he had so recently shared with Hölderlin and Schelling. "Force," apparently, should be reconceived as some sort of natural "vitality" in order to resolve the antinomies of the understanding. As Pöggeler succinctly puts it, at this point the Notion under consideration appears to be "*everything* that is basically is self-consciousness."[2]

Consider such extraordinary accounts of "the determination of Life," "that simple fluid substance of pure movement within itself," as the following:

> Essence is infinity as the supersession of all distinctions, the pure movement of axial rotation [*die reine achsendrehende Bewegung*], its self-repose being an absolutely restless infinity; independence itself, in which the differences of the movement are resolved, the simple essence of time which, in this equality with itself, has the stable shape of space. (*PhG*, 105; *PS*, 106)

Or:

Life consists rather in being the self-developing whole which dissolves its development and in this movement simply preserves itself. (*PhG*, 107; *PS*, 108)

We shall need to see more of what Hegel is doing in the chapter as a whole before such claims can begin to make sense. However, even now, before looking at how the discussion of "desire" helps illuminate these claims, the context of such passages already makes it highly unlikely that the *PhG*'s turning point, the transition upon which all else will depend, is such a "life" or ultimately "spirit" metaphysics, despite the turgid character of such pronouncements. The proper context for these claims is set by an earlier passage where the critical nature of Hegel's idealism is much more clearly on view. It is important enough for the remainder of the chapter to be quoted at length:

Hence otherness is for it [consciousness] in the form of a being, or as a distinct moment; but there is also for consciousness the unity of itself with this difference as a second distinct moment. With that first moment, self-consciousness is in the form of consciousness, and the whole expanse of the sensuous world is preserved for it, but at the same time only as related to the second moment, the unity of self-consciousness with itself; and hence the sensuous is for it an enduring existence which, however, is only an appearance, or a difference which in itself is not difference. (*PhG*, 104; *PS*, 105)

This introductory passage makes it clear that Hegel's position has not turned, even temporarily, toward some metaphysical monism. The "whole expanse" of the sensuous world is clearly "preserved" in the present context, not literally "canceled" within an infinite whole. The problem Hegel introduces is how to understand the connection between consciousness of this manifold and the "second moment," so problematic since Kant, the self-relating upon which the determinate diversity (the categoriality or Notionality) of such a manifold depends.[3] The external world *exists*, it "has the form of a being," as Hegel puts it, but its determinacy, its "differences," are as variable and undetermined as, at this point, the undetermined second moment. It is in this sense that Hegel can say, in proposing the topic he is to explain and justify, that the "being" of sense certainty, the "universality" of Perception, and the "empty inner being of the understanding" are now no longer "essences" but are to be understood as "moments of self-consciousness" (*PhG*, 104; *PS*, 105). How they are to be so understood is the difficulty.

So, given this introduction to the problem, we need to understand how Hegel is led to the particular topics of the chapter, especially the hermetic passages on life. (If he does not mean to refer to a romantic, metaphysical solution, what *is* he referring to?) In doing so, we should keep in mind the general, now familiar problem that Hegel's approach, from his original Jena position on, naturally generates: how to account for the *determinacy* of what he is now explicitly calling the "moments of self-consciousness," the forms of the self-relating inherent in any possible claim about objects, if such a self-relating must be empirically or materially undetermined, "autonomous" in Hegel's reconstrual of the a priori.[4] And the first move in the development of that problem involves, yet again, what appears to be a startling shift of topics. He says:

> This antithesis of its appearance and its truth has, however, for its essence only the unity of self-consciousness with itself for its truth; this unity must become essential for it; that is, *self-consciousness is desire in general.*
>
> (*PhG*, 104; *PS*, 105; my emphasis)

Later Hegel says that such a self-consciousness will "exhibit itself as the movement in which this antithesis is removed, and the identity of itself with itself becomes for it such an identity" (ibid.). And although this clearly seems like a promise to resolve the skepticism problem inherent in idealism, the relevance of *desire* (*Begierde*) to such a demonstration is not explained. Hegel simply suddenly asserts, without one line of preparation or explanation, that this "unity" of self-conscious determinations and "truth" will become essential, undeniable for consciousness, somehow because, or once we understand that, "it [self-consciousness] is desire in general."

In large part, the explanation for the introduction of this topic derives from the general purpose of the *PhG*, Hegel's methodology in considering the truth of possible shapes of Spirit, and the particular issues raised thus far in the work. Hegel takes himself to have already established the interdependency of, on the one hand, the possibility of determinacy in the experience of objects (from a simple sense experience to a theoretical determination) with, on the other hand, the activity of an empirically undetermined, self-conscious subject. He considers himself to have done this by showing how the denial of such an epistemic interdependency leads to the unacceptable paradoxes of inverted worlds. In terms of the general intention of the *PhG*, the justification of Absolute Idealism, this interdependency means for Hegel that the realist notion of objectivity assumed in much modern skepticism (the fundamental assumption of "consciousness") is a fabrication, an ungrounded counterpossibility with no concrete *ratio dubitandi.* Insofar as skeptical doubts about a mediated knowledge of objects are concrete, their consideration and partial resolution have led us to this point in the *PhG*. But at this point, as noted already, what Hegel has not done is to demonstrate how an empirically and metaphysically "ungrounded" subject can be said to be "self-grounded," in what way specific conditions of experience can be accounted for.

It is in the pursuit of this idealist project that Hegel begins, true to his form throughout, by trying to understand this problem (the problem, let us say, of a subject's "self-*determination*," a nonempirical and nonmetaphysical account of the ground of a subject's Notional determinations of actuality) in its "immediacy." However, Hegel provides so little in the way of transitional argument at this point that we can understand the details of this beginning only by anticipating a substantial portion of what will follow and by keeping in mind the issues developed thus far. The latter is especially important, since Hegel is at the point where he begins his own version of idealism by shifting the way its crucial issues are presented, away from

Kant's transcendental subjectivity and formal categoriality and toward a consideration of the *achievement* of some fundamental "like-mindedness" as the condition of knowledge, where such a condition must be seen as a *result* of a certain kind of conceptual change, and away from a transcendental deduction and toward some account of the *genesis* of such a like-mindedness in justifying the objectivity of such "shapes of Spirit." I suggest that we look at this shift in the following way.

Since Hegel refers so early to self-consciousness *as* the problem of "Spirit," his term of art for social existence, for collectively achieved practices (whatever else the notion may also mean), he appears to be already reconceiving the proper statement of such a condition. We now assume, at least provisionally, that any claim-making activity can *count* as a possibly objective judgment only within the "*practice*" or "*institution*" governing such judging, and that there is such a practice only insofar as a community of participants take themselves to be participating in it, within constraints that define it as that and no other practice. If this is so, we need some reconstructive way of understanding *why* any such participants would come to take such a practice as constraining possible judgments about objects (as well as, ultimately, acceptable acts, justifiable political institutions, etc.). This account can serve as a deduction if we can show some rational inevitability, even necessity, in the development of the stages of such a progressive self-consciousness. So, the pursuit of knowledge will, as a result of this chapter's claims, be reconceived as participation in a social practice or institution, a rule-governed, collective, teleological activity. And, as we shall see in detail, given this reconstrual, assessing the rationality of such practices will ultimately involve considering such self-consciously held criteria as, in effect, *social norms*, possible bases for what Hegel will call "mutual recognition." In the terms used by Hegel, this will mean the progressive elimination of bases of recognition linked to the mere exercise of power (the rule of the master or claims for a radical social "independence") or abstract, unreal, "beyonds," hopes expressed by those laboring in "dependence." The result, genuine mutual recognition, will require a genuinely universal basis of recognition, a form of self-understanding that will again return us to Hegel's account of "thought" and its "self-determinations."[5]

This already introduces a tremendous complication into the very statement of the problem. For Hegel *both* makes use of a highly idealized reconstruction of the genesis of such practices (no more literally historical than classical state of nature or contemporary original position arguments)[6] *and* appeals later to historical details (in Chapter 6) in what appears to be a continuation of the Deduction of Absolute Knowledge. This is a duality in the Hegelian understanding of "development" (*Entwicklung*) and a potential ambiguity in Hegel's famous conjunction of the problems of history and rationality that will have to be addressed.[7] At this point, however, we need note only that Hegel also assumes that such an issue cannot be answered by replying that such putative participants come to take such conditions as constitutive "because they discover that following such practices yield true judgments."

That very possibility is originally at issue. And we have seen, in great detail by now, why Hegel will not accept empirical or Kantian "formal" answers to the question concerning the determinacy of such fundamental criteria. So, he raises the issue of such a self-conscious, self-determining subjectivity, a relating to and distinguishing from objects around it, in the simplest, most direct way that such a self-determined practice of comprehending objects can be said to arise for such a subject, in its "experience." The subject in question as a result of Chapter 3, the subject *pursuing* knowledge but "inverting" its attempt by attempting to rely on the "here and now" (*Diesseits*) and the "beyond" (*Jenseits*) *is* pursuing such knowledge because of an original *lack*, because it determines "for itself," in a particular way, to pursue knowledge purposively, all within a certain self-understanding of such knowledge. And if the basic classifications and distinctions of experience are to be understood as somehow due to the experiencing subject in some constitutive sense, we should look, Hegel suggests now, to the nature of this pursuit, the kind of lack experienced by any subject, to the subject's *desire*, its purposiveness, in accounting for the origin of such like-mindedness, the genesis of our taking some criterion of knowledge to be constitutive.

All of this is, admittedly, still not easy to understand, but at least it looks like we are on the verge, finally, of a recognizable philosophic claim. Simply put, it looks like Hegel is carrying over the antirealist dimensions of the first three chapters into an explicit, full-blown anti-realism, pragmatism. Hegel appears to be saying that the problem of objectivity, of what we are willing to count as an objective claim in the first place, *is* the problem of the satisfaction of desire, that the "truth" is wholly relativized to pragmatic ends. Somewhat less crudely, viewed in the light of the explanation paradoxes of Chapter 3, it looks like Hegel is claiming, as many have done in the nineteenth and twentieth centuries, that what counts as a successful explanation depends on what practical problem we want solved, that the explanation that solves such a problem (e.g., prediction and control of nature) is what counts as the correct, or even true explanation, that "knowledge" is a function of "human interests."[8] Although such an appearance helps explain Hegel's influence on the "theory–praxis" problems that followed him, and even looks ahead to such nonpragmatic but similar theories as Heidegger's, with its anti-Cartesian notions of "world" and "care" as originally constitutive of the possibility of knowledge,[9] ascribing such a move to the domain of praxis to Hegel at this point would be quite premature.

For one thing, as already noted, although Hegel indeed is beginning to suggest that the inherent self-consciousness of experience cannot be understood without attention to the acting, desiring, purposive nature of a self-conscious subject, he clearly introduces "desire" as the general term for such activity in an intentionally provisional way, as the most immediate, and so ultimately untenable, characterization of such activity.[10] Stated directly, if we read even a little further in Hegel's text, it will become increasingly difficult to understand Hegel as introducing pragmatic or existential resolutions of epistemological problems, since it will soon turn out that *which* desires a subject determines to pursue, which ends to satisfy, and indeed what counts as true satisfaction are no more a possible independent ground for account giving than the empirical manifold or the rational beyond. They too, it will turn out, are *results* of the collective, historical, social subject's self-determination and have no independent, natural status. So, although it is partly true that the impossibility of a purely theoretical (or realist) understanding of cognitive intentionality has motivated this turn to the practical, to the issue of a subject's success in dealing with the world, and so to its desires and satisfactions, Hegel is *also* engaged in an idealist reformulation of the notions of the practical, desire, life, and purposiveness, and it is that transformation that, we shall see, helps explain the kind of *dissatisfaction* with the immediacy of desire that leads to the reintroduction of explicitly philosophical or theoretical considerations.[11]

We can also get a better sense of this turning point by recalling the connection between this topic and the issues left hanging at the end of Chapter 3 of the *PhG*. Roughly, that connection involves Hegel's attempt to show how the possibility of account giving, explanation, or, generally, objective judgments must be understood to be fundamentally conditioned by what a subject could accept, could take to be an account or explanation. He tries to show this by demonstrating the impossibility of grounding such accounts or systems of judgments in the substantive notions of basic forces or kinds, or in the empirical understanding of lawlike ordering and prediction. Both such attempts "invert" (or subvert) themselves, and it is in these terms that Hegel tries to suggest that the true "supersensible" world required for the explanation of the sensible is the "world of self-consciousness," and that it is not an external or "other world" but originally a condition of the possibility of such a sensory world. What that now means is that we should try to understand the Notions determining what *counts* as an objective judgment or correct explanation by reconstructing that issue in terms of some kind of internal history of a socially mediated subject's "*self*-constituting," let us say. To do that, we need to begin by considering the simplest, most immediate form of such a "self-understanding" experienced by a finite subject. (Of course, there is not and never was such an "immediate" subject, but that is not a criticism of what Hegel is doing. Indeed, part of his account involves the attempt to show why there could not be a subject understood so immediately.) Such a subject comprehends the world around it in terms of its desires. Objects are understood or grasped immediately as objects of desire, and the most comprehensive object of desire at such an immediate level is simply life itself. The eventual problem here is that such constitutive forms of self-understanding can be properly understood only if our reconstruction can explain such a "self-relation" in relation to a genuine *other*, if we can show how an initial *self*-determination is progressively "objective." Or, clearly, relation to objects, objectivity, cannot simply be "whatever a subject, or even a group of unanimously agreeing subjects, desire it to be."[12]

Thus if we keep these two general issues in mind – Hegel's idealist formulation of the problem of "the unity of self-consciousness with itself" and his methodological reasons for beginning his account of that problem with the problem of desire – his remarks on *life* look, I hope, less mysterious. First, we should recall that the notion of a "living totality" was already introduced at the end of Chapter 3 of the *PhG*, that, according to Hegel, when the "supersensible world" could be properly understood as "overarching" the sensible world, and not as its "other," the various necessary categorial "differences" could be understood as "inner difference, or difference in its own self, or difference as an infinity" (*PhG*, 99; *PS*, 99). They could, that is, be understood as results of Spirit's experience of itself, wholly due to the internal development of spirit and so "infinitely self-determined," in the language Hegel still owes us an explanation for. (As we shall see in much more detail when we look at the *Logic*, when Hegel wants to stress the empirical independence of such an autonomously developing categoriality, he invokes this notion of "infinity," thought purely determining itself or even "revolving on its own axis.") And this is, of course, the problem we have anticipated since Hegel rejected Kant's account of categories and his use of pure intuitions to justify them.

This is the key to the notion of life, since, also at the end of Chapter 3 Hegel identifies this topic of a "self-differentiating" subjectivity, and so an "infinite subject" with an organic living whole. "This simple infinity, or the absolute Notion, may be called the simple essence of life, the soul of the world, the universal blood" (*PhG*, 99; *PS*, 100). In the passage quoted earlier on page 144 Hegel had focused on those aspects of such a "living" model for subjectivity central to the idealism he has been developing. It is a "restless" infinity, "pure movement" (but a movement of "*axial* rotation," a self-determining movement), a "sublation of distinctions" and, especially, "*independence itself*." He is, I suggest, trying to indicate by these notions a characterization of such a subjectivity borrowed loosely and even metaphorically from Aristotle. A living being has its "principle of motion" within itself. Its purposiveness, its "leading" of its life, is not acquired but internal. In Hegel's version, of course, there is no reliance on natural teleology, but the notion of a *growing* being purposively pursuing its own life is an important even if very preliminary metaphorical introduction of his own account of subjectivity. Alternatively, the notion of such a "living subjectivity" is simply the image by which Hegel introduces us to the basic idea of a historically self-determining subjectivity, one whose "self-determination" ought first of all to be considered "immediately," a subject whose fundamental self-certainty, and so whose sense of the "other," is manifested only "negatively," in its desires. In Hegel's language, such a subject, or living being, is simply and immediately "for itself" in its relation to objects. This means that it senses itself only in desiring, and that its other, objects of all kind, are objects simply to be negated, overcome, controlled, mastered.[13]

To be sure, the reason Hegel does not state this point simply as a claim about the issues of subjectivity, ground, and development is that he always has one eye on what we can call, for want of a better word, the "religious" implications of such claims. Hegel is also out to show that the classic religious notion of finitude, the "unhappy consciousness" that connects all of pre-Hegelian thought, from Plato and Christ to Kant, Fichte, and Schelling, is not the eternal fate of human desire. In the two cases critical for Hegel's development, Christ and Kant, he thinks he can show how their own notions of finitude were possible only by presupposing a true human "infinite," and so an "absolutizing" of the finite, without any beyond or Other. The language of life, infinity, Absolute Spirit, and even God are all, I am suggesting, attempts by Hegel to make use of the appropriate theological notions in order to state his idealist position in a way of direct relevance to the basically Christian notions of tragic human limitation and Divine Life. Of course, since Hegel is maintaining that *at some level* (the Notion) human beings do understand themselves absolutely he is thoroughly sublating or transcending such a religious view, not accommodating his position to it. Accordingly, here and throughout, I shall assume that the idealist position that allows him to make such claims about the overcoming of religious, representational thought is what is of real interest in his position.[14]

And stating his position this way introduces us now to all the obvious problems. The one Hegel first stresses is the logical issue of how such a putative living unity does differentiate itself. The abstract idea of individuals participating in the developing, universal "life of the species" gets us nowhere, by itself, in explaining the determinate moments of that life or the nature of the relations between individuals and that life, those collective practices and institutions that make up such a life. To understand how such determinate, fundamental constituents of universal life (what Hegel more clearly refers to in Chapter 5 as simply the "life of a people")[15] come about, are taken to be fundamental by a developing community, we must understand the active pursuit of life, the overcoming of external objects as obstacles to life, or the use of them as means, and so their negation as independent. *Subjects* (as opposed to animals or living beings without histories) do not simply "live" or exist within the life of the species; they must determine how they shall live, and so must overcome in specific ways the limitations of unsatisfied desires. And this creates a second problem with the notion of a living subject.

A subject that "experiences itself" only as a kind a desire-satisfying organism and construes all objects of intention in those terms, as objects of satisfaction or obstacles, has not, Hegel argues, *established* any concrete self-relation or relation to objects. That subject's self-relation is a mere immediate self-sentiment of life and has no sense of what we characterized earlier as a "*self*-constraint," a grounded relation to itself and the world. That occurs only when it does not merely desire, but understands itself to be desiring, and does not merely appropriate objects in the satisfaction of its desire, but takes objects *to be* objects of its desire and worth pursuing. To account for the conditions under which this could occur (the mere occurrence of a desire is not tantamount to the desire's being a self-conscious motive), Hegel proposes another dramatic shift in perspective. A subject's desire, its "absorption" in the pursuit of its life, is a desire or a pursuit "for it," and so a genuinely intentional relation, only in the presence of another living self-consciousness, when there are two desiring agents whose desires clash. In one of the most influential moments in the *PhG*, Hegel now suggests that the way in which a subject can be said to "determine itself" in the relevant Notional sense is necessarily a social experience, and that it is in such a social experience that the basic skepticism problem of the *PhG*, suitably transformed, is resolved. Or, in a sentence: "Self-consciousness achieves its *satisfaction* only in another self-consciousness" (*PhG*, 108; *PS*, 110; my emphasis). And this introduction of some kind of social analysis of what had been epistemological issues – although still quite an ideal or transcendental-social analysis – brings us to Hegel's claim about the turning point of the *PhG*, the introduction of an "I that is a We and a We that is an I," or of Spirit (*PhG*, 108–9; *PS*, 110).

Understanding Hegel's justification for this last claim requires an extended examination of the next section of the chapter. But before doing so, I want to make sure that I have made clear the sense of the various Hegelianisms central to the very statement of the problem at issue. Admittedly, on the face of it, terms like "forms of self-relating," the "autonomy, or empirically undetermined nature of self-consciousness," and especially the autonomously, even "infinitely" *self-determining* nature of Spirit, are by no means transparent technical terms. I have tried to use the post-Kantian problematic to develop an interpretation of such notions, but the further we move into Hegel, the thinner that thread can seem, and it should not vanish altogether. This is particularly important here, as Hegel introduces his account of *Geist*, the term responsible for so many theological and metaphysical interpretations. So, I note in review the following.

First, it is important to remember that when Hegel says "with self-consciousness we have therefore entered the native realm of truth" (*PhG*, 103; *PS*, 104), he is not proposing to investigate the problem of how a self directly observes itself or identifies itself as this individual, nor is he entering the realm of any mentalistic reduction of all objects to thoughts. Given what I hope to have established as the Kantian legacy, when Hegel says that a "relation to objects" presupposes also (as a "*second* moment") a "self-relation," he is not talking about a parallel, bipolar self-regarding. The general example used in Chapter 2 is important to recall here, as Hegel begins his expansive "completion" of Kant. That is, one can restate the self-consciousness condition by noting that participating in a practice can count as such only if the practice is undertaken in a certain way, within, if you like, the "horizon" of various assumptions taken by the participants to be those assumptions. This introduces the problem of the extent to which such a self-understanding must be statable in some way, or expressed in some action, for it to fulfill such a condition, but it also, I hope, introduces the sense of self-consciousness (the "implicit reflexivity") relevant to the skeptical "highway of despair" set out in the *PhG*.

I also hope that it is clear that by referring to the "activity of an empirically undetermined, self-conscious subject" I am not referring to a subject (or, now, a collective, social subject) arbitrarily "creative" ex nihilo. Hegel's stress on "independence as such" as he put it, on the autonomy of such a subject, is meant to refer to a kind of epistemic and metaphysical independence. In other words, although there may indeed only *be* material, spatio-temporal beings (I leave aside for the moment Hegel's position on that issue),[16] and although such beings may be in all sorts of causal relations with sensory objects around them, the point Hegel is stressing is that no reference to such materiality or to such interaction can account for a body movement or an utterance being *this* such an act by that subject or this epistemic claim made by that subject. These material beings (let us say) establish practices over historical time, create institutions and a historical memory within which, and only within which, the significance and normative force of various deeds can be understood and assessed.[17] Understanding these collective "doings," understanding what they are, what their point is, and assessing the legitimacy of the self-understanding within which they are done is what Hegel means to cover by the term "Spirit." Since an appeal to an empirical fact or a material object is itself, for Hegel, a component of such a historically achieved practice, it cannot count as a ground or explanation of such a practice. Hence the antireductionist emphasis on independence, autonomy, even "infinity."

Hence also the language of "self-determining," a language even more prominent in the *SL*. This is an even stronger formulation of what had originally been Kant's "spontaneity" claim, and Hegel often makes loose, quite ambiguous use of the practical language of self-determination (i.e., "freedom") to stress that the issue of how some fundamental determination of a practice, a "shape of Spirit," in his language, comes to be taken as fundamental is not one that can be answered by looking at empirical success or at metaphysical substrates. As we have already seen in this chapter, he is looking toward an internalist answer, one that makes use only of comparison with other available "doings" by Spirit to account for the shape and, ultimately, the rationality of a particular practice. It is in *this* sense, a sense that presumes a collective subject, or even an institution viewed as if it were a subject, that one can speak of "self-determination," or at least of "not being determined by anything other" than Spirit's attempt to correct its practices. Or: particular empirical claims about the world are, Hegel takes himself to have shown, always embedded in, conditioned by, the purposive activity of reason (again, a theme that derives from the Kantian claim about the relation of Reason to the Understanding). In Hegel's language, this is all expressed by saying that in trying to account for the world, a subject encounters not just the world, but itself, the "self-legislation" of Reason determining what is a successful account and why. Since Chapter 4 in this study, we have seen that Hegel refuses to consider such a practical or purposive context as some mere subjective gloss on the empirical/analytic work of the understanding; the kind of "goals" or "ends" that Reason sets for itself determine the possibility of such work. The task now is to reconstruct how such goals might be set or, again, "self-determined." (In other words, we reach here, finally, the Hegelian appropriation and extension of Fichte's revisions of the Kantian theory of self-consciousness, and indeed of the Kantian account of knowledge itself.)

2. The fear of the Lord is the beginning of wisdom

As we have seen, the central problem of the *PhG* is the problem of knowledge, *Wissen*, ultimately the justification of the standpoint of Absolute Knowledge. As any reader of the *PhG* knows, however, this topic covers a very wide variety of what, for other philosophers, would be quite different issues. For one thing, Hegel obviously treats ethical issues as in some way cognitive and teleological, and so as decisively linked to the *Wissen* problematic.[18] The "self-relation in relation to an other" formula appears throughout Hegel's idealism and is certainly relevant to the way in which Hegel poses the problem of a right or justifiable recognition of another human being, or the general problem of an objective grounding of ethical life itself.

This fact – that Hegel clearly thinks his general idealist position is the foundation of ethical and social-philosophical issues (in the latter half of "Reason" and in all of "Spirit" and "Religion") – together with the obvious social dimensions of this section of the *PhG*, has led many commentators to view it as the beginning and ultimately the core of that social theory, as the place in the *PhG* where Hegel simply turns his attention to a novel, powerful way of assessing the legitimacy of various forms of social relations.[19] That assessment is supposedly based on a criterion of completely reciprocal "recognition," a criterion that Hegel appropriated from Fichte in the Jena years,[20] but that he argued for on the basis of a "social ontology" presented in a Hobbes-like parable of an original "struggle to the death."[21] In such views of the "Independence and Dependence of Self-Consciousness" section, Hegel supposedly tried to establish the claim that the very possibility of practical self-determination, the possibility of being a person or a moral agent at all (what one commentator calls the possibility of "ego identity," *Ich Identität*),[22] requires reciprocal recognition, or is possible only within a social community. Since such a claim is at the center of many traditional Hegelian attacks on the "individualist" moral and political tradition, these passages, presumably justifying the basis of such attacks, have drawn far more attention in the *PhG* than any other. Moreover, and more famously, the way in which Hegel makes such a case, how he presents his argument for the implicit features of the community that can achieve such recognition, with his reliance on the notions of class (as some interpret "Master" and "Slave"), violence, the Master's impasse, and the historical labor of the Slave, clearly set much of the agenda for Marx's program and again help account for the attention this section has received.[23]

In short, for many readers, this section presents a kind of archetypal modern parable of social life, an account of what is implicit in modern institutions – their potential violence, their actual domination, and (contrary to Hobbes) their historical character, their development – and an account of why such institutions have such features and in what sense such features are legitimate. Now, very little of what I have said so far about the development of the problem of self-consciousness in the *PhG* prepares us for such a major beginning in social theory. I am thus committed to arguing that a correct reading of this section does not view it as a wholesale shift to the concerns of social and ethical theory, that it is much more a continuous development of the idealism/objectivity issues posed in "Consciousness," and that it thus ought to be kept separate from Hegel's explicit extension of his idealism into ethical or social-ontological or ego-identity areas.

Textually, there is ample support for the claim that it would be extremely premature to look here toward Hegel's social concerns and away from the specific problems developed in the first three chapters. Most obviously, if there is an identifiable continuous argument running throughout the chapter, it in no way concludes in any account of the specific institutions that would provide the reciprocal recognition that arises as such a dramatic issue in this section. Straightforwardly, at this point in the book, Hegel thinks that the argument in this chapter properly concludes with the "Certainty and Truth of *Reason*." In *this* version of the problem of recognition, as we shall see, Hegel's primary interest is in the problem of *universality*, the way in which the purposive activity introduced in the preceding section, although mediated through forms of social interaction can be successfully purposive only if what Hegel calls the "particular will" becomes the "universal and essential will." Thereby, Hegel asserts at the end of this chapter,

> there has arisen for consciousness the idea of Reason, of the certainty that, in its particular individuality, it has being absolutely in itself, or is all reality.
> (*PhG*, 131; *PS*, 138)

Clearly, Hegel intends some connection between the issue of the "universality" of some kind of developing like-mindedness (which he ultimately calls "Absolute Spirit") and this fundamental, even if preliminary, statement of his own idealist position. This direction in his argument is already clearly signaled at a decisive juncture in Chapter 4, the initial stages of what he calls "The Freedom of Self-Consciousness," where in a preliminary and still unsatisfactory way, subjects begin to realize that the only foundation of genuine recognition, and so the only realization of freedom itself, is the "pure *universality of thought*" (*PhG* 118; *PS*, 121).[24] This means that the basic question that should govern any attempt to interpret the chapter is simply: What is the significance of the problems of recognition and independence/dependence with respect to the "deductive" intentions of the *PhG*, with respect to the general problematic of "Absolute Knowledge"?

Moreover there is also ample textual evidence that Hegel himself understood quite well the difference between the relevance of "the struggle to the death for recognition" for social philosophy and as a component of the *PhG*'s deduction of idealism. In one early version of the recognition theory (the 1803–4 *PS*), his claim about the struggle for recognition is made in explicitly social terms that are absent from the *PhG* account; it concerns heads of families, is based on a notion of such an individual as a "totality" (a notion that does not appear in the *PhG*), is presented in terms of a complex theory about language and labor as social activities, and concludes in claims about the "spirit of a people," an "absolute" *Volkgeist* he explicitly calls "the absolutely universal element," in marked contrast to the *PhG*'s claims about reason.[25] Likewise, in the 1804–5 account of *PS*, Hegel presents the problem of recognition and its resolution in explicitly political and legal terms, concentrating on presenting the theory in terms of crime, law, and constitution.[26] None of these distinctly social and political elements play any role in the *PhG*'s account. However, to be sure, the earlier social-theoretical account of recognition, and the general Hegelian claim that the realization of my own freedom depends on a successful recognition of the freedom of others, do indeed play important roles in a different way, later in the *PhG*. The theme dominates one of the most important sections of "Spirit," "Conscience," until, after the account of "forgiveness," Hegel can introduce the theme of "Absolute Spirit" simply be calling it "reciprocal recognition" (*PhG*, 361; *PS*, 408).[27]

So then, if the account in this chapter is not intended as an introduction to a philosophic anthropology or a theory of moral identity, what exactly is it an account of? If the key problem is the universality of self-consciousness's "will," what *is* that problem and why does it involve such strange claims about a showdown of opposed self-consciousnesses, a necessary risk of life, and the opposition of Master and Slave?

Put another way, the issue is simply: What *is* an ideal reconstruction of the collectively "self-determined" subjective conditions of experience? If objects are being considered now as "determinate" *only* for consciousness, as dependent for any fundamental determinacy on the way in which a subject takes itself to be in relation to that object, and if we begin to consider how that determination occurs "immediately," with such self-relation understood simply as desire, a sentiment of life, and objects as mere objects of desire (or obstacles to desire), in what way does Hegel propose to reconstruct a "transition" from such a wholly, even crudely subjective determination to a universal, genuinely objective determination? As Hegel himself implies, his original position "solves" the *PhG*'s realism problem all too easily: Objects are only provisionally "other" than a desiring being takes them to be; soon they are simply "devoured," destroyed or ignored, and so *not* other. End of problem.

As already noted, Hegel begins simply by pointing out that in such a scenario, no relation to objects has been established *for* consciousness; objects are simply obliterated, and consciousness, as a merely living being, pursues whatever desires it has or whichever is strongest, and so cannot be said to determine itself self-consciously. He states such a claim this way:

Appearing thus immediately on the scene, they [self-consciousnesses] are for one another like ordinary objects, independent shapes, individuals submerged [*versenkte*] in the being of life. . . . They are for each other shapes of consciousness which have not yet accomplished the movement of absolute abstraction, of rooting out all immediate being, and of being merely the purely negative being of self-identical consciousness; in other words they have not as yet exposed themselves to each other in the form of pure being-for-self, or a self-consciousness. (*PhG*, 111; *PS*, 113)

Accordingly, on this view of a living subject, we have not begun to explain the "self-relation in relation to an other" required by the account given in the *PhG* thus far. There is no real self-relation (however implicit or "horizonal" we construe it); and there is no real, mediated relation to objects. This all changes when we consider, again ideally and quite abstractly at this point, such a radically and immediately "idealizing subject" (e.g., objects are objects for it only in terms of its immediate self-sentiment, desire) in the presence of another such desiring subject. In Hegel's reconstruction at this point, two things can be said to happen: We introduce, by considering this new element, the possibility of conflict, of opposed desires; and, even more importantly, that conflict alters the experience of desire itself for a subject. For a self-conscious subject,[28] the threat posed by another self-conscious subject is not merely a threat to this or that satisfaction of desire; it is a threat, potentially, to any future satisfaction of desire. If this is so, such a pervasive threat requires not just a resolution of this or that conflict but eventually a fundamental resolution, a securing of some practice of mutual satisfaction of desire or mutual, and so finally rational, universal recognition.

The general picture emerging from this scenario, and its relevance to the *PhG*'s general deductive problematic, also comes more into focus with the introduction of this struggle/recognition issue. Having argued against what we can call both realist and empiricist accounts of ground, and having also shown, he believes, the necessity of forms of self-consciousness for any determinate experience, criteria constraining what fundamentally can count as a determinate object, Hegel retreats in a sense to a kind of "ground zero" position, a consideration of what experience would look like if such subjectively determined constraints were simply and exclusively a living being's contingent desires, the most immediate form of its self-sentiment. He first concludes, in effect, that this alone would not be what we were looking for; construed so radically, it would not count as an experience, a genuine relating to and distinguishing from objects.

Hegel is thus accepting as a premise, justified by the earlier establishment of a necessary "self-relation in relation to any other," that even the most immediate form of this self-relation or self-sentiment must be a genuine *self*-relation, that the desire for an object must be a desire for-me, self-consciously pursued. He argues that this condition cannot be fulfilled on the model of a solitary subject responding impulsively to its strongest contingent desire. In his terms, it would be "sunk" in life, not leading its life. If we provisionally consider such a subject as a solitary, self-conscious subject, taking itself to be pursuing these desires, construed in this way and so on, we then open up the possibility Hegel is interested in: another self-conscious, desiring subject negating that pursuit and even that construal. Only in the presence of this other, it will turn out, can there be a determinate, grounded self-relation and relation-to-other.

Hegel then shows how conflict with another desiring subject does introduce this issue of its desire *for* consciousness, forces on such a subject the issue of its desire in light of such a threat (and thus, within such a conflict, the general problem of the *objectivity* of a subject's self-determined, negative relation to the world is introduced). What he goes on to consider is what, within the *methodological constraints* of his approach, we must conclude as a consequence of such a struggle. That is, given the assumption that, at this point, subjects can rely on no common or "universal" point of view to resolve any conflict, with the collapse of the options represented by consciousness in the *PhG*, all we can assume as a result of any conflict is war, a struggle to mastery. A self-grounding subjectivity looks, first of all, simply like a plurality of opposed subjects, each acting to secure its purposive projects, and to secure them by forcefully securing recognition of them from others. Just as consciousness had begun with the simplest possible sense of knowledge being "determined by the object," so this initial consideration of self-consciousness introduces the simplest, even crudest, sense of the subject's "determining the possibility of objects" in knowledge. In Hegel's extraordinary reconstruction, he will consider first the possibility of a radical *independence* for such an essential subjectivity; as if subjects simply *do* directly determine, qua subjects, the character of their experience. The story of the chapter is the story of the "self-negation" of such a view of independent determination. It is negated immediately by the mere presence of other subjects, and the attempt to reestablish such independence by simple Mastery, or by spiritual independence, or spiritual negation (in Stoicism and Skepticism) are likewise "sublated."[29]

So, to sum up, I am suggesting that we view the problem Hegel is pursuing this way. The question is: How should we regard an ideal community (at this stage, a community considered with minimal theoretical presuppositions, or considered "immediately") as coming to establish the constitutive principles of its various practices, activities, and institutions, particularly, given the interest of the *PhG* as a whole, the claims to knowledge constitutive of all its basic institutions. We have reached this question because Hegel has argued that the self-relation (apperception, self-consciousness) necessary for there to be a determinate, cognitive relation to an object cannot be understood as determined on empirical or rational grounds, and is an empty or wholly indeterminate self-relation if considered apart from intersubjective mutual determination or outside such a historically self-determining community. Having reached this way of looking at the question, what Hegel wants to do in this section as a whole is thus basic to his whole enterprise: to show why, in this reconstruction of such fundamental practices, opposed self-consciousnesses would reach a kind of impasse, a barrier to any successful objective resolution of their own violent struggles, one that can be resolved only by reconceiving the very terms of recognition, by understanding the centrality of "thought itself," to use his terminology, in the possibility of such a struggle and its resolution. And, although such a realization of the need to understand the nature of thought itself in our reconstruction of such institutions and practices can only be quite obscure at this point, it is at least clear that once this link between the possibility of self-consciousness ("in relation to" any object or other subject) and pure thought is established (and explained and refined, but not substantively extended, in "Reason"), the deduction of the Absolute Standpoint, and so the proper introduction to the *Logic*, will have been achieved.[30]

Looking at this issue this way allows us to focus attention on the two crucial elements of the project. The first considers Hegel's reasons for introducing the problem of "other self-consciousnesses" in the way he does. The second concerns the initial resolution of the problem of self-consciousness "in thought," most obviously in that statement of idealism in "Reason," and most generally in the move to an "idealist logic" as the final resolution of the *PhG*'s task.

The first problem contains a number of distinct issues. I have already tried to indicate why Hegel introduces the problem of subjectivity first in terms of desire and then by considering the significance of another desiring being in the satisfaction of such desire. But we clearly also need to understand why Hegel thinks that such a relation of "opposed self-consciousnesses" should be understood to issue in a "struggle" for recognition, why the risk of life is so important in such a struggle, why it results in the opposition of Master and Slave, why this relation represents a kind of impasse for both (no successful "realization" of self-consciousness), why the labor of the Slave is important to Hegel in resolving this impasse (at least for the slave), and finally, to come to the second large topic, what the connection is between this interpretation of the significance or meaning of human work and the introduction of "the absolute universality of thought."

Hegel begins his discussion of all these themes by restating clearly the central claim of the chapter:

> Self-consciousness exists in and for itself when, and by the fact that, it is in and for itself for another; that is, it exists only in being acknowledged.
>
> (*PhG*, 109; *PS*, 111)

I have interpreted this claim about recognition as a component of the *PhG*'s version of the problem of a "possible knowledge of objects." Such knowledge is conditioned by some form of self-consciousness, a self-relating Hegel originally considers in its immediacy, as purposive and practical, a "desiring" self-understanding. But on such an immediate view of a subject's determination of its own experience, objects are simply abstractly negated by a subject, and so subjects remain "sunk" in "life," and cannot be said to establish a "self-relation in relation to an other." This can occur only when the subject's self-sentiment is itself negated by an other, when its pursuit of satisfaction is challenged by another subject. Its desires are in that situation "for itself," are either as they are taken to be or not, can either be acted on or not, given such a threat, and so a mediated relation of "self to self" and "self to other" can be said to result. This established the issue of how a mutual like-mindedness can be said to arise in such a situation, a like-mindedness with respect to each other and to objects. Knowledge of objects is conditioned by forms of self-consciousness, and forms of such self-consciousness are to be understood as the product of opposed self-consciousnesses attempting to resolve such opposition, ultimately in "thought." "Recognition" is Hegel's name for the achievement of such collective subjectivity.[31] Assuming that individuals pursue their desires and are capable of understanding the threat to their desires posed by an other, we can reconstruct the development of a resolution of such conflict, of final satisfaction, in a form of self-understanding that Hegel calls "Spirit," the necessary conceptual moments of which he presents in the *SL*.[32]

However, since we are assuming here, for purposes of this reconstruction, that the achievement of such recognition can take for granted no common desires or natural interests (any such claims would have to presuppose a common recognition with respect to conditions for such claims), any such attempt at a social self-understanding, particularly of a kind that is to be relevant to the broad range of issues suggested by Hegel, faces what he regards as a profound paradox. The basic structure of that paradox emerges quickly from the first paragraphs of the Master/Slave section. Roughly: A self-determination that is indifferent to, independent of, the other is the mere self-sentiment, "sunk in life" described earlier, and so, although "self-certain," possesses no "truth"; but a self-determination dependent on recognition by an other is not *self*-determined, and so not a determination of what "we" think or must think in our interaction and claims about objects, but a submission simply to what "they" think, to the contingent desires of others. (This latter *itself* is paradoxical in Hegel's formulation, since my "dependence" on the other robs the other, in effect, of the "independence" of the other that *he* requires of me as a component of recognition.) *Mutual* recognition, genuinely *universal* like-mindedness, thus requires both the independence and dependence of the parties involved, and initially that seems quite hard to account for. We want to account for both "recognizing themselves as mutually recognizing each other" (*PhG*, 110; *PS*, 114), but, without a way of resolving this paradox, the struggle for recognition devolves into a recognizing and a recognized component, a Master and a Slave. (At this point, given Hegel's methodological assumptions, there simply is no *basis* for recognition other than "who wins.")[33]

It is this struggle that Hegel refers to as a "trial by death," about which he claims that "it is only through staking one's life that freedom is won" (*PhG*, 111; *PS*, 114). This component of Hegel's reconstruction, however idealized it is supposed to be, is difficult to understand. Straightforwardly, given the latter claim it seems as if he wants to maintain that a condition of practical rationality ("freedom") is a willingness to risk one's life, that only if one is willing to "demonstrate" one's indifference to natural life can one be said to be truly self-determining, independent of such life. And although there is an old tradition that holds that "only he who is free of the fear of death is truly free," it is hard to see what that kind of claim is doing here and why Hegel feels entitled to make it. Just being willing to die does not demonstrate my freedom, self-determination, or rationality. I might be willing to take that risk only because some other natural desire, including perhaps a lust for honor and power, or a biological attachment to my family, is so overwhelming that I cannot resist it. And what would make the willingness to die a condition of practical rationality? It seems obvious that a minimum condition of such rationality is: It is not rational to do that which makes it unlikely that I can continue as a rational agent.[34]

But there is little indication that Hegel thinks of himself as trying to provide a general theory of the conditions of human freedom here. For one thing, he introduces the risk of life issue only to quickly "sublate" its significance. If I do act in complete indifference to my natural life, Hegel goes on to say, one of two things can result. Either I will die, in which case I obviously have not achieved mutual recognition and so the final satisfaction of my pursuits, or I will conquer the other, I will become a Master. But in that case, as Hegel's famous account of the Master's impasse goes, I will also not have achieved mutual or universally grounded recognition. I *will* be recognized by an other (he whom I defeated, the Slave), but not by someone I myself recognize. In Hegel's terms, "In this experience, self-consciousness learns that life is as essential to it as pure self-consciousness" (*PhG* 112; *PS* 115).[35]

Hegel is, though, pointing to something quite important by this representation of the risk of life. That becomes somewhat clearer in a later passage, where Hegel describes the "labor" of the Slave. Like the Master, the Slave has not achieved recognition. He recognizes one who does not recognize him. Unlike the Master, however, the Slave does not merely "enjoy" objects; he must work, transform the natural world, or, in the phrase that has come to sum up much of the problem of objectivity since Descartes introduced it, he must "master nature." It is in describing this toil that Hegel says:

> [The point of view of the Slave] does in fact contain within itself this truth of pure negativity of being-for-self, for it has experienced this, its own essential nature. For this consciousness has been fearful, not of this or that particular thing or just at odd moments, but its whole being has been seized with dread [*Angst*]; for it has experienced the fear [*Furcht*] of death, the absolute Lord. (*PhG*, 114; *PS*, 117)

In the kind of subjectivity Hegel is summarizing by the notion of the Slave, something essential about the "nature of self-consciousness, absolute negativity, pure-being-for-self" (ibid.) is confronted. He signals what he is trying to get at by such appositives as "absolute negativity" and "pure-being-for-self," as well as by noting that in the Slave's experience "everything solid and stable has been shaken to its foundations." The Slave's labor, in other words, is without firm, external foundations. There is no external purpose or point to his labor that justifies or redeems it; the significance of human labor, the active transformation of the objective world (a transformation that, with its success, promises some sort of mediated subject–object identity), is initially merely the avoidance of death (*the* modern, secular Lord). Such an attachment to life is so completely indeterminate, however, that there is nothing specific *in* life that could be said to direct or determine the course of the Slave's labor. (That is why, after all, a "dependent self-consciousness" is dependent, or slavish; its attachment to life or fear of death is unconditional, absolute.) But this also means that the course of the Slave's labor, the specific forms of the "self-relation in relation to an other" assumed in the transformation of the natural world, are not predetermined by some goal or natural interest either. They arise wholly as a result of and within the self-defined experience of the collective activity of labor. It is by laboring, transforming the world in the service of the Master (finally the ultimate Master, death), a labor that requires a determinate understanding of nature, and of knowledge itself, that a truly independent and so self-determining self-consciousness arises. The Slave begins by being attached to *nothing* of significance in life but life; in Hegel's secular parable, then, only he can realize that he and he alone is the source or ground for the structure and worth of his "products." History, in other words, is and is nothing but the result of the self-determination of subjects in their transformation of nature, and that self-determination, viewed as originating in "the fear of death," is wholly undetermined by any specific telos or preset value, some absolute of greater value than life. Indeed, "Through his service, he [the Slave] rids himself of his attachment to natural existence in every single detail; and gets rid of it by working on it" (ibid.). (Or: "the fear of the Lord is indeed the beginning of wisdom," in this case, wisdom concerning the true nature of the independence of self-consciousness.)

So, the fact that Hegel describes the struggle of opposed self-consciousnesses as a struggle to the death, and describes the Slave's labor as essentially involving the fear of death, does not mean he is introducing any claim about human psychology or motivation in general. On the assumption he carries over from the Consciousness section, that self-consciousness cannot be said to be wholly or fundamentally determined to be as it is by objects or by any "beyond," it looks as if such a supposedly independent self-consciousness is determined by nothing objective at all, and that there is no way to assume some common commitment (or natural interest, or objective goal, or obvious eudaimonia) on the part of the struggling parties that would *prevent* a hypothetical struggle to the death. (We can, on the idealist assumptions now in force, assume such a goal only by showing how subjects would determine themselves to pursue it.) But, he goes on to show, independence achieved in the light of such a radical ungroundedness is no real independence. The Master is dependent on the Slave (or on a continual fight with other Masters), the Slave on the Master and on his own successful transformation of nature. But, he argues in the closing paragraphs of this section, the Slave, in contrast to the Master, is at least capable of realizing both the futility of the Master's abstract independence (he realizes that the Master is dependent on him) and, ultimately, the nature of true independence in relation to the other – other subjects and the objective world.

This anthropological representation of the problem of an empirically and metaphysically ungrounded and self-determining subjectivity brings together so many historical and conceptual assumptions that it is hard to see just where in the account Hegel is trying to defend many of his claims, or even just what issues he takes to be at stake. Yet the outline of the *PhG*'s continuation of the idealism problem, the focus on the issue of an independent self-consciousness, and the move to some developmental or historical-genetic account of why a subject would take itself to be in some relation or other to objects, together with what Hegel regards as his rejection of realist suspicions about the worth of such a topic, are all, I think, visible in his account. Such idealist issues are much more apparent in the topics he discusses next.

3. Idealism and the Absolute Standpoint

So the situation is supposed to be this: On the assumption that a constitutive subjectivity must be self-determining, that the categorial structure of any subject's experience cannot be said to be grounded on a beyond or a given, we must consider the possibility of a chaotic struggle for supremacy among opposed self-consciousnesses, a struggle not just for simply supremacy at a time, but for permanent supremacy and so recognition. The internal paradoxes created by such a hypothetical situation require that we next consider the problem of the *basis* on which truly mutual recognition, and so a truly self-determining, universal subjectivity, can be achieved. What Hegel now wants to begin to show is that such subjects would, just *by* attempting to pursue their individual desires, ultimately come to "experience" such a basis as "Reason," a Reason finally not external to but identical with "actuality as it is in itself," "objects in their truth." Having shown this, he can go on to show what he regards as the necessary components of such a rational, self-conscious, self-determining subjectivity, components he considers the "logical moments" of the "self-actualizing Notion," or the *SL*.

He signals this decisive turn to a position much closer to his own final idealism by saying:

> We are in the presence of self-consciousness in a new shape, a consciousness which, as the infinitude of consciousness or as its own pure movement, is aware of itself as essential being, a being which thinks, or is a free self-consciousness.
>
> (*PhG*, 116; *PS*, 120)

Hegel has given an unusual, novel representation of the problem of subjectivity to which his account has led, and the real significance of that account now begins to emerge in passages like this one. That is, the unrecognized, dissatisfied Slave, Hegel's representation of a dependent self-consciousness (one whose self-understanding and relation to objects is neither freely nor rationally determined), does not merely labor, but self-consciously labors. He thinks; in particular, he struggles to understand the significance of his labor. This means that not only is the labor of the Slave progressively rationalized – the Slave masters nature more successfully and so actually establishes his independence from it, the condition for a free self-determination – but that he begins to struggle to understand the significance of his labor and how that labor shall be determined (by *him*, not the Master, who grows increasingly dependent on the Slave's expertise).

Predictably, as Hegel begins his account of the Slave's realization of his "independent self-consciousness," we encounter an "immediate" and abstract form of the Slave's "negation" of his dependent existence. The Slave's initial realization of the truth that his labor is ultimately dependent not only on him, but on his "thought," involves a highly abstract version of independent thought:

> In thinking I am free, because I am not in an other, but remain simply and solely in communion with myself, and the object that is for me the essential being is in undivided unity my being-for-myself; and my activity in conceptual thinking is a movement within myself. (*PhG*, 117; *PS*, 120)

This version of free self-consciousness is stoicism, and although it is, because so wholly abstract and negative a version of independence, indeterminate and even "tedious" in its emptiness, it is also already clearly indicative of the position toward which Hegel is heading. Indeed, if the preceding passage were lifted out of context and the subsequent qualifications and sublations were ignored, the quotation might be mistaken for one of Hegel's own summary claims about what is going on in the *Logic*.

At this point, however, he continues to present the unresolved dialectic of independence and dependence, Master and Slave, self-determining subjectivity and objectivity in this newly fashioned language of "thought." That is, since Hegel thinks he has shown that the Slave cannot count his position as thinking laborer as a resolution of the struggle for recognition, that the Slave's growing independence contradicts his position of dependence, and since he thinks he has shown that the Slave's growing independence, his direction of his own labor, is tied to the development of the Slave's self-consciousness, his thought, he begins to explore the possible forms of such an independent level of thought. In doing so, he replays in effect the dialectic of Master and Slave (itself a replay of the inverted world). Stoicism represents a "masterly" attempt simply to negate the world, to realize the actual independence inherent in the slave's position simply by a complete indifference to life, by retreating to "pure thought." Whatever the Master does to me, he cannot make me think anything; there alone am I truly free, myself a Master. But this position leaves it undetermined *what* I am to think (except that *I* am to think it), and so is empty, tedious. Skepticism represents a slavish response to this impasse, a "thought" with content, but only the negative determinacy of the skeptic, a demonstration that there is nothing finally worth believing or doing (and so no real superiority in the Master's power).

> It is clear that just as Stoicism corresponds to the Notion of the independent consciousness which appeared as the Master and Slave relationship, so Scepticism corresponds to its realization as a negative attitude towards otherness to desire and work. (*PhG*, 119; *PS*, 123)

But, Hegel proceeds to show, a thoroughly skeptical attempt to establish such independence is ultimately self-negating as well, so purely and finally inconsistently "negative" that the value or worth of such a negative activity itself also "vanishes." Skepticism thus does not solve the problem of the Slave's independence and recognition, but now in Hegel's narrative, the subject in question knows *this*, realizes the power and independence of its thought, and its negative independence from the real world, but cannot determinately make use of such thinking to satisfy itself *in* its work. Consciousness is thus deeply divided against itself, unable to accept the status of its relation to the world and others, and unable to rest content with its mere ability to demonstrate to itself the unsatisfactory character of its status. It is an "unhappy consciousness."

This term finally sums up dramatically the basic problem of all the *PhG*, and, even more than the beginning sections of this chapter, clearly indicates how far we have come from the initial problems of Kant's Deduction, what a different view of philosophical account giving Hegel is now proposing. For Hegel, the great emerging Kantian discovery of the freedom and spontaneity of subjectivity, the independence of thought, succeeds initially (i.e., in its earliest manifestations) only in leaving such subjects "homeless," undirected, and alienated, that the entire significance of a subject's spiritual and physical labor seems to it mere futility, wholly purposeless. To be sure, such a realization is only implicit or "in-itself," "for us" at this stage of the *PhG*'s reconstruction. For itself, self-consciousness simply appears to itself as "the changeable," ungrounded, contingent shapes of Spirit, skeptically self-destructive. Yet, such a self-consciousness also realizes that such a self-negating skepticism accounts for nothing and simply leaves unresolved the problem of mutual recognition. Within such a position, recognition is sought in a third, beyond, inaccessible to a wholly negative, skeptical thought, but a hoped-for resolution required if self-consciousness is not to dissolve into a renewal of the struggle to the death. (Hegel thus is locating the origin of the modern epistemological principle, subjectivity, or self-consciousness, much earlier than is traditional. It is, he is claiming, implicit in an unresolved way to Stoic, Skeptic, and Christian practices, but wholly negatively, without a full self-understanding.) In the grand Hegelian picture of Western intellectual history now emerging, human beings are viewed as progressively realizing the limitations and inconsistencies of various views of themselves as dependent even though initial manifestations of the truth of independent subjectivity are indeterminate or self-destructive. They thus merely prepare the way for a kind of indeterminate faith in the unchangeable, a belief that holds out some hope that universal mutual recognition, the problem created by independent subjectivity, can be resolved.

In the remainder of the chapter, Hegel discusses various ways in which a self-conscious subject could be said to ground its independence and the significance of its labor in an other, in which, basically, a religious attitude (typified best, probably, by Pascal's skepticism) could be said to resolve the philosophical and practical problems created by any "realization of the truth of self-consciousness." Actually, although his account is quite appropriate to early Christianity (Jesus's great teaching was that he was *both* Master and Servant, and early Christianity was dominated by the idea of Jesus's absence *and* immanent return), the topics he introduces range over Judaism, historical events (the Crusades, the pathetic but clearly understandable search for the absent Christ, at once a physical place and the symbol of God's absence), and clear references to Catholic and Protestant religious practices and to romanticism. What is important for us in the course of the discussion, as Hegel demonstrates the ironies and inconsistencies in the attempt to "find" outside or beyond the labors of Spirit the significance or redemption of those labors, is that at the conclusion of the account he returns us directly to the problem of idealism, having now demonstrated in effect that it is a problem that cannot be resolved empirically, metaphysically, pragmatically, conventionally, or religiously. In general, what he tries to show is that self-consciousness realizes (or must realize in order to avoid the incoherence into which it is otherwise led) that the "object" of its devotion and hope, the source of the worth and the warrant for the truth of its various "independently" determined practices, is *itself*, a claim that introduces the idealism issue that will dominate the rest of the *PhG* and all the *SL*. As quoted earlier, Hegel closes this chapter by claiming:

> But in this object, in which it finds that its own action and being, as being that of this particular consciousness, *are being and action in themselves*, there has arisen for consciousness the idea of reason, of the certainty that, in its particular individuality, it has being absolutely *in itself*, or is all reality. (*PhG*, 131; *PS*, 138)

The question, of course, is what such a claim means. However, what the rest of the *PhG* demonstrates is that such an identity between reason and reality *would be* the only resolution of the problems created by a "Spirit opposed to itself," that Spirit ultimately comes to understand that all its institutions are products of its own activity, including modern political, scientific, and philosophic institutions, and thus continually creates for itself forms of the unhappy consciousness, a dissatisfaction with the merely "produced" character of such institutions, unless Spirit understands its products as "in themselves all reality."[36] But the *PhG* itself does not provide us with an account of what such an "identity" actually means. It continues to show us in great, often brilliant, detail what the development of Reason, of Spirit's political and cultural history, and of religion, look like, *given* that Spirit does not understand that it is "in itself" all reality, and so it remains fundamentally dissatisfied with itself. But, in Hegel's own terms, his account is thus incomplete. It may be that the truth of Hegelian idealism, suitably interpreted in a nonmetaphysical way, *would* resolve that dissatisfaction, but it also may be, it is at this point fair to suspect, that such an idealism has no viable content of its own, other than the *PhG*'s promise. Human beings may simply *be* the unhappy consciousness; Hegel may be right about their "self-diremption" but wrong about its possible resolution.

Hegel clearly thinks that his speculative logic (an "Absolute Standpoint") is some kind of answer to this question, and our last task here is to understand how he motivates that answer in the *PhG*. As noted, he tries to motivate it mostly by an extensive account of what the implicit denial of a "subject–object" identity and a "self-determining" subjectivity entail. Such "non-realizations" of the Absolute Standpoint continue to create inversions, paradoxes, and contradictions that make impossible any satisfaction with such potential resolutions, and they can all be shown to demonstrate determinately that some such realization of the Absolute Standpoint would be the only effective, internally coherent satisfaction. Moreover, Hegel also tries to show that such a claim about internal paradoxes and dissatisfactions resulting from Spirit's realization of the truth of its "independence," but inability to understand that independence, is in fact the way we ought to understand "actual" forms of historical conflict (e.g., "tragedy") and actual "shapes" of historical self-understanding (the Enlightenment, the French Revolution, morality).[37] Just as we can undermine the point of view embodied by the epistemological realist skeptic (who doubts that the world is as we must think it to be), so we can undermine a historical realist skeptic, who doubts that actual forms of human dissatisfaction have anything to do with Hegel's idealist problematic. The great discovery of Kantian self-consciousness is not threatened by realist skepticism, but it *is* an unresolved problem throughout most of the *PhG*. It is threatened by itself, by its own lack of understanding of its own forms and the relation of those forms to historical actuality. Self-consciousness will be satisfied only when it is satisfied in being a self-consciousness, to return to the ambiguous genitive of my subtitle.

But, as noted, the *PhG* promises this final satisfaction without telling us much about it. Hegel anticipates his own idealist position at the beginning of "Reason," and, more famously, in the chapter "Absolute Knowledge." In the former, his speculative language is much in evidence. "Reason is the certainty of consciousness that it is all reality; thus does idealism express its Notion" (*PhG*, 133; *PS*, 140). And there is much talk about "otherness, as intrinsic being," "vanishing" (ibid.). These claims return us to several issues discussed in Chapter 4, where the problem of what Hegel meant by this use of "is" in "is all reality" was first addressed. As in the passages examined there, his formulations are far from clear, but we also find, even in these introductory claims, evidence that he is not asserting a monistic identity of thought and being. He also notes that "self-consciousness and being are *the same essence*," and not simply numerically identical (*PhG*, 134; *PS*, 142), that it is the "unity of self-consciousness" that "is all reality" (ibid.) and that "only in the unity of apperception lies the truth of knowing" (*PhG*, 136; *PS*, 144–5), all suggesting the Kantian interpretation claimed throughout here.

However, these initial statements of idealism are also limited in that Hegel himself stresses that such formulae express what is yet a mere "certainty" by self-conscious Reason that it "is" reality. The position under consideration no longer considers knowledge to be of a potentially inaccessible other, but there is as yet no determinate understanding of Reason's "identity" with reality. Consequently, as Hegel proceeds to point out, Reason's determination of itself in relation to reality replays (now at a self-conscious level) much of the earlier dialectic of consciousness and self-consciousness, as it struggles to formulate for itself its own relation to objects and to other subjects. So again, we get a programmatic statement of the goal of such determinate identity, but no real indication of how Hegel understands that final position (except, of course, by multitudinous contrast with what it cannot be).

In the last chapter, we fare a bit better. There, instead of the "Reason–reality" identifications, Hegel states his position on "Absolute Knowing" in terms of Spirit's knowledge of itself, and so an "overcoming" (*Ueberwindung*) of the object of consciousness and its presumed independence. But now he reminds us that such an overcoming is not to be thought of as "one-sided," as if the "object showed itself as returning into the self" (*PhG*, 422; *PS*, 479). The idealism he presents here does involve something called the "externalization of self-consciousness," but what is posited in such a movement is said to be the "thinghood" (*Dingheit*) of the object, not its literal existence. Hegel's identity claim is now introduced as the issue of the "reconciliation" (*Versöhnung*) of consciousness (a relating to and distinguishing from an *external object*) and self-consciousness, the "second moment" at issue since the beginning of Hegel's appropriation of Kant (*PhG*, 425; *PS*, 482). To be sure, such a reconciliation is, he admits, still only programmatic at this point; "the unification that is still lacking is the simple unity of the Notion" (*PhG*, 425; *PS*, 483). But such initial formulations confirm that by Absolute Knowledge Hegel is not referring to a knowledge of an absolute substance-Subject, a Divine Mind, or a Spirit-Monad. As he has since the latter half of his Jena years, he is referring to the conditions of human knowledge "absolutized," no longer threatened by Kant's thing-in-itself skepticism. In his clearest formulation of the subject matter of this chapter, he writes:

> This last shape of Spirit – the Spirit which at the same time gives its complete and true content the form of the self and thereby realizes its Notion as remaining in its Notion in this realization – this is absolute knowing; it is Spirit that knows itself in the shape of Spirit, or a comprehensive knowing. (*PhG*, 427; *PS*, 485)

When he specifies later in this passage what he means by "Spirit knowing itself in the shape of Spirit" as becoming a comprehensive knowing, he says simply:

As a result, that which is the very essence, viz. the Notion, has become the element of existence, or has become *the form of objectivity for consciousness*. Spirit, manifesting or appearing in consciousness in this element, or what is the same thing, produced in it by consciousness, is Science.

(*PhG*, 427–8; *PS*, 485–6; my emphasis)

The fact that Hegel glosses the issue of the "existence" (or objective reality) of the Notion with "becoming the form of objectivity," and the very fact that he describes the subject matter of Science, the *Logic*, in these terms, directly confirms the reading we have been giving to Hegel throughout.[38]

But it does not, so far, resolve the issue of how Hegel understands the "content" of this Science, how these "forms of objectivity" will be presented in a way consistent with the *PhG*'s account of knowledge. Since the beginning of his engagement with Kant, and his acceptance of the principle of a spontaneous apperception in all experience and action, together with his acceptance of Fichte's attack on the understanding/intuition distinction, Hegel has been faced with this problem of determinately distinguishing the merely logically possible from the really possible, or from the "forms of *objectivity*," what determines not merely the thinkable but the objective. And we have seen what is, in effect, the phenomenological version of this account of the development of forms of thought, a way of trying to show the indispensability of some form or other in the possible apprehension of any determinate object. What he has demonstrated is that there must be some such Notional determination of the real for there to be concrete experience and self-determined action, and that such determinations are not open to a realist skepticism or to suspicions of mere conventionalism. But, as his remarks now admit, he has not yet established how such a self-determined Notion can be accounted for. The *PhG* may have argued for the necessity of an impossibility.

In fact, there are a number of problems left open in Hegel's *PhG* account. As we have just seen, Hegel claims that Spirit, the "I that is a We and the We that is an I," a community of mutually recognizing individuals, all of whose basic institutions embody such universal recognition, simply *is* "Science" and that the Notion has become the "element of existence" and the "form of objectivity of consciousness."[39] From what we have seen, the general motivation for such claims by Hegel is clear enough. His idealist argument connects the very possibility of any number of basic institutions with their forms of self-understanding with, peculiar as it is to say, the institutions' self-consciousness. And it is clear that he thinks that such a conditioning self-consciousness introduces a kind of dissatisfaction, or self-negating impetus, into these institutions in ways that cannot be resolved until there is a full "scientific" account by thought of the basic categorial distinctions involved in such self-understanding and an account of the ground of such distinctions, their rationality, at least as defended in Hegel's "self-moving" account. And, looking ahead, it is even possible to see how the logical issues of finite/infinite, same/other, essence/appearance, and especially individual/universal might be quite relevant to what appears to have emerged in this chapter as Spirit's fundamental practical problem – mutual recognition. But the details of this connection between Hegel's *Logic* and his account of knowledge as, basically, a social institution (or of rationality *as* recognition) are not easy to understand, particularly as one makes one's way through the details of the *Logic*. The subjectivity presupposed by the *Logic*, the subject presumably determining for itself, in Hegel's ideal reconstruction, its own fundamental Notions is supposedly the Spirit introduced and developed in the *PhG*, a collective, *socially* self-realizing subject. In one sense, this just means that Hegel considers philosophy, realized in Absolute Knowledge, the decisive single institution within the interrelated collective attempt at mutual recognition by a historical community. Its resolution of the terms within which any form of self or other knowledge can occur is the sine qua non of self-satisfaction. And this somewhat Platonic aspect of his idealism was certainly among the most noticed and debated by subsequent Hegelians, especially young or leftist Hegelians. But the threads connecting Hegel's account of thought or rationality as, originally, a problem of social recognition and the logical Notions that "any such Spiritual community" must employ in its quest for mutual recognition are thin and often impossible to make out. They are there, I think, and can be made out (particularly as Hegel reverses direction and reconnects the issues with his *Encyclopedia* account of "objective Spirit"), but doing so is difficult enough to require a separate study.[40]

There is a more internal problem on the horizon, given the way Hegel has introduced the topic of a *Science of Logic*. He has claimed that these empirically independent, interconnected, developing "forms of objectivity" determine the possible "thinghood" of objects. This presumably means that he is arguing as follows: For there to be empirical differentiation and empirical explanation, there must be, prior to such investigation, criteria in place to determine what can count as a determinate object or explanation, and these criteria can be understood and legitimated only within the "movement of thought" itself, by reference to other possible attempts at such "criteria setting," and their internal incompleteness. But if this is so, it will still determine only the criteria or Notions for "thinghood," or *possible* objects. To be sure, this will *exclude* a great deal as a potential "possible object of a determinate, intelligible, self-conscious thinking" (e.g., atomism will not be a possible Notion of objects), but it will still leave an enormous amount *open*. Even if Hegel can deliver on his promise to formulate a criterion of pure Notionality, an account of forms of intelligibility far more detailed and specific than that required by the avoidance of contradiction or any other purely rational standard, it would seem that, ironically, this will mean that a great deal of the evidence necessary for deciding whether some controversial but logically (Hegel-logically, that is) possible object is a "real" object must be empirical evidence; at least empirical evidence of a kind, suitably constrained by Hegel's transcendentalism.

In a way remarkably similar (again) to Kant's worries about the relation between his principles and his philosophy of science, Hegel refused to leave *so* much to empirical ajudication (although, as we shall see, he leaves open far more than is often claimed).[41] In Chapter 8 he already looks ahead to the "incompleteness" of the *SL*, and the fact that the "self-knowing Spirit" knows "not only itself but also the negative of itself, or its limit" (*PhG*, 433; *PS*, 492). And he refers explicitly to the philosophies of Nature and Spirit. This seems to means that once we have determined the "self-constitution" of the "forms of objectivity," we can determine the specific implications of such Notions for Nature and Spirit in some nonempirical manner. Although this is not an issue I shall pursue here (the "self-constitution" business will be problematic enough), I want to note that Hegel himself thinks that the issues of the *Logic* and the *Philosophy of Nature* represent different issues; they are separable philosophically, and the resolution of one need not involve a specific answer to the other. And, given the disrepute of Hegel's *Philosophy of Nature*, it should also be noted that he is not simply merrily out to deduce the specific existence of objects in the world in the latter. The problem he faced is faced by anyone who holds that some non-empirically determined principles determine the possibility of empirical experience: to wit, how to reconcile such determination with actual and potentially "revolutionary" empirical discoveries.

But, as noted, the problem internal to the *Logic* is serious enough by itself. For Hegel describes such an interdetermined set of conceptual conditions in some fairly extravagant ways. He says that the moments of the *Logic* "spontaneously impel themselves along" (*PhG*, 428; *PS*, 487), and the "specific Notions" are said to be understood in "their organic self-grounded movement" (*PhG*, 432; *PS*, 491). As we have seen throughout, *something* like this developmental notion of conceptuality is necessary if Hegel is genuinely to replace Kant's deduction of the objectivity of the "forms of self-consciousness." Such interdeveloped forms would be the only ways in which a subject could take itself to be in relation to objects, and the *PhG* has already demonstrated (to Hegel's satisfaction) that such necessary forms of self-relation determine "reality as it is in itself." It is clear enough, then, that this is what *would* complete Kant; the question now is whether it does.

III
Idealist logic

8
Objective logic

1. What is a speculative logic?

For the most part, Hegel's designation for his theoretical philosophy is "Science" (*Wissenschaft*). As we have seen from the *PhG*, to be strictly accurate, science is not "philosophy," or the love of wisdom, but the completion of philosophy, or the achievement of wisdom in a comprehensive, systematic account by "thought" of itself, the completion of what we have been variously calling, since the discussion of the Jena material, the "self-legitimation of reason" or the "self-grounding of absolute subjectivity." Such an enterprise is to be distinguished from traditional speculation, metaphysics, since the latter treats the objects of thought, including mind itself, as substances, indeed as substances beyond or transcending finite particulars, whereas Hegelian science, often also called "speculation" or even "speculative philosophy," has succeeded in thinking of traditional substance "as subject," and by doing so has completely rejected any notion of the metaphysically real beyond, or behind, or "more real" than what can be understood in "Spirit's experience of itself," or, now, by "thought's examination of itself." And, although the title of the *Encyclopedia* makes it clear that in Hegel's view there can be many "philosophical sciences," there is only one comprehensive account of his basic scientific position, his "logic," expressed in the *Science of Logic* of 1812–16 and in his more schematic but often more intelligible version, the *Encyclopedia Logic* (1817, 1821, and 1830).

Hegel's summary term for the subject matter of this science is, simply, "actuality" (*Wirklichkeit*), a term he often glosses with "what objects are, in their truth" (*PhG*, 53; *PS*, 46) and, in his most famous claim, identifies with "reason," or rationality (*Vernunftigkeit*). What is "actuality"? Well, in *EL*, section 6, Hegel is very careful to distinguish this subject matter from what simply exists, and explicitly brings up his real/rational claim in *PR* and remarks that nothing in such a claim should be taken to deny the possibility of philosophical criticism of "what exists," which may indeed itself be far from its *own* "actuality," what it "is" in truth. And yet he is also careful to point out that this does not mean that science concerns itself with "ideals," that its "actuality" is the realm of mere thoughts, ought-to-bes. In one of his clearest formulations, in section 1 of *PR*, he notes that although philosophy (or again, more properly, *philosophische Rechtswissenschaft* in this case) has "ideas" as its objects, these are not "mere notions" but "the Notion" which "alone has actuality, and further gives itself this actuality" (*dass er sich diese selbst gibt*) (*PR*, 18; *PhR*, 14). Actuality, as Hegel understands it, *is* the "immanent development of the Notion," and philosophy can become science by pursuing this "self-construing path" (*WL*, I, 7; *SL*, 28). At the conclusion of *SL*, he explains what this "Notional actuality" involves in the following way. He says that the Logic, "in its entire course,"

> in which *all possible shapes of a given content and of objects* came up for consideration, has demonstrated their transition and their untruth; also that it was not merely impossible for a given object to be the foundation to which the absolute form stood in a merely external and contingent relationship, but that on the contrary, the absolute form has proved itself to be the absolute foundation and ultimate truth.
>
> (*WL*, II, 486; *SL*, 826; my emphasis)

I have already indicated in some detail why I believe that these official statements of Hegel's basic position preserve, even while greatly transforming, a Kantian project; that a Notional "foundation" (*Grundlage*) of actuality refers to the conceptual conditions required for there to be possibly determinate objects of cognition in the first place, prior to empirical specification, and that the key element in such an investigation will continue to be a focus on the self-reflexive character of any possible judgment and what *that* condition requires. [Hegel himself remarks explicitly that fully two-thirds of the *Logic*, the "objective logic," "would correspond in part" to what Kant calls "transcendental logic" (*WL*, I, 44–5; *SL*, 61–2).][1] This goal is, I think, what Hegel is after when, in the same section of the *SL*, he claims, about any subject matter, that "it is in the determinations of thought and the Notion that it *is* what it *is*" (*WL*, II, 493; *SL*, 833) or that there is a "supreme and sole urge" for the Notion to "find and cognize itself by means of itself in everything" (*WL*, II, 486; *SL*, 826). The problem now is simply whether this proposed interpretation, although clearly visible in such summary statements, can be supported by the vast detail in the texts of the *SL* and *EL*.

Initially, it is not at all clear that it can be. For one thing, whatever problems there were in Kant's Deduction, Hegel's response seems to have made matters much worse. The *PhG* may have established the necessary role of "Spirit's spontaneous self-determination" in the possibility of cognition and purposeful action, but trying to determine the "logical requirements" of such determination, which "thought determinations," as Hegel calls them, are necessary for there to be such conditions, seems quite a difficult task. According to Hegel, such required Notions are "identical with" (in his speculative sense) "what there is in truth." This means that he has to be able to distinguish between, to use Kantian language, a condition merely necessary *for a subject* to make judgments about objects and conditions necessary for objects to be objects at all, and to explain why he is not presenting an unusual version of the former, despite what he says about "actuality." And it would seem difficult to preserve Kant's own distinction between general and transcendental logic without Kant's intuition doctrine, much less to transform the latter into a speculative logic of "absolute and ultimate truth."

For another thing, there are two other approaches to the *Logic* that have, understandably, looked more promising to many commentators. The first appears to be motivated by such passages as the following, one of the most quoted of Hegel's summary claims about the *Logic*:

> Accordingly, logic is to be understood as the system of pure reason, as the realm of pure thought. The realm is truth as it is without veil and in its own absolute nature. It can therefore be said that this content is the exposition of God as he is in his eternal essence before the creation of nature and a finite mind.
>
> (*WL*, I, 31; *SL*, 50)

And, just to add some confusion about Hegel's attitude toward traditional metaphysics, at the same time that he wrote to Goethe that "we philosophers have a common enemy, metaphysics" (Br., II, n. 381, 251), he wrote in the *EL*:

> Logic therefore coincides with metaphysics, the science of things in thought – thoughts which are assumed to be able to express the essentialities of things.
>
> (*EL*, 81; *Enl*, 36)

All such claims about thought's determination of actuality, the "Absolute Knowledge" of "objects in their truth," and this association of logic with God's mind and, paradoxically, with metaphysics, together with Hegel's more well-known passages about Absolute or World Spirit in his philosophy of history and other unpublished works, tend to make it seem inevitable that Hegel's full theoretical position depends essentially on some metaphysical doctrine of spiritual substance (an Absolute Subject), "active" in history and nature, the "blueprint" for whose activity can be found in the *Logic*. Such a position on the *Logic* is again best expressed by Taylor:

> The rational, truly universal thought which is expressed insofar as we think categories is thus spirit's knowledge of itself. Since the external reality to which these categories apply is not only an embodiment of *Geist*, but is posited by *Geist* as its embodiment, and hence reflects the rational necessity of thought, in grasping the categories of thought about things, we are also grasping the ground plan or essential structure to which the world conforms in its unfolding.[2]

Again, although I have already indicated that such a view of Hegel's project must be rejected, it is not at all clear, in the face of the passages just cited and such a reasonable reconstruction of their meaning, that an alternative can be devised.

Moreover, on the face of it, there is another plausible way to interpret the task of the *Logic*, quite popular in recent years, that also does not rely so heavily on Hegel's Kantian origins. The *Logic* simply appears to be a peculiar kind of category analysis, an account by thought of itself, and *just* that. The main point of such a theory would be to establish that there are peculiar sorts of relations among primitive or somehow basic concepts, relations that are in their own way necessary, but are not entailment relations or much at all like what is discussed in formal logic. In this country, the most prominent representative of such a Wittgensteinean, somewhat "informalist," approach has been J.N. Findlay.[3] In Germany, its major proponent (with a very different notion of "category" and "category theory") has been Klaus Hartmann, who goes so far as to call his isolation of the *Logic*'s category theory from any account of reality "anti-metaphysical."[4] Since both such approaches, together with the less programmatic, highly detailed "category analysis" of scholars like Henrich and Rohs,[5] have focused so much attention on the problem of the specific transitions, they have produced important results in understanding that work and the theory of conceptual interdetermination detailed in it.

The problem with the position is not what it explains but what it doesn't explain, especially with respect to Hegel's systematic pretensions. The whole point of the transition from the standpoint of the *PhG* to the *Logic* had been to prevent our understanding the *Logic* as a category theory alone. However difficult it is to interpret and even partially defend Hegel's pronouncements about Absolute Idealism, the evidence is overwhelming that he would reject any construal of it as a particular way of uncovering and analyzing our "thought game." (It is fair, in some sense, to say that it *is* that. The question is what "that" establishes, how we should understand the significance of the results.)[6] The metaphysical interpretation at least has the merit of trying to account for what one might call the "source" or ground of the Idea's self-realization and for the status of those results.[7]

Hence the problem: If the metaphysical view attributes to Hegel a precritical monism, indefensible in itself and at odds with much of what Hegel actually says about his project, and the category approach leaves too much of Hegel's problem with "objectivity," or the epistemological status of the Notion, unexplained, is there a defensible view of Hegel's project that attributes to him less than the former but more than the latter?[8]

So much for the general problems confronting such an interpretation and its possible competitors. The specific problems facing any account of the *Logic* can be stated briefly. If Spirit's experience of itself can be said to result in the proper understanding of the role of the subject and its "pure thoughts" in all experience, then what simply *are* such pure thoughts, "logical" thoughts, pure "thought determinations"? In what determinate ways can Hegel's ideal subject be said to "determine itself" to think in various ways about what there is? We now supposedly know that such a self-determination is how we ought to understand such logical forms, and we have supposedly dealt successfully with the kind of skepticism that such a subject-centered approach generates. But such preparatory work just brings us to the threshold of Spirit's most important form of self-knowledge, its knowledge of its *own* "thoughts." What kind of knowledge is that?

Other questions follow immediately. The first stems from the fact that so much of the idealist understanding of self-consciousness and spontaneity is preserved in Hegel's understanding of the *Logic*'s program. Spirit is said to "come to itself, in the deepest sense of the word," in *Logic*, and this because Spirit's "unadulterated self-ness is thinking" (*EL*, 55; *EnL*, 15). Later, introducing a notion that will be central to his claims about *Logic*, Hegel says that the purity of this self-relation, the way in which thought and thought alone determines itself, means that pure thought is "infinite," not constrained by an other, a limit, as in ordinary thought. "Thinking (*das Denken*, that is, speculative thought) is on its own (*bei sich selbst*), relates itself to itself, and has itself for an object. Insofar as I have thought for my object, I am at home with myself, on my own (*bei sich selbst*)" (*EL*, 95; *EnL*, 49).[9] And in a passage that still shows the continuing influence of Fichte:

> This pure being-on-our-own (*reine Beisichsein*) belongs to free thought, to it in its free sailing out on its own, where there is nothing under it or above it, and where we stand in solitude with ourselves alone. (*EL*, 98; *EnL*, 52)

Given such claims, the obvious question is whether anything determinate can be said to result from such a pure self-determination. One might admit that there are subject-constituted elements of experience, a conceptual structure that cannot be challenged by experience since constitutive of it, and yet look for the determinate *source* for such a structure in pure intuition, pragmatic ends, the structure of the brain, the current status of the forces of production, survival value, the will to power, or the gifts of Being. But it does not seem promising to look for such an explanation in the ideal "self's unlimited, infinite relation to itself." Even if we recall that Hegel is presupposing in such an account quite a different notion of self or subject than that prominent in the modern, post-Cartesian tradition, and quite a different notion of reflection than that prominent in the post-Kantian tradition, the sheer oddity of such claims is striking, and, for a commentator, intimidating.

Besides an account of this unusual notion of infinity, we can see immediately that we shall also need an account that distinguishes the results of such self-determinations (if it can be shown that there are determinate results) from the concepts we form "finitely," in a way tied to the oppositions and limitations of finite objects, and an account of the relation among these various conceptual levels. This last is important to resolve since Hegel also, despite the preceding remarks on the independence of thought, occasionally concedes that philosophy can "thank, for its development, the empirical sciences," even while he maintains that philosophy gives these sciences the "shape of the freedom (of the a priori character) of thinking," a thinking he continues to call a "completely self-supporting activity" (*EL*, 58; *EnL*, 18).[10]

Ultimately, these claims about the "self-supporting" activity of thought, its infinity, autonomy, self-determining character, and so on represent the most controversial and most difficult to understand in Hegel. He simply appears to think that he can ideally reconstruct how any attempt to think, to make a determinate judgment about, an "actual" object will involve presuppositions and categorial commitments that are not and cannot be determined by the extraconceptual and yet constitute the "real possibility" of an extraconceptual actuality. This categorial projection of what could be an intelligible actuality introduces all the classic Hegelian controversies, especially with respect to one of his most influential claims.

For there is another distinctive feature of "logical thoughts" often stressed by Hegel. Relations among such thoughts are unique. In particular, a variety of exclusion relations we would normally expect to obtain do not. Where we would expect concept A, by being A, to exclude that concept's also being B, we find instead that no account of A's being A can succeed unless A is also B, even though B appears its contrary, logically excluded by it. There is, then, an unusual sort of fluidity in the logical marks of such concepts, a special kind of interdefinability that presupposes a distinct, speculative theory of negation and that distinct sort of relation known famously by the name "dialectic." At the speculative level, thought "entangles itself in contradictions, that is, it loses itself in the set non-identity of its thoughts"; or the "nature of thought itself is dialectical" (*EL*, 55; *EnL*, 15). Hegel himself asserts that this claim about the dialectical nature of thought is one of the "main elements" of *Logic*, and so he must be able to defend in detail this feature of thought's self-determination.

If there is such an unusual logical relation among the thoughts of any possible object, we face a third crucial problem – how can we understand the specific derivation of thoughts from each other. Or, more simply, why does the *Logic* have the structure that it does? This problem involves much more than the architectonic issue alone when we realize that, according to the last chapter of the *PhG*, the *Logic* not only represents thought's articulation of itself, but, in being such a self-articulation, determines comprehensively any possible actuality. Thus the issues of dialectical relation and development have an ontological dimension as well that the *Logic* must clarify. So, the fact that the *thought*, or theory, of classic metaphysical realism (the doctrine of "Being") must give way to, cannot be consistently maintained apart from its completion in, a reflective determination of Being as Essence/Appearance, can be said to reveal something about what reality must be like. (*It* must be reflected by a subject to be determinately real.)[11] Since Hegel rejects Kant's notion of phenomena, this again looks like a return to a precritical notion of category, a purely rational determination of the real.[12] And by now, this is a familiar problem: how to understand Hegel's rejection of the finite subjective idealism of his predecessors without what would amount to a precritical theology or a postcritical romantic metaphysics. This will all bring us again to the identity theory problem, now articulated in its final terms, those of the *SL*.

In this articulation, it will at least be clearer why Hegel's formulation of "Absolute idealism" has produced so many divergent interpretations of what he himself keeps calling the "heart" or "spirit" or "soul" of his position. All of the issues opened up earlier must be resolved in terms of Hegel's account of what he calls the "self-realization of the Absolute Idea," which is what the *Logic* is supposed to be about, and it is the maddening complexities of this doctrine that has sent so many to such various interpretations and revisions. Since Schelling's critical lectures influenced the likes of Feuerbach and Kierkegaard,[13] it has seemed impossible to be able to accept either that the Idea can determine itself or that the self-determinations of the Idea have anything to do with the world of finite, individual, existing objects, especially subjects. The first claim produces all the charges of Hegel's mystified logicism so prominent in the Marxist tradition.[14] The latter now familiar issue has a long history in the post-Hegelian European tradition, starting with the Schellingean, proto-existentialist critique of Hegel on existence, continuing through the famous attack by Kierkegaard and the more recent insistence by Heidegger on the priority of "difference" or non-identity. It is also the obvious source of wholesale unacceptability, even unthinkability, of Hegel for anyone educated in some version of the empiricist philosophical tradition, where Hegel's "thought determinations" are tied either directly to experience, as in classical empiricism, or, through a theory of language and meaning, to the possibility of empirical verification. And Hegel's position seems even less likely to get a hearing if it is true that the question of "why we think as we do" about things should be explained in the same way we explain the world itself, by science, as is claimed by modern versions of scientific realism.

Unfortunately, Hegel does not discuss problems such as those raised earlier in any direct or explicit way. If we want to understand how thought can determine itself, Hegel suggests, ever contemptuous of "introductions" (in his many introductions), we read his account of how it does so. If we are confused about what is involved in a "dialectical" relation among concepts, again, we should look to the details. So, it is time to turn to the details.

In doing so, I note in advance the obvious: that I do not pretend to be able to offer a commentary on the *Logic*. I want mainly to show that the project of the *Logic* is consistent with the idealism I have attributed to Hegel, and that many of the major and, for a long time, most contentious specific issues of the *Logic* are better understood as contributing to such an idealist argument. Specifically, this will mean a discussion of (1) Hegel's critical interpretation of the classical, metaphysically realist tradition in Book I, his demonstration that the "logic" of "being as it is in itself" is an incomplete and so inadequate logic (all this a kind of introductory motivation for the beginning of Hegel's own idealism, playing much the same strategy as Kant in the Antinomies); (2) his account of both the advance and incompleteness of a "reflective logic," a grand settling of accounts with all attempts to conceive of being as necessarily "reflected being," and so the introduction of his own initial claim about the "identity" of reflected essence and existence in "actuality" (a claim I take simply to state, in an initial form, Hegel's idealist position); and (3) his own final statement of the relation between categorial "universality" and "particularity," an "identity within difference" that has prompted so much of the "Hegel myth." Hegel, in the interpretation I am defending, will try to show how the determinate problems of realist metaphysics ground the claim for being as reflected, or mediated, or ideally determined being; will then raise the great problem of that position – *Schein* – the skepticism issue again; and will then try to preserve the idealist mediation without the skeptical remainder, or will perform his infamous "absolute reflection," and so complete the case for his "absolute idealism." Or, at least, so he intends.

2. Being and thinking

In the *SL*, Hegel devotes a good deal of preliminary attention to a problem that, in his lifetime, had become the most controversial aspect of any supposedly systematic science – the beginning. It has certainly become the most frequently discussed and most often criticized aspect of his own *Logic*, the beginning with being and the first logical transition to becoming. In the *EL*, however, Hegel is content simply to summarize the results of those discussions, as if the issue is relatively unproblematic.

> Pure being makes the beginning, because it is not only pure thought, but also undetermined, simple immediacy, and the beginning cannot be anything mediated and further determined. (*EL*, 182; *EnL*, 124)

In the Addition to this paragraph, he clarifies a bit what he means by "undetermined":

> The indeterminate (*Bestimmungslose*) which we are dealing with here is the immediate (*das Unmittelbare*), not mediated indeterminacy, not the cancelling of all determinacy, but the immediacy of indeterminacy, indeterminacy prior to all determination, indeterminacy as the very first of all. This we name being. (*EL*, 185; *EnL*, 125).

Such characterizations of the beginning, however preliminary and still ambiguous, nonetheless sketch a plausible opening to what other texts and his own introductory remarks have proposed as a *Science of Logic*. That program helps explain the two reasons given for the beginning with being: It is "pure thought" and "simple immediacy." The *Logic*, that is, is to explain the most central and mysterious of Hegel's doctrines, the "self-determination" of the Notion. One way of posing this problem is to ask: On the assumption that a prior categorial determinacy is required for the self-conscious apprehension of any object (and its empirical determinations), can there be a completely indeterminate, all-inclusive such categorial determination functioning as such a condition (the Concept "being")? Does the mere "thought" of any "actuality" require a variety of other "thoughts" just to *be* the thought of an actuality? As we have seen by reviewing the *PhG*, the assumption guiding this question is that it cannot be empirical information or some extraconceptual determination that accounts for "what else" is required if the thought of anything at all is to be the determinate thought of anything at all.

Looked at this way, we can begin to anticipate that ultimately, the final claim of the *Logic*, its major thesis, is that in attempting to render *determinate* any possible object of self-conscious thought, thought comes to understand the "truth" that it is "thinking itself," thinking its own activity. As usual, Hegel tries to establish that position by beginning with its opposite, here by assuming that thought can directly or intuitively think "being itself." If the *Logic* is right, being itself will turn out to be inconceivable except as "actuality," conceptually mediated objectivity, and so, in the Kantian sense I have defended, the Notion, fully realized (or the first division of the *Logic* will be "completed" by the third).[15] This approach will raise a number of questions as its development unfolds, chief among them being how such implicitly presupposed, more determinate thoughts are argued for, and in what way Hegel begins to argue for a structure, a whole for all such transitions. But his remarks about the task of the *Logic* do illuminate the appropriateness of mere being. It is a "pure thought"; nothing about the content of the notion of being is determined by anything other than the rational requirements of "anything at all," any possible object. In Hegel's version of the contemporary ontological question, we get roughly the same answer: If the question is just "What is there?," the answer is simply and indeterminately – everything. Or, if we wish to investigate how thought can be said to determine itself, we begin by assuming no specific determination, and then we see if we still have a possible thought of an object.

As Hegel's famous argument proceeds, however, it quickly becomes clear that we do not, that the mere thought of anything at all is not a determinate thought of anything. There is nothing such a thought excludes – *everything* is – and so the thought itself can be said to be "nothing" – *Nichts*. In trying to think all the possible contents of thought "at once," as it were, and so in excluding any specification not drawn from thought alone (as in a beginning with matter, or the I, or God), we end up in a familiar Hegelian predicament, defeating ourselves, in this case thinking "nothing at all." But, again in a familiar way, we at least know what we require, the most inclusive conceptual determination of anything at all that *is* some kind of determination. By the requirements of the *Logic*'s program, this should be a minimal determination, one "close" conceptually to the extreme generality of the *Logic*'s beginning, but responsive to the instability, one could call it, of mere being as an object of thought, responsive to the result that, armed with no conceptual markers with which to fix and categorize, any being so (putatively) thought "turns into" nothing. Hegel calls this instability "becoming" and so completes the infamous first dialectical transition.

It is infamous for a number of reasons. Most simply, the whole thing seems so artificial. As in many other places in his books, Hegel pretends, in a sense, to be accepting and entertaining a notion he considers impossible or inadequate. After all, one way of putting the whole point of German Idealism from Kant on is to note the denial by all those thinkers that there can *be* anything like "unmediated immediacy." The denial of the possibility of immediacy, or an intuitive apprehension of pure being, is the heart of the program. So there is no great dialectical result produced in the first transition. Hegel simply, on this view, restates the manifesto of that philosophical movement, and so again reveals his idealist commitments. Pure being is not a possible object of thought, thanks to its complete indeterminacy. Therefore, since the *PhG* has determined that any representation of objects requires the spontaneous determinations of pure thought (a priori conditions), and this condition is not met by being, then, as Hegel puts the issue, *thought* must produce some minimally determinate notion of anything at all. Hegel is clearly trying to dismantle the possibility of such an ontology, and so to show how the terms of that dismantling lead ultimately to his idealism, but the suspicion has always been that he is pulling that rabbit out of the hat because he put it there.

This sort of objection means that one is denying that the beginning of the *Logic* is really a beginning at all, and it is probably the most frequently raised criticism of this section of the *Logic*. As Dieter Henrich summarizes these objections, they amount either to outright denials that the supposed transition between being and nothing can be any sort of transition, or to revisions of Hegel that adandon his claim to begin in pure immediacy, and argue that the beginning of the *Logic* is already necessarily mediated.[16]

To the first camp belong those who claim that the beginning is just a play on words, that being and nothing are just two ways of saying the same thing, featureless or indeterminate immediacy, and so it is no surprise to find that in thinking being, I am thinking nothing, since that featurelessness is what being means by stipulation. To the latter belong those who regard the beginning of the *Logic* as only an apparent beginning. The *Logic* truly begins with some theory of thinking, and it is that theory that determines that being must be "reflected" as nothing, that is, as self-consciously or explicitly indeterminate, if we are to understand what we are thinking.

The first objection misrepresents what Hegel means by immediacy. He is quite clear that he does not mean by being, featurelessness, as if we are to consider the results of *abstracting* from every concrete determination and think the result. He explicitly excludes this in the Addition to section 86 quoted earlier. We are not just thinking "the absence of determination" twice in thinking being and nothing because being is supposed to be what Hegel calls "indeterminacy as the very first of all," "prior to all determinateness" (*vor aller Bestimmtheit*). But this means that Hegel *does* mean that we think something different in thinking being as nothing, and that is still quite problematic.

I have already suggested that we should understand that transition in terms of the overall goal of the *Logic*, thought's attempt to determine a priori what can be a possible thought of anything at all. On this reading, the infamous first transition is not nearly as momentous as so many commentators assume. The transition in question simply involves a greater degree of self-consciousness about such a possible object of thought. *Given* the original intention of the *Logic*, we find that any attempt to formulate the object of thought as being is really not a coherent thought. At first, we assume it may be (being); then we are forced to admit that it is not (nothing). The thought of "nothing" is thus just the thought *that* the thought of being designates no possible object of thought. It is thus the "determinate negation" of being, not a separate thought that somehow one would intuit in thinking being. This is what, I think, is expressed by Hegel when he says in the first section, that is, the section *on being*, that there is "nothing to be intuited in it," that nothing is "the same as pure being," and especially that being does *not* "pass over" into Nothing, but "has passed over," already (*sondern übergegangen ist*) (*WL*, I, 90; *SL*, 103).[17]

But this interpretation, which is similar to some of those Henrich groups in the second category earlier,[18] faces a number of problems. The first is interpretive. What is left of the sense of "immediacy" and of the kind of demonstration of the necessary, logical mediations of immediacy the *Logic* was to have provided? The interpretation presented sounds like a claim that the beginning of the *Logic* presupposes the whole *Logic* and so cannot be a beginning in any sense. Second, how can we begin with a thought that is really *not* a thought, an impossibility? The "thought determinations" of the *Logic* are supposed to preserve a "correspondence between Thought and reality," according to one commentator, and this would seem contradicted if being cannot be thought.[19] And such an approach seems to make difficult an understanding of the relation between the *PhG* and the *Logic*. The former was to have enabled us to reach the standpoint of Absolute Knowledge, and it would seem odd, to say the least, to begin our articulation of Absolute Knowledge with the unthinkable. Finally, and most interesting philosophically, given that this view of the *Logic*'s beginning minimizes its importance so much (what is "concluded" requires no great dialectical insight to see; we simply become more explicit about what Hegel has known all along cannot be a possible thought), can the approach explain how we go on from here? What about the conclusion that in thinking a purely immediate being, we are in fact thinking nothing should move us to the thought of "becoming," whatever that is? As Taylor has pointedly asked, why shouldn't we just conclude with the general notion of "determinate being" (*Dasein*), and bypass the metaphysical excursion into becoming?[20]

The first objection involves more than differing interpretations about the technical meaning of "beginning" in Hegel. Viewing the account of being and nothing as a reflective determination of the thinkability of being raises more serious problems about the purpose of the *Logic* itself. As Henrich puts the objection:

> If the *Logic* intends to develop thought-determinations for themselves and from one another, the reflection on their being-thought cannot be the moving force of the progress. That is much more the standpoint of a phenomenological dialectic.[21]

Henrich means that if the "test" of such thoughts appeals to their *Gedachtsein*, as Henrich calls it, their possibly being thought, then the touchstone for the system is *thought*. Yet the *Logic* seems to claim an "absolute" status for itself, to be a doctrine about *becoming*, *finitude*, *essence*, *form*, and not about the "thought relations" involved in the *thought* of becoming, essence, and so on. (Or, as Henrich puts it, down this path lies neo-Kantianism, not Hegel.)[22] Moreover, the true beginning of the *Logic* would be highly mediated, would have to involve an implicit appeal to thinkability and subjectivity, all of which would render confusing Hegel's strong insistence on the immediacy of the beginning.

However, Hegel himself is not at all reticent about undercutting the supposed immediacy of the beginning. As we have noted, this should not be surprising, since he does not believe an immediate beginning is possible, even though the program of the *Logic* demands that he entertain its possibility. In the preparatory "With What Must Science Begin?" in the *WL*, he states clearly that "there is nothing, nothing in heaven or in nature or in mind or anywhere else which does not equally contain both immediacy and mediation" (*WL*, I, 51; *SL*, 68). And he goes on to note that the "logical" beginning of the work is "pure knowing," which is said to be "mediated, because pure knowing is the ultimate, absolute truth of consciousness" (ibid.). And he even goes so far as to say that "Simple immediacy is itself an expression of reflection" (*WL*, I, 52; *SL*, 69). Moreover, the fact that "pure being" is an admittedly "mediated" determination of thought, and that the issue being raised in the opening of the *Logic* concerns its reflective adequacy *for thought*, need not mean that we are construing the program of the *Logic* in a neo-Kantian way. (Although it would be fair to say that this emphasis on thought's developing self-consciousness of itself associates the *Logic*'s approach with the *PhG*. The difference between the works is not the abandonment of reference to "Spirit's experience of itself" but the nature of the "experience." In Hegel's language, it is not the experience by "consciousness" of itself, skeptically posing its experience against "reality," but "pure thought's" experience of itself, without such skeptical doubts.)[23] We could not fully evaluate such a charge unless we introduced a good deal more detail about the Hegelian account of subjectivity, thought, and pure thought's objectivity. But it is clear that neo-Kantian category analysis differs from Hegel on all such counts, as we shall see in subsequent sections of the *Logic*. In sum, since Hegel has assumed that he has proved the centrality and priority of a kind of self-determining self-consciousness in all experience, he begins with the task of trying to isolate this self-determining element, to specify ideally Spirit's own self-transformations as it tries to determine itself in its relation to all possible objects. It is not yet at all clear what this project involves, but Hegel does not seem hesitant about admitting that it already determines the beginning of the *Logic*, "mediates" it, and about admitting that we are already invoking thought's inherent self-reflection in determining the possibility of any such moments.

As he puts it himself, then, Hegel's notion of a "logical advance" is that it is a "retreat" (*Ruckgang)* into the ground, one in which the supposed beginning in immediacy turns out not to have been a beginning, to "lose" the "one-sidedness" of its appearance, to "become something mediated." [He even says, in a phrase that greatly confuses hard and fast distinctions between the methodology of the *PhG* and the *Logic*, that it is "*consciousness*" that is "led back" to absolute knowledge as the "innermost truth" of *its* supposed immediacy (*WL*, I, 35; *SL*, 71).]

All of which already takes care of the second objection. On the view of the *Logic* noted earlier, it is incorrect from the start to worry about what Rosen calls the "realism" of the *Logic* and so to worry about how Being could be "unthinkable." The *Logic* is idealist in its function and goal, and that at least means that thinking about the relations between the thought determinations of the *Logic* and "reality" cannot be construed as a problem of "correspondence." For Hegel, any "reality" side of such a dyad is just another thought determination. "Truth," he says, is the "agreement of a thought-content with itself" (*EL*, 86; *EnL*, 41). When thought fails to be able to think "what is there before us," as Hegel puts it in *SL (WL*, I, 53–4; *SL*, 69), it is not thereby "realistically" determining the nature of things, but itself. The *reason* such a self-determination turns out to constitute what could be real (in Hegel's technical sense of *wirklich*) depends, as we have seen, on the argument in the *PhG*, and, as we shall see, on how he introduces the notions of "actuality" and the relation between the Notion and reality in the next two books of the *Logic*. Accordingly, nothing about this "impossible" beginning confuses the *PhG*'s relation to the *Logic*. The result of the *PhG* was not simply to introduce us to pure immediacy, but as Hegel says in a passage Rosen quotes, that result is the beginning *of the Logic*, or "Thought for itself" (*SL*, 70; *WL*, I, 54).[24]

The final objection raises more difficult problems. As noted in discussing both objections previously, reading the *Logic* as thought's reflective determination of itself, where that self-determination involves progressively more self-consciousness about what it can think "on its own" and about its own self-determining activity, seems not to take into account the ontological dimension of the *Logic* itself (as opposed to the ontological implications of the *Logic* of thought). On the face of it, there are several places where Hegel, in discussing the limitations of a Notion or its development, slips frequently from a "logical" to a material mode, going far beyond a claim about thought or thinkability, and making a *direct* claim about the necessary nature of things, direct in the sense that no reference is made to a "deduced" relation between thought and thing. A claim is simply made, on the supposed basis of logical necessity, about things. One obvious example is the one mentioned in summarizing the objection. From a consideration of the complete indeterminacy of being, from self-consciousness about the "nothingness" of that Notion, Hegel appears to move directly to a consideration of *a* being's passing into non-being, or its coming to be from what it wasn't. That is, where his argument, on the logical level, should simply introduce the requirement of determinacy in the thought of anything at all, and should go on to investigate the possible logical markers of determinacy, he introduces a claim about the real relation of coming to be and passing away, and *then* returns to the logical issue of determinacy. Why does he do this?

This is a natural question that arises on any reading of the *Logic*, but it is particularly pressing for the interpretation of Hegel's idealism for which I have been arguing. Not only would what I have been saying have no way to deal with such passages, this would appear to be a chronic problem throughout the *Logic*. Even more famous in the first section is Hegel's account of the necessary contradictions of the finite, of any finite thing, and by virtue of his claims about "limit" and finitude, his account of the necessary interrelation of everything, "infinitely." This even more clearly appears to involve a metaphysical theory about the monistic nature of being, the impossibility of "real" independence for things, and would seem flatly inconsistent with the approach I have taken. The best one could say about Hegel is that he "forces his argument beyond what it can strictly yield,"[25] by confusing the requirement that any being be characterized "contrastively," in a way that will distinguish it from some other, with the claim that *beings* actually oppose and negate each other and, in their opposition and negation, are essentially related, could not be what they are outside such a relation. The latter claim, then, not only represents a conflation with the first, but is itself suspect, since it again confuses logical with ontological issues. It appears to claim that a thing's not being something else is a property of it, part of what make it what it is.

3. Thoughts about *Dasein*

I shall deal with both issues separately, beginning with Hegel's account of becoming and concluding with a general discussion of his notion of finitude, as it appears in the first section of the *Logic*. As noted, it should be admitted that there are indeed a number of passages that naturally generate questions like those asked previously but do not adequately answer then, passages where Hegel appears to go far beyond what many of his own characterizations of the *Logic* would allow. However, I shall argue, even in some of the most apparently extravagant such passages, it is still possible to continue to make out the argument for the the kind of "logical idealism" attributed to Hegel thus far. The two under consideration now will serve as test cases for such a claim.

What is initially unusual about Hegel's discussion of becoming is that he claims not to be discussing the becoming of *things*, the coming to be and passing away of finite objects. In his first Remark on the issue in *SL*, he cautions us not to think of a "something" becoming nothing, or ceasing to be (*WL*, I, 45; *SL*, 83). If that is so, he must be investigating how thought can think actuality in its initially assumed pure indeterminateness, yet be thinking of something; not of some being, but still of "being itself," self-consciously taken to be indeterminate (nothing). To do so, we can try to think being *in* its indeterminateness; we can try to conceive being in such a way that its continuing instability as an object of reference is captured by our category. Upon reflection, this is what the category, becoming, attempts to do. It is not, Hegel points out, the thought of the becoming of things, but the thought of being as what we might call a minimally determinate, indeterminate thing. Being can be minimally determined by the "moments" of its indeterminacy. Being as flux, or becoming, can be thought in terms of the moments of that flux, not as a plurality of things but as one internally changing, unstable thing, being. As always, the question the *Logic* is trying to answer must be kept in mind in such passages. That question asks, in a radically idealized context, how thought on its own can determine objects of thought. With no determination supplied exogenously, it is left thinking being *in* its indeterminateness, and Hegel simply *calls* that "becoming." He tells us in the *EL* that becoming is thus "the first concrete thought, and therefore the first notion," since being and nothing before it were merely "empty abstractions" (*EL*, 192; *EnL*, 132). As he puts it in a discussion of Jacobi in *SL*, the very indeterminateness of being *is* a kind of determinateness, and this is what I think he is trying to capture by the notion of becoming (*WL*, I, 85; *SL*, 99).

Not that the Notion of becoming is a successful determination; like being and nothing, it too turns out to be a self-defeating thought of anything at all. The indeterminate moments of becoming are not true moments; they cannot be concretely specified, since such moments "are always changing into each other and reciprocally cancelling each other."[26] Because of this, he tells us, "Becoming stands before us in utter restlessness – unable, however, to maintain itself in this abstract restlessness" (*EL*, 192; *EnL*, 134). Thus there is, as of this point, no attempt by Hegel to confuse the logical problem with ontological issues. Far from attempting to evoke and *affirm* a Heraclitean vision of a ceaselessly changing reality, Hegel's introduction of the notion of becoming at this point still only aims to provide what thought initially requires, a "self-determined" object, and to demonstrate that a "pure" Notion of becoming itself does not provide such an object.[27] It is then the *failure* of Parmenides and now Heraclitus to *think* being itself that motivates, for thought, the Notion of being as always *a* being, determinately specifiable by means of properties or qualities. To be sure, there is the same tour de force artificiality about this "result" as there was about the "beginning," but Hegel has barely started. He has gone so far as to argue that being itself is not a possible object of thought, and given the standpoint of the *Logic*'s idealism, for him that is sufficient to dismiss the question of "being itself." It is certainly possible to object to this, as Heidegger would, but that objection must focus on the standpoint of the *Logic*. There is not much, given that standpoint, that one can object to in these opening moves. Contrary to the notion that Hegel is smuggling in complicated and controversial metaphysical claims, I think the most meaningful criticism of these passages is that Hegel is not doing very much at all. He is introducing some classical problems in ancient ontology and offering his own unusual description of their *source*: They are what we would expect from thought's first attempts to determine itself with respect to all possible objects, and given the failure of these attempts, he takes himself as providing a rational justification for necessarily thinking of being as a determinate or qualitative being, specifiable by determinate properties. As we have been saying throughout, such a necessity stems not from metaphysical commitments but from what other thoughts are possible or impossible.

But, an objector could say, what happens when we proceed beyond the abstractness of becoming and consider Hegel's famous remarks on the contradictoriness of finitude itself, and its necessarily "perishing" nature? What of such passages as this:

When we say of things that they are finite, so we must be understood to mean not only that they have determinateness, not only that they have a quality as their reality and a self-subsistent determination, not merely that they are limited – have their existence determined beyond their limits – but that it is much more the case that this non-being (*Nichtsein*) makes up their nature, their being. Finite things are, but their self-relation consists in the fact that they are negatively related to themselves, that just in this relation to themselves, they propel themselves beyond themselves, beyond their very being. They are, but the truth of this being is their end (*Ende*). The finite not only changes, like something in general; but it perishes, and it is not merely possible that it perishes, so that it could be without perishing, but the being of finite things is such that they have the germ of perishing as their essence (*Insichsein*). The hour of their birth is the hour of their death. (*WL*, I, 116–17; *SL*, 129)

Moreover, Hegel not only appears to claim that, by virtue of some conceptual necessity, we can determine that reality must be itself necessarily perishing, he introduces the whole discussion of finitude by claiming that the finite character of reality is inherently contradictory:

Something with its immanent limit posited as the contradiction of itself, through which it is directed and forced out beyond itself, is the finite.

(*WL*, I, 116; *SL*, 129)

And this whole discussion appears to be central to the basic theme of idealism, since Hegel points out in both versions of the *Logic* that to properly understand the insufficiency of the finite, its passing over into the infinite, is to understand the truth of idealism. For many, this means a Hegelian claim about the exclusive reality of Absolute Spirit, and so the unreality of finite individuals.

As we have seen often before, the solution to this problem, the problem of an apparent conflation between an account of concepts and a direct (i.e., not transcendentally deduced) claim about reality, depends a great deal on how one interprets the function of this section of the *Logic*. Obviously there is something wrong with using the text as a kind of Hegelian dictionary, as if, when one wants to know what Hegel's position is on a topic, one searches through the Table of Contents and consults the particular argument, in this case an argument against a particular philosophical notion. Even though there is little doubt that Hegel believes that there is something conceptually insufficient about an understanding of the world wholly determined by the Notion of independent, limited, finite individuals, it is also true that "finitude," or that original metaphysical orientation, as a "moment" of thought's self-determination, is to be somehow preserved in any fully adequate understanding of a possible object of thought. Thus it cannot be the case that Hegel is trying to attack or argue against the possibility of finite individuals, all in favor of the true reality of one infinite spiritual whole. As he himself points out, *that* position represents simply a "finitization" of the infinite, a consideration of it as the one (hence finite) thing that is. In *EL*, Hegel notes that the position that ascribes to the finite no "independent actuality," no "absolute being," "forgets" this when it poses the infinite over against it, as if they were opposed alternatives, and so "comes to an infinite which is only a finite" (*EL*, 201–2; *EnL*, 139). They are not opposed alternatives; or at least, that is what one must try to understand in understanding this section.[28]

But what, then, should we make of what appear to be direct claims about (1) the necessarily perishing nature of the finite and (2) the necessarily interrelated nature of the finite, the "dependence" of individuals on other individuals (a position that, as noted, seems to confuse grossly properties of properties, like "otherness," with real dependence)? The first issue clearly depends on how we understand the claim about "perishing" (*Vergehen*). The first thing to note about the claim is that, throughout this section Hegel's primary interest is overwhelmingly focused on the second issue, on (2), as a way of denying the sufficiency of the Notion of finite individuals. His central claim, I shall argue, is that the *determinacy* of individual beings cannot be *accounted* for by unreflected or immediate predicates alone, qualities a thing can be said simply to have, without any attention to the implications of having such properties. Individuals cannot be "qualitatively" what they are unless the properties they possess do some contrastive and ultimately relational work, can actually be used to exclude one individual from another. Throughout the discussion of "something/other," "being-for-self" and "being-for-other," and "determination, constitution, limit," the emphasis is on the claim that determinate individuals cannot *be determined* as such (thought as such) unless the properties that specify them are in some actually contrastive relation with the properties of other individuals. And, Hegel wants to show, such a contrastive relation cannot be understood within the limitations of the *Dasein* point of view.

It is in this context, let us say the context of arguing for the "dependence" of the "thought determinations" used to specify finite individuals as such, on other thought determinations, that Hegel introduces the notion of "perishing." More specifically, he introduces it as a "development" of the discussion of "limit" that had preceded it.[29] The general discussion is, we need to recall, the possible ways in which determinate being can be thought determinately, as a something, not an other, as *this* something – a requirement that leads Hegel first to the abstract notion of "determination" in general (*Bestimmung*); then to the more concrete notions of "constitution" (*Beschaffenheit*) and "limit" (*Grenze*), that is, to those determinations or properties that can function to distinguish a something from an other (that "hold the other within it," "brings the otherness . . . into the determination, which consequently, is reduced to constitution" (*WL*, I, 112; *SL*, 124); and so to the idea of a limited thing, a thing determinately limited by not-being, as specified by its determinations, what it is not.[30]

What is most important about these abstract progressions is that Hegel, appropriately, makes no reference to what might seem here a natural way of accounting for this determinate limit, the notion of essence, of those determinations that constitute the thing essentially, and so help us refer to and describe it, and only it (at least qua *this* kind). Within the "unreflected" assumptions of "determinate being," he cannot make use of the notion of descriptive determinations necessary to specify the referent of a referring term, "this instance of E," say, such that if it loses the determinations of E, it ceases to be that finite thing. He makes no such reference because, as we shall see, essence is a "reflected" notion; or, a thing does not "announce" its own essence, it is not an immediately presented determination, but the result of the work of thought, a reflection *on* immediacy.

It is only in the light of this implicit absence, I would suggest, that Hegel can claim that the concept of immediate finitude, *thus defined* or restricted, must be the concept of an altering, finally perishing something. The actual inference from the general account of the role of a negative relation to an other in determining any being as individual, to the "dying" nature of the finite, occurs in quite compressed, elliptical sentences in both versions of the *Logic*. But I believe the context, as sketched previously, reveals what Hegel is getting at. In the *EL* he writes:

> With this [Plato's claim that all is composed of "one" and "other"] is the nature of the finite in general expressed, which as something does not stand over against its other indifferently, but in itself is the other of itself and *therefore changes (hiermit sich verändert)*. (*EL*, 198; *EnL*, 137; my emphasis)

In the *SL*, the inference is even more difficult to understand:

> *Dasein* is determinate; something has a quality and in it is not only determined, but limited. Its quality is its limit, with which it remains, in the first place, an affirmative, stable *Dasein*. But the negation develops, so that the opposition of *Dasein* and its negation as a limit immanent to it, is the in-itself of the something, which something is *thus* (*somit*) only in itself becoming, and this constitutes its finitude. (*WL* I, 116; *SL*, 129)

In both passages, Hegel argues (on the face of it, mysteriously) that if we are thinking of something as a stable *Dasein* opposed by virtue of its determinations to all others, we must "develop" the thought of this negative relation to others and, when we do, we shall come to see it as "in itself" characteristic of the something as such, that opposition is the *Insichsein* of a something, and *therefore* such a something must be understood as an altering, perishing thing. Some notion of "internalizing" the negative relation to any other is supposed to do the work of introducing us to finitude as unstable, mutable, perishing.

To understand this claim, we have to remember that Hegel is investigating the notion of being as such, prior to theoretical or reflective characterization. A thing just has the qualities it immediately has, and those qualities are what we must use to distinguish it as something. But because we have no conceptual ability, as yet, to identify the central or essential, or theoretically relevant, or objective or primary properties, there is no basis for asserting what Hegel continually calls in subsequent sections "affirmative being." Since a thing is contrastable with others by any and all properties that will do the job, *any* reconception of properties alters *the thing's determinate being*. When Hegel says that a thing is "negatively related to itself" and thus must "cease to be," I take him to mean that there is no way conceptually to *assign* any permanent structure to any thing, and therefore the only consistent overall thought of being at this stage is the thought of the radically unstable, the impermanent, as incapable of maintaining itself as such, and so as always "passing away."[31]

Of course, there is no strict deduction here of the necessity for properties to alter, or for their relation to other properties to change, and when Hegel gives that impression, as to be sure he sometimes does, I think we should reject his claim. I am suggesting that the only defensible sense that can be give to what he clearly believes are inferences in the passages cited previously is the sense just attributed to them, and that is, despite more extravagant tendencies, clearly present in the text: that it is the impossibility, within the notion of "immediate being as such," to stabilize any identifying *criteria* of determinacy that ensures that finite being so conceived is radically *un*stable, *conceived* in such a way as to present being as never simply "what it is," but always becoming other than it is, determined as such by other properties. "Finitude" is the only way that thought, given the resources attributed to it thus far, can conceive of a "limited being," a "something" with a determinate constitution or limit. Thought is, as it were, on this self-understanding, stuck with a wide variety of immediate, contingent properties. Because no property can be reflected as essential to the thing, all properties used to determine a limit are contingent, and so thought can only think of the being's determination as contingent. This utter contingency, the possibility of a thing's determining qualities becoming other than they are, or ceasing to be, is what, I think, Hegel means by "finitude" and why he tries to infer its succession from "limit." It also explains why the only real determination possible at this point is characterized by Hegel this way:

> The being-in-itself of the something in its determination reduces itself therefore to an ought-to-be (*Sollen*). (*WL*, I, 120; *SL*, 133)[32]

That is, such a determination is a "mere ought" that *thought* can never actualize if thought must be of immediate being.

Thus, if there is a logical problem in Hegel's introduction of finitude, it does not lie in carelessly confusing the conceptual with the real order.[33] I have tried to show that the issues are conceptual throughout and determined by the overall conceptual strategy of the *Logic*. Hegel himself indicates that if the question is whether he wishes to make some claim about finite reality, or about the unsuccessful attempt by thought to think being finitely, as independent, monadic units, the answer must be the latter. He frequently refers to finitude as "the most stubborn *category* of the understanding" (*WL*, I, 117; *SL*, 129) or explains that "determination and constitution showed themselves as sides of *external reflection*" (*WL*, I, 119; *SL*, 131).[34] In this section, the problem is that although it might be plausible to introduce the notion of the mutability of objects as a likely successor notion to our inability to fix a truly "affirmative" being, strictly speaking, Hegel's inference from the latter to the former is a non sequitur. From our inability to *determine* any permanence in the finite, it does not follow that we are therefore working "implicitly," already with a concept of impermanence, of a mutable finite. Even when we have enough material at our disposal to address the issue of the nature of "dialectical negation," I don't believe we can go beyond a claim for a "plausible next topic" here and claim a "logical inference."

As already indicated, though, the real problem in this section, the core of the charge of a crudely idealistic conflation between thought and thing, occurs in the account of finitude itself, with Hegel's claim to show that finite things are dependent on other things just to be what they are, and his apparent assertion that the nature of that dependence turns on the "relation," supposedly, of "otherness." On such claims rests the attribution to Hegel of the metaphysical theory of "internal relations," as well as the monistic implications of the view, as sketched earlier.

And in describing a thing's exclusion of its other, its not-being what it is not, Hegel does say things such as the following:

> So something relates itself from itself to the other; because being other is posited as its own moment in it. . . . The negation of its other is now the quality of the something, for it is as this sublating of its other that it is something.
>
> (*WL*, I, 113; *SL*, 125)[35]

Moreover, whatever this negative relation to an other turns out to be, it seems to function decisively in Hegel's remarks about the "infinite," in his claim that, because of this dependence of a thing on its other" things cannot be said to be what they are except in infinite relation to all others. Thus "being" finally does not refer to individual beings but to an infinitely self-related whole. It is this claim, that the "negation of its other" is a *quality*, that seems so important and so problematic.

It is problematic, obviously, because it appears to claim that, besides the properties a thing can be said to have "affirmatively," as when a lake is said to be full of water, two thousand meters wide, brackish, and so on, it must also be said to have at least one more quality or property, the property of being other than the meadow it borders. Not only does this open the door to a wild proliferation of properties (the lake is also other than lake B or C or . . . ; it is other than meadow B or C or . . . and other than mountain B or C or . . .), it mistakes properties of the thing for simply not having properties, judgments about which can be made without representing negative states. We do not learn anything *about* S by learning that S is not P, such a standard objection goes; we just learn the *fact* that S is not P, *whatever* S is.

If Hegel is building his rejection of the possibility of, say, a Leibnizean world of independent individuals on this premise, and if he is beginning his own claim about the necessarily interrelated infinite whole on this kind of negative relation, then he appears to be in some trouble.[36] Again, however, if the interpretation I am pursuing is correct, it should not be insignificant that, in the passages quoted previously, Hegel notes that the other is "posited" (*gesetzt*) as a moment of anything or that the negation of the other is described as a "sublating" (*aufheben*). As noted throughout here, such locutions are evidence that Hegel's discussion is still confined to an analysis of the limitations of the *notion* of determinacy available to a metaphysically realistic *theory*. Thinking through the implications of determining a being by reference to its qualities, we reach a point where those properties must be conceived in some contrastive way for them really to determine, to set apart, that being. A mere list of the properties that a *something* has and something else doesn't would presuppose the determinacy of the thing that we are seeking to explain. It must be having these properties that makes this something this and *so* not that, and being able to specify this will ultimately depend on understanding on what *basis* different constitutive properties exclude, render impossible, a thing's being anything but that kind of thing, that qualitative being.

We have reached this point by means of a succession of not always clearly distinguished topics in the *Logic*, although most are discussed adequately only in *SL*: something, determination, constitution, limit, and finally finitude. We begin with the most abstract notion of a determinate something, defined simply by its not being what is other than it. (It is a matter of indifference what is something or other; at this stage, determinateness just means distinguishability from an other.) But such distinguishability presupposes some specific qualitative means for separating a something from an other, some "determination," at the very least, of a list of properties this something has and others do not.

> The *in-itself* into which something is reflected into itself out of its being-for-other is no longer an abstract in-itself, but as negation of its being-for-other is mediated by the latter, which is thus its moment. (*WL*, I, 110; *SL*, 122)

This opaque definition of "determination" confirms that Hegel is moving from the abstract stipulation that a something can be determinate only as contrastable with others to a more concrete "in-itself" that can positively accomplish this differentiation. He pursues this investigation by noting that a mere list of positive determinations will not establish this "in-itself," this qualitative identity. We must be able to distinguish the "external *Dasein*" from such an in-itself determinateness, which Hegel now calls "constitution" (*WL*, I, 111; *SL*, 124). Finally, he returns to the question of determinateness by considering the role of such constituting qualities in "limiting" the thing, distinguishing it from other somethings, now also conceived in terms of their constitutive qualities. This brings him to the full statement of the role of the notion of "limit" in determinate being.

> There is a single determinateness of both [both something and its other] which on the one hand is identical with the being-with-self of the somethings as negation of the negation, and on the other hand, since these negations are opposed to one another as other somethings, conjoins and equally disjoins them through their own nature, each negating the other: this determinateness is limit. (*WL*, I, 113; *SL*, 126)

And the problem that will develop is whether this internally contrastive function can be understood within the "thought of being itself," whether the "other" can truly be posited or thought as a moment of finitude. As indicated earlier, without the introduction of "reflection" (which would be regarded as a subjective distortion of being as it is in itself, at this point in the *Logic*), this task cannot be fulfilled, and determinate being as a "thought determination" reveals itself as incomplete, and a "contradiction" if its completeness is asserted. This is indeed what we should expect – that Hegel is here only beginning to motivate the rational necessity of a reflective determination of being, the necessity for thinking of being as essence and appearance.

Put another way, then, Hegel means just the opposite of claiming, in his own voice, that being other than some other *is* itself a property of the thing (in fact, as we shall see that notion is precisely where the idea of a "spurious infinite" emerges, since, by so considering a thing's relation to an other, we render it indeterminately, or "indifferently" other than an infinity of others). Hegel means instead to insist that the properties immediately attributed to a thing must themselves be capable of some contrastive work, some determinate way of excluding other properties concretely, and so of distinguishing the thing from other things that have such properties, and that the thought of immediate *Dasein* cannot accomplish this task.

That this interpretation is correct is confirmed most clearly in passages from Division 2, where Hegel is explaining why the "otherness" or contrast at issue in Division 1 begins to be more correctly understood with the notion of "opposition" (*Entgegensetzung*), about which he writes:

> In opposition the different does not only have an other over against it, but *its* other. Ordinary consciousness regards different things as indifferent with respect to each other. Thus we say: I am a man, and around me are air, water, animals, and all sorts of things. But the goal of philosophy is to banish indifference and to understand the necessity of things, so that the other appears standing over against *its* other. So for example inorganic nature is not to be considered just as something other than the organic, but as the necessary other of it. (*EL*, 246; *EnL* 174; my emphasis)

If we look at Hegel's account this way, it becomes clearer why he thinks that the general view of "finitude" is radically incomplete, and so "contradicts" itself when it is assumed to be complete. It is incomplete because understanding the contrastive effect that having a property carries with it requires that we understand *why* having such a property functions as it does in prohibiting having others. If something is an acid, then it is a *feature of its acidity* that determines which other possible such states the thing determinately cannot be, like a base, and which others cannot be excluded from possibly being that kind of thing, on the basis of that determination alone, like being this acid or that acid. It is not by having a property that a thing can be determinately limited and distinguished from other things. To understand such determination, we need to understand the ground of a being's possible "external" properties, including the relations with other beings that such a ground makes possible or excludes. But on the assumptions of being, things just are as they are, independent of any ground or relation to others.

We are thus brought to the point where the thought of determinacy as a function of qualitative properties requires a more concrete understanding of the various contrasting relations among those properties. But in this context, there is no ontological status possible for such relations. The only "finite" way in which this "exclusion necessity" (necessary for determinacy) *is* understood is to make "having properties other than some other thing" itself an immediate property of a thing, but this move is precisely, Hegel is trying to show, the most concrete evidence of the insufficiency of the thought of radically independent determinate beings. With no more reflective understanding of "negative" determinacy, or the ground of the contrastive effects of property possession, a thing can only be said to be "indifferently" other than everything, infinitely other than everything that it is not, and that is just what Hegel means by a bad or incoherent infinite. In this case, it is incoherent because the introduction of such an infinite defeats the original purpose; a thing being infinitely "other than all it is not" offers up no determining mark therewith at all.[37]

Further, something like this must be what Hegel has in mind since, neither in the *SL* nor in the *EL*, does he argue that the contradictions developed in the notion of real determinacy "pass over" into true infinity, or what he, Hegel, will mean by infinity (a concept that will require the idea of thought's self-determination). At this point, all that the insufficiency of the finite yields, given the point of view of being itself, is the "spurious infinite" of the indefinite alternation of finite determination, and infinite otherness, infinite as the endless progression of excluded determinations.

In the passage where this is discussed most directly, Hegel is, unfortunately, at his most opaque. The gist of the passage is that whenever a limit is proposed as a determining feature, "We pass from the finite to the infinite," we understand the thing so limited as infinitely other than what is not so limited. Hegel calls this the "void beyond the finite." But, he goes on, "because this infinite remaining aloof on its own side is itself limited" – because, that is, such an infinite is itself defined in such a limited way, as what is infinitely determined to be other than such a finite limited thing – "there arises a limit," that is, a new limit or candidate determination. "And so we are faced with a relapse into the previous determination which had been sublated in vain." And as we might expect, "so again there arises the void, the nothing, in which similarly the said determination, a new limit, is encountered – and so on to infinity" (*WL*, I, 130; *SL*, 141).

There is thus nothing surprising in the fact that, within the limitations of the thought of being as it is in itself, or "positive," immediate being, the required contrast, or negative relation to others, necessary for determinacy, can only be thought as itself a positive property, so that a thing is conceived as in a spuriously infinite relation with all other things. Eventually, in this process of thought's self-determination, the immediacy of this notion of reality will have to be abandoned before such a contrastive relation can be explained. A reflective reliance on essence, or ground, or causal laws, the determinations of "reflection" in general, will make possible far more successfully a coherent self-understanding of what there will be called the "identity" and "difference" of any object of thought.

Likewise, understanding this section as sketched previously should make clearer the programmatic and elusive nature of Hegel's remarks about the "true infinite." Although it would be more than a little surprising if, in this initial section of the work, we could make out clearly the full implications of the Hegelian infinite (and must more surprising indeed if Hegel intended to introduce his full account as a result of the insufficiencies of the notion of finitude), it is nevertheless important to notice what Hegel does say about that notion. For what he says is consistent with his use of the notion in the Introduction and with the interpretation of his idealism presented here. He had earlier introduced true infinity as referring to "thought's pure self-relation"; it expressed the infinity of full or absolute self-consciousness. Indeed, with that in mind, the shape of the progression of his whole argument in the *Logic* begins to come into view at this point. If it turns out that the possibility of a coherent notion of determinate being requires that such beings be determinately contrastable with other beings, on the basis of some identification of their *Insichsein* or in-itself constitution, and if it turns out that such an *Insichsein* and the contrastive determinacy it makes possible can be understood only as a *product* of reflection, as thought's determination of the mediated "essence" behind immediate appearances, then the pivotal point in Hegel's *Logic* will be an understanding of *how* such products or reflected thought determinations are possible. As we would expect by now, he will try to show that, just as immediate determinations of being must be embedded in a reflective account of essence, such reflective products depend on, are embedded in, thought's pure self-determinations, are ultimately grounded in nothing other than the most universal self-determinations of thought itself, or thought determined by nothing other than "other" thought determinations. It is in this last section that we should encounter what the Introduction first called "infinity" and that should be alluded to in these remarks about true infinity.

Such allusions are indeed made. Hegel even says explicitly, when introducing the "infinite in general":

> At the name of the infinite, the mind and spirit light up, for in the infinite, spirit is not only abstractly at home (*bei sich*), but raises itself to itself, to the light of its own thinking, its universality, its freedom. (*SL*, 137–8; *WL*, I, 126)

Moreover, the other frequently mentioned characteristic of the true infinite is also quite consistent with this approach. The infinite is not opposed to the finite but represents the finite's own self-transcendence. If the previous passage is any indication that this will mean that pure thought is not "all there is," as if there were no finite individuals, or that pure thought determines the real, be the real as it may. Rather, if successful, Hegel will show that infinity is the "truth" of finitude, that the determinations of finitude required for there to be finite individuals ultimately themselves depend logically on the self-transformations of thought, on Notional conditions.[38] And this is indicated when Hegel himself introduces the notion of ideality by saying that "Ideality can be called the quality of infinity" (*WL*, I, 140; *SL*, 150) or that "ideal being is the finite as it is in the true infinite" (*WL*, I, 139; *SL*, 149–50). Accordingly, Hegel does indeed mean to point to his eventual thesis, that finite objects cannot be conceived as radically independent, but he is, I am maintaining, for the most part quite consistent in arguing for this by showing how the determinacy of any such object requires a conceptual structure not limited to a series of immediate qualities, but one that makes possible the various contrastive relations necessary for such determinacy. In the language of the last section of the *Logic*, "individuals" are related to each other "in" the universality on the Notion, and not by virtue of any realist, metaphysical relation with each other.

Although a full interpretation of what such a Notionally determined rather than traditionally ontological "relation" amounts to must await a consideration of that section of the *Logic* it is important here to note why, just from what has already been examined, it is so inaccurate to associate Hegel's position with a traditional monism, particularly one that depends on the thesis of "internal relations." The central claim of such a position, that there is only one substance, often also entails the claim that all parts or determinations of that substance are what they are only in their relation (and even possible relations) to all other determinations of that substance, that there exist no relations apart from, ontologically independent of, relata. On such an account, the identity conditions of any putative object necessarily involve that object's relation with all the objects, and vice versa. However, as we have just seen, Hegel completely rejects the adequacy of the realist notions of substance, property, and relation on which such an account is based. He clearly believes that such a position reduces individual objects to merely abstract determinations of substance and so sacrifices any chance of accounting for their qualitative determinacy. Thus, although it has become a kind of cliché in textbook summaries of Hegel to note that he believes that "finite things" and "other" finite things are linked in a monistic system of internal relations, there is a great deal of evidence, much of it compellingly summarized by Horstmann, against attributing such a "Bradleyean" view to Hegel.[39]

But Hegel introduces these remarks on the "true infinite" only to make clear its difference from the "bad" or "spurious" infinite to which the thought of determinate being is led.[40] And it is this problem, sometimes called the problem of the "indifference" of a thing to its determinations, that continues to arise throughout Hegel's assessment of unreflected or immediate being. He suggests next that the only immediate candidate for a thing's "in-itself" determinateness appropriate to this level of thought is "quantity," a calculation of a thing's determinate being that can in some sense be said to take in all of a thing's qualities at once, to think them together in another way, to specify the thing-with-its-qualities not contrastively or negatively, but by degree, by specifying a thing's "how much" as an immediate standard of contrast with other things' "how much."[41] It will turn out, though, that quantitative determination is a "mere collection of numerical facts" (*EL*, 224; *EnL*, 157) if such quantitative specifications cannot be used to think a thing concretely. For Hegel this means understanding how quantitative alteration alters a thing's quality as well (the way two substances can combine in specific quantities to form a third that is qualitatively different from the sum of the first two, that has itself qualities neither of the first two did). Understanding this is understanding "measure," the relations between quantitative and qualitative alteration and relation. But since we are still restricted to immediate being, the ground of these determinations is as elusive as ever, and we are able only to report an endless series of quantitative/qualitative measures, none of which successfully isolates a determinate being in its interactive and contrastive relations with others. We need to consider a thing's essence to get such determinacy. Hegel introduces this "moment" of thought, and sums up the whole problem of being, when thought "in itself," in a passage of unusual clarity:

> things really are not what they immediately show themselves. So the matter at hand [in *Logic*] is also not concluded with a mere roving about from one quality to the other, and with a mere advance from the qualitative to the quantitative and back again; but there is in things something permanent [*bleibendes*] and this is, first of all, essence. (*EL*, 232; *EnL*, 163)

Such a claim concludes Hegel's "logical" attack on the "positivity" of being, on the internal coherence, for reflective thought, of the very notion of "immediate being." As we have seen, it is not an attack on the possibility of an extraconceptual reality "in itself," but on the internal coherence of the notion of such an object as an object of thought. Such a putative object is, from the start of the "*Seinslogik*" to the end, indeterminate, "available" to us only if we "rove about" (*Herumtreiben*) endlessly in infinite qualitative determinations. Thought must fix for itself the categorial structure that makes possible determinate objects of its intentions if it is to have objects. How it does so makes up the second half of "objective logic."

9
Reflected being

1. Essence and the problem of idealism

The "Logic of Being" had been an account of the interrelated concepts necessarily involved in the attempt to think being as it is in itself, immediately. It had been, that is, a logic of the concepts and the relation among concepts involved in the attempt to think determinately about reality, when reality is generally construed within a certain kind of theory, a precritical realism. However, aside from a "bad," infinite list of qualities, or a quantitative specification that turns out to be "indifferently" related to its qualitative implications, determinacy is just what the project of being had not achieved. (If the object of thought is so stipulated, there could not be thought of such an object, and so in the idealist sense of the claim as I am attributing it to Hegel, there could not "be" such an "actual" object.) Such determination, it was argued, required more than the specification of directly apprehended qualities, qualities that one object had and another did not. The object itself would not be picked out unless it it were (impossibly) distinguished from literally everything by such a procedure. We need to know the ground by virtue of which we can claim that having such properties distinguishes this thing as such and can be used to contrast a "qualitative thing" (a kind of thing) with its contraries. And such a basis for the contrastive use of properties involves more than attention to the properties themselves; it involves, we now hear, what Hegel calls an "act of reflection." Some kind of independent reflective activity (logically and causally independent of what can be directly apprehended), thought's own projection of the structure within which the determinacy of its objects can be fixed, is required in order for thought to have objects (i.e., to be able to make cognitive claims about objects). It is, Hegel now wants to argue, due to thought's reflective activity that a thing can be known to have an identity (to be a possible object of experience, in more Kantian terms) through its different appearances, and the terms of this identity-fixing activity thus need to be analyzed. It is simply such an activist, theorizing "approach to the Absolute," as Hegel might put it, that is the subject matter of Book II.

Initially, however, such a sweeping topic seems to take in so much as to be very nearly unintelligible, and the situation is made more complicated still by the place of such an account in Hegel's overall argument. Again informally, this analysis is supposed to contribute to the claim that, in some sense to be specified in Book III, this self-examination of spontaneous thought is gradually coming to understand that the "origin" of the notions fundamentally necessary for it to think a world reflectively can only be somehow internal to the autonomous development of thought itself, understood as a dialectically interrelated, historically progressive, socially mediated activity. However, in Book II, such a fully idealist claim is still only implicit in the determinations of reflection. And this intermediary status for the "Logic of Essence" can often cause serious interpretive problems as one tries to figure out what Hegel is trying to affirm and deny (or dialectically overcome) in his account of these issues. For one thing, although reflection introduces a large number of Cartesian, Lockean, and Kantian themes, themes that appear deeply connected with the "subjective" term in philosophy, this is still what Hegel calls an "objective" logic. That does not mean that it is, like Book I, an "entity" logic. Essence and appearance, say, are not understood as separate beings, but as "moments" of any being that reflection can identify and understand. But the activity of thinking under examination is still governed by an assumption of dependence, an orientation toward its objects that separates and categorizes the dual moments of "being itself." "Essence," Hegel notes at the beginning of the section in *EL*, "is the Notion as posited (*gesetzter*) Notion, the determinations in essence are only relative, not yet simply reflected in itself; accordingly the Notion is not yet the Notion for itself" (*EL*, 231; *EnL*, 162).[1] As we shall see, it is often the case that reflection's misunderstanding of its own ground (in *the* Notion) and the status of its results is what leads it into paradoxes and dilemmas that force revisions in its self-understanding until a speculative, nonreflective account can begin to be given. As he notes, again in the *EL*:

> The sphere of essence thus turns out to be a still imperfect combination of immediacy and mediation. . . . And so it is also the sphere of the posited contradiction, which was only implicit in the sphere of Being. (*EL*, 235; *EnL*, 165)

It should also be part of the task of this section to introduce such a final speculative dimension carefully enough, with enough attention to the problem of determinate appearances, the contingent world of "nonthought," that this final claim about the truly independent self-determination of thought loses its extravagant tone, its wildly idealist indifference to the world as, in *some* sense at least, the ultimate reference and arbiter of our notions. If, that is, as I have been arguing, Hegel's position is not simply wildly idealistic.

Such a general sketch of Hegel's project in Book II can, however broad-brushed, now give us a way to introduce the major problems his account must deal with. As noted earlier, we have supposedly come to understand the insufficiencies of a realist conception of "positive" being, somehow inherently determinate, accessible either to sensation or to pure reason as it is in itself. Contrary to the *PhG*, this has been demonstrated not by an analysis of the kind of experience such a Notion would entail, but by attention to the conceptual coherence of the Notion itself, to the question of whether the account of determinacy implied therein is adequate or requires presuppositions other than those defensible within the Notion itself. Hegel now wants to explain what these new presuppositions are, and so is introducing and proposing to analyze a revolutionary reorientation in Western philosophy. Historically, he is trying to account for and then explore the modern Cartesian and skeptical attack on the reliability of the commonsense orientation from the given, sensible looks of things so important for classical thought. Merely "being there," the immediate, must now be viewed as only an *appearance*, as other than what there really or essentially is. As is well known, however, Hegel does not believe in incommensurable, revolutionary paradigm shifts (in philosophy or science), and so tries to connect the insurmountable problems created in the "Being Logic" with the determinate reorientation proposed in the "Essence Logic." He does so in what is for him a typical way. He announces that the results of the "Being Logic" should be characterized first in the strictly negative terms we actually end up with: What had been *Sein*, "being itself," is now indistinguishable from *Schein*, "illusory being." That is, all we end up with in thinking through the implications of the logic of being are negative results, insufficiencies. That is what *Schein* means. What there *immediately* is cannot *be* what there is; it is only illusory being, a mere show of determinacy, or a vanishing determinacy. As we shall see, Hegel's next move, the one that is supposed to establish a dialectical, necessary connection between these fundamental notions, is to argue that this very "negativity," or indeterminacy, or insufficiency, is *itself* impossible (in the sense of incoherent, impossible to understand) unless that "inherent negativity" is understood as itself already dependent on a further condition, ultimately the activity of reflection itself. Presumably, we wouldn't be able to understand the results of the "Logic of Being," we couldn't understand its insufficiency, unless we were already able to use (or now find that we can use and have been using) the basic appearance/essence distinction.[2]

There is certainly a great deal packed into these opening transitions in Book II, especially since this first major transition in the book clearly reveals something of how Hegel thinks the "teleology" of the Notion, the internal self-development of thought, works. But aside from that issue (which comes up explicitly as a theme in Book III), this kind of approach to what Hegel considers the modern philosophy of reflection, introduces a number of problems just in its own terms. First, what precisely does Hegel mean by "appearances"? To view any directly apprehended (i.e., nonreflectively or nontheoretically determined) object as an appearance might mean any number of things. Modernity aside for the moment, the notion itself has such a long history that Hegel's use of it could refer to appearance or *ta phainomena* as wholly "unreal," as in Parmenides, as of a lower degree of reality, as in Plato, as not yet fully real, as in Aristotle; or it might mean an object on one side of the "veil of perception," a mental state or phenomenon; or it might mean a nonmental object, but one known only in terms of subjective, finite forms of knowledge, as in Kant; or it might simply mean that we know only illusions, as in mirages and hallucinations.

It is hard to identify where Hegel fits into such a possible spectrum because his introduction of the problem with a discussion of *Schein* is so abstract and idiosyncratic. In initially describing the problem he thinks he is working on, he portrays *Schein* in a wholly conceptual way, in terms of his logical terminology alone, as a kind of "immediately self-canceling object of thought," an object that cannot be grasped without being "negated," or referred beyond itself to a mediated, thought-determined structure of explanation. As Henrich puts it, Hegel now shifts his notion of an immediate object of thought, shifts the meaning of immediacy away from the relationless positivity of the logic of being to a notion of "immediate self-relation."[3] This is, I think, true, but at this point in Hegel's presentation, it is extremely hard to figure out just what it means.[4]

The self-relation in question is the negative one noted earlier: the immediate insufficiency of such an object, its elusiveness when considered apart from reflective determination. But this is still such an abstract characterization that it is not clear how we are to understand this "insufficiency." We have seen, from the beginning of the *Logic*, that Hegel accepts as his central problem an adequate understanding of "determinacy." In fact, this looms as a problem as soon as he accepts wholesale so many of Fichte's revisions of Kant's understanding/sensibility distinction but rejects Fichte's solution. The project of a speculative logic, as we have seen throughout, had been to show how thought can and must "determine itself." For Hegel, the way this problem is formulated is by reference to the problem of "differentiation," or, in his logical terms, the "negative." An object of thought is determinate if the terms of its determination can successfully pick it out as other than all others, as not what it is not. (Again, all of this is, of course, what Kant thought impossible for thought. Only logically possible, not real, determinacy, could be achieved by thought alone.) Here Hegel wants to understand the possibility of determinacy in a more satisfactory way than as a specification by contingent properties or by an external relation to an other. Now determinacy is supposed to be "self-relating," or to be originally due to the thing's "internal" essence, or primary qualities, or substance and substance modifications. The idea of an object being, directly and *immediately*, only a "partial" or insufficient manifestation of what the object truly is, is, I take it, what Henrich is trying to capture with this notion of a self-relating negativity. Hegel is thus beginning to point to the constitutive role of reflection in such an apprehension of "illusory being" by noting the inadequacy of any realist construal of *Schein*. Conequently, he ends up with his incredibly compressed formulations of what *Schein* logically involves. He is trying to say everything at once (again), and so describes its insufficiency in ways that cannot possibly be clear on this point and will require much explanation later. Here is one of Hegel's typical formulations of the unusual character of this immediacy:

> Or, since the self-relation is precisely this negating of negation, the *negation as negation* is present in such wise that it has its being in its negatedness, as illusory being. Here, therefore, the other is not *being with a negation*, or limit, but *negation with the negation*. (*WL*, II, 13; *SL*, 399)

Second, *how* is the mediated ground of such immediacy, the essence of appearances, to be determined? Hegel himself states this problem in the introductory remarks in *SL*:

Essence as the completed return of being into itself is at first indeterminate essence. The determinations of being are sublated in it; they are contained in essence in principle [*an sich*] but are not posited in it. Absolute essence in this simplicity with itself has no determinate being [*Dasein*]. But it must develop determinate being, for it is both in and for itself, i.e., it differentiates the determinations which it contains in itself. (*WL*, II, 4–5; *SL*, 390)

How we are to "develop" these determinations (or "go over to *Dasein*," as the passage literally reads) will be one of the major issues of the section.

I should also note here something clearly assumed in the preceding interpretation of Hegel's problem: We ought not to be misled by the relatively archaic language of "essence" and, later, "identity," and "form." As is manifest throughout the text, Hegel uses *Wesen* as his designation for "reflected being" in general, that is, to specify the issue of the contributions made to the possibility of a determinate object of thought by thought itself, by reflection. The fact that "essence" is understood as a product of reflection, and that Hegel discusses the issue from the start in terms of the (for him) Kantian problematic of "immediacy" and "mediation," supports the interpretation here presented – that Hegel is introducing his version of "subjective conditions" for objects, the fundamental, purely determined conceptual structure indispensable in the differentiation, the qualitative identification, necessary for there to be determinate objects of cognition. Like Kant, he is interested in demonstrating that such essences are neither merely subjective ("posited" is his word), be the world as it may, nor derived in all cases empirically ("externally reflected" is his term). If it would not explain the obscure by the more obscure, it would be appropriate to characterize the Hegelian problem of essence as the Kantian problem of the "a priori synthesis."[5]

But these are familiar and obvious problems in any division of being into appearing and true being. Explaining what we mean by attributing a "negative" or illusory status to the world as it immediately appears, full of "whole" objects that are not really whole but parts, solid objects that are not solid, apparently linked events that are not linked, an "inner life" that is not really inner, and so forth, and explaining what status the nonappearing, or essential, should be understood to have (as truly real, most useful to believe, best confirmed, and so on) are not new to Hegel's inquiry. The Hegelian version of such issues is quickly apparent in the comprehensive solution to both, and to the whole division, that Hegel announces in the beginning and pursues throughout. Although he maintains from the beginning that essence is "posited" (*gesetztes*) and "mediated" (*vermitteltes*), and so "confronts illusory being," he also claims throughout the section that what we must finally understand is that reflection's duality of essence and appearance can be overcome, that "illusory being is, however, essence's own positing" (*WL*, II, 7; *SL*, 393).[6] Or, "illusory being (*Schein*) is not something external to or other than essence; on the contrary it is essence's own illusory being. The showing (*Scheinen*) of essence in illusory being is reflection" (*WL*, II, 7; *SL*, 394). As is typical with Hegel, we begin with this putative separation (or "standing over against," *gegenüberstehen*) of essence and appearance, somehow come to understand the insufficiency of their separation and the true dialectical nature of their unity, comprehensively articulated in the category of "actuality," *Wirklichkeit*. Then, in turn, we shall come to understand the truth of that unity in the Notion's self-determination. Thus the simplest version of the entire argument of the *Logic*: For there to be determinate being, objects about which possibly true or false claims can be made, we must be able to distinguish a reflected essence from the illusory being that immediately appears. This essence, even though somehow subjective, a product of reflection, is not imposed on appearances or merely posited, a Hegelian claim much in the fashion of Kant's (usual) claim that his "subjective conditions" are not merely imposed on a manifold. And yet, the basic essential structure of possible appearances is not fixed, or knowable transcendentally, a priori. What will count as such an essential structure depends on the development of thought's self-consciousness about itself, and especially on the "ends" or purposes that thought sets for itself, whatever such a teleology will turn out to be.

The basic claim in this argument (basic, anyway, for the view of idealism I am attributing to Hegel), the identity of essence and appearance, although couched in what Hegel admits to be the most difficult language of his philosophy, and although paradoxical and peculiar, could easily qualify as that single claim in the *Logic* most important for properly understanding everything else Hegel wants to say. Indeed, contrary to many popular interpretations of Hegel (the ones with world spirit behind the scenes, pulling the historical strings), it appears that the major point of this section is to argue that there is literally *nothing* "beyond" or "behind" or responsible for the human experience of the world of appearances, and certainly not an Absolute Spirit. There must be some way of understanding the totality of appearances themselves as "absolute," without reliance on the familiar representations from traditional metaphysics or theology, if this unusual identity claim is to be properly understood.[7]

Thus, in one of his few informal characterizations of the problem he takes himself to be solving, Hegel states in the *EL*, that he agrees with those who insist that a man's conduct cannot be adequately understood simply by noticing what he does. His character, or inner self, is not necessarily revealed in these acts. Because, say, he performs unjust acts, it does not follow that he is essentially an unjust man. The concept we have to construct, his character (or essence), cannot be adequately constructed by simply adding together, synthesizing, the external appearances. Yet, Hegel says, he also believes that "the only means by which the essence and the inner self can be verified is their appearance in outward reality," and he expresses his usual suspicion that those who retreat too far into the unobserved inner life do so only to elude responsibility for the consequences of their acts. The fact that this character or essence depends on reflection, is not immediately given, does not mean that we are free to determine that essence independently of one's acts. All of this certainly sounds like the position one would like to defend (say, somewhere between Kant on the primacy of intention and Sartre on the primacy of action in the world, but without the theoretical vagueness of Aristotle), but *how* can such a "dialectical" position be defended?

This central thesis, that essence "shows itself in its appearances," also returns us to a familiar problem in Hegel's idealism. For one thing, the topic of reflection raises again the central issue in this interpretation of that idealism: the self-conscious spontaneity of thought. "Reflection" is simply the *Logic*'s name for that topic, and this discussion of it is one of the most comprehensive, if most abstract, that Hegel provides. Accordingly, since essence is a product of reflection, a thought determination, any claim for a unity or even identity between such a wholly theoretical construct and the world of existing appearances returns us again to what has been throughout a constant suspicion about Hegel's idealism. Given that Hegel calls his final position on "actuality" "the unity of essence and existence" (*WL*, II, 156; *SL*, 529), it would appear again that Hegel is either defending some kind of pre-Kantian rationalism, and so, in Kant's specific terminology, "amphibolously" confusing the conditions of thought with the conditions of existence,[8] or he is appealing to a notion of metaphysical dependence between existence and essence, a view of existing things as created by, or posited by, Absolute Spirit, assuring that the results of Absolute Spirit's rational reflection coincide with what exists. At least, it is this dimension of the many problems raised by Hegel's account of reflective thought that I want to pursue in the following discussion.

In sum, Hegel believes that he has formulated a comprehensive perspective on the activity of reflection and its chief dualism, essence and appearance, and can show us a way out of the paradoxes created by such a dualism, can reveal the true identity of essence and appearance. Since, I have argued, Hegel is also clearly progressing toward a claim about the final origin of reflective determinations of reality in thought alone, this problem of essence and its relation to existence or appearance should be understood in terms of the idealism problematic; here in terms of the problem of reconciling what Hegel says about the independence and purity of thought's self-determination with its objectivity, with the claim that such results can finally be understood as "standing over against" what there simply and contingently is, but "showing itself" within such appearances. What is such a showing? How are appearances understood? How does reflection, according to Hegel, determine what is at first merely an indeterminate essence? And can the final unity of essence and existence in actuality be understood as something other than an amphibolous version of what Kant criticized in Leibniz and Spinoza?

2. Reflection and immediacy

As just noted, the theme of "reflection" stretches so far back into Hegel's early philosophical career that his elaborate treatment of it in the *SL* has been understandably much commented on. But it is not just for historical reasons that so much interpretive energy has been invested in this book of the *Logic*. As we shall see, virtually all of the major problems raised by Hegel's idealism begin to receive here what Hegel himself clearly regards as a final, decisive hearing. Most important is the theme introduced earlier, where Hegel had claimed that essence must be understood not as an indeterminate *je ne sais quoi* but as determinate. From the perspective on Hegel defended in this study, this issue of determinacy is indeed decisive. Simply put, if we follow Hegel (and Fichte) in arguing that the spontaneous self-relation inherent in all conscious apprehending makes impossible a secure separation between the activity of pure thought and some a priori form of the given, we face not only Kant's Deduction problem anew (the objective validity of pure thought determinations) but a different version of problems he confronted in the Metaphysical Deduction and Schematism. In Kant, the pure functions of thought, the rules of judgment, can only be understood as determinate concepts of objects by means of a detailed reflection on the possibility of experience, and that reflection is everywhere guided by consequences implied by the existence of pure forms of sensible intuition. Ultimately, for Kant, formal functions of judgment can be determinately understood as the "essence" of the appearing world of objects thanks *only* to a unique kind of representation of all possible objects given *to* thought, schemata, yet another reincarnation of those problematic pure intuitions.[9] It is only by reference to such a formal determination of all possible objects of thought that the objective determinacy of specific categories can be defended.[10] As we have seen in many different ways by now, Hegel does not believe that such a "mediated" representation of immediacy is possible. But if that is so, how can reflection "determine itself," produce a determinate "essence" of appearances, if not by reference to independent conditions of immediacy or to the immediately given itself, as in empiricist theories of abstraction or induction? We know by now that Hegel proposes some kind of "intraconceptual" theory of such determination; that he believes a concept's determinate role in fixing the thought of *objects* is in some way a function of its relation to other *concepts* and of the proper understanding of the status of that conceptual system's objectivity; but that abstract program needs much more explanation in this book and the next. If, in other words, we abandon all of Kant's gestures in the direction of the *theoretical* role of immediacy in the determinations of pure reflection, whence such determinacy and why claim that we have still saved rather than simply ignored the appearances (indeed, that we can *identify* reflection's results with appearances)?

The key to Hegel's answer, of course, must involve his own understanding of immediacy and its relation to reflective activity. (In less logical terminology, such a theme introduces how Hegel wants to reinterpret the fundamental notions of truth, objectivity, and rationality, all now understood in Fichtean terms: the nature of the constraint imposed by thought or theorizing on its own spontaneous activity.) And that is another reason why this section is so important. We now get a chance to ask directly a question that has come up in different ways a number of times: If Hegel is to be understood as a thoroughgoing critic of any reliance on the immediate in grounding or directing or determining knowledge, if he challenges the very possibility of a purely given, an exclusively self-presenting manifold, an immediately certain experience, and so forth, what then *is* the role of immediacy, even if not pure or exclusive or independent, *within* his systematic account? From the critique of Fichte on in his career, Hegel has been clearly struggling to find a satisfactory way of understanding "mediated immediacy" rather than abandoning the notion in some wholesale way. He takes another stab at the issue, his most important, I think, with the notion of *Schein* and the relation between *Schein* and reflection.[11]

Hegel wants to characterize immediate being, what putatively should be just "there" for thought (*Dasein*), as itself immediately insufficient, or, as noted previously, as somehow immediately self-negating or self-canceling. His complex formulations in his introduction of the notion of *Schein* all point toward such a new notion of the indeterminacy of the immediate, new because now not the result of the inadequacy of Book I's ontological realism, but an immediate being in which that indeterminacy is itself an immediate characteristic. So, he writes:

> The being of illusory being consists solely in the sublatedness of being, in its nothingness; this nothingness it has in essence and apart from essence, illusory being is not. It is the negative posited as negative. (*WL*, II, 9; *SL*, 395)

The paradoxical nature of such a claim is even clearer in other formulations, as when he writes that "illusory being is this immediate not-qualitative being (*nicht Dasein*) in the determinateness of being" or when, a few lines later, summing up the paradox pointedly, *Schein* is said to be "reflected immediacy, that is, immediacy which is only by means of its negation" (*WL*, II, 9; *SL*, 395–6).

If we adopt here the most plausible reading of this claim, it is hard to see how we have done much more than restate Kant's founding claim in a perversely dense way. That is, if we attempt to categorize any possible object of thought (as usual, throughout, construed quite broadly as cognitive consciousness, a possibly true or false intending) as an "indeterminate appearance" or a self-canceling immediate being, one that cannot be determined as such, in its immediacy, it appears that we have just restated as an impossible alternative Kant's claim that intuitions without concepts are blind (in Hegelian language, "indeterminate," or "the immediate *nicht Dasein* in the determinateness of being"). There *are* intuitions, according to Kant; he does not claim that they are impossible. But although components of the determinate thought of anything objective, they are not themselves possible objects of thought.[12]

But this interpretation would just restate a reflective claim about the impossibility of intuitional or immediate knowledge. We will seem to have only a programmatic statement of what Hegel wants – some new version of the post-Kantian immediacy/mediation problem, a way of understanding the mediating activity of reflection that involves neither the metaphor of subjective imposition, and so estrangement from the world in itself, nor the rationalist metaphor of the mind's eye, in which the mediated structure of the immediate is intellectually (more "clearly") intuited. Perhaps the account of reflection itself will make this clearer.

There are two important components in Hegel's initial account of reflection; he distinguishes three basic types of reflective activity (positing, external, and determining reflection), and he identifies what he calls the "essentialities" of reflection, basically, the "laws" of all reflective thought, as they were sometimes called (identity, difference, and contradiction). In the first discussion, we begin to see what Hegel had meant by calling *Schein* a kind of self-negating immediacy. First, despite the extreme generality of his earlier remarks, he now tells us that by "illusory being" he had simply meant to refer to "the phenomenon of skepticism," and so to an object that was rightly characterized as an "immediacy," but "not an indifferent being that would still be, apart from its determinateness and connection with the subject" (*WL*, II, 9; *SL*, 396). This remark and the paragraph that follows it help considerably to clarify the object of Hegel's attention here. For although a "subjective" skepticism considers the immediate objects of experience illusory because somehow subject dependent (and the consequence of Book I had been to insist on the unavoidability of this subject dependence, and so to raise the problem of skepticism), it also admits that such appearances are *determinate*, even if determined by exclusively mentalistic, ideational, or phenomenal predicates. For Hegel this means that they are "immediately" determinate, and that is the source of all the problems, since according to Hegel, determinacy must be a result, or mediated, a negation of the immediate. Hence skepticism's correct insistence on the "phenomenal" nature of all experience, or the "subjective" character of experience, nevertheless does not go far enough in exploring the potential contradiction in its own formulations; it leaves unexplained the conditions under which any immediate datum can be determinately identified as such, whether as this impression, or empirical manifold, or monadic representation.[13] Indeed, using Leibniz as an example, Hegel points to the unexplained nature of the determinate origin of a monad's immediate representations; they seem to arise simply "like bubbles" (*WL*, II, 10; *SL*, 396).[14]

This is why he refers to illusory being in the incredibly opaque way quoted on page 204; it is a "negating of its own negation." Its original "negativity" refers to the illusion problem inherent in the skeptic's charge (the appearances are not or cannot be known to be, what there is). But these immediate objects, supposedly the only origin and ultimate arbiter of reflective thought, are also *self*-negating in Hegel's sense because their supposed independence and ultimacy are self-defeating, cannot be maintained successfully by the skeptic. The "other" of this immediate illusory being (here the mediated or reflected) is thus not external to it, as another object (e.g., as was the case with "limit"), but a characteristic of the immediacy itself. In this case, that means that the determinacy of any immediate *Schein* already ensures that, put as paradoxically as Hegel does, *Schein* only appears to be *Schein*, the immediate subjective content of consciousness.[15] As a determinate content it cannot but be mediated, requiring an account of what turn out yet again to be reflective or spontaneous mediations. [Again, in Hegel's language: "Here therefore the other is not being with a negation, or limit, but negation with the negation" (*WL*, II, 13; *SL*, 399). He then goes on to say, somewhat more clearly, that this means that *Schein* is *not*, as claimed by skeptics and subjective idealists, "a first from which a beginning was made and which passed over into its negation, nor is it an affirmatively present substrate that moves through reflection".] Put one final way, skepticism as Hegel understands it is simply correct; there are no "essences" beyond or behind the appearances, at least none that can do any cognitive work. There are just the appearances; but the necessary determinacy of these supposedly immediate appearances indicates that essence, or some fixed structure that will allow identification and so determinacy, already "shines through" such appearances, is an inherent, necessary characteristic for illusory being just to be, and so requires its own account. That is, illusory being, immediate appearances, themselves can be said to be determinate only as a moment of the subject's *self*-determining. Or "Illusory being is the same thing as reflection." [To be sure, Hegel's casual use of the language of essence and reflection at this point is incredibly premature. He begins here flirting with a problem that emerges often throughout Book II, what we might call a conflation of an argument for the necessity of "mediation" in general (conceptual activity, *überhaupt*) with a case for *essential* mediation, the determinate categorial conditions required for there to be determinate "thought objects." He will have something to say about this issue later, but I do not think it is satisfactory.]

Indeed, as Hegel moves further into his account of reflection, he becomes clearer that the immediacy of subjective appearances should not be understood as their incorrigibility, or noninferentially warranted status. Their determinacy means that they cannot be immediate in that sense. As putative objects of consciousness, they are mediated. The particular immediacy they point to is *reflection's* immediate *self*-determination.[16] And this will pose its own problems as Hegel tries to account for what appears to be a kind of ungrounded, self-generated determinacy. He puts all this in his usually infelicitous way by telling us that "the self-relation of the negative is, therefore, its return into itself," and so we have a "self-sublating immediacy" (*WL*, II, 14; *SL*, 401). Because of this self-sublating quality, it is the originary self-determination of reflection that

> is that immediacy which constitutes the determinateness of illusory being and which previously seemed to be the starting point of the reflective movement. But this immediacy, instead of being able to form the starting point is, on the contrary, immediacy only as the return or as reflection itself. (*WL*, II, 15; *SL*, 401)

According to this claim, we have "returned" from the supposed immediacy of *Schein*, as a putative object, to the "immediacy of reflection" itself, Hegel's term for its causal and epistemic autonomy with respect to the given. In other words, the necessary determinacy of any appearing object requires an explanation of the terms of such determining, the classifying structure by virtue of which a reflective subject can identify and discriminate. He refers to the "immediacy" of reflection as a way of indicating that such a subjective condition cannot be understood as "mediated" *by* the given. *Schein* cannot be such a "starting point" because its determinacy is a result, and so the determining activity itself is, initially at least, immediately self-determined. (It is only initially so, since it itself is finally conditioned by the system of reflective possibilities, or the Notion.)

Lest we get lost in the incredible detail of this section, I should mention here that we have already seen enough of Hegel's project to suspect that what we quoted earlier as his solution to the problem of essence/appearance will, as with so many other aspects of his enterprise, begin to look, however radically revised, decidedly Kantian. Clearly, the passages discussed previously indicate that for Hegel, once we argue for the necessity of the determinations of reflection in any "science of objects," the problem with "essence" (*the* determination of reflection) is the problem of objectivity. And the claim that there is an identity between essence and appearance will mean something very similar to the early constructions of his "identity theory," where he took as his guide Kant's "Highest Principle of Synthetic Judgments." In this case, that will mean that ultimately we come to see that there can be no conflict between the products of reflection (initially essence, later ground, and finally "absolute relation") and what we apprehend "immediately," or even, say, empirical truth, because the possibility of such apprehension or of empirical truth depends on such products. The key points Hegel must discuss thus include a demonstration that this claim is so, an account of how there can be, speaking simply, a genuinely two-sided "identity" involved in "thought" as the ground of appearance, rather than some imposition, constitution, or production relation, and how within that identity, understood as the claim that any direct empirical apprehension depends for its possibility on the subject's reflective activity, there can nevertheless by a way of ensuring that reflection's activity is not wholly and in all cases simply self-determined, but self-determined in being related to "what appears."[17]

Hegel has varying success with each of these claims. As is typical of much of the *Logic*, most of them emerge quickly, right at the beginning of his discussion, and then reappear in much the same, though more developed, form later. In this case, the impossibility of a purely *self*-determined reflective condition is discussed under the rubric of "positing reflection"; the impossibility of reflection simply *being* determined by the immediate, or the empirically given (or, say, of reflected scientific laws required to explain and determine the appearances themselves being the logical product of atomic sentences), is discussed as "external" reflection; and the balanced position that avoids both extremes is introduced, and then explored in the rest of Book II, as "determining reflection."

To add to the problems, there is a scholarly issue that must also be mentioned here, although a full discussion of it would require an independent chapter. The difficulty is the following: When writing his first version of the *EL* a few years after the *SL*, Hegel radically altered the organization of Book II, eliminating almost all of his discussion of "illusory being" and the three kinds of reflection (Section One, Chapter I in *SL*), and significantly reorganizing his discussion of "existence" and "the thing." There are some, chief among them McTaggart, who argue that this alteration represents a great improvement in Hegel's exposition, particularly since the *SL*'s discussion of reflection is, as we have already seen, probably the most obscure section in all of Hegel.[18] Others, Henrich most prominently (Rohs in the most detail),[19] have argued persuasively that although Hegel's theory itself might be more clearly *stated* in the *EL*, Hegel's *defense* of the position is virtually lost in what is, after all, a textbook summary. As is already clear, I side with the latter commentators. Since Hegel, when writing the second edition (1831), did not alter the presentation of the original *SL*, despite his frequent versions of a different presentation in *EL*, there is strong prima facie evidence that he regarded the passages I discuss subsequently as essential to the full defense of his case. And since I have argued that, in all cases of this kind of dispute about architectonic descriptions, transitions, and so on, the most important issues involve the details of the best existing Hegelian argument, I simply propose to see how much of the position outlined previously he can defend in his fullest presentation of his case, the greater *Logic.*

So, to come the issue at hand, given the problem of reflection as sketched earlier, what *is* "positing reflection" and why does it fail to "determine essence" fully? In the concluding section of the Chapter I, Hegel writes that "External reflection starts from immediate being, positing reflection *from nothing*" (*WL*, II, 20; *SL*, 405; my emphasis). And in his discussion of positing reflection, Hegel makes a great deal of this relation to "nothing," so much so that the text often threatens to disintegrate under the opprobrious weight of the "nothings," "negations," "nonbeings," and "negatives." One of Hegel's summary accounts of this form of reflection is as follows:

> Reflection, as sublating the negative, is a sublating of its other, of immediacy. Since, therefore, it is immediacy as a returning movement, as a coincidence of the negative with itself, it is equally a negative of the negative as negative. Thus it is presupposing.
> (*WL*, II, 15; *SL*, 401)

The "Thus" ("So") in this passage introduces the conclusion that Hegel thinks the mysterious prior claim establishes, and it is in fact the central claim of the section. It is *because* positing reflection is a "presupposing" that it is insufficient; in this case, it is *not* wholly "positing," it depends on an "externality" it seeks to deny, and we are thus led next to consider the "logic" of "external reflection."

In the key claim about the self-sublating character of positing reflection, Hegel is, I think, trying to point to an internal tension in the attempt to explain qualitative determinacy wholly in terms of the projecting, theorizing activity of any subject of knowledge. Such a positing act, whether it refers to a Fichtean, transcendental activity (as it undoubtedly does throughout),[20] or to a collective social practice (what theoretical structures "we" constitute and then allow each other to make use of), or to a radically observation-independent scientific theory (to cite two more modern examples), must all explain why *such* projective activities are determinately required in the first place. And this requirement is, Hegel thinks, where all the problems start, since such a necessity *presupposes* a certain determinate view of the "nothing" one would have without such a specifying, explanatory structure. The original "negative" (here Hegel's even more abstract term for *Schein*) is not simply a kind of epistemic "absence," as if we start off in some sort of Fichtean void, projecting an indeterminate number of possible identifying systems. The fact that the "given" is always already theoretically or at least minimally conceptually determined, is not available as an incorrigible foundation, does *not* mean, we now see asserted quite clearly, that the activity of thought (theorizing, reflection) should be regarded as a pure positing, as an autonomous, Fichtean *Tätigkeit*. When Hegel had claimed, then, that the immediacy of illusory being was spurious (because always already determinate) and thus introduced the immediacy of reflection itself, the independent self-determinations of autonomous thought, he was, we now find, only provisionally describing such activity. It is not a pure or immediate positing, because it is also a "presupposing," it always involves an orientation from a certain presupposed given insufficiency and toward a certain presupposed goal. The identification of illusory being with reflection thus has its dialectical counterpart: that the conceptual specifications of any possible manifold presuppose a specific *kind* of "conceptualizing" requirement, a notion of what specifically would be required if the otherwise uninformed, illusory being (the negative) *is* to be essentially determined. The immediacy of the self-determining act of reflection, its initial autonomy, is thus "self-sublated." Or, in less Hegelian terms, all such reflective activity already presupposes a certain goal (we don't just start "reflecting" and then stop periodically to see which "posits" we ought to prefer among those we've got), and this goal must be already informed by the nature of the (paradoxically) original "nothing." Stated in more specific ways, only given a presupposed theory of, say, sensation will the sensory given *be* insufficient for the possibility of experience; only given a certain theory of observation will some theories be observationally equivalent; only given a certain theoretical claim about the discreteness of impressions will experience be unable to support what the mind constructs. (We thus have here a repetition of the kind of argument presented in Book I. The alleged independence of "being itself" as the origin of determinate thought was undercut, or sublated, in a way similar to what is now claimed about the possibility of an allegedly independent thought positing itself. The moment of postivism, we might say, in both realism and idealism, is being denied; in the former through the resulting indeterminacy, in the latter by pointing to the presupposing inherent in such positing.)

To return to Hegel's (even more) infelicitous language, "reflection into self is essentially the presupposing of that from which it is the return" (*WL*, II, 16; *SL*, 401). In a somewhat fuller statement of the same point:

> Reflection therefore finds before it an immediate which it transcends and from which it is the return. But this return is only the presupposing *of what reflection finds before it*. What is thus found only comes to be through being left behind; its immediacy is sublated immediacy. (*WL*, II, 16; *SL*, 401; my emphasis)

Thus, when Hegel had said that this kind of reflection was a "negative (1) of the negative (2) as negative (3)," he was claiming that the reflective, self-determined activity, as a *negating* of immediacy (1), overcomes the *insufficiencies* of the appearances as such, of *Schein* (2), but only as those appearances are already understood to be insufficient in a certain way, *as negative* (3). And this does not mean that Hegel is trying to argue that such reflective activity is, despite its own claims, still tied to some pretheoretical given, since it also turns out that what reflection here presupposes as some other is also, itself, a result of a "positing."

Before he can explain what this interrelation of positing and presupposing involves, though, he pauses to consider a much more straightforward version of how reflection works: external reflection. This version ties reflective possibilities to the immediate and interprets the activity by virtue of which we reach the required theoretical structure as either a version of abstraction or of empirical induction. To make his point against the sufficiency of this approach, he turns though to Kant and uses his *Third Critique* example of "reflective judgment" to press the very general issue he is trying to raise. Here the discussion is brief and more familiar, since Hegel is replaying a number of themes established in Book I and seems to include them here only because of some architectural obsession with threeness.[21]

Kant had generally defined external reflection (what he called "reflective judgment") as the attempt to determine the appropriate "universal" for a "given particular." (This was contrasted with "determining judgment," the attempt to apply a "given universal" properly.) What Hegel objects to in Kant's presentation, which he treats as paradigmatic for all external reflection, is that the specification of this universal (a qualitative essence in Hegel's terms) is taken to be due to exclusively "subjective" or regulative interests; it is "external" to the particular itself, and cannot be derived from it. But if the (in Kant's case, say) aesthetic or teleological universal is "indifferent" to the particular, is only what the subject finds for itself indispensably necessary, then there is no longer any determinate connection, even a putatively external one, between the universal and the particular. Precisely to the extent that reflection is successful *in any sense* in identifying *the* determinately *appropriate* universal for some particular, "the externality of reflection over against the immediate is sublated" (*WL*, II, 18; *SL*, 404). In a way intended to be symmetrical to what occurred in positing reflection, just as there the attempt to determine a "negative" immediacy by a positing activity was shown to involve a "return" to a determinate presupposition from which reflection was oriented, so here the attempt to determine a particular externally involves a "return" to the particular in a way that connects the results of reflection to that particular, as its essence, and so sublates the presumed externality.

> But in external reflection there is also implicit the notion of absolute reflection; for the universal, the principle or rule and law to which it advances in its determining, counts as the essence of that immediate which forms the starting point; and the immediate therefore counts as a nullity, and it is only the return from it, its determining by reflection, that is the positing of the immediate in accordance with its true being. Therefore, what reflection does to the immediate, and the determinations which issue from reflection, are not anything external to the immediate but are its own proper being. (*WL*, II, 19; *SL*, 405)

Such a positing that presupposes something "external," or not-posited, and a reflection on such externality that "sublates" its externality, form the basis of Hegel's account of "determining reflection." And in a way, this "solution" to the antinomies of reflection is already familiar to us as a central claim in all of Hegel's idealism and is clearly present in the last sentence of the preceding quotation. The necessity of self-conscious reflection for any possible determinacy does not mean either (1) that being itself thus proves inaccessible, that reflection is always "external" (that standard of "being itself" which we supposedly cannot meet is in itself incoherent), or (2) that reflection is itself unconstrained, a pure positing, and that epistemological anarchy is around the corner (that notion of a purely positing reflection is, again in itself, incoherent). There is and must be a kind of spontaneous, positing reflection necessary for the determinacy of any determinate being to be accounted for, but it is not "external" to such being or self-generated in some mysterious way from its own *nihil*. This is, in a nutshell, Hegel's idealism; he takes himself to have argued that this is the possible position we are led to by the failure of its competitors, and, since it is obviously still quite programmatic, he starts trying to fill it out in describing "determining reflection."[22]

To be sure, he does keep trying to explain what he means by determining reflection by repeating the "neither-nor" account summarized previously: There must be reflection, a self-conscious determination of essence, and it cannot be positing or external reflection, so it must be "that form of reflection that is neither the one nor the other." And although it is, I think, fair to argue that it is a typical, serious deficiency of all Hegel's philosophy that he is better at telling us what cannot be an acceptable solution to a problem than he is at describing the details of what can be and is (and that, with his account of "determinate negation," he sometimes seems to think that the positive answer just *is* the realization of such determinate insufficiency),[23] in this case we need much more than such a programmatic outline of what *would* be an acceptable position. Hegel concentrates on claiming that the "posited" character of the results of reflection should not and cannot be characterized as mere positedness, that the positing of reflection must be understood as the "reflection into self" of being, but there are only faint indications of how this resolution is to be concretely understood. (Especially, again, there is surprisingly little discussion of how we are to distinguish a correct or appropriate "reflection of essence," or objectively valid category, from an incorrect one.) Hegel either just asserts, without explaining very much, the possibility of a position like this:

> In so far, therefore, as it is the positedness that is at the same time reflection-into-self, the determinateness of reflection is *the relation to its otherness within itself*.
> (*WL*, II, 22; *SL*, 408)

or he makes use of a strikingly odd metaphor to suggest how this is all supposed to be possible:

> The determination of reflection, on the other hand, has taken its otherness back into itself. It is *positedness*, negation, which however bends back into itself the relation to other, and negation which is equal to itself, the unity of itself and its other, and only through this is an *essentiality*. (*WL*, II, 23; *SL*, 408)

Of course, it is only fair to note that Hegel is just beginning to try to motivate such claims, to explain and further defend them. In fine, that is what all the rest of Book II is supposed to do. In the terms that will emerge shortly, Hegel commits himself to demonstrating that various candidates for reflective conditions, "ground," "form," and "condition," *can* be understood as having a determinate "relation to other," and so can be a "*real* ground," a "form *of*," or a "condition *for*." At least we already know, not just from the *SL* but from everything else we have seen so far, that Hegel's solution to this problem, in trying to avoid the "imposition" and "intuition" alternatives (including the Schellingean self-intuition often confused with Hegel's position), will not try to offer simply a third alternative for understanding the relation between "thought" and its "other." A complete reformulation of the way the terms of the problem are usually posed is being proposed, such that the intraconceptually determined "essence," if properly understood, *is* the self-reflection of what is "other than thought" (is all that it could be understood to be).

Everything thus comes down to how such self-determination is to be properly understood and how its results are to be evaluated. These two problems dominate the rest of Hegel's discussion, and they introduce far more than can be dealt with adequately here. In lieu of a complete commentary, I discuss in the rest of this chapter the two most obvious problems Hegel's account generates and see what he has to say about them. The first is: How does he understand reflection, since it is not a mere positing, to constrain itself, to determine essence *determinately*? Whence such determinacy without external reflection, without some reliance on an independent foundation? The second is: What entitles Hegel to say that such results *count* as the essence *of* the appearances, such that when this relation of essence to appearance is understood, "actuality" itself (*Wirklichkeit*) will have been understood? The second problem will obviously be incomplete (obviously because otherwise the *Logic*'s job would be finished), and will lead to the set of topics Hegel discusses in Book III.

3. Grounded appearances

In his discussion of what he calls the "essentialities" of reflection, Hegel to a large extent repeats much of the analysis he had given in regard to "illusory being." However, he advances his discussion significantly because, while discussing the identifying (or essence-identifying) function of positing reflection, and the differentiating introduced by what is "external" to reflection, he introduces the notion of determining reflection now as "opposition" (*Gegensatz*), and so discusses the whole reflective process by invoking the greatest bugbear of Hegelian terminology, "contradiction" (*Widerspruch*). [In the *SL*, he tells us that "In opposition, the *determinate reflection*, difference, finds its completion" (*WL*, II, 40; *SL*, 424).] What this development will help reveal is that the "resolution" suggested by determining reflection is not really a resolution at all, as if we should, on understanding it, go forth and determine, specify methodically, the essences of appearances. In fact, the very notion of opposition begins to suggest that a lack of a final resolution is part of what Hegel wants to argue for, that a reflective (scientific or philosophic) attempt to "identify" a "differentiating" essence is always, necessarily, indeterminate, incomplete on its own terms, all in a way that will eventually lead to an "absolute reflection" *about* or "Notion" *of* such continual "movement" in thought. He begins, that is, to make his case that the issue of the adequacy of reflective determination, given this perpetual opposition, can be understood only within the movement of the historicity of thought, internal to that constant "opposition."

In the much shorter presentation of the *EL*, Hegel gives us a kind of map for where he thinks the turning points in this argument are. He remarks that,

> as will be seen, it [concrete identity] is first possible as ground, and then in the higher truth of the Notion. (*EL*, 237; *EnL*, 167)

That is, there is a kind of insufficiency prominent in the discussion of reflective identity, provisionally addressed by the Notion of ground, but finally only comprehensible in the final section of the *Logic*. Our task now is to find this key "insufficiency" in the central argument of Book II.

The problem of identity, the insufficiency that is to lead us through the rest of Book II, is, initially at least, a familiar one. It has been with us from the early Jena discussions of identity and the limitations of reflection. What Hegel proposes to do again is to break down the apparent independence (from each other) and foundational autonomy of the basic "axioms" of reflective thought, the logical "laws" of identity, difference (excluded middle), and noncontradiction. All such principles are just restatements, for Hegel, of reflection's attempt to "posit" identities, or essences, in a way that is not merely positing but tied to the presupposed external diversity that originally required such specification. First, he notes that a *purely* "posited" or reflectively "pure" identification of a thing's essence could only be a tautologous definition, one that excluded "difference" or differentia, and pronounced that "A planet is a planet; Magnetism is magnetism; Mind is mind" (*EL*, 237; *EnL*, 167). Such "abstract identity," Hegel claims in *SL*, "immediately collapses within itself" (*WL*, II, 27; *SL*, 412) or cannot count as establishing a thing's identity, since nothing is excluded. In Hegel's understanding of the terms, we need genuinely synthetic identities, reflected categories that do differentiate all possible objects. For that differentiation to occur, the categories or principles must embody such a concretely differentiating function, or must "contain difference," as Hegel says.

However, if the interpretation developed thus far is correct, the most standard gloss on his explanation of this relation between identity and difference is completely wrong. It is often assumed that this section of the *Logic* is where we find *the* argument in support of Hegel's rhetorical association of himself with Heraclitus and a "metaphysics of becoming." Here is where Hegel is supposed to argue for the necessity of a realist ontology of ceaseless change, in which all putatively stable things are shown to be mere moments in the development of Absolute Mind and thus never (except in reflection's falsified representation) to be what they are, but always in the process of becoming what they are not, and so "in contradiction." As we have already seen, though, identity for Hegel is a concept of reflection, of self-conscious active thought, not a category of determinate being. This would already seem to imply that Hegel's topic in this discussion is not qualitative metaphysical identity simpliciter, but the conditions of qualitative identification, of what is involved in our constructing a schema for identifying, that the former issue cannot be adequately understood except as a result of the resolution of the latter. And if this is true, it will further shift the question at issue for Hegel away from an "objective logic" altogether toward the relative autonomy of "thought's" own generation of its criteria of identity and the larger theoretical structure such criteria depend on, toward a "subjective logic." Not only is such an interpretation confirmed by the very organization of the book (the two-part structure of "Objective and Subjective Logic") and by what we have already seen in the first two books, Hegel's own discussion here and in his accounts of "appearance" and especially "actuality" confirm this idealist direction.[24]

His discussion revolves continually around a pair of typical claims, each of which occurs after some attempt to show why the notions of identity and difference cannot be understood in isolation from each other. Having made such a claim, Hegel then turns to the consequences of this interdependence. A representative claim about identity is the following:

In other words, identity is the reflection-into-self, that is identity only as internal repulsion, and is this repulsion as reflection-into-self, repulsion which immediately takes itself back into itself. Thus it is identity as difference that is identical with itself. (*WL*, II, 27–8; *SL*, 413)

The same kind of dialectical flourish characterizes his remarks about difference:

Difference is therefore itself and identity. Both together constitute difference; it is the whole, and its moment. It can equally be said that difference, as simple, is now difference; it is this only when it is in relation with identity, but the truth is rather that, as difference, it contains equally identity and this relation itself. (*WL*, II, 33; *SL*, 417)

As noted such claims repeat, somewhat more abstractly, the earlier account of the limitations of an exclusively positing and external reflection. No identity (or identifying rule of reflection, categorial ground rule of qualitative identity) is simply posited; it is "reflected" in the light of the determinate differences "presupposed" to require it and it alone. Yet the differences taken to require some sort of conceptual "identification" are themselves always apprehended *as such*, in a way that already depends on the identification of such differences. His reasons for this introductory defense of what will be his claim about the "moving," internally interdependent nature of categorial thought have already been sketched in his original account of the limitations of reflection. What is significant now are the conclusions he draws.

We should note two assumptions of the approach taken here to Hegel's discussion. First, I have obviously been assuming throughout that Hegel is interested in the conditions for the possibility of *qualitative* identification, not numerical identification. The issue for him is not how we formulate the means to refer successfully to numerically individual objects. A variety of descriptions, idexicals, or combinations will do that job without the issue of reflective *knowledge* necessarily arising. As has been clear since the relevant discussion in the *PhG*, in an appropriate context, "That over there" is sufficient for a particular to be identified without our having to answer "what" that is. (Of course, explaining adequately successful reference to particulars is, as the twentieth century attests, no small feat. And Hegel has his own enormous problems with the issue. But those touch on the status of space and time in his philosophy of nature and cannot be pursued here.)[25] And again, as in the *PhG*, Hegel's view is clearly that the "context" in such an example can allow for such successful reference because of an already achieved, perhaps unexpressed, qualitative differentiation that needs its own account. If "That over there" is, say, ambiguous, it is so because of a schema already assumed to be in place, one that identifies tables and books and computer terminals as *the* "different" kinds of things and so provides the relevant structure within which "that" is insufficiently informative; if it is not ambiguous, it is because the appropriate qualitative constraints are assumed in a way that makes direct reference clear. And again, such a constraint requires its own explanation.

Indeed, we can see that it is the issue of qualitative identity (the issue of the ground for claiming that things "are" of the same categorial kind) that Hegel is interested in (what will become the problem of "universal and particular" in Book III) by noting how the lack of an adequate account of the relation between identification and differentiation leaves us with what he calls mere "diversity" (*Verschiedenheit*), or qualitatively undifferentiated particularity, and that he regards this as a wholly unsatisfactory result (or that such numerical identity cannot be understood on its own, is parasitic on some qualitatively identifying scheme). That is, in the text, the first consequence Hegel draws from the impossibility of keeping separate posited identity and external difference is that there just is mere diversity, diverse moments "indifferent to one another and to their determinateness" (*WL*, II, 24; *SL*, 419). In this context, conceptual classification is wholly "external" (as we predictably begin to repeat the Hegelian dialectic again), a matter of mere "likeness" or relative likeness and unlikeness of diverse particulars. Again predictably, Hegel denies that there can be such diversity "indifferent" to its own determinateness. He attacks the so-called law of diversity (Leibniz's law), which holds that any thing is utterly unlike any other, as an insufficient formulation; it leaves unaccounted for the original conditions for the thing being taken to be a *thing* in the first place. This leaf may be unlike any other leaf, but its distinctness clearly already depends on its qualitative identification as a "leaf." "Two things are not merely two . . . but they are different *through a determination*" (*WL*, II, 39; *SL*, 422; my emphasis), and what Hegel continues to pursue is how such an original "determination" (*Bestimmung*) can occur.[26]

Second, given this context, it is clear that Hegel is not stupidly confusing the issues of predication and identification. Although his language is far from precise, and he can seem to be claiming that because a thing is differentiated by a predicate with which, qua predicate, *it* is not identical, a thing is what it is (predicatively) by not being (not being identical with) what it is not (a universal term). As I have argued elsewhere, Hegel is interested throughout in essential predication[27]; in the Kantian terms I have used to interpret that interest, this means that he is interested in the requirement that there be a structure for identification in place before the actual qualitative determination of experience proceeds. Such a structure can neither be wholly posited, indifferent to the differentiations it can or cannot effect in experience; nor wholly "reflected externally," as if such qualitative identification results abstractively or inductively. It is *this tension between the identifying and differentiating functions of reflection* (as necessary conditions for the determinate thought of any object) that Hegel begins to discuss as producing a kind of "opposition" (*Gegensatz*) and finally a "contradiction."

"Opposition," Hegel now tells us, is "determination in general" (*WL*, II, 41; *SL*, 424). Or, any such determin*ing* (as I am interpreting *Bestimmung*) can occur only by introducing what Hegel is here calling an opposition between "positive" and "negative," between the always required spontaneous positing of thought and "the negative," the differences that externally require such positing. There is an "opposition" because there is no way, within the self-understanding of reflection, to specify what is posited and what is external to positing. A qualitative identity can be posited that will differentiate the fundamental kinds from all others only if all others are *already* understood in a certain way, as the negative of that kind. And they can be such only if the required qualitative identification has already gone on.[28] Hegel also continues his alteration of the fixity of the Kantian picture of this relation between spontaneity and receptivity by recalling again that any such positing is already a presupposing of the differences that require it, and such differences are apprehensible as such only by means of prior "posited" concepts. This state of affairs introduces what turns out to be the signal problem of reflective adequacy. Just as "indifference" was the concluding problem of the "Logic of Being" (the failure to distinguish, except indifferently, something and other), so now a complete *relativity* attends the opposed relation between position and what is assumed to negate that position.[29]

In non-Hegelian terms, the basic idea is that what turns out to be a constraint on theorizing or conceptualizing (i.e., reflection), a limit on what can be a successful "essential determining," is itself a *product* of some prior reflection; and the theorizing or conceptualizing is itself already guided by some presupposed sense of the determinate "differences" that constrain it. Hegel introduces here this sense of the relativity of positive and negative, I think, to begin to show the *dependence* of the identification he is interested in (again the equivalent of what Kant would call the a priori synthesis) on some comprehensive, developing theory, one that can ground and defend the way in which this potential relativity is overcome, in which the constantly relative distinctions of reflection can be, at least in some sense, fixed. In somewhat broader terms, what Hegel is trying to do here is to demonstrate the rationale for an oft-repeated claim of his, that "thought" is in a kind of perpetual "opposition" to itself. As we have seen throughout, given the unavailability of the Kantian "anchor" in empirical or pure intuition, this is exactly the conclusion we should expect. Far from its being the case that such an alteration in Kantian theory opens the door to a purely posited dogmatism, a kind of self-satisfaction unchallenged by the world, the reflective or self-conscious nature of thought for Hegel makes that option impossible. Any "positing" or identifying is possible only by its "presupposing" or the "differences" it determinately assumes. It must then "negate" or undercut its results constantly, since it is self-conscious of such a limitation, at least at this stage of reflection, without some criterion to determine how such contradiction or instability shall be overcome. And, as we have also seen, and will examine in more detail in the next chapter, Hegel's understanding of the progressive nature of the development of this opposition involves a growing self-consciousness about *itself*, about thought itself and the nature of its development. The line of development, through various forms of insufficient realisms and positing and external idealisms, is such a "meta-line." Or so I am claiming, Hegel will try to show in Book III.

Here what I am claiming is that Hegel's notion of contradiction is meant to refer to the relativity and so indeterminacy that attends any reflective attempt to specify the differentia for a posited determination, or qualitative identification (or Kantian concept). That is, to review, given a claim that a reflected view of being is required, a "mediation" of the "immediate" for the immediate to be determinate, and that such a specification of "essence" is in some sense independent of such immediacy, autonomous, a condition of determinacy, the topic in Book II was the nature of this reflective mediation. Any such classification or posited law, though, required informative differentia, a differentiation that can effectively contrast such a class of events from *all* others, from all possible kinds of objects of experience (a causal series, say, and not an objective, though causally unconnected, series). But this can occur only if it is presupposed that the relevant kinds are already specified, and, put simply, we don't know yet how that occurs. Without that account, we are always "contradicting" ourselves: Any presumed positing is really only a presupposing; any presumed differentiating rests on some hidden positing. Or, Hegel goes on, what must be explored further is the insufficiency of the idea of the "self-subsistence" of essence. What counts as the reflected essence of appearances, in a word, changes. This introduces "contradiction" because Hegel is *so* relativizing the truth of claims about essence to the comprehensive theory (what he will introduce as the "grounding" theory in a moment) that makes reflection possible. That is, Hegel's account of how we end up apparently committing ourselves to something like "S is P" and "S is not P" depends on his reading each proposition to have the "logical form" "S *is reflectively determined as* P," and this essentially, as providing the identifying marks of S qua S. But given the inaccessibility of a complete ground, Hegel is assuming that S can also be reflectively determined as non-P, given some other grounding theory. Since there is no appeal to S itself outside some reflective structure, S itself must be said to be (to be reflectively, essentially determinable as) P and non-P. And, even though Hegel likes to trumpet his fondness for instability and contradiction, such rhetorical passages should not obscure the fact that Hegel regards this result as a *problem*, an unacceptable crisis in his ideal reconstruction of the possibility of determinate thought.[30] In the almost unintelligible passage where he introduces this "advance," he writes:

> The excluding reflection of the self-subsistent opposition converts this into a negative, into something posited; it thereby reduces its primarily self-subsistent determinations, the positive and the negative, to the status of mere determinations; and the positedness, being thus made into a positedness, has simply returned into its unity with itself; it is simple essence, but essence as ground. (*WL*, II, 52; *SL*, 434)

To *avoid* what Hegel is calling "mere positedness," the instability of equally possible, inconsistent determinations, essence must be understood as ground. In the *EL*, Hegel puts this in a different way by claiming that essence is not now "abstract reflection into self, but into *an other*" (*EL*, 248; *EnL*, 175; my emphasis). Or, a thing, we have found, cannot be qualitatively identified, and so cannot be a possible object of experience, when considered in isolation ("reflected into self") or by virtue simply of some classificatory schema posited by pure reason. That schema succeeds by virtue of the differentia it identifies as relevant to that thing's identity and those differentia ground the thing's identity, function as a basis of a reflective articulation of its possible relation to others.

As usual, this claim is so abstract that it is only dimly possible to see what Hegel is driving at. Despite the scholastic tone of the remarks, though, it is again possible to make some sense out of these claims if we keep in mind (1) that the remainder of Hegel's argument intends to present a theory of "existent things" as always grounded in some determinate way in another, just to be conceivable as this sort of existing thing. So, consistent with the approach taken here throughout, it is not some other event or thing that counts as an object's ground, but what Hegel will ultimately call the law or principle by virtue of which it can be "thought" as this-such a thing; (2) that a grounded existent is an "appearance" (*Erscheinung*), a somehow not fully "actual" manifestation of its ground; and (3) that a full comprehension of essence and appearance, of ground as condition and grounded as conditioned or limited appearance, is what "actuality" (*Wirklichkeit*) is. That is, keeping in mind the direction of the rest of Book II raises again the familiar Kantian tone, however altered, of Hegel's case: The "groundedness" of existence in certain conditions renders them "appearances," though a proper understanding of the objectivity of such conditions, such as the causal principle, allows us to avoid the inference that such appearances are not real; in fact, they constitute the only possible "actuality" (necessary connection according to laws) there is. And presumably, if an adequate ground can be determined, the relativity of reflection's results, its contradictoriness, can be in some way "sublated." (That is, the necessarily developing nature of thought can be done justice to without resulting in simple relativity.)

Given this general sketch of Hegel's presentation of the remainder of his remarks on essence, we can see that his introduction of ground in this context draws on a number of themes that have been important to his idealism since the earliest Jena formulations. All this occurs even though such a claim about the idealist dimensions of these passages might sound strange, given the standard metaphysical reading of this section. I am claiming that the passages are misread if the preceding direction of Hegel's case is not kept firmly in mind. That is, although much of Book II continues to make heavy use of "objectivist" notions of ground (as if Hegel were speculating a priori on the in-itself nature of form, force, etc.), the conditionedness of such grounds in *grounding principles* is more and more prominent in the text as a way of preparing for the transition to "the Notion" as the only true or "absolute" ground. And, as we have seen from the very beginning of this study, Hegel describes *that* ground in distinctly Kantian terms, as the transcendental unity of apperception (and not as Absolute Spirit's creative act).

What such a direction means for the account of ground is that we ought, I think, to view it *from the start* in Kantian terms, suitably altered in terms of the Jena modifications. That is, as Hegel makes clear only much later (*WL*, II, 227; *SL*, 589), ground here has the same status as the Kantian pure synthesis, and so ground is *ultimately* (though certainly not initially) a kind of necessary subjective activity.[31] [Indeed, unless interpreted this way, there would be no coherent way to understand Hegel's frequent references to the "activity" (*Tätigkeit*) of form or to the "movement" (*Bewegung*) of form and matter (*WL*, II, 73; *SL*, 453).][32] Or, a thing is grounded in the conceptual conditions of its possibility. (Again, this is already different from Kant, as Rohs points out. For Kant, a pure synthesis must itself be grounded in pure intuition. For Hegel, the only ground of a synthesis is the result of another synthesis. Or, as has come up frequently before, Hegel is trying to replace the Kantian reliance on pure intuition with a self-grounding conception of thought.)[33] Throughout, I have taken that to refer to a reliance on the concrete negation of *prior* attempts at "pure syntheses." To reflection, or the fixed oppositions of the understanding, this claim can seem an insoluble contradiction, a contradiction between the "external" and the "posited," "differences" and "identities," "intuitions" and "concepts," or "appearances" and "essences." (A contradiction because such *oppositions* are *identified* in statements of ground, as in Kant's highest "grounding" principle – "the conditions of the possibility of experience are at the same time the conditions of the possibility of objects of experience.") And the breakdown of such reflective oppositions means the beginning of the possibility of understanding such oppositions as identities, even while admitting such differences.

Hegel himself indicates that such speculative identity is where he wants to be able to end up by beginning his discussion of ground with a reference to the vacuousness of a claim for a ground that rests on a purely reflective or abstract identity. In such a case, the ground for a man drowning is that man is so constituted (*eingerichtet*) that he cannot live under water (*EL*, 249; *EnL*, 176). On the other hand, when difference is introduced into such claims, when the ground is genuinely other than the grounded, and so proffers a genuine explanation, the same kind of relativity discussed earlier is also introduced. To make this point, Hegel uses the example of the "grounds" of a theft, and notes how many factors might be relevant to explaining or grounding it as theft. He notes:

> The violation of property is unquestionably the decisive point of view before which the others must give way; but this decision cannot be made on the basis of the law of ground itself. (*EL*, 250; *EnL*, 177)

(I note that in his example, Hegel immediately assumes that the question of the right ground is, as interpreted earlier, the question of the right "conceptual ground," the description essential to the act being rightly understood as "theft.") He goes on to sum up and point out the direction of the rest of Book II – what will finally, justifiably, allow such a decision – in the terms we suggested previously:

> On the one hand, any ground suffices; on the other, no ground suffices as mere ground; because, as already said, it is yet void of a content in and for itself determined, and is therefore not self-acting [*selbstätig*] and productive. A content thus in and for itself determined, and hence self-acting, will hereafter come before us as the notion. (*EL*, 250; *EnL*, 177)[34]

Such a reference to the "self-acting" clearly links the account of ground to the long-standing Hegelian claim about the spontaneity of intellect and all the "self-determining" problems that claim has raised for us throughout.

But before he addresses the issue explicitly, he develops the consequences of the basic logic of essence in ways that confirm and extend the interpretation suggested earlier. Since I believe that the interpretation advanced thus far represents the core of what Hegel wants to claim throughout Book II, I want now only to indicate briefly how the course of the rest of the book proceeds.

4. Actuality

Hegel begins the second section of Book II by summarizing the results with a new term: "existence." We now know that "whatever exists has a ground and is conditioned," that "existence cannot be considered merely as immediate" (*WL*, II, 102, 103; *SL*, 481, 482). But it is also not the case that just because we have no access to an "immediate" ground in itself, the mediation of ground is indeterminate, either wholly posited or externally reflected, and in either case collapsing into its other, or contradictory. (Hegel plays around with the notion of a "downfall," *Untergang*, of ground into an "abyss," or *Abgrund*, as a way of introducing the need to consider the topic of how we determine the nature of the relation between a putative ground and the determinate existent it is to ground.) Hegel begins, that is, to explore whether there are constraints on what could count as such a general grounding relation. In doing so, he considers in an interesting way the idea of the "thing in itself" as a ground of existent objects. What is important about his comments is how they help reveal the direction of Hegel's investigation into this topic. In rejecting the idea of a thing in itself as a ground, arguing that it is either unknowable and so wholly "indifferent" to the determinations it is supposed to ground, or not indifferent, but the concrete ground of these determinations and so neither unknowable nor wholly "in-itself" (since concrete, such a ground is itself grounded), he makes two remarks that are suggestive about his own self-understanding. He contrasts the subjective idealism of Kant with what he calls (and clearly means to affirm) "the consciousness of freedom," about which he says according to which I know myself rather as the universal and undetermined, and separate off from myself those manifold and necessary determinations, recognizing them as something external for me and belonging only to things. In this consciousness of its freedom, the ego is to itself that true identity reflected into itself, which the thing in itself was supposed to be. (*WL*, II, 111–12; *SL*, 489)

Here Hegel again points to what he regards as the finally acceptable candidate for ground, the self's relation to itself. This "free" self-relation functions as the thing in itself was meant to (e.g., as "ungrounded ground"). But Hegel also, significantly, distinguishes between the universal and (initially) undetermined character of this freedom and the manifold and necessary determinations of the external, "belonging only to things." As with his rejection of a wholly positing reflection, Hegel is rejecting the idea of the self as some productive ground of immediately existing objects; it is only a ground of the essence "shining forth" in existence, or of appearances, *Erscheinungen*, and by being such a ground is not in any sense responsible for all the manifold characteristics of the grounded.

By "appearances," Hegel is careful to point out, we should not understand illusory being, or some subject-dependent state. It is the reflected object itself that must be considered an appearance, not the state the object might produce. Any object can be apprehended as such an object only as reflected; as "essentially identified," ultimately, as we have seen, as grounded, conditioned by thought. Since such a reflective condition is a necessary conceptual condition for the object's being an apprehensible object at all (the condition is a "determining reflection"), it is not "external" to the object, an essence behind or underneath the appearances. But since objects are apprehensible only as subject to these conditions, *and* since such conditions are, at this point, themselves incompletely determined, the object is "only" an appearance. Thus the general definition of appearance is "existence as essential existence is appearance," and the *limitation* implied in the very notion of appearance is explained this way:

Something is only appearance – in the sense that existence as such is only a posited being, not a being in and for itself (*an-und-für-sich-Seindes*). This constitutes its essentiality, to have within itself the negativity of reflection, the nature of essence. (*WL*, II, 122–3; *SL*, 498)

This reference to a kind of transcending of the "appearing" character of objects by finally understanding them as beings in and for themselves introduces again the final theme of the *Logic* – the full Hegelian story of the "free self-relation" of thought and its objectivity – and the reference to the "negativity" of reflection is a reference to the fact that reflection is still everywhere conditioned by presuppositions it has not discharged. [Much later in the text, Hegel distinguishes what he means by the appearing or phenomenal character of "objects conditioned by thought" by contrasting Kant's position – which he claims defines such phenomenality as a result of this conditionedness *alone*, because categories are "merely determinations originating in self-consciousness" – with his own view, which is that "intellectual cognition and experience" has an "appearing content" (*erscheinenden Inhalt*) "because the categories themselves are only *finite*" (*WL*, II, 227; *SL*, 589).]

All of this seems to make the resolution of this dispute between Kant on the conditioned, finite, and so, in that sense, ideal character of experience, and Hegel on the completeness, "infinity," and absolute character of "thought" as "ground" turn on their differing understanding of the "*un*-conditioned" *in* experience. In the next chapter, that is exactly what we shall find: that the structure of Hegel's entire discussion is determined by Kant's analysis of the "subjective necessity" of reason's ascent to the unconditioned.

Prior to moving to that topic, however, Hegel finally begins to provide a much clearer, more direct interpretation of what has become, to pack everything into one phrase, the "required, determinately reflected essential ground." It is clearer because the idealist, conceptual character of ground comes to the fore; more direct because the topic shifts to issues less specific to Hegel's unique terminology.

Having understood all possible objects of cognitive representation, of thought, as "appearances" because necessarily apprehended as "grounded," or conditioned by a conceptual structure neither wholly posited nor externally reflected, and so, at this point in the analysis, indeterminate, finite, Hegel now proceeds:

> Appearance now determines itself further. It is essential existence; the latter's essentiality is distinguished from appearance as unessential and these two sides enter into relation with each other. (*WL*, II, 123–4; *SL*, 50)

It is this introduction of the notion of a "relation" between the essential and unessential "sides" (*Seiten*) of an appearance that is supposed to move Hegel's account further along. Without such a relation, the actual determination of the essence of appearances would have to involve some *posited* "form" or "species" or qualitatively identical substrate that could only function as a ground of determinate appearances, the particular existence of the object, as an indifferent "beyond." The way in which such a ground could *ground*, could account for, say, this water's forming a compound with this liquid, would only be because it is of the essence of water to be able to do so. Or such an essence would be wholly *externally* reflected, a mere sum of observed appearances, and essence as explicans would amount only to the claim that no water has ever been observed to be incapable of forming such a compound. Since Hegel takes himself to have shown that neither option can count as the required ground, he now notes that what is lacking in them is an account of the determinate relation between the "essential" and "unessential," and so introduces the two notions that dominate the rest of his discussion in Book II – "law" and "relation." It is, he now argues, only when ground is understood as law, and law is conceived in terms of the actual, possible, and necessary relations among objects, that the required conceptual ground for a consistent, determinate thought of an object can be understood.

It is this introduction of "lawful relation among appearances" *as* essence that is supposed to return us to all the earlier formulations of the problem of essence and suggest their resolution. That is, with essence now understood as relational law, Hegel can claim that "appearance and law have one and the same content. Law is the reflection of appearance into identity-with-self" (*WL*, II, 127; *SL*, 503). Or, he has now formulated his version of the initially abstract claim that appearance is the "showing" of essence and that essence is its showing in appearance. An essential conceptual condition or ground for an object or event being what it is is the *law*; a thing is *understood as what it is* (in the now familiar idealist turn from realist essence talk) by being understood in its possible, actual, and necessary relations with other things, by virtue of the law that accounts for these relations. Such an essence, law, is not some substrate behind or always "in" the appearances; there *are* just appearances, but they are determinate by virtue of the determinate ways they are understood in law like relations to others. (And, again, the incompleteness and potential relativity of such laws are what render the appearances mere appearances.) Or:

> Accordingly, law is not beyond appearance but is immediately present [*gegenwärtig*] in it; the realm of law is the stable image of the world of existence or appearance. But the fact is rather that both form a single totality, and the existent world is itself the realm of laws. (*WL*, II, 127; *SL*, 503)[35]

(Thus, attempting to understand the ground of someone's actions by reference to his character should not be understood as a reference to an independent substrate. It is necessary to understand him in terms of a character or "substrate," but that character can be understood by understanding the relation among his actions; he is not simply identical with his actions, but he is identical with the totality of those actions insofar as those actions themselves reveal a pattern or law that can be used to construct a possible determinate totality.)

As Hegel proceeds to examine possible specifications of such "essential relations," in terms of whole/parts relations, "force" and its expression, and, later, substantiality, causality, and reciprocity, and as he tries to demonstrate the unity of the modal relations such notions help specify, it is important to note, in concluding this interpretation of Book II, how many of the previously identified idealist themes Hegel takes himself to have established. As we have noted throughout, the fact that such relational laws, functioning as essential ground or condition for the determinate representing of objects, are products of reflection, of the self-conscious spontaneity of thought, does not mean that Hegel considers such results as, to use his terminology, "indifferent" to the relata so comprehended. In the first place, Hegel explicitly rejects the model of a wholly positing reflection and continually insists that "actuality" involves the determinate identity of essence and appearance, or some concrete relation between some projected law and its actual success in accounting for "existing" objects and events. As we shall see in Book III, Hegel's idealism is still quite radical in that it argues that what will count as "success" is itself a "self-determined Notion," but this will not mean that the products of some theoretical projection, although underdetermined by empirically contingent particulars, possesses some autonomous status, indifferent to the "real" world of appearances. In the first place, there *is* such a determinate world only as conditioned by such a ground; but in the second place, although such a condition is necessary for the "identification" of some object, any putative particular condition is, at this stage, "finite," only incompletely successful in its grounding function. Since Hegel has so tied together appearances and essences in his language, identifying them, the nature of this insufficiency, or internal self-negation, cannot be straightforward empirical inadequacy, but however much his explanation of this inadequacy will still involve all the language of the "self-relation of thought" and so forth, we now know that it is the self-relation of thought *in* it *being able* to relate concrete appearances to one another. Exactly what this means has yet to be determined but his long argument about the inseparability of essence and appearance throughout Book II must be kept in mind in exploring that notion.

All of this simply returns us to the central issue in all of Hegel's idealism. How can he argue for any kind of autonomy or self-determination of "thought," and still explain (1) the determinacy of such "thinkings" and (2) the objectivity of such determinations? I have been arguing that he has adopted an essentially Kantian strategy with regard to (2), both in the *PhG*'s rejection of a skeptical-realist alternative to idealism and in the argument for the conceptual incoherence of a realist ontology in Book I. But such an interpretation does not, of course, commit Hegel simply to the view that *any* nonderived, conceptually interrelated structure, at a sufficiently fundamental level, accomplishing a certain kind of determinacy in thought, can be said to be objective. We may now know that he envisions this autonomy of thought not as some sort of positing reflection but as self-determining *in* its attempt to ground successfully the totality of actual appearances, an attempt that must somehow be capable of being restrained by "existence," but all of that still does not tell us how such a requirement for reflection is to be fulfilled. It is clear by now why Kant's reliance on the forms of intuition and his schematism are not acceptable for Hegel, and that some sort of internalism or holism about the determinacy of concepts is envisioned, but thus far, all this is still quite programmatic.

In the latter sections of both the *EL* and the *SL*, this problem is introduced by explicit reference to the problem of the purposiveness or teleological development of thought, a reference that yet again introduces Kantian themes, this time the notion of the "unconditioned." In his discussion in *EL* of the logic of the relational law of "force and its expression," Hegel begins to indicate what he regards as a fully satisfactory conceptual condition when he criticizes the "defectiveness" of the form of this relation, suggesting that the always conditioned nature of some particular force, its being the product itself of some other force's expression, limits the explanatory power of such a notion. For a full explanation, Hegel implies, we need a notion that is "in and for itself determinate," or a "notion" (*Begriff*) *and* an "end" (*Zweck*) (*EL*, 270; *EnL*, 193). For the latter unconditioned condition, we need again an end or *Zweck* that is not itself conditioned but "self-determining" (*das sich in sich selbst Bestimmende*) (*EL*, 271; *EnL*, 194). As in Kant then, reason is said to seek inevitably (as a goal or *Zweck*) the unconditioned; unlike Kant, such a search does not terminate in antinomies and paralogisms, but in *the* "Notion, the realm of subjectivity or of freedom" (*WL*, II, 205; *SL*, 571) that constitutes an absolute, not illusory, "ascent."

10
Hegel's idea

1. The notion of the Notion

In his *SL* remarks on the "Notion in general," Hegel introduces the central topic of Book III, the "notion of the Notion." His remarks on what such a topic involve all indicate that this book will contain a decisive discussion and defense of the core of his claim about the necessary "Notionality" of all "actuality." And, as quickly as he introduces the topic, he insists on that version of the issue stressed throughout this study:

> The Notion, when it has developed into a concrete existence that is itself free, is none other than the I or pure self-consciousness. (*SL*, 583; *WL*, II, 220)

This is, of course, the passage where Hegel so strongly identifies his own account of the Notion with Kant's doctrine of apperception, a passage I have stressed and used as a point of orientation since Chapter 2, and it is also the section where he produces one of the simplest formulations of his own idealism:

> The object therefore has its objectivity in the Notion and this is the unity of self-consciousness into which it has been received; consequently its objectivity, or the Notion, is itself none other than the nature of self-consciousness, has no other moments or determinations than the I itself. (*SL*, 585; *WL*, II, 222)

We should thus discover in this book, in terms of these claims, the speculative idealist solution to the problems inherent in rationalist and empiricist accounts of such notionality (Book I) and in the various finite idealist insufficiencies detailed in Book II's account of external and positing reflection. And, again, that solution will explain the Hegelian Notion in terms of "the unity of self-consciousness," the original source of Hegel's hermetic claims about thought's self-determination. It will also make clearer that the inadequacy of the logic of being and the logic of essence was a *result* of the unacknowledged and, within such positions, the unacknowledgeable role of such spontaneous self-consciousness in the possibility of those positions.[1]

In order for this project to succeed, Hegel will have to solve the problems he posed for himself in appropriating Kant's Transcendental Logic. As we have seen throughout, Kant's claims about spontaneity and apperception have been transformed into a claim about the "self-determining" or even infinitely self-relating nature of pure thought, and his claims about the necessary unity of apperception have been transformed into a claim about the systematic or holistic "dialectical" interrelatedness of any possible Notion. Thus, not only must these transformations be finally explained and justified in Book III, Hegel must do so while also explaining his claim about the completion of the *Logic* in the "identity" of Notion and Reality in the Absolute Idea.

In his first remarks on the Notion in *EL*, Hegel introduces us to such problems with his typical timidity. The Notion, he proclaims, is the "free, existing for itself substantial power" (*Macht*), that it is, "in its identity with itself in and for itself determined," and so that the problem is understanding what he now begins to call more frequently the "life" of the Notion, the term he finally introduces in Section 3 to help explain what he means by such organic self-determination and self-realization.

This "in and for itself determined" nature of the Notion is the problem of the Notion's content mentioned previously and finally calls in a long overdue debt in this interpretation. Throughout the previous chapters on the *Logic*, I have understood this claim about the internal development of the Notion, the "self-development of thought," in terms of Hegel's appropriation of Kant's spontaneity and self-consciousness themes. This originally signaled a negative thesis: attributing to Hegel a "conceptual scheme idealism" that attempts to account for the determinacy and legitimacy of any conceptual scheme nonempirically and without metaphysical substance commitments. More positively, this attributes to Hegel the view that being able to understand and being able to argue plausibly for the legitimacy of some putatively absolute, isolated "Notional" candidate can be shown to fail unless that original Notion is supplemented and expanded in some way by the understanding of another such Notion, one that originally would have been considered an incompatible alternative, and that comprehending *this relation* is all that "accounting" for such an expanded Notion, understanding it and its adequacy, amount to.[2] Hegel has now raised to explicitness (self-consciousness) the fact that fundamental kinds of account givings are what they are only "within" the process of "thought's autonomous development." The Kantian apperception theme is what generates the extreme claims for the autonomy of this development, and the rejection of Kant's reliance on intuition is what places so much weight on the claim that thought can determine its own objective notions developmentally, that there is some sort of progressive self-negation in this reconstruction of a subject's Notional determination of possible objects. This internality is what Hegel now begins to discuss in the model of some kind of "living" and, especially, purposive, totality (*EL*, 307; *EnL*, 223). Such an internal, developmental theory is, as we have seen before, to be Hegel's replacement for Kant's "anchor," pure intuition, and, for all its obscurity and limitations, is the most suggestive of any in Hegel. [It is, he says here, the "standpoint of absolute idealism" (ibid.).]

So, besides a final account of how there could be such necessary Notionality in any successful, "knowing" determination of an object, and what it would mean to consider that empirically independent level as somehow "self-correcting," the interpretive context sketched previously also introduces a number of other questions long troublesome in Hegel interpretation. For not only does Hegel claim that there are such nonstandard relations among such wholly "self-grounded" Notions, he also faces a final explanation of the central claim of his "Absolute idealism," that "what there is, in truth" *is* the Notion. Understanding this is the final "realization" of the Absolute Idea. For many commentators, understanding this claim in the light of Book III requires appreciating how radically Hegel rejects the standard view of concepts and the relation between concepts and particularity. According to many, Hegel can make this claim about the Notion because he believes that concepts are not abstracted forms, Aristotle's secondary *ousia*, nor are they Kantian subjective forms, rules for synthesis. (And they are surely not "mere names," to cite the position most opposed to Hegel's.) But *concepts determine their own instances*, are even "dialectically identical" *with* such instances. Needless to say, this bizarre claim is difficult to explain, much less justify, but it appears at least to commit Hegel either to the view that particulars are nothing but dialectical relations among concepts (in which case their particularity is impossible to account for) or to the view that it can somehow be shown that there is some conceptual requirement for these and those particulars, that an empirically undetermined result of a concept's very nature so determines the vast expanse of the natural and human world.[3] From the analysis of the Jena materials on, I have been suggesting a different reading of Hegel's view of concepts and their relation to particulars, and that reading must now be applied to the things Hegel says about the "concrete universal."

And this problem brings us back to the general issue of Hegel's metalevel account of the *process* of thought's self-determination, the issue on the agenda for Book III. If the determinate thought of any actual object presupposes a certain Notional structure as its condition, if we know something about the limitations of the Notional structures inherent in the "Being Logic" and the "Essence Logic," and if those limitations stem in large part from the lack of self-consciousness reflected in those structures about the autonomy, the independent spontaneity of thought required for the possibility of their own projects, then we are supposedly prepared for this final account of thought's self-consciousness, where the subject matter is thought itself, the *way* in which the various moments of being and essence are to be seen as moments in that autonomous process.

Or so I am proposing to read Hegel's most condensed statement of his idealism, the section on "The Absolute Idea." Before doing so explicitly, I want to put that section in context by discussing the structure of Book III, and especially those sections where Hegel appears to think that thought somehow resolves the "diremptions" it creates for itself. That is, there are two "resolution" sections in this book that should help to clarify how Hegel views the "resolution" of Notional self-consciousness, in his strange language, the identity of thought with itself, one that makes possible the discussion of the Absolute Idea. These are the accounts of the syllogism and teleology, the conclusions, or resolutions, of the discussions of the subjective and objective Notion.

2. The subjective Notion

In his wide-ranging discussion of the "doctrine of the Notion," Hegel has many things to say about the state of syllogistic logic in his day, and even about the way some aspects of that theory have decisively shaped aspects of science and the philosophy of science. For our purposes, however, the first section is important for the way it begins to introduce Hegel's concluding discussion of the Absolute Idea. In that account, he must attempt to reconcile the two components of his idealism that he constantly stresses and that, to some extent, work against one another: the radical internality of the Notion's development and the determinacy of such development. Only with an account of such determinacy will we know how the *PhGs* requirement is to be satisfied: a self-determining conceptual structure, whose determinate content can be understood to constitute "actuality," not merely "the thinkable."

As was the case in the *PhG*, Hegel's account of the internal coherence of thought's fundamental self-transformations, its determinacy, and the objectivity, at a certain level, of that determinacy, looks not to the origin or grounds of thought, to anything external to thought, but to its *end.* "Reason," he had told us in the Preface to the *PhG*, is "purposive activity." Accordingly, what is of greatest significance in the first two sections of Book III is the way in which Hegel develops a line of thought that will introduce explicitly the problem of logical development itself. That is, what Hegel must explain more concretely is simply what has implicitly been transpiring in the *SL* so far, how it is that any subject, relying, as such a subject must, on some minimal a priori concept of objects (initially, being), would be unable to make determinate use of such a Notion unless it was progressively developed in the ways the *Logic* describes. Clearly, this idealized account of thought's self-determining progression presupposes a purposiveness and potential resolution of "thought's dissatisfaction with itself" that must be accounted for independently. As noted earlier, part of that account begins in the concluding or resolution chapters of the first two sections. There we can examine the supposed realization of the "Notion" in the "Syllogism," and later the realization of the Objective Notion in "Teleology."

We should also note initially the manifold importance of this topic. In the first place, it introduces the properly Hegelian sense of totality, of the whole, Reason's completion in itself, a completion that should finally be distinguishable from the objective idealism with which he has so often been saddled.[4] To return to the concept-instance problem mentioned earlier, this should mean that Hegel's infamous attack on the "reality" of finite particulars is an "idealist" attack[5]; he is claiming that their concrete particularity, what they are *taken* to be, is dependent on the "development of the Notion," the conceptual resources available for thinking that particular determinately;

and so, what such a particular "truly is" should be understood in terms of the end of such development, the completion of Reason's development. *That* is the "whole" compared to which the particular itself, in this attenuated sense, is "unreal."[6]

Further, much of Hegel's equally infamous account of determinate negation depends on such a notion of development, as we have already seen in a number of different contexts. To claim that the insufficiency of some position or other results not in the mere insufficiency of that position, but is already a determinate indication of its successor, presumes that such an insufficiency can be identified and confirmed only if there is some standard of complete sufficiency implicit in some determinate Notion, all such that "experiencing" or "logically determining" the failure to meet that standard can tell us much more determinately what it is (for it may be quite implicit and unrecognized as such) and more determinately about how to meet it, given this particular failure. All, that is, if such a teleology can be explained and defended. It is this topic that will supposedly complete the idealist project in Hegel. The great question of the rational adequacy of some Notion or conceptual structure is, we have seen, supposed to be a matter of intra-Notional adequacy in Hegel, not determined by origins or "the beyond." But that answers the question of *rational* adequacy, and not *just adequacy with respect to some alternative or other*, only if there is some way of understanding such continuous transformations in Notions that can defend the claim of *development* (particularly the claims for a specific development), of the "higher" resolutions promised by the very term *Aufhebung*, and this can all occur only if there is some direction to this development, some *terminus ad quem.*[7]

This is also the issue that provides Hegel with the opening for his favorite metaphor in explaining such development. One of his frequent complaints about the presumed stability and classificatory "deadness" of traditional categorial schemes is that they do a great injustice to the "organic" nature of thought, that thought should be understood, to say everything at once, as "life." No traditional reflective category can capture the nature of thought's "living" activity. To reflective understanding, such a view of things seems simply contradictory, not merely because such thought's categorial structure changes, but because reason determines itself to *be* each of the moments of its "growth," and not simply now one and now the other (all presumably in the "organic" way a person can be said to continue to be who he was, and yet not be *that* person anymore). It is this highly metaphorical notion of the "organically growing" life of the Notion that is to make clearer reason's telos in the "idea of the true" and the "idea of the good," or in the final realization of the unity of both in the Absolute Idea. That, Hegel hopes, is what can be introduced in this section of Book III and the next. In other words, the Notion Hegel is interested in cannot be accounted for by reliance on empirical intuition, cannot be grounded in the metaphysical beyond of substance, cannot be a mental construct, or subjective positing, or pragmatic criterion. But now it looks like Hegel will tell us how it can be accounted for by relying on the "internal telos of the Notion's life."[8] This hardly seems promising.

We can attempt to motivate such a claim by returning to the first chapter on the "Subjective Notion." For the most part, Hegel is interested here in showing how the traditional understanding of thought's most fundamental distinctions, the fixed classifications of logical kinds, Notion, judgment, and syllogism, and the internal distinctions within each classification (especially universality and particularity, predicate and subject) are inadequately understood within the standard term "logic." Such Notions are far more inherently interrelated and interdefinable than had been recognized (and so, in his terms, are also aspects of the process of thought's self-determining). More importantly, many of the metaphysical consequences that are often entailed by simply adopting unreflectively the fixed distinctions contained in that scheme can also be shown to be undermined by revealing the incompleteness and internal inadequacy of the distinctions upon which such commitments rest. The outcome of such an analysis will be to show that a proper account of "actuality," of "what there is in truth" (as opposed to what simply exists), cannot be formulated within a traditional judgment form. Such forms carry ultimately untenable metaphysical commitments and improperly isolate the judgment as the bearer of truth or falsity, obscuring the dependence of Notions and their use in judgments on the conceptual scheme as a whole, and so on fundamental or Notional distinctions.

Accounting for all the details of Hegel's attempt to justify claims like these would, as in the previous two chapters, amount to a book in itself.[9] Here I restrict myself to what I believe is significant in his account for the idealism problems developed earlier. The first point of relevance can be stated quite directly. Hegel gives us here a logical example of what he had meant when, in the preliminary remarks to the *EL*, he had claimed that "Thought, considered as an *activity*, is accordingly the *active* universal (*das tätige Allgemeine*), and indeed the *self*-acting universal, because the deed, what is produced, is itself a universal" (*EL*, 73; *EnL*, 29). Part of what he means by such a claim is evident here in his treatment of all concepts (not just that special class, Notions) *functionally.* In this context, that means that for Hegel, concepts can be determinate concepts only as judgmental functions, as rules for judgmental activity, and indeed that the possibility of determinate judgments presupposes an even larger "thought activity," inferential presuppositions, a systematic interconnection of judgments, or the syllogism.

That is, when examining the traditional understanding of concepts, Hegel objects to any abstract distinction between sheer particularity, on the one hand, and the universality of concepts, on the other, as if the latter are abstracted common features of the former. The determinacy of the concept is not (or is not wholly and not fundamentally) a function of such abstraction, according to Hegel; instead the concept's determinacy (its own particularity or content) is primarily a function of the role it can and cannot play in judgments, judgments that originally determine the particular as the distinct particular it is. Hegel is following Kant here in understanding concepts as "predicates of possible judgments" and likewise insisting that to understand a concept is not to represent some abstracted common quality, but to understand how to use it in a variety of judgments. This does not mean that there cannot be abstracted concepts, but it does assert that such abstractions cannot originate a determinate concept unless there are specific judgmental roles for that concept to play within a range of judgments (ultimately requiring pure categorial distinctions) and a system of inferences grounding such possible judgments. Moreover, the qualities picked out and held together in some concept acquire a determinate sense only by virtue of the role such a concept can and cannot play in an interrelated network of judgments. (We could abstract some feature ϕ from A and B and C and D, but if that concept could play no role in a variety of possible judgments, a judgmental system, it could not count as a possible kind.) Specific abstractions, as it were, "fill in" possible judgmental functions that must already be determinate for there to be an original determination of particulars.

Thus Hegel's speculative language in *SL*, when he claims that the Notion, as individual or as determinate, can only "return to itself" or be a "totality" in an "original *partition* of itself," or in the divisions (*Urteile*) of different *judgments* (*WL*, II, 264; *SL*, 622). Or "this posited particularity of the notion is the judgment" (*EL*, 315; *EnL*, 230) and "The judgment is the notion in its particularity" (ibid.).

But judgments too are not isolated aspects of "thought's activity." Being able to predicate an attribute of a subject justifiably, in the most obvious case, presupposes a determination that an object is *such* a subject, that is, the kind that has attributes. In more complicated cases, the relevant chain of inferences necessary to judge specifically might be quite complex. And in this Hegel also follows Kant, who had claimed that, say, the possibility of any specific, objective causal judgment was hardly established by the Second Analogy (or by the transcendental conditions for the possibility of judgment alone), that the judgment determining which cause was responsible for which effect (as opposed to a proof that there must be one) required a system of causal laws, a *theory*, neither originally warranted inductively nor in any direct way warranted by transcendental philosophy. Such a theory was a "product" of pure reason, and Kant also turned to the architectonic of syllogistic inferences to provide a model for how such a required theorizing activity might link judgments together.

There is a passage in *EL* where Hegel summarizes his views on such an interconnected activity and highlights usefully what we are concerned with. I note especially how he stresses the hierarchy of issues involved, culminating in his own idealist problem. He first notes, in summarizing:

> This is the continuous determination (*Fortbestimmung*), by which the judgment, through a content-full (*inhaltsvolle*) copula, comes to be a syllogism.

This summarizes his claim that we cannot understand how it is that predication does "determine" a subject if we consider such predication in an isolated and abstract way. (In the obvious case, telling us that Socrates is mortal presupposes that he is a man and that men are mortal, that he is a man because he is a rational animal and men are rational animals, and so on.) Hegel goes on:

> Primarily occurring in the judgment, this continuous determination of itself involves the determining of an at first abstract, sensuous universality in terms of allness, of species, of genus, and finally of the developed universality of the Notion.
> (*EL*, 321; *EnL*, 235)[10]

But, again, what is such a developed universality? How does it develop, and what sort of universality are we talking about? Hegel makes a number of specific points in this section of relevance to such questions.

First, he reminds us that such genuine determination must be understood to occur in judgments, and he distinguishes such judgments from propositions. Judgments are assertions made by a subject; propositions isolate what is asserted, the fact of the matter, and abstract from the claim-making characteristic of judgments (and from the subjects who make them). So "I slept well last night" or "A carriage is passing by" are mere propositions and can be considered judgments only if they are being *asserted against* some possible doubt. Apparently, giving information about particulars or stating the facts about a particular is not (or is not usually) making a judgment. Keeping in mind that judgments are assertions, even "spiritual activities" of a certain kind, is important, since it affects the way Hegel introduces the truth of judgments.

For Hegel also distinguishes what he calls the "value" (*Werte*) of judgments, a distinction he bases on what he calls "the logical significance of the predicate." In an odd Remark he simply asserts that a person who runs around making judgments like "This wall is green" would not be considered a person with a "genuine capacity of judgment," as would someone whose judgments are "This is good" or "This is beautiful." The latter requires "a comparison of the objects with what they ought to be; i.e., with their Notion" (*EL*, 322; *EnL*, 236). Later, Hegel makes clearer the distinction he has in mind by stating that "It is only when things are studied from the point of view of their kind, and as with necessity determined by the kind, that the judgment first begins to be a true judgment (*wahrhaft*)" (*EL*, 329; *EnL*, 242). It is on the basis of this distinction, one that clearly refers to the hierarchy noted previously, that Hegel also distinguishes between "truth" (*Wahrheit*) and "correctness" (*Richtigkeit*). The latter term is the appropriate designation for the lower-level judgments mentioned earlier (some so low as to count as propositions, not necessary to assert) and involves what Hegel calls the "agreement of concept and content"; the former is the designation for the truth of the Notion. Again, Hegel says that in the latter case, "Truth is the agreement of the object with itself, i.e., with its Notion" (*EL*, 323; *EnL*, 237).

So, in sum, all of this means that what Hegel had earlier described as the "continuous determination" that occurs through linked judgments ultimately requires the "truth" of the Notional distinctions upon which all such specification depends. This truth is not and cannot be "correctness," because the Notion determines the possibility of content, and so cannot merely "coincide" with it. So, to ask whether the fundamental elements of our conceptual scheme are true is to ask if they "agree with themselves" or proceed from the self-determining power of the Notion itself.[11]

The specific model or logical form used by Hegel in this section to account for such a continuous determination is the syllogism. His attempt to link together various kinds of syllogism in a dialectically progressive way is not as important in this context as the way it reveals again the issues at stake in Hegel's account of what in the *PhG* had been the "speculative proposition" and is now the theory of the "concrete universal." What he ultimately is interested in is how the syllogism links judgments together in a way that must finally have some "speculative import" if it is to be successful. Particulars can be judged to be such and such only mediately on Hegel's account, through the use of some Notion determined judgmentally to be what *it* is, and so on until the full "concreteness" of the Notion is achieved. Whereas Kant would argue that objects of intuition can be objects of experience only as subject to the categories, and can be determinately subject to categories only in terms of some theory regulatively governed by forms of syllogistic inference, Hegel, although following much of such an argument, is finally only interested in one kind of "syllogistic" mediation: the connection between what there is in truth and the Notion, mediated by the determinations of being and essence. The possibility of an object of judgment is, he claims, "continuously determined" until finally understood to be what it is *because of* the Notion's self-determination, the Notion's "truth" as agreement with itself.

These are all, to say the least, obscure criteria of truth.[12] To some extent, as we have seen, what Hegel is saying is that the question of the adequacy of a conceptual scheme can only be a matter of its determinate relation to some other possible scheme (actually, another variant on the one conceptual scheme), that such a Notion of a determinate relation is to be understood in terms of a *developmental* connection, and that the basic story of such development involves the consequences of a developing self-consciousness within the scheme about itself, about its being a scheme or a Notion. Also, we have seen that Hegel is willing to accept the counterintuitive consequence of this Notion of development. That is, if the correctness of propositions and humdrum judgments depends on Notional criteria that change, then what was "true" relative to one moment in the Notion's development turns out not to be true relative to another. Since some prior Notion is not really an "alternative" to a later one, but both are "necessary" in the Notion's full development, then both kinds of claims are indeed true, even if contradictory. (This is not a full-blown contradiction, since it is not the case that both judgments are true "in the same respect," but the rejection of bivalence is clear nonetheless.)

But much of this just reformulates Hegel's position in a different way and does not, remarkably, advance us very far in answering the questions asked previously. It is still not clear what will count as a truly Notional judgment, according to Hegel. It *is* clear that he is relying on considerations similar to Plato's attack on the imperfections of the sensible world to gesture toward those criteria, but that isn't very helpful. That is, just as Plato argued that a sensible particular could not "really" be as it was said to be because it instantiated the property only imperfectly (Helen is beautiful with respect to apes, but not beautiful with respect to Aphrodite, and so on for tall, or large, or other qualities), only the Idea could "be" perfectly what it was; so, Hegel wants to import some such considerations into this Kantian context.[13] Consistent with his denial of Kantian skepticism about the thing in itself, he too wants to claim that the Notional determination of the real truly *is* what there is, and *only* such a determination "is" what there is. Any other determinations of "man," say, are merely external and contingent determinations that depend on man being originally identified *as* man in terms of his notion. In the *SL* account, he says that a judgment that can account for an object at a truly Notional level, wherein a subject is not "partly" representable through a predicate, but is "wholly" determined as what it is by such a predicate, is a judgment that has achieved truly "concrete universality," a term of art Hegel often uses in other contexts to indicate the kind of determination he is interested in (*SL*, 662; *WL*, II, 306). Identifying such a Notional level had been the goal of Hegel's enterprise since he first ventured into the identity theory thicket at Jena, and is, I have argued, the proper way to understand Hegel's claims about the Notion determining its own content and about such a self-determined Notion "being" its instances or being the "actuality" of those instances. But again, remarkably, we can still ask directly what such a "Notional" level of determination *is*, and not get much of an answer. If there is such a hierarchy of conceptual types, and if, in reconstructing that hierarchy at some level, we reach a domain presupposed for the discriminations "beneath" it, what *is* that level? Just pointing to the distinctions used in the *Logic* is no good, first because that begs the question, second because Hegel descends rather far "down" in the *Logic* itself to a conceptual level that one cannot possibly argue is wholly undetermined by what there just contingently is, and third because the examples Hegel gives of Notional determination are not consistent.

When he wants to talk like a Kantian, Hegel claims that "*the* Notion" comprises the major categories of the *Logic* itself, being and essence (e.g., at *EL*, 307; *EnL*, 223). This is, as we have seen, the major line of attack in the *SL*. Following it means that the basic claim is: For there to be any possible judgment about objects, there must be possible an original determinacy, a pure discrimination presupposed prior to any empirical or specific judgmental discrimination. Minimally, this means that any such object of judgment, and so, in Hegel's idealist treatment, any being, must be qualitatively determined, distinguishable by its attributes from others. The failure of "immediate" discriminations to ground such determinacy "leads" (in Hegel's controversial dialectical sense) to the attempt to make use of quantitative categories, and finally to a "measure" of the connection between qualitative and quantitative determinacy in order to fulfill this requirement. It can then be shown that such qualitative-quantitative determination radically underdetermine the possibility of a concrete object of judgment unless the reflective distinction between essence and appearance is invoked, a distinction that itself cannot be effective unless essence is understood as the "law"-governed relations among "appearances." All of this leads to Hegel's basic claim that the originally required qualitative determinacy itself ultimately depends on (in some sense) subjectively projected theories, in particular causal theories, some level of which is a function of "spontaneous thought itself," presumably at a very abstract level of generality. This is the basic, stripped-down version of Hegel's idealist case for the required Notional interdependence of being and essence.[14]

But, as just noted, Hegel is happy to go far beyond what is, in essence, his own reconstitution of the Kantian categories of quality, quantity, relation, and modality. And he is often also given to waxing Platonic about such Notions. He claims that "man" is a Notion in the relevant technical sense, and he praises Christianity for first treating man in terms of his Notion. But in that same section, more consistent with the former emphasis, he claims:

> What are called notions, and in fact specific notions, such as *man*, house, animal, etc. are simply determinations and abstract representations. These abstractions retain, out of all of the functions of the Notion, only that of universality; they leave particularity and individuality out of account and do not develop in these directions and thereby just abstract from the Notion. (*EL*, 314–15; *EnL*, 229; my emphasis)

It would indeed be odd if the transcendental-logical requirements for a conceptual scheme *could* develop in a way that would not only have consequences for *how* man might be *defined*, or accounted for, but could actually provide the definition. This is a serious problem in Hegel and one I shall return to later. Just as significantly, with individual truth claims relativized to Notional self-determination, then, put simply, *all* Hegel has left to save his position from a "conceptual scheme–incommensurable paradigm" relativism is his account of the interdeveloping nature of the conceptual scheme. Without an adequate account of such a developmental structure and of the "completion," in some sense, of that structure in the Absolute Idea, the claim that rival Notions are really part of One Notion, and cannot be incommensurable paradigms, and so on, is empty, and his position, once cut loose from Kantian intuitions, cannot secure itself again by such a reliance on teleology. The self-grounded looks more and more like the groundless.

3. Purpose and logical life

As we have seen already, Hegel's understanding of the Notion's "reality" is complex. A large component of that issue involves Hegel's treatment of the skepticism problem and his deduction of the objective reality of the Notion. Another aspect of the issue involves distinguishing between those elements in a conceptual scheme that essentially constitute "actuality," the very possibility of objects of judgment, and concepts that are simply highly abstract determinations of what there contingently is ("finite," say, versus "energy," or, perhaps, "species"). Yet another aspect involves a problem that arises if the preceding two can be solved: the problem of how we are to understand the consequences of Hegel's idealist conclusions for an empirical investigation of nature and human activity. What do such investigations of "reality" look like if Hegel is right about the role of reason's autonomous development? Hegel gives us a kind of a preview of that issue in this book with his account of the Objective Notion. He makes explicit the division of labor he has in mind in section 213 of the *EL*, where he distinguishes the "ideal" content of the Notion, "nothing other than the Notion in its determinations," from its "real content," the "presentation which the Notion gives itself in the form of external existence" (*EL*, 367; *EnL*, 274–5). This is again one of those issues worthy of an independent book, particularly since the exact "architectonic" place of this discussion is not easy to see.[15] But it is important to understand how, in bringing this particular aspect of the Notion–reality issue to a close, Hegel introduces and expands on the problem of teleology.

There are actually two different dimensions to Hegel's treatment of the issue of purpose (*Zweck*). The subject matter of his discussion proper concerns the objective status of teleological judgments, and involves a highly abstract version of Kant's argument that an adequate knowledge of nature is (in some sense) impossible unless an "internal purpose" is attributed to certain "organized beings." It also involves Hegel's by now quite familiar rejection of Kant's own understanding of this "impossibility" as stemming from a regulative or "merely subjective" necessity. Hegel's version of a defense of the objectivity of claims about natural teleology, however, also involves his own account of the Notional requirements for the investigation of anything. Accordingly, he treats the problem of teleology as a version of the problem of the "presentation which the *Notion gives itself* in the form of external existence," mentioned previously. Here that means showing *how* the "internal" requirements of Notionality somehow "play themselves out" when the object of study, "external existence," is the observable natural world. Thus Hegel hopes to show that there is some Notional justification, one required by "thought itself," for the intelligible investigation of anything at all, for attributing to that object "mechanical," "chemical," and "internally purposive" properties.

Hegel's success in such a demonstration seems to me quite limited. But there is another dimension to his discussion, one of much greater importance for his project as a whole. The issue of purposiveness allows Hegel to raise quite explicitly the issue of his own understanding of "Reason's self-legislated demands," to use the Kantian language, that is, its own "ends" and his own understanding of the objectivity of such ends. As he puts it in the *EL*:

> Purpose is the Notion, being-for itself, having emerged into free existence by means of the negation of immediate objectivity. (*EL*, 359; *EnL*, 267)

Insisting that the Notion be understood as a "being for itself . . . free existence" has been a dominant motif of the *Logic* since its beginning, and Hegel now points to purposiveness as the "moment" where this demand is finally first met, where thought self-consciously realizes its own requirements in the objective comprehension of the world.

Or, with the Notion of purpose, the general issue of Reason's own purposiveness – in Hegel's *Logic*, its internal development – and the nature of the idealist claim made for the objectivity of the results of such a development, are both now clearly in focus. This is so because Hegel admits that initially the idea of purposiveness appears to be a mere requirement of ours in rationally organizing the results of empirical inquiry, and so it introduces both the themes of Reason's own subjective purposiveness and the overcoming of such an appearance of subjectivity.

In fact, his discussion ranges over the question of the objectivity of "internal purpose," to, once the subjectivity problem had been raised, purposiveness in action (or from the question of purposiveness in Nature to purposiveness in Spirit). On the former issue, Hegel reminds the reader frequently that he means to follow Kant's distinction between internal and external purposiveness, that he wants no part of an "extramundane" (*ausserweltlich*) intelligence as the explanation of purpose or order. No references to God's purpose or the purposes of Nature as a whole are intended. The only purposiveness that can function in a true "comprehension" of Nature's order is one based on "immanent determinateness" (*WL*, II, 385; *SL*, 735). (As in the relevant sections of Kant's *Critique of Judgment*, the issue is not, say, the natural purpose of chickens in providing man food, or of rivers in facilitating social intercourse, or the purpose of Nature as a whole, but the necessity of invoking the idea of purpose in accounting for the internal relation of parts of some material being, a being for which a mechanical explanation alone would leave unaccounted for the functional interdependence of the parts.)[16] Hegel's attraction to such an issue in Kant can be seen by noting Kant's claim that

> the principle is no doubt, as regards its occasion, derived from experience, viz. from the methodized experience called observation; but on account of the universality and necessity which it ascribes to such purposiveness, it cannot rest solely on empirical grounds, but must have at its basis an a priori principle, although it be merely regulative. . . .[17]

For Hegel, on the other hand, purpose is "the concrete universal," and so not posited "for the convenience of our cognitive faculty." It is "the truth existing in and for itself that judges objectively and determines external objectivity absolutely" (*WL*, II, 390; *SL*, 739).

Hegel can make such large claims about this topic because, again, the problem of internal purpose and its objectivity brings to a clear focus the purposive self-determination of the Notion and *its* objectivity. Indeed, to bring out even more dramatically the issue of whether such a Notional requirement is "external" to objects, as it first appears (cf. *WL*, II, 393; *SL*, 742), or "identical" with the actuality of the object, and so a truly concrete universal, Hegel raises the issue of purposiveness in action and considers cases in which the pursuit of an end seems totally external to objects except as mere means or obstacles. I say "more dramatically" because Hegel goes to great lengths to emphasize this appearance of externality. He calls the use of an object as a means for a subjective end "violence" against objects (*WL*, II, 397–8; *SL*, 746).

But, he goes on to point out, an end formulated in complete indifference to its objective realizability would not be a true end, an "actual" end that could be pursued. For Hegel, the most visible manifestation of the necessary "mediation" between subjective end and objective world is "the tool." In his words, "In his tools man possesses power over external nature, even though in respect of his ends he is, on the contrary, subject to it" (*WL*, II, 398; *SL*, 747). This concrete manifestation of the mediated nature of end and actuality is, supposedly, the first indication of the "sublating of the illusory show of externality" (ibid.) that had characterized the standard understanding of Reason's purposes in cognition and action.

Yet, for all the help such a clear example might give the reader in trying to understand Hegel's account, much of this discussion seems to be mere conceptual wheel spinning. Hegel is making use of the issue of teleological judgments and their objectivity, and practical ends and their sublation into the "realized end," to *state* repeatedly that this objective expression of determining judgment should not be understood as merely subjective, regulative, wholly indifferent to its realization, and so on. Reliance on objective purposiveness, indeed, provides Hegel with what he clearly regards as a successful enough account of the identity of such Notional determinations and actuality to proceed to a final, recollective account of this achieved identity, what Hegel had been promising throughout as "the Idea." Presumably this means that, to use the relevant Hegelese, in the account of teleology we can see most successfully how thought's return to itself as self-determining origin (a "return," since originally opposed to an external other) "sublates" such an opposition. This is indeed what Hegel thinks, but again, he just states this result for the most part, and states it in some of his most sweeping, inclusive language yet:

> The movement of the end has now reached the stage where the moment of externality is not merely posited in the Notion, where the end is not merely an ought-to-be and a striving to realize itself, but as a concrete totality is identical with the immediate objectivity. This identity is on the one hand the simple Notion and the equally immediate objectivity, but on the other hand it is just as essentially a mediation, and only through the latter as a self-sublating mediation is it that simple immediacy; the Notion is essentially this: to be distinct as an explicit [*fürsichseinden*] identity

from its implicit [*ansichseinden*] objectivity, and thereby to possess externality, yet in this external totality to be the totality's self-determining identity. As such the Notion is now the Idea. (*WL*, II, 405–6; *SL*, 753–4)

This almost hopelessly dense introduction to Hegel's last topic clearly brings to its conclusion a major claim about Notionality involved in the *Logic*. If there must be Notional determinations in order for there to be possibly self-conscious judgments about determinate objects – the claim established by the *PhG* – then the Kantian problem of differentiating merely logical from transcendental-logical concepts can be resolved by showing how and why some determinate Notion is required for there to be a Notional determination of anything at all. This can be shown by developing the inadequacies of "objective being" Notions in a progressively more adequate way. The result of this development is now said to be a "concrete totality" that is "identical with the immediate objectivity." This does not mean that it is identical with "externality" as such, which is preserved. That is, such Notional determinations constitute the original moments required by thought for there to be empirical determinations of externality. Teleology thus brings to a sharp focus Hegel's view of thought's purposiveness and its objectivity: how thought determines for itself the conditions under which any subject must think in order to think objectively at all.

But it is also apparent that this summary statement remains tremendously abstract. Notionality is here being discussed at an exclusively metalogical level. In the speculative account of the syllogism, Hegel's discussion concluded with the claim that the possibility of particular determinacy was ultimately dependent on the Notion, on empirically undetermined principles, and that the mediation of possible particularity through the determinations of the being logic and the essence logic revealed the necessity of this spontaneous, self-determined condition. The syllogism, speculatively interpreted, was a way of stating this dependence. But this, in effect, shifted Hegel's discussion to Notionality itself, not to *a* notion that would "resolve" the instability of the essence logic, basically that would solve the problem of determining reflection. Likewise, in the conclusion to the "Objective Notion" section, Hegel makes use of teleological judgments to state again the necessary conformity of being to, in general, "thought's purposiveness." But he does not state in any concrete way what such purposiveness is, beyond thought's realization of its constitutive role. In effect, then, these two concluding, supposedly "resolution," sections (on the syllogism and teleology) reveal something strikingly odd about what Hegel thinks such a resolution consists in. It appears to consist in a self-consciousness about the spontaneity of Notional determination, a generally antiempiricist, antinaturalist account of any possible conceptual scheme, and a self-consciousness about the wholly internal ground of thought in itself – that Notional distinctions can be understood and assessed only in terms of each other – and such self-consciousness appears to be the *extent* of the "resolution." The entire "Subjective Logic" section would thus appear to be a reflective account of the subjectivity of the Objective Logic, and beyond such a metalevel claim, not to resolve or conclude, in some permanent, traditionally "absolute" way, thought's "process."[18]

Of course, it is also undeniable that Hegel thought there were a number of "object-level" implications of his logical account of the Notion, and that he was even given to making sweeping claims about the completion of philosophy itself, and indeed the end of history. But no part of those grandiose assertions is, I am claiming, playing any significant role in the position defended by the *PhG* and the *Logic*. Just as in the *PhG*, Hegel had argued that Spirit's final "satisfaction" was in a kind of self-consciousness, not reflective in the traditional sense and not the awareness of a subject-substance, but the comprehensions of its own subjectivity, a comprehension possible only as a result of interconnected and *ongoing* attempts at self-definition. Here in the *Logic*, such attempts, understood at what Hegel regards as their fundamental level, a subject's self-definition as a subject of knowledge, are shown to require "logical determinations" of a certain character, but his argument concludes only with an account of "logical subjectivity," an account of *what it is* to be a thinking subject.

In a certain sense, although this appears to bowdlerize the account of Absolute Knowledge (that it is an absolute or final account of what it is to know, and not a knowledge of a divine Absolute), this result should, from another familiar Hegelian point of view, be expected. All of Hegel's favorite metaphors, neologisms, and important summary claims stress again and again that "the Absolute" *is* a process, movement, activity, and so forth, and it is thus appropriate that his account of Absolute Knowledge involves a self-consciousness about such a process rather than its final completion and so termination. In one of the most important of such claims, in his introduction to the Idea, he writes:

> The identity of the Idea with itself is one with the process; the thought which liberates actuality from the illusory show of purposeless mutability and transfigures it into the Idea must not represent this truth of actuality as a dead repose, as a mere picture, lifeless, without impulse or movement, as a genius or number, or an abstract thought; by virtue of the freedom which the Notion attains in the Idea, the Idea possesses within itself also the most stubborn opposition; *its repose consists in the security and certainty with which it eternally creates and eternally overcomes that opposition, in it meeting with itself.* (*WL*, II, 412; *SL*, 759; my emphasis)

Such a remarkable claim would appear to mean that since the required Notions cannot be conceived of as grounded in substance, the beyond, the given, Notional adequacy must be always in a kind of flux or continual self-determination (must *be* "negativity"), without that realization (again the content of Absolute Knowledge) reraising the skepticism problem. If thought is truly "self-determining" in the peculiar sense that Hegel has defended, then it is continuously self-determining in that sense. (As we shall see, this is why Hegel's final account of the Absolute Idea is about the *method* of this determining.)

4. The Absolute Idea

The foregoing discussion raises the question: In what sense can self-consciousness about the nature of Notionality function as the telos of the *Logic* itself? Does such an account help at all to resolve the various doubts raised here about, for example, Hegel's claim for the progressively more inclusive nature of his analysis, or about the "level" (or "value") at which a concept can be said to be a Notion? To address such questions, it should again be noted that most of Hegel's remarks about the Notion are remarks about his having demonstrated (1) the "free existence" of the Notion – the Hegelian descendant of what we have been tracing throughout this study as Kant's original spontaneity claim, the claim for the priority and empirical unrevisability of a "subjectively determined" conceptual scheme – and (2) the nature of the internally related elements of any such scheme, the way in which understanding any such Notion requires understanding its function in an idealized determination of what is required in order for a subject to judge self-consciously about objects. I have noted several times that much of Hegel's case for the latter ultimately depends on what he thinks about the telos or outcome of such an attempt. And the question now is whether the remarks he has made about the "*eternally* self-opposing" nature of this Notional scheme, as such an outcome, are of any help with these larger questions.

In Chapter Three, "The Absolute Idea," Hegel states such an outcome in unambiguously metalogical, or what we might call "logically self-conscious," terms. That is, he writes:

> More exactly, the Absolute Idea has for its content only [*nur*] this, *that* the form determination is its own completed totality, the pure Notion.
>
> (*WL*, II, 485; *SL*, 825; my emphasis)

Such an emphasis on the universality of form is carried to such a length that Hegel at one point goes so far as to claim that "anything whatever is comprehended and known in its truth only when it is completely subjugated to the method" (*WL*, II, 486; *SL*, 826). When compared with Hegel's criticisms of Kant for the formality of his method, and the supposed Kantian failure to show that content could be considered as subjugated to form, these remarks look quite out of place. But they are also consistent with the Kantian dimension of the *Logic*'s enterprise and confirm again that Hegel's rhetorical bark is worse than his appropriating bite when it comes to Kant. Here, though, the point is to see how Hegel's account of the Absolute Idea, his version of "thought's realization of its own nature and its own relation to content," is meant to conclude the *Logic* itself.

That the discussion of such a self-consciousness is meant to be such a conclusion is apparent from several passages. Summarizing again the course of the *Logic* from the beginning in being to this resolution in the "realization of the Notion," the Idea, he writes:

As a matter of fact, the demand that being should be exhibited for us to see has a further, inner meaning involving more than this abstract determination; what is meant by it is in general the demand for the realization of the Notion, which realization does not lie at the beginning itself, but is rather the goal and task of the entire further development of cognition. (*WL*, II, 488–9; *SL*, 828)

Thus, it would appear, the development itself, Hegel's infamous notion of a dialectical progression, can be understood in terms of such a telos. Presumably, this means that a putative Notional account of objects is insufficient, fails in some determinate way to be a Notion of objects, *because*, for that Notion to be the Notion it is, certain presuppositions about Notionality itself would have to be made that cannot finally be made within the presupposed limitations of that original Notion. "Failure," of course, is too strong a word, since Hegel prefers to speak of the incompleteness of the Notional self-consciousness, the metalogical adequacy, inherent in some Notion or other, but the point now is to see how this metalevel issue is supposed to be crucial in the *Logic*'s development. Or dialectical self-negation is somehow a result of such metalogical incompleteness, a claim confirmed by remarks such as the following:

Since however, it [the "consciousness of the Notion" or the "method"] is the objective immanent form, the immediacy of the beginning must be in its own self deficient and endowed with the urge [*Triebe*] to carry itself further. (*WL*, II, 489; *SL*, 829; my emphasis)

The advance *consists rather in the universal determining itself and being for itself the universal*, that is, equally an individual and a subject. Only in its consummation is it the absolute. (ibid.; my emphasis)

But all of this simply confirms textually that Hegel does in fact think of the "consummation" (*Vollendung*) of the *Logic* as some kind of a metalogical claim, and that he thinks such a telos will account for the self-negating, developmental structure of the preceding sections of the *Logic*. Moreover, it is possible now, after so many examples, to see generally how Hegel understands such a developmental progression. In some suitably defined context, we begin with some presumed "immediacy" as foundation, realize the internal impossibility of such an immediacy, that it requires a determinate mediation to *be* determinate, and then come to understand the source or origin of such mediation, to become fully self-conscious about the mediating activity. Having developed such a progression this way, mostly in order to demonstrate internally the insufficiency of such putative immediacy and such incompletely mediated mediation, we can then recollectively assert that it was *not* comprehending the possibility of such immediacy within a self-consciously grounded mediation that was the true source of the required negations throughout Spirit's experience of itself, or thought's self-determination, or a subject's attempt to act rightly, and so forth.[19] But such a high aerial view of matters does not advance us very far into the details of how this process is supposed to work. A slight advance is achieved when Hegel officially introduces his notion of "dialectic" by means of the old Kantian war horse, the analytic/synthetic distinction.

To see how he makes use of that distinction, we need to keep in mind Hegel's revision of some other notions central to Kant's transcendental logic. As we have noted throughout, Hegel tends to use the notion of "absolute" as a replacement for the Kantian "a priori." His understanding of an absolute or a priori Notion, involving as it does his claims about the "autonomy," independence, and even "freedom" of such Notions, clearly involves the same kind of insistence on *empirical unrevisability*, as in Kant's theory of pure concepts. And, as I have been stressing, Notions have this status for basically Kantian reasons, because for Hegel, the issue of the "determinations of any possible object" (the classical Aristotelian category issue) has been critically transformed into the issue of the "determinations of any object of a possibly self-conscious judgment." Notions shown to play a necessary role in the possibility of such judgments thus constitute "what there is, in truth," and cannot be revised on the basis of any experience. (Their "*self*-revising movement" is, of course, another story.)

Again the issue now is what "shown to play a necessary role" actually amounts to, but we should first note that Hegel has also, with his use of "absolute," transformed the Kantian idea of necessity. For Hegel, "Notional judgments," as he had called them, are indeed "necessarily true," although as with Kant, it would not be correct to take him to mean what contemporary philosophy understands as metaphysical necessity, true in all possible worlds. Again, a significant appropriation and revision of Kant is the key to what he does mean. Instead of the restricted Kantian sense of necessity, "necessarily true of any possible world we could sensibly experience," Hegel's revision of Kant's account of sensible intuition means that his "qualifier" for necessity is "necessarily true of any possible world that a self-conscious judger could determine." And he has, contra Kant, his own reasons for arguing that any skepticism about such results (about their holding only for "our" world, for self-conscious judgers "like us") is, although logically coherent, epistemically idle.

So much for a priority and necessity. How does his use of analytic/synthetic introduce the notion of dialectic? From the preceding summary, it might appear that Hegel's understanding of Notional development might very well *be* an analytic understanding, that such determinations are the result of a complex analysis of the concept of an apperceptive subject. And Hegel certainly does say such things as "The essential point is that the absolute method finds and cognizes the determination of the universal within the latter itself" (*WL*, II, 490–1; *SL*, 830) and

> The method of absolute cognition is to this extent analytic. That it finds the further determination of its initial determination simply and solely in the universal, is the absolute objectivity of the Notion, of which objectivity the method is the certainty. (*WL*, II, 491; *SL*, 830)

However, he goes on to explain what he had meant by the earlier "to this extent" restriction:

> But the method is no less synthetic, since its subject matter, determined immediately as a simple universal, by virtue of the determinateness which it possesses in its very immediacy and universality, *exhibits itself as an other* [*als ein Anderes sich zeigt*].
> (*WL*, II, 491; *SL*, 830; my emphasis)

The task is to find a way of understanding the underscored phrase. Clearly, Hegel does not mean that, upon analysis of some putative Notion, we find that it presupposes, say, "other" Notions that do not immediately "show themselves" (*sich zeigen*) in an initial comprehension of the notion. If that is what he meant, the force of the claim about an *other* and syntheticity would be lost. But consider again the Kantian context for the distinction. As Kant understands it, the only legitimate way that some "other" determination, some genuinely nonanalytic extension of a concept in a true judgment, could be made is by some actual appeal to the "evidence" of the extraconceptual. In the simplest sense, this means actual experience, as in synthetic a posteriori judgments. In a priori judgments, the "third thing" that allows such a connection is the "possibility of experience," although, as we have seen since Chapter 2, for that notion to function as Kant wants, his concept of a "pure sensible intuition" must be defensible.

Now, to make final use of the evidence accumulated over the last two chapters, I think that the best way to understand what Hegel is getting at with his "dialectical" Notion of otherness is to see it in the context illuminated by the Kantian framework. That is, to put the point negatively first, if the *Logic* were to be understood as an extended analysis of the conceptual presuppositions of the Notion of a self-conscious, judging subject, it would be unclear from that "analysis" alone, whether such results had to do with anything *other* than the Notion of a self-conscious subject. Nothing whatsoever about objects would follow from such analysis. However, Hegel assumes that he has already, prior to the start of the *Logic*, justified the general claim that no consideration of the determinations of objects is possible unless undertaken in terms of the requirements of a self-conscious judger of objects, and that such requirements do determine what could be a determinate object. Thus if we can determine that, at this empirically unrevisable, required Notional level, a Notion cannot function *as a Notion*, fulfill the criteria of Notionality demanded by the *PhG*'s deduction, and in that failure can suggest an extension into an "other" Notion, this will all have been a further determination *of possible objects*, and so a synthetic claim. A Notion like finitude, or quantity, or positing reflection can be known a priori actually to *be*, in Hegel's extraordinarily compressed sense, an "other" Notion, infinity, or measure, or external reflection, but only by virtue of comprehending the original Notion as a determination of possible objects. So there is no possible analysis of the Notion without reliance on Hegel's claim that "thought can determine its other," that Notional conditions are objective. It is by reliance on this logically presupposed claim about Notions that an extension to a genuine "other" is made; it is the counterpart of Kant's reliance on "the possibility of sensible experience."[20]

So, in sum, an extension of some Notion can in some sense be viewed as a result on an analysis of the Notion, since Hegel is not relying on an appeal to the extraconceptual to ground that extension, but since that extension also relies on the ultimate criterion of an adequate Notional determination *of objects*, it presupposes a nonanalytic claim about the proper way to understand the relation between spontaneous human thought and objectivity, and so is synthetic. The Notion's extension is a genuine, nonanalytic *other* because it is being assessed in terms of the general, nonanalytic requirement *that* thought determine its other.[21]

This moves us some of the way down the Hegelian path, but there are still miles to go and one large hurdle left. The preceding discussion helps to account for some of the things Hegel says about why Notional self-consciousness, a somewhat formal understanding of the nature of any possible conceptual scheme, is both the telos of the *Logic*'s development and the source of the earlier incompleteness of various Notional candidates. His remarks in Chapter Three do help make clearer why the *Logic* moves from a realist understanding of conceptual determination, to a more self-consciously idealist moment, to, finally, thought's exclusive concern with itself as the "true" foundation of what conceptual determination is all about. But Hegel not only says that he can construct an ideal account of the development of "Notional determinations of the real" in terms of a developing self-consciousness or metalogical awareness about Notionality itself. He also claims that the way this development occurs is necessarily by way of "opposition." He claims that a Notion, when found to be incomplete, must be synthetically extended not just by *an* other Notion, but by *its* other, its contrary, or that the respective Notional judgments are contradictory. We hear again that "the thinking of contradiction is the essential moment of the Notion" (*SL*, 835; *WL*, II, 496), and indeed, Hegel again in this chapter seems to claim that this instability in Notional determinations is a permanent ("eternal") feature of them, that the Absolute Idea "contains within itself the highest degree of opposition" (*WL*, II, 484; *SL*, 824).

Yet as noted earlier, to add to the complexity, Hegel also suggests that, when properly understood, it can be seen that such Notional contrariety stems from a *mis*understanding of the origin of such Notions in the spontaneity of the Notion's self-development. Within such self-consciousness they are not such contraries; their abstract opposition emerges only because of thought's ignorance about itself.

> Thus all the oppositions that are assumed as fixed, as for example finite and infinite, individual and universal, are not in contradiction through, say, an external connection; on the contrary, as an examination of their nature has shown, they are in and for themselves a transition; the synthesis and the subject in which they appear is the product of their Notion's own reflection. (*WL*, II, 494; *SL*, 833)

So the question now is: What do such remarks suggest about Hegel's "dialectic," at least as that notion is presented in *SL*? It is, first of all, clear that claims about both the opposition and contradiction of Notional determinations are playing quite a different role in the Absolute Idea account than they had in the account of the essentialities of reflection. In the latter context, Hegel had tried to show how the attempt to "determine reflectively" stable, essential identities, criteria for identification within what would otherwise be "illusory being," was not successful, that the attempt resulted in a contradiction between identification and differentiation, between what was to have been a positing reflection and its presupposings. But in that context, the instability or relativity of such identification was shown to originate in an insufficient understanding of the ground of reflective activity, and in that sense to "require" a consideration of ground. In his search for various ways to understand such ground, and the proper relation between ground and grounded, the appearance, Hegel tries to demonstrate that a notion of *relation* among appearances, law-governed unity, is the account we are led to as most adequately responsive to the original problem of reflection. Yet again, the "absolute ground" of law in the Notion had not been shown, and so the determinations or moments of this account of "actuality" break down into the (basically) original opposition of positing and external reflection.

However, in *this* chapter Hegel is treating the issue of opposition recollectively, or metalogically. (By the latter term I mean that his understanding of the origin of opposition at this point is of a different order than the exhibition of a particular kind of opposition.) Indeed, as we saw in Section 2, Hegel thinks that he has accounted for the original, fundamental opposition, that between Notional self-determination and objective particulars, the opposition that would have to be accounted for if the proper Notionality of any Notion were to be understood. And he thinks he has done so in a way that, by comprehending such an opposition and the "identity" upon which that opposition is based, in some sense resolves it. Thus, from the point of view achieved in the Absolute Idea, what looks like a "contradiction" from the incomplete position of reflection now looks like a "transition"; the *relativity* and *partiality* of the claims that generated the opposition are now understood. (Or, as was clear in the discussion of syntheticity, since, throughout, the self-negation of various Notions was a result of their inability, as so isolated, to function as the required pure Notions of determinate objects, we are led by Hegel's analysis to a more adequate resolution and finally a more adequate self-consciousness about what such a resolution must involve.)[22]

So the theory, stated with its Hegelian flourishes, is supposed to be this: What from a "finite" point of view might look like simply antinomial results of pure Reason is finally comprehended as required moments in the attempt by an Absolute Subjectivity to understand itself. Within such a comprehension the oppositions are affirmed as required for such self-understanding, but sublated as mere opposition since their origin in an identical source, Absolute Subjectivity, is now understood. Thus Kant was right to see that pure reason must pose for itself antinomial candidates as the original unconditioned ground for all empirical investigation, but wrong to try to account for such opposition by grounding them indeterminately in "the" nature of pure Reason, and wrong to try to overcome such oppositions by restricting possible knowledge to the domain of sensible experience. The difference between understanding such oppositions as an unresolvable antinomial problem and understanding them as originating in "thought's self-determining necessary transitions" is the difference between contradiction as a problem internal to reflection and as comprehended by speculation.

This introduces what is another book-length topic – how Hegel understands the speculative sublation of the most important reflective opposition, freedom and necessity[23] – but for present purposes, what the account does is to reveal how tremendously abstract Hegel's logical account of dialectic is, and how the abstractness leaves a number of questions unanswered and raises several more that seem unanswerable. First, given that it is this kind of telos that is supposed to account for why thought found its attempt to determine its Notions self-negating, nothing very specific follows about the general nature of this self-negating activity. All that Hegel's final remarks suggest is that "thought opposes itself" in one general sense because of its misunderstanding of its own self-determining nature. This means that recollectively, we can understand that the insufficiencies encountered in the Being Logic were all the result of an inadequate understanding of reflective mediation as a necessary condition of all determinacy, and the inadequacies of the Essence Logic were all the result of an inadequate understanding of the Notional self-determination of particularity.

This means, first of all, that no general method of "dialectic" is being employed to produce such results. What kind of opposition is generated by thought and *why* are highly dependent on the particular assumptions about Notionality and determination we may make in trying to explain and defend some particular Notion. Hegel himself remarks on these widely differing kinds of "negation" in section 240 of the *EL*:

> In Being, the abstract form of the advance is an other, and a transition into an other; in Essence it is appearing (*Scheinen*) in *that* which is opposed; in the Notion the distinction between individuality and Notion, which continues itself as such in what is differentiated from it, and as an identity with it. (*EL*, 391; *EnL*, 295)

And there can thus be varying degrees of success in Hegel's various attempts to demonstrate such an opposition. As noted earlier, sometimes Hegel attempts illicitly to conclude that from a lack of determination, a positive indetermination follows; sometimes the internal difficulties exhibited in some Notion directly show that the contrary of some Notion is being presupposed (as in positing and external reflection); sometimes a Notion is completed or extended by a plausible replacement, a distinct other, but *not* a contrary (quality/quantity), sometimes by an "other" neither a contrary nor an "alternative" but a "resolutive" other (as in "measure" or "ground").

The meaning of otherness and negation and the criteria of success vary so much in all such accounts that it does not seem to me fruitful to try to make any general assessment of Hegel's dialectical method. His account in the *Logic* presupposes the requirement of pure concepts as original criteria of determinacy, and he constructs an idealized "progression" of candidates that is supposed to show the interrelation of each in, ultimately (as the preceding passages state), an awareness of Notional self-determination itself. It is not dialectic, then, that is the problem to be addressed (there is no such single problem); it is this supposed "demonstration."[24]

That is, the previous interpretation means that the full justification of such insufficiencies and transitions cannot be fully presented internally, as a *result* simply of some Notion's internal inadequacy as a Notion. In that case, we would just have specific kinds of inadequacies, not "determinate negation." Hegel's remarks in this chapter on the telos of the *Logic*'s development thus make it clearer how and why Hegel has constructed the *Logic* as he has, but he does not seem to notice that his very recollective *explanation* also undercuts the *justification* of the claim *that* there is a fundamental empirically unrevisable, internally self-determining, "free" Notional level, constitutive of all possible knowledge of objects. The *Logic* was to demonstrate that this was so by showing how the assumption that this was not so, that this Notional level was, in Hegel's terms "unfree" (realistically determined) or only relatively free (subjectively "posited" or "reflected"), was self-defeating, could be shown to presuppose such a wholly "free" Notionality. But now we find that this demonstration presupposed its result.[25]

Indeed, throughout the *Logic*, this dependence has been continually apparent. Although Hegel sometimes writes as if dialectical development in the *Logic* proceeds by showing that "in thinking" one Notion one would really *be* "thinking its other," we have found that this does not reflect his actual procedure. In trying to understand why the thought of "being as nothing" was a problem, and why Hegel would think that such a problem could be sublated by the thought of becoming, or why the thought of becoming required the determinations of *Dasein*, we found that we had to refer to what would be an adequate, pure Notional determination of objects. The same was true of such issues as the insufficiency of a qualitatively finite Notion of objects. It is certainly possible, that is, that the world can be such that particulars can be qualitatively limited only by an infinite contrast with all other particulars, and so simply cannot be determinately comprehended by us. It is also possible that there simply is no "absolute ground," and that the "relativity" of grounds and the resulting contrariety of theories and objects determined by them are simply the truth of the matter as we are able to apprehend it. The "urge" that Hegel speaks of for the Notion to comprehend itself in these moments is, in other words, an urge Hegel cannot demonstrate if he presupposes it throughout. And both our account here and, finally, his own words in this section indicate that he does.[26]

But perhaps a "self-articulation" by thought of its own nature is all the

Logic should be about, rather than also an internal justification that thought is as it is exhibited to be. Or perhaps the two issues coincide in some way for Hegel. He is, after all, not at all reticent about admitting the "circularity" of his system, and he insists that at the "end" of the *Logic* we have indeed reached the "beginning."[27] And moreover, as I have interpreted him, he believes that the *PhG* has already established the legitimacy of the *Logic*'s "standpoint." So maybe such a self-articulation is all he wants and all he needs. This, though, would be an insufficient response. In the first place, as we have seen, the *PhG*'s justification of such a standpoint is burdened with its version of the very same problem. In the second place, the *PhG* does not simply entail the structure of the *Logic*. Its case against empiricist and subjective idealist accounts of experience requires that there be a logically autonomous Notion, but the *Logic* must determine and demonstrate what this Notional structure is, given that there must be one. And Hegel's case for the logical relation of immediacy, mediation, and an understanding of the origin of such mediation demonstrates such a structure by presupposing it.

Thus the dilemma: Either Hegel's claim about the final comprehension of Notionality itself is justified by the determinate negations of prior, insufficiently comprehended Notions, in which case we are committed to a highly implausible view of determinate negation and one that does not usually match what goes on in the text, or Hegel's claims about determinate negations are themselves justified by an implicit (or "in itself") assumption about thought's final self-understanding, in which case it is unclear why *that* version of thought's completion is the correct one, since it certainly cannot be defended by appeal to the transitions articulated by reference to it.

But this dilemma conceals another problem. Just how are we to understand the "content" of this claim about the Absolute Idea? What does thought's final understanding of itself and its own autonomy amount to? This is a problem because we have seen indications here, and throughout Hegel's work, of two very different ways to understand this *Vollendung*. At one point in the chapter, Hegel claims that in the course of the *Logic* "all possible shapes of a given content and of objects came up for consideration," and that, having demonstrated "their transition and untruth," he has thereby demonstrated that the "absolute form has proved itself to be the absolute foundation and ultimate truth," and that the "self-knowing Notion" has "both subjective and objective" for its "object" (*WL*, II, 486; *SL*, 826). The fact that Hegel claims that "all" possible notions have been discussed, and that an "absolute foundation and ultimate truth" have been attained, certainly suggest that the insufficiencies of the Being Logic and the Essence Logic have now been resolved in the "self-knowing Notion." But this cannot be correct. The self-knowing Notion is not "another Notion," but the comprehension of the nature of the limitations of metaphysical and reflective notions. Indeed, throughout Book III, resolution of opposition in the Notion is a highly ambiguous resolution. The account of the syllogism and teleology were far too formal and abstract to resolve or complete anything, except at this speculatively reflective level of comprehension.

All of this suggests that the resolution in question is an absolute comprehension of the nature of the incompleteness of thought's determination of itself, of the necessity for reflectively determined Notions, and yet the instability and ultimate inadequacy of those Notions. Hegel's *Logic*, that is, does not conclude by proposing a "new" logic; the reflective logic of concept, judgment, and syllogism is all we've got. It proposes only a comprehension of the limitations of such a logic for a full "self-understanding." Such a strain in Hegel is inconsistent with what appears to be the surface meaning of his claims about completion and Absolute Truth, but it is quite consistent with all the earlier quoted passages about the *eternal* opposition of thought with itself and about the importance of method. It would mean, for example, that a truly determinate reflection is not a resolution of the opposition between positing and external reflection, but a continuation of such a constantly unstable reflective enterprise in a suitably self-conscious (and so, in a speculative sense, satisfied) way.

The latter sense of completion would also mean that the force of the earlier dilemma is weakened. In this reading, Hegel's doctrine of the "concrete universal," say, is a doctrine about "concrete universality." It is a claim about the proper way to understand Notional determination of objectivity, not necessarily a claim that such determination has been completed. Thus prior sections of the *Logic* need to be appealed to as instances of such determination, and as instances of Notional interdetermination, some more successful than others in establishing such relationships, but all evidence for the general, metalogical assessment of Book III.

Although both senses of completion are present in the text, I think that the evidence compiled here is that the latter is more consistent with the philosophically valuable aspects of his project. To many, no doubt, it will seem that attributing such a view to Hegel yet again too closely associates him with Kant's views on the inevitability of Reason's self-opposition when an appeal to intuition is not possible, that Hegel is simply providing a different account of the source of such opposition and a different assessment of such a result. After everything said so far here about the Kant–Hegel relation, that should be neither surprising nor by now, I hope, a problem.

5. Unresolved problems

But there are still enough problems left in Hegel's account. I shall conclude with a brief inventory of the most outstanding ones, problems that would remain even if the preceding dilemma, and the interpretive ambiguity, could be resolved.

Throughout, I have argued that Hegel's project cannot be properly assessed unless different levels and different kinds of claims are distinguished, that Hegel's own all-or-nothing demands about his philosophy ought to be rejected. Most obviously, this has involved examining separately Hegel's account of concepts, their objectivity, the role of claims about self-consciousness and subjectivity in such accounts – Hegel's idealism – from various consequences Hegel draws from such an account, and various uses to which he puts it. As such a summary already indicates, it also involves distinguishing various distinct claims within Hegel's idealism. I have tried to interpret and assess these claims both separately and in their obvious interconnection: Hegel's theory about the role of pure concepts in any possible experience; his reliance on what he regards as the idealist consequences of the necessarily self-conscious nature of possible experience in establishing claims about such concepts; his unusual case for the objectivity of such a self-determined level of thought, a case that involves a general theory about "Spirit's experience of itself"; how the latter argument also involves an account of human subjectivity, particularly as a "self-defining," necessarily historical subject; whether an Absolute Subjectivity is possible; what a resolution of skeptical doubts about a subject's self-determination would mean; and finally, what the "logic" of such an absolute thought thinking itself would look like, what it means for thought to determine itself absolutely, and how, without reliance on pure or sensible intuition, the determinacy of such a Notional level could be established.

Many of the problems surrounding the latter two issues have already been addressed, but one mentioned earlier has also not been resolved. It is connected with the issue of whether Hegel can support a claim stronger than one *about* Notional interdetermination, about its nature and general features, and stronger than a demonstration, in various instances, of such self-determination, but an account of such a Notional structure itself, a "table of Notions" that results from the account of Notionality that Hegel does provide. The same kind of problem arises when we go beyond Hegel's general idealist claim about Notionality and objectivity and ask about what, *theoretically*, counts as an a priori constraint on possible empirical experience. I have already indicated why I do not consider it philosophically credible to answer: whatever is a dialectical result of thought's initial attempt to determine objects as being (although it is surely an answer Hegel occasionally seemed to offer). At *some* level of universality that might be a possible claim, but Hegel goes far beyond such a possible level when he includes as Notions such concepts as "elective affinity," "the constitution of things out of matters," the "solicitation of force," "the chemical process," or even "man." So many such concepts are clearly as they are because the world is as it is, and cannot possibly be considered categorial results of thought's pure self-determination, that Hegel's project cries out for a more explicit, clear-cut account of when and why we should regard our fundamental ways of taking things to be "due" wholly to us, in the relevant Hegelian sense.[28]

Moreover, Hegel's account of the Notional determination of objectivity is expressed in the speculative language of "identity" and "difference." I have interpreted the former, as Hegel originally did, in terms of the transcendental claim about the objectivity of pure concepts, and the latter as the descendant of the claim that such concepts are the necessary conditions of experience, not the sufficient ones, that Notions were "identical" with the *Notional* structure of actuality, not the vast range of determinate particularity, that there was still a clear difference between Notion and Reality. If, however, we accept this interpretation, it raises the following question: Why *shouldn't* the development of Absolute Subjectivity, since it is a development and not a Kantian condition, be in some way *subject* to genuine discoveries about objects? To be sure, Hegel would reject, with some powerful reasons, the view that empirical discovery could simply determine a "logical moment," and he would insist that there are always general logical constraints on what could be a discovery at some time or other. But although a theory about "empirically responsive though not empirically legitimated" Notions might be quite complex, it is hard to see how or why Hegel should reject it, as he apparently does. He stresses, that is, from all we have seen, the "identity" side of his own dialectical formula, and seems insensitive to what the "difference" side ought to open up. It might indeed be that some Notion could be prompted by a recalcitrant problem in empirical research, even though such a Notion could get to be a Notion, get to be unrevisable and be thought of as constitutive, only by virtue of its "dialectical" integration with our general conceptual scheme. Put another way, no serious student of Hegel should, it seems to me, want to deny that the results of Darwin or the experience of the holocaust can be "Notionally" relevant, even while preserving a great deal of what Hegel wants to claim.

To be sure, Hegel is not of much help here. His own view of the relation between "content" and "absolute form" is not easy to summarize and exhibits a general philosophical problem in the post-Kantian tradition. We might designate it as the problem of "returning" to the empirical world, once one rejects empiricism or a naturalist realism in favor of original, constitutive conditions. Kant's infamous *Übergang* problem resurfaces in Hegel, especially in the notorious claims that seem to be embodied in his *Encyclopedia* project. The approach I have taken to Hegel ought to mean that a philosophic consideration of Nature and Spirit is not a deduction of the content and details of each, but a consideration of the particular ways in which necessary constraints imposed by a subject on itself, pure Notions, determine the form such investigations could take in various contexts. Thus, for example, the *PhG* and the *Logic* might provide us with a "logical framework" within which some domain of spirit must be investigated; certain assumptions about the significance of self-consciousness and thought's constitutive role are required for an investigation of, say, ethical life, without that meaning that the content of ethical experience is determined by the requirements of the *Logic*.[29] I believe that Hegel's texts has the resources for reading him this way without anachronism, and with philosophical merit, but it is certainly true that Hegel himself seems often much more ambitious about his system, that the major direction of his *Realphilosophie* involves a theory of systematic necessity that is not, I think it is safe to say, philosophically defensible. It is also true that such an inquiry is yet another book-length topic. I mention it here only as another unsolved problem.

Finally, we should note the import of this reading of Hegel for his major claim. Hegel is the last philosopher in our tradition to have offered a positive account of the "whole." That is, he tried to understand the unity of such different domains as science, ethics, art, religion, politics, and philosophy. They could not be for him different, fragmented investigations of different spheres of interest since, so construed, there was no way to understand the significance, the point, of each, and since the assumptions of many such activities are, on the face of it, sometimes inconsistent. For Hegel, such a unity could be made out if it could be shown, as he believed he had, that such fundamental human activities were essentially cognitive and that all such attempts at knowledge were, again at some appropriate level, grounded in Absolute Subjectivity's attempt at self-knowledge. But Hegel also appears to have thought, in much of his work, particularly his later work, that he could show this only if he could show that this is *all* that such attempts were, that his account of the whole could not succeed unless such a concrete, all-inclusive, systematic totality could be defended. I have suggested numerous times that such an ambition is not a necessary principle of, or a necessary consequence of, Hegel's idealism. This means that there might be some other way to understand the *implications* of Hegel's idealism than that officially attributed to Hegel, and so another way to understand his holism, his account of an "originary, universal, purposive subjectivity." But that too is a much longer story.

Notes

Chapter 1. Introduction

1. Sussman (1982).
2. For similar formulations of this "Hegel reception irony," see Henrich (1971c), 132 and Horstmann (1984), 139.
3. Cf. Düsing (1976), Theunissen (1978b), 39, and Chapter 2, n. 22, this volume.
4. It is not hard to understand this kind of interpretation. Even leaving aside Hegel's "totality" terminology, he associates himself with Spinoza in a remarkably enthusiastic fashion. He calls "Spinozism" the "essential beginning of all philosophizing" and claims that "When one begins to philosophize, one must be a Spinozist." *JA*, 19, 376. As with many other such enthusiastic identifications with historical figures (Parmenides, Heraclitus, Plato, Aristotle, Descartes, Kant), however, the connection between Hegel's own project and his unusual reading of the history of philosophy must always be kept in mind. Cf. Rohs's (1969) comments on the Spinoza connection, 17, and see Hegel's explanation of his "refutation" of Spinozism in *WL*, II, 218; *SL*, 581.
5. Some of Hegel's reputation problem stems from a pedagogical problem; there is simply very little in Hegel that can be manageably taught in a contemporary curriculum, given the background necessary, the length and difficulty of his major works, and the nature of modern survey courses. This has led to the popularity of *Reason in History* in such courses, a work that, as Brockard (1970) shows in detail and convincingly, is very unrepresentative of the philosophical core of Hegel's position and can lead to a disastrous reading of his other works. See 118ff. See also his remarks about the much discussed "early" versus "later" Hegel issue and the "metaphysical tendencies" of the latter, 176.
6. Kojève (1969).
7. To a large extent, the European revival of Hegel in twentieth-century Germany is made up of such commentators, those primarily interested in Hegel's social and/or existential philosophy – e.g., Lukacs, Marcuse, to a certain extent, Dilthey and Hiedegger, Ritter, Riedel, Habermas, Theunissen, Siep, and, most recently, Wildt. In English, the most representative "social-philosophic" interpretation can be found in Plant (1973). Taylor (1975) deals with almost all aspects of Hegel's system, but his basic interpretation of Hegel's philosophic contribution, much influenced by Isiah Berlin's reading of German romanticism (especially the importance of Herder), greatly stresses Hegel's romantic vision of community, his social theory, and his theory of purposive action. In France, interpretations of the *PhG* have tended to dominate discussions of Hegel completely, as in Kojève, Wahl, Hyppolite, Ricouer, and the Hegelianism of the early Sartre and of Merleau-Ponty, although recently the speculative Hegel has been the object of interest again, mostly as a whipping boy for Battaille, Deleuze,

and Derrida. However, in the last twenty-five years or so there have been several attempts, mostly in the German literature, to interpret Hegel's logical or speculative position in ways that are either not subject to the standard objections or in ways that explore Hegel's failure more thoroughly and with more sensitivity to the genuine philosophic problems he faced. I shall be especially concerned with this latter work in the discussions that follow.

8. Such a difference in approaches to Hegel is also visible in recent English language commentary; on the one hand, there is Taylor's influential "cosmic spirit" reading (1975), or at what must be counted the extreme end of such metaphysical-monist (and philosophically implausible) readings, Inwood (1983); on the other hand, there is Solomon's "existential-pragmatic" reading of the *PhG* (1983).
9. Cf. Marcuse (1987), Pippin (1985), Lukacs (1971, 1975), and, more recently, the interesting work of Bernstein (1984a, 1984b), and Rose (1981).
10. There are several interesting versions of what I would regard as nonmetaphysical readings of Hegel: Brockard (1970), Fulda (1978b), Theunissen (1978b). [Especially since the publication of Theunissen's book, there has been a good deal of discussion about the "critical" rather than metaphysical function of the *SL*. See Fulda et al. (1980).] See also the important articles by Buchdahl (1984, 1985), J. Heinrichs's work on the *PhG* (1974), Kolb's recent study (1986), Findlay's influential work (1958), and Hösle (1987). The phrase has come to be especially associated with one of the most important and helpful proponents of the view: Klaus Hartmann. See inter alia (1976a, 1976c), and the work of several of those influenced by him: Pinkard (1979, 1981, 1985), Bole (1974, 1985, 1987), and White (1983a).
11. Hegel, of course, calls his theoretical position a number of things: "science," "speculation," "knowledge of the absolute," even "wisdom." Although the "absolute idealism" characterization is, as far as I can determine, limited to the *EL*, it is a particularly apt one. See *EL*, 307; *EnL*, 223.
12. *WL*, I, 145; *SL*, 154–5.
13. *DS*, 6; *Diff*, 80.
14. *WL*, II, 221; *SL*, 584.
15. Obviously, I am not the first to suggest that the Kant (or Kant–Fichte) relation is central to understanding Hegel. Such a claim plays a large role in the work of many of the commentators discussed in the following chapters. But the nature of that relation, and in particular the question of what Hegel's "logical" position *appropriated* from Kant, rather than rejected, is a matter of great, unresolved controversy.

    In general, the relatively noncontroversial aspect of reading Hegel as a post-Kantian idealist involves attributing to him various arguments intended to deny the fundamentality or ultimacy of empirical knowledge, or of a "naturalist" or "materialist" explanation. The controversial aspect involves the claim that Hegel is, like Kant, an "antirealist," not a metaphysical realist, even though he rejects Kant's "thing-in-itself" skepticism, and so proposes to "overcome" any presumed realist/antirealist opposition.
16. *L*, 33.
17. As noted subsequently, there are so many different strands connecting Kant and Hegel that emphasizing any one of them can be misleading. This issue of objectivity, or the concept–intuition relation, is a good example, since many of Hegel's own remarks about such an issue refer, often in a confusing, simultaneous, very compressed form, to topics in Kant's first and third *Critiques* that

Kant would much prefer to keep separate. Indeed, Wohlfart (1981) has written a valuable book that everywhere attempts to interpret Hegel's speculative position in the light of his Kant critique, but that virtually ignores the first *Critique* in favor of the third. I shall be arguing that, although it is true that Hegel's account of speculation can be helpfully interpreted in the light of Kant's attempt to separate "reflective" from "determining" judgment (what Hegel would call "external" and "positing" reflection), as Wohlfart argues in detail, Hegel's critique of that distinction and his arguments *in support* of that criticism cannot be understood without an attempt to reconstruct Hegel's view of the Transcendental Deduction and his view of what went wrong in the Deduction. Cf. Chapter 4, this volume.

18. Cf. Ameriks (1985), 4; Harris (1983), 3–73.
19. Pippin (1982).
20. Roughly, the approach I am suggesting would mean that the situation in Hegel's philosophy of nature (and so, ultimately, his use of the philosophy of nature in his systematic account of freedom) faces problems very similar to Kant's in his tortuous "transition" problem: Once we claim that there are "pure principles of experience," that there are empirically independent constraints on what could be the investigation of nature, what exactly is their relevance to and role in a progressing, empirically self-correcting natural science? See Buchdahl (1984, 1985) and the recent massive work by Hösle (1987). [Hösle is mostly interested in demonstrating Hegel's failure to provide an adequate account of "intersubjectivity" and in showing how that failure leads to *aporiai* and gaps in Hegel's systematic project. I discuss his interpretation extensively in a review article. See Pippin (forthcoming c).] I am not suggesting that Hegel has a definitive answer to this question, any more than Kant does (as the *Opus Postumum* reveals), but it is the nature of the problem that is important to get right. For the purposes of the present study, I am treating Hegel's "transition" problem itself (especially as it concerns his influential claims in the "Philosophy of Objective Spirit") as a separate problem, one I hope to address in future work.

Chapter 2. Kantian and Hegelian idealism

1. *L*, 35.
2. The relation between the theoretical issues I discuss here and issues in the practical philosophy begins to emerge in the next chapter on Fichte and especially in Chapter 4's discussion of the *Critique of Judgment*, even though I must minimize the discussion of that relation in order to keep the scope of the idealism issue manageable. Such issues turn on another Hegelian denial of a strict Kantian dualism, that between the understanding and reason. See Chapter 4, Section 3, and notes. For some helpful remarks about the issue, see Görland (1966), 37ff. and 55, and Wohlfart (1981), 1–65.
3. The Hegelian and Fichtean emphasis on the idealist consequences of the Deduction invite a good deal of controversy, particularly the claim that such an emphasis grossly neglects Kant's Transcendental Aesthetic and that it misreads the function of the Deduction in Kant's argument. I shall attempt a preliminary defense of Hegel's position on both counts here.
4. Cf. Görland's account (1966) of Hegel's reformulation of some of his pre-Jena problems (especially his notion of "life") once he began to rethink seriously the transcendental position, especially the implications of the "transcendental unity

of apperception," 15. Düsing (1976), 114, stresses helpfully the same issues, as does Harris (1983), 3–73, who also provides some compelling details about Hegel's relation to Schelling, details that help explain why the "transcendental" or "logical" element in Hegel's position (as opposed to the romantic, philosophy of nature element) was not as obvious or clear as early as it might have been, prior to Schelling's 1803 departure from Jena. xix–lxx.

5. There are, of course, all sorts of ways to count these things but, aside from such general discussions as the account of critical philosophy in the *PhG*, I have in mind the section on "Kantian Philosophy" in the 1802 *GW*; a series of "Remarks" in the *SL* (1812–16); the passage on the "Notion in general" in the same work; paragraphs 40–60, entitled "The Critical Philosophy," in the introductory remarks to the *EL* (especially the 1827 edition); paragraphs 413–24 in the "Philosophy of Spirit" in the same work (the so-called Berlin Phenomenology); and the section on Kant in the *Lectures on the History of Philosophy*. I should note that the quality of these discussions varies widely. In the last, for example, Hegel characterizes Kant in what appear to be grossly inaccurate terms, as a subjective-idealist and empirical-psychologist, and so seems subject to the pointed criticisms raised against him by Bird (1987). My argument later will be that Hegel has a particular problem in mind when raising the issue of subjective idealism (the problem of transcendental skepticism), and the charge of empirical psychologism is meant to be the conclusion of a rather extended attack on Kant's own version of transcendentalism. See the account in Chapter 5, this volume, especially n. 1. In this chapter, I shall try to show that, on the central issue between them, self-consciousness, Hegel did not crudely misread Kant or even reject as much of Kant's account as is commonly held.
6. Walsh (1982), 93–109, highlights this passage helpfully and demonstrates that the issue of an "intuitive understanding" is central in Hegel. But his interpretation commits Hegel to a notion of intellectual intuition, or an a priori determination of a concept's instances, that seems to me too extreme. Or so I shall try to argue in Chapter 4, where Hegel's own account of intellectual intuition can be examined. See also Walsh's much earlier (1946), 49–63, Walsh (1983), and Düsing's problem with the same issue (1976), 120.
7. The strategy would be even less promising were it committed to some form of Richard Kroner's famous "Hegelian" interpretation of the development of German Idealism, and were some internal necessity in the Kant–Fichte–Schelling–Hegel connection being argued. See Kroner (1961). Although my interest is in Hegel and I thereby concentrate, as Kroner does, on the early Fichte and the Jena Schelling, I am trying to focus on historical and thematic aspects of Hegel's position that have gone relatively unnoticed and can simply be used to clarify what I regard as the philosophically valuable dimensions of Hegel's theory. I am making no claim about deficiencies in Kant that "led" necessarily to Fichte, Schelling, or Hegel, or suggesting that Fichte and Schelling themselves can be adequately understood by focusing only on their early works.
8. Cf. Düsing (1976), 228ff., on Hegel's remarks in the earliest version of the *EL* (the Heidelberg *EL*) that by understanding the "philosophical I" as "pure apperception," Kant has reconstrued knowledge of this I so that it is no longer focused on the I as a "Seeelending," with "*metaphysischen Prädikate, ob es materiell sei oder nicht*," but that such an I is simply *die reine Identität des Selbstbewusstseins mit sich, die Freiheit*. (*JA*, 6, 45; my emphasis) Cf. the discussion in Chapter 4, Section 2.

9. Cf. Allison (1983), 137.
10. Cf. Guyer's position (1980), Ameriks's rebuttal (1983), Aquila's similar rejection of the "Cartesian-conflationist" and "logical condition" approach (1987), and, on similar issues, Allison (1983), 272–93, and Pippin (1982), 151–87. I should note here something that will become more obvious as this reconstruction of the Kant–Fichte–Hegel relation proceeds. In much of the recent Kant literature, led by Strawson and Henrich, and including Guyer, Hossenfelder, Hoppe, Kitcher, and others, there has been an attempt to dissociate completely the "constituting activity" dimension of Kant's Deduction from some supposedly more respectable "austere" intention. Clearly, on my reading, very little of later German Idealism is worth much attention if this dimension in Kant is a philosophical dead end. I am arguing that, since what Kant means by the "apperceptive nature of consciousness" is not the "conflationism" these authors often attribute to him, it is not subject to the by now standard attacks.
11. See Henrich's (1976b) approach.
12. This emphasis on the reflexivity of experience can be found throughout Kant's writings. In the *Opus Postumuum*, Kant was still arguing that there must be some form of self-consciousness in conscious experience, and was still insisting that this was not an explicit awareness, but what was called a "logical act." *AA*, vol. xxii, 77, 89, 98. And in the much discussed *Reflexion*, "Is It an Experience That We Think?" Kant can be taken to mean just what is suggested here: that the apperception inherent in experience is a constituent aspect of experience without itself being experienced. [Although here again, Kant is better at creating neologisms than he is at explaining just what such apperception is, if it is not an "experience." Here he calls it "transcendental consciousness, not experience" (*AA*, vol. xxiii; *Reflexion* 5661, 318–19).] Pothast in (1971) has tried to argue that Kant was simply ambiguous about whether apperception was an explicit self-perception or the implicit form of all thinking. Cf. 13. I do not see how the passages he cites in evidence of the former (A342 and A343) support such a reading, since they are clearly preparing the way for what rational psychologists believe. However, Kant's insistence that apperception is a form of self-relation in all experience, though not an instance of self-reference or a consciousness of mental states, provides enough of a problem for a book in itself. A good one has recently been written by Dieter Sturma (1985). Kant, Sturma argues, has much to contribute to the post-Wittgensteinean issue of the proper account of the "subjectivity" of experience, the *Erlebnisperspektive* of all experience, and does so without subscribing to a theory of self-consciousness that is either referential and cognitive or nonreferential and noncognitive. See especially his discussions on 93–106 and 142–56. I am in agreement with much of what Sturma says about Kant, but would argue that (1) his use of such notions of as a "quasi-object" of awareness (for the self) and many of his negative formulations about self-consciousness indicate that later idealists were right, that Kant's positive theory, although suggestive, is incomplete, and (2) that the later idealists, especially Fichte and Hegel, preserved the Kantian project on spontaneity, rather than retreated to a Cartesian version of it. See the discussion of Fichte and Henrich in the following chapter. Finally, a full historical account of the issue would have to include Leibniz's influence on Kant. That influence is crucial for all later German philosophy, from idealism to ideology critique, because Leibniz first formulated a version of the self-reflexive character of experience that was *not* committed to the Cartesian thesis about the "transparency" of the mental.

This meant that the mind could "apperceive" itself without having itself as an intentional object, and with that, much of the later German tradition was begun.

13. For a discussion of the complications that develop for Hegel upon his acceptance of the self-consciousness condition as a condition of experience, and his rejection of Cartesian or all "reflective" accounts of the nature of self-consciousness, see Cramer (1976), 219–21.
14. See Pippin (1987) for a full discussion of the passages on spontaneity. It should be noted that Kant never seemed to come up with a designation for this "transcendental consciousness" that pleased him, and occasionally slipped into some odd, empirical descriptions he should have stayed away from. See especially the *Prolegomena*, where he says that the representation of apperception is "nothing more than *the feeling of an existence* without the least concept and is only the representation of that to which all thinking stands in relation (relatione accidentis)" (*AA*, IV, 334n; emphasis mine). For a representative passage in Hegel, demonstrating how much his own unusual account of thought's "freedom" is influenced by this Kantian notion, see *SL*, 738; *WL*, II, 388.
15. Cf. the discussion of Sellars in the article noted in n.14 and Sturma (1985), 8ff.
16. This interpretation would also help to clarify some of the problems faced in a full Kantian account of intentionality. That is, Kant's problem not only can be posed as "What are the conditions for subjective representations having content?," that is "being objective," possibly true or false, but also as "What are the conditions for a representation being *my* representations?" Without the right focus on the problem of apperception, this can seem an uninteresting question. Whose representations could yours be but yours? But the proper issue centers not on the fact that this is the case, but on how. It asks about the nature of your "taking yourself" to be representing, and so on, in some intentional mode or other. (It also helps to clarify the nature of the difference between the Transcendental Deduction and the Refutation of Idealism, since the latter is, and the former is not, an argument based on my explicit awareness of my "inner" states.)
17. See Pippin (1982), Chapter Three. The commentator who has taken most seriously the necessity of the doctrine of pure intuition in any successful interpretation of Kant is Henry Allison (1983). I sketch my disagreements with his approach in Pippin (1986).
18. Cf. Dieter Henrich (1969), 640–59; Allison (1983), 133–72; and Pippin (1982), 166–87.
19. The most explicit passage by Hegel on this section of the Deduction occurs in *GW*, 327 (*BK*, 69). I discuss these remarks and the context in which they occur in Chapter 4, Section 4.
20. See Pippin (1982), 172–87, for a detailed discussion of the issues raised here.
21. I do not believe it would be sufficient to argue, as Allison does, that the synthetic extension in Kant's argument comes from his reliance on "the synthetic fact" that space and time are intuited as unities. (The idea is that we proceed from this nonanalytically derivable fact to the conditions for our consciousness of this unity, and so have a synthetic argument, a claim about a genuine "link" between our conceptual conditions and the intuited manifold as intuited.) Such an interpretation turns on the claim that there is no "logical contradiction" in the thought of appearances being given in different spaces or times. But this claim is too weak, it seems to me, to do the job. Logical contradiction is not here of interest to Kant. His claim throughout is that we could not *experience*

(in the required "apperceived" way) such a disconnected time, and that this requirement is again one we impose as a condition of ours on the possibility of representation. See Allison (1986), 11, and (1983), 162ff.

22. Again, one of the most helpful commentators on this aspect of Hegel's position is Düsing (1976), particularly the section on "Hegel's Umdeutung des kantischen Prinzips der reinen Apperzeption zum spekulativen Begriff," and in his English article (1983). As noted earlier, however, Düsing's final position on the Hegelian problem of objectivity accepts a traditional view of Hegel as an "ontotheological" metaphysician, an interpretation I reject. Aside from Henrich's work, one of the best accounts known to me of the relation between Hegel's post-Kantian theory of subjectivity and his ontology is that of Brockard (1970). Cf. Horstmann's apposite remarks on the work of Düsing and Brockard (1984), 86.
23. Ameriks (1985), in an article that raises a number of important questions about Hegel's relation to Kant, claims that the Deduction alone does not commit Kant to transcendental idealism, at least not without the additional arguments of the Aesthetic and the Antinomies. See 3ff. Hegel, I am arguing, is assuming that the Deduction involves an idealist commitment because (1) the unity of apperception condition requires, for its possibility, "pure concepts," concepts that cannot be empirically derived and that, from the argument used, can only be said to be "conditions for the possibility of a human (discursive) experience." And so, no *claim* about *their* having noumenal objectivity can be made, although obviously it does not thereby follow that nothing *else* – say, other pure concepts – can have noumenal objectivity (although Kant, given his account in the Aesthetic, would clearly already be suspicious). The point is that the results *of the Deduction* have only an "ideal" status, whatever else does or does not, and that is all Hegel needs. And (2) Hegel believes that the success of the Deduction depends on the use of pure intuitions, which, given how Kant understands intuition, necessarily idealizes the argument. On both counts, I think Hegel is right about Kant. I might also mention that Ameriks's article clearly reveals how intertwined are the issues of Hegel's critique of Kant and Hegel's own absolute idealism. See Ameriks's own brief summary on 22, that Hegel believes "in the in principle transparency of all reality to our rational faculty." In a way this is true, but it is deeply ambiguous, since it can mean either some kind of (say Spinoza-like) precritical rationalism or an *antirealist* relativization of "claims about reality" to "*our* rational standards." Ameriks's reference to Dummett's Frege here (n. 76) is most instructive given the *same* ambiguity in Frege (witness the recent Sluga–Dummett controversy on just this point). Roughly, I want to defend the latter view of Hegel's project.
24. Cf. the Zusatz to section 42 in the *EL*, especially the last paragraph, and section 424 of the *BPhG*, 55. Some of the most helpful discussions of this issue in Hegel occur in a series of articles by Konrad Cramer (1974), (1976), (1979).
25. Such a discussion is still, I hasten to note yet again, a preliminary account of the full dimensions of the Kant–Hegel relation, which, historically, was deeply influenced by issues in practical philosophy. I am arguing that the best way to view such further dimensions is by beginning with what I regard as the foundational dispute over subjectivity, transcendental logic, and the objectivity problem. With that understood, the most important dimensions of Hegelian idealism so far left out by adopting this focus – the "monistic" implications of Hegel's approach and his account of the "teleology" of the Concept – can be better

explained. On such an issue, compare Düsing (1976), 289ff, and Horstmann (1984), 70–82.

26. That Hegel himself believes that such a progressive determination (*Fortbestimmung*), or a "movement of the Concept itself," is possible is everywhere apparent in the discussion that follows. What is not so apparent is what Hegel means by such a claim.
27. The Hegelian account of a priority is a complex one and clearly needs more of an explanation than is given here. The issue shall return again often throughout the following, especially in Chapter 10. For a helpful discussion of the issue in Kant, see Kitcher (1981).
28. "Instances" is not quite the right notion here, given the way Hegel will come to understand the relation between universal and particular. See Chapter 10, Section 2.
29. To be sure, a good deal of the best recent German scholarship on Hegel (especially the "Heidelberg school" and their respondents) has focused an enormous amount of attention on the various problems and paradoxes in the post-Kantian treatment of self-consciousness. But there has not yet been in these discussions, I shall argue, enough attention focused on the connections between the self-consciousness theme and the problem of idealism, especially the legacy of the "Deduction issue," once Kant's doctrine of pure intuition is abandoned. See, for example, Cramer's insightful concluding discussion (1976), where he shows how much of Hegel's "dialectical logic" originates in the problem of self-consciousness, a self-relating that is not a *blosse Selbtsbeziehung*, that is also a complex kind of "self-negating" (598). But since, for Hegel, a key issue in accounting for the self-conscious subjectivity of experience is a self-relation in the determination of objects, the issue of self-consciousness should not be detached from the general idealist problems of objectivity and categorial determinacy. Or so I am trying to show here. Cf. the account in Winterhager (1979), who also distinguishes between the problem of an intentional self-relating and apperception, but ultimately accepts Henrich's criticism of Hegelian "reflection" (40), a criticism I dispute in the following chapter.

Chapter 3. Fichte's contribution

1. Perhaps more directly than anywhere else in his corpus, Hegel settles accounts with Kant and Fichte in his *SL* arguments against "external reflection" and "positing reflection," and begins to sketch his own position with the provisional account of "determining reflection," a reconstrual of the problem of reflection that introduces what will become the topic of "speculative" thought. See my discussion in Chapter 9, Section 2.
2. There are many passages from the *Logic* that show the influence of Fichte's formulation of the problem of thought. One of the clearest occurs in the *EL*:

   This pure being-on-our-own (*reine Beisichsein*) belongs to free thought, to it in its free sailing out on its own, where there is nothing under it or above it, and where we stand in solitude with ourselves alone. (*EL*, 52; *EnL*, 98)

   Cf. my discussion in Chapter 8, Section 1.

3. Hegel's best-known early formulations of his idealism make indispensable use of Kant and Fichte as foils. They are subjective idealists, Schelling is an objective idealist, and his position is to be understood as avoiding or overcoming such alternatives. There is, of course, a great deal of controversy about whether Hegel's characterization does any justice to the historical Fichte, even the early Fichte. Probably the definitive "Fichtean" side of this issue is presented by Janke (1970). See also Girndt (1965), 55–107. In fact, there has been a minor growth industry in recent German scholarship defending even the early Fichte from the Hegelian charge that he was a "subjective idealist." In the reading I am presenting, Fichte is not guilty of the usual summary version of Hegel's charge; but given a proper reading of Fichte's *WL*, and of Hegel's early idealist intentions, there is still a good deal of weight left in the charge.
4. The year 1801 is the more relevant date with respect to Fichte's influence on Hegel; 1804 is the more important date for Fichte's own turn away from an idealist position. A very valuable account of this turn, one that also demonstrates what Fichte never bothers to show – the relevance of the later Fichte to Hegel's attempt at systematic philosophy – is provided by Siep (1970). Particularly important is the way Siep highlights the later Fichte's implicit imputation of a kind of Spinozism to Hegel, stating that Hegel's central claim about the appearances or the manifoldness of the Absolute as a moment of the Absolute itself cannot be sustained, and that systematic philosophy is thus impossible.
5. *Werke*, I, 4, 183. *SK*, 3.
6. *Werke*, I, 4, 184. *SK*, 4.
7. *Werke*, I, 4, 184–5. *SK*, 4.
8. *Werke*, I, 4, 190–1. *SK*, 11.
9. *Werke*, I, 4, 213. *SK*, 46.
10. *Werke*, I, 4, 200. *SK*, 21.
11. Ibid.
12. Ibid.
13. *Werke*, I, 4, 219. *SK*, 41.
14. As previously noted, I have tried to provide part of this account in Pippin (1987a).
15. *Werke*, I, 4, 196. *SK*, 17.
16. Ibid. (I have altered the translation slightly.) Fichte's formulations on this issue were not helped by his being so influenced in his early work by Reinhold's *Elementarphilosophie* and his famous *Satz des Bewusstseins*. Cf. also the discussion in Wildt (1982), 207–8, 220. With the 1797 *Versuch einer neueren Darstellung der Wissenschaftslehre*, he is much less inclined to give the Reinholdean impression that the problem of self-consciousness crucial to transcendental philosophy is a species of the general problem of consciousness. Cf. Wildt's discussion, and especially the passage cited from the 1790–1800 *Nachlass*, 208.
17. Henrich (1966a), 188–232.
18. Henrich (1966b), 193–5. This is not to say that these objections should simply count as decisive against the reflective theory. See Wildt's response (1982), 215ff.
19. *Werke*, I, 2, 260. *SK*, 99.
20. Henrich (1966b), 201.
21. Such an isolation of Fichte's self-consciousness discussion from the larger intentions of the *SK* does not characterize Wildt's interpretation (1982). However, in this section of Wildt's discussion (which is somewhat disconnected from his major project), he moves rapidly to a somewhat confined discussion of the

definitional problems of self-consciousness, the common problem that Schmitz, Henrich, Pothast, and others critical of the first-person point of view have raised. That is, from the fact that "A posits itself" is not a "fact" about itself that A could report like any other fact, Wildt concludes that Fichte is radicalizing Descartes's account of self-certainty. Since Descartes's certainty of his own existence is "immediate," that is, involves no inference, and is indubitably a presupposition of all consciousness or thinking, Wildt reasons that Fichte's emphasis on the nonexperiential nature of self-positing must be a similar attempt. Thus "A posits itself" becomes "A is empirically certain that something exists." (Cf. 221ff.) I have argued that the proper model here is Kant, not Descartes. By stressing the supposedly Cartesian origins of Fichte's project, Wildt is, I would argue, again unduly restricting the scope of the self-consciousness problematic in Fichte, here as a special kind of first premise, from which other components of experience must be derived. For further discussion of the Cartesianism/reflection issue, see Sturma (1985), 111ff., particularly with respect to his questions about the historical *Adressaten* of Henrich's critique. (But see also 123ff., where Sturma seems to slip back into a Cartesian reading of Fichte's problem.)

22. *Werke*, I, 4, 214. *SK*, 34–5.
23. Ibid.
24. *Werke*, I, 4, 277.
25. *Werke*, I, 5, 53. Cf. also the general discussion of the theme "Ich finde mich selbst, als mich selbst, nur wollend," 37–69.
26. Ibid., 41.
27. Cf. Janke (1970), 25. It might also be said that Henrich's assumptions about the conditions of any possible self-relation betray a "Platonism" about the possible object of such knowledge, that such an object is a "form" or monadic unity, assumptions that foreclose even consideration of Hegel's radical reformulations of such an "object." Rosen has suggested this pointedly in (1974a), 115.
28. Henrich (1966b), 202 ff.
29. Siep (1970) points out that in such an argument Fichte is only entitled to draw conclusions about the consciousness of the self's limitations in its positings, although he (Fichte) often uses this form of the argument to "deduce" the fact of the limitation itself, as if the I produces its own *Anstoss*. Cf. 23. This problem is the clear forerunner of similar difficulties in Hegel, i.e., in passages where formal and material mode distinctions are not clearly drawn or are obviously confused. See the discussion in Chapter 8, Section 3.
30. Henrich (1966b), 206ff. Cf. again Sturma's general account (1985) of Henrich's reading, particularly with respect to Kant, 120ff.
31. Another commentator who believes that Fichte exhibits a general tendency in German Idealism to confuse the issue of self-consciousness by reliance on a crude, "bipolar," subject–object model of knowledge is Ulrich Pothast (1971). Pothast cites some particularly confusing passages in support of his very strong criticisms, particularly from the 1798 and 1801 *Doctrines of Knowledge*, but, like Henrich, he does not attempt to interpret the status of Fichte's interest in the self-relation problem as a component of a generally idealist position. Accordingly, objections against a supposed Fichtean theory of self-awareness in all experience are taken as evidence against any theory of apperception. See 68ff.

I would also argue that Pothast's own theory of reflection – his "intensification" theory – does not make sense without already presupposing the reflexive apperception I have described. Putting the issue as Pothast does sets up Tugendhat's characterization (1979) of the false alternatives he thinks have been bequeathed to the German tradition, ego-centered or egoless theories of consciousness. The issue in that tradition, though, is not, from the first, an "egology."

32. Thus it is true, as Karl Ameriks has argued, that Fichte, like Reinhold, makes use of a "shorter" argument for idealism (than Kant) and ends up with a more "radical" result. In this case, the shorter argument is based on the "original act" whereby all consciousness is made possible (and not, as in Reinhold, on the fact of representing as such), and the more radical idealism is the claim that it is not just creatures with our forms of intuition who are restricted in their knowledge to appearances. Any self-conscious judger is thereby limited to the "results" of his positings. But Fichte is not simply ignoring the relevance of Kant's complicated case for the ideality of the forms of intuition. As discussed subsequently, he is denying the possibility of the kind of separation between sensibility and understanding that makes possible Kant's Aesthetic. See Ameriks (forthcoming) and Breazeale (1981), 545–68. A typical passage in Fichte where this claim about Kant's distinction is made explicitly is *Werke*, I, 4, 275. One commentator, by the way, who realizes just how badly Reinhold misses the "transcendental" dimension in Fichte is Hegel, in *DS*, 41; *Diff*, 127–8.
33. Cf. Kant's *Prolegomena to Any Future Metaphysics*, *AA*, vol. IV, 276.
34. *Werke*, I, 2, 255. *SK*, 93. The fact that this first principle does not admit of proof (*beweisen*) or determination (*bestimmen*) does not mean that the principle cannot be supported, or in any other "transcendental" way defended. But Fichte surely opens himself up here to the later Hegelian charge that his system relies on an inadequate understanding of "ground."
35. Fichte here leaves completely open the nature of A's "division" from itself and does not himself introduce the issue of temporality. I mean this only as an example. Fichte's own discussions of time turn on other issues, in particular, several mentioned earlier. The most important is his claim that the Kantian "matter of experience" (*Empfindung*) and the supposedly immediate forms of our apprehending such matter must also be construed as moments in a subject's self-positing. See especially the *Grundrisse des Eigenthümlichen der Wissenschaftslehre*, *Werke*, I, 3, 147–51, and the "Deduktion der Anschauung," 151–93.
36. *Werke*, I, 2, 257. *SK*, 95.
37. The issue of identification and its possibility is important for historical reasons as well. Fichte's characterization of the problem is linked to the Kantian question of the possibility of "synthetically unified" objects of experience and the Hegelian exploration of the possibility of determinate thought throughout the *SL*.
38. *Werke*, I, 2, 266–7. *SK*, 104.
39. For a clear discussion of Fichte's own attempts to solve this problem without, speaking generally, "Hegelianism," see Siep (1970), Part II.
40. Cf. Ameriks's discussion (1988).
41. *Werke*, I, 2, 269. *SK*, 108.
42. *Werke*, I, 2, 270. *SK*, 108.
43. *Werke*, I, 2, 287. *SK*, 123.
44. *Werke*, I, 2, 287. *SK*, 124. This tension in Fichte's formulations appears frequently. Cf. the contrast between *Werke*, I, 2, 325, 327. *SK*, 161, 163.

45. A typical formulation of this point by Hegel is presented in *DS*, 56; *Diff*, 146.
46. *Werke*, I, 2, 328. *SK*, 164. Stanley Rosen, in keeping with his generally "logical" reading of German Idealism, interprets this problem in Fichte as representative of rationalist aporiai that stretch back to Plato – in this case, the difficulty in accounting for the relation between identifying and differentiating criteria for objects. Cf. Rosen (1974a), 101.
47. To anticipate again Hegel's point of view, much of Fichte's problem stems from an inadequate, "reflective" understanding of identity.
48. The more the later Fichte tries to solve this problem, the less idealist he becomes (replacing the I/not-I relation with the problem of the Absolute and its appearances) and, appropriately, the more the Kantian critical worry emerges: how Fichte can justifiably claim what he does about such an Absolute. See Siep (1970), 80, 89.
49. For an important account of the details of such Kantian aporiai in the neo-Kantian sociological tradition, see Gillian Rose (1981). Rose's account poses the issue in terms of the problem of "value" and "validity," but as her book proceeds, it is clear that the foundational issue is subjectivity and the way in which a subject can be said to determine itself (to *be* a subject), or what in this chapter could be called the "Fichtean dimension," and yet how a subject can be said also to be a real, concrete, and so, in some sense, determined subject (what has here emerged as Fichte's aporia). To think both aspects together, indeed even to be able to recognize that they must be thought together, requires, as Rose points out with great thoroughness and insight, the move to Hegel's "speculative" position.
50. As will begin to be clear in the next chapter, Hegel's response to the Fichtean problem is to argue that the self-relation necessarily presupposed in all possible experience is neither a formal condition, with certain "transcendental constraints" on *its* possibility (categories), nor an "original act" of some kind, but that it is *both* a kind of *condition* of experience, presupposed in all instances of thinking a thought or experiencing an object, *and* a *result* of (historical) experience.
51. Since I have concentrated here on Fichte's theoretical position, and have tried to argue that his formulation of the "epistemic" issue of self-consciousness significantly determines much of what is important in later idealism, especially Hegel, I should note the contrary view. It is put best by Wildt (1982), who, by and large, follows Henrich's lead (1963) and argues that the most fruitful philosophic dimension of the Fichte–Hegel relation concerns Hegel's account of *Sittlichkeit* and Fichte's theory of the will in the *System der Sittenlehre*. Wildt claims that one can detach the practical issues of *ich-Identität* from the Fichtean project, and that given the *Absurditäten* (332) to which the "speculative" dimension of self-consciousness leads, such a separation is valuable. Wildt clearly believes that such "absurdities" are generated (e.g., the *fatale Subjekt–Objekt Dialektik*, 334) because he accepts a number of extremely tendentious and crudely unsympathetic characterizations of Hegel's speculative position. Twice he simply cites the work of Becker (1970) and Tugendhat (1979) as if their criticisms of Hegel were obviously decisive (289 and 334). I also do not believe that there *finally* is such a thing as a speculative logic, but there is far more philosophic interest in Hegel's attempt to resolve the theoretical antinomies of Kant's and Fichte's critical philosophy than can be countered by the

mere citation of these authors. For a brief counter to Becker, see Hartmann (1973), and to Tugendhat, Siep (1981).

52. Fichte's own reactions to the problems of his early idealism involve a complete break with the idealist alternative. Or so Siep (1970), 104ff., shows. For a more reconciliationist reading of the two (or three or four) Fichtes, see Janke (1970).

Chapter 4. The Jena formulations

1. How Hegel, still deeply concerned with the theological and social issues of his Frankfurt period, "became" the philosophical Hegel of the *PhG* and beyond is a matter of very great controversy, complicated by difficult philological, textual problems. I am not primarily concerned here with this developmental issue, which centers on when and why Hegel began to develop a positive account of dialectic, to think of speculative philosophy itself as a "logic," and to regard such speculation as about "Absolute Subjectivity," rather than as the "overcoming" of subjectivity. Rather than try to sort out the changing relation among the various projects Hegel was working on continuously in this period (philosophy of nature, of spirit, logic, political theory, aesthetics), I shall emphasize aspects of Hegel's understanding of his idealist predecessors that will be helpful in understanding the motivation for and the meaning of his own later idealism. In situating this issue in the Jena work, I have relied heavily on the work of Harris (1983), Düsing (1969, 1976), Kimmerle (1969, 1970), Horstmann (1972, 1977, 1980, 1982), and Pöggeler (1973b, 1973c).
2. The clearest example of such a relation is found in the 1802–3 *System der Sittlichkeit*, in which the concept/intuition problem, so prominent in Hegel's theoretical discussions of Kant, forms the basis for the structure of this work in practical philosophy. In the later Jena period, after what Pöggeler describes as a *gewisse Ruckwendung zu Fichte*, and so a turn away from Schelling, Hegel would consider the "structure of subjectivity" problem an issue *in* speculative philosophy, and so would attempt an "idealist" solution to problems earlier addressed in the context of *Lebensphilosophie*, aesthetics or religion. He would, that is, come to see the possibility of a "science of the experience of consciousness." Cf. Pöggeler (1973c), especially 294.
3. This interest explains my attention to *DS* and *GW*, to the exclusion of the 1804–5 Jena system and other works. The former works reveal a great deal, I shall argue, about what Hegel thought idealism could *not* be, although it is true that they alone do not do much more than that, that Hegel had not yet worked out adequately the implications of his criticisms. So Hegel could still, early in the Jena period, propose an "incarnated God" philosophy of nature that is not consistent with what I take to be the direction of his critique in the former works. See Harris (1983), 75–101. However, it was not long at all before *Geist*, not Nature, became the central problem of speculative philosophy, and this because of, as Horstmann argues, a growing attention to problems of the "self" and self-consciousness. See Horstmann (1972), 115. Cf. also Pöggeler (1973c), 279. Indeed, it is now relatively standard in the commentators I cite in this chapter to characterize the later Jena period as involving a return by Hegel to transcendental issues. This is true, but I think it can also be shown that much of the "idealism problem" as Hegel originally understood it in Jena reflects such

a transcendental orientation. Cf. Wildt (1982) on the early Jena writings as in fact, despite appearances, a *Radikalisierung Fichtescher Intentionen*, 303ff.

4. Harris in his "Processional Prelude" (1983), xix–lxx, describes well the details of such expectations, particularly by Goethe and Schiller. Although scholars disagree about whether there was a continuous development or a more radical break during this period, the standard view is that the Jena period ought to be divided into at least two phases: roughly, 1801–3, the years more closely associated with Schelling, when Hegel had a Schelling-like negative position on the limitations of all reflective thinking; and 1804–5 – with the writing of the *Systementwürfe II* – to 1807, when Hegel's approach to the problem of identity philosophy was much more obviously a matter of logic, or of thought's self-determination and realization. See Horstmann (1977), his introduction to the Meiner edition of the *Jenaer Realphilosophie*; Kimmerle (1970), 15–38 and 283–99; and Pöggeler (1973b, 1973c).
5. Cf. Düsing (1976), 121, 134, especially his remarks on the importance of Spinoza in such a project (or at least Jacobi's version of Lessing's Spinozism).
6. Düsing (1976), inter alia, 236.
7. Most of Hegel's clear references to Schelling in the works considered here are to the *System der transzendentalen Idealismus* (1800) and the *Darstellung meines System der Philosophie* (1801).
8. The indispensable work on Schelling's development away from German Idealism is Schulz (1975).
9. *SW*, I, 335, 337 (*Abhandlung zur Erlauterung des Idealismus der Wissenschaftslehre*).
10. *SW*, 2, 35 (*Ideen zu einer Philosophie der Natur*).
11. For a clear exposition, see White (1983b), 7–55.
12. This "relationship" question is, again, one of complicated scholarly dimensions. For a helpful overview, see Kimmerle (1970), especially 15–38; White's discussion (1983a) is also helpful, as is Düsing's (1969).
13. On the important relation between the "aesthetic object" in Kant and the Hegelian notion of a "concrete universal," see Wohlfart (1981).
14. *STI*, 355.
15. *STI*, 450–1.
16. *STI*, 455.
17. *STI*, 369.
18. *STI*, 600.
19. *STI*, 376.
20. *STI*, 600–1; cf. 350–1.
21. For Hegel's "logical" account of the problem of reflection, see Chapter 9, Section 2.
22. Out of such doubts about philosophic reflection grew Schelling's later position and the "end" of Idealism. See Schulz (1975), 11–20, 95–186; Marx (1986); and my discussion of his position in Pippin (1987b).
23. See, for example, his remarks on the artist, feeling, and sentimentality in *GW*, 323; *BK*, 65. For more on Hegel's motives in the break, already apparent in *DS*, from the Frankfurt period, Hölderlin-influenced concern with a "living" unity, see Düsing (1976), 70ff. and 135.
24. To return to the original issue that calls Schelling so quickly to mind, "freedom," one can simply note that the concluding paragraph of *GW*, with its dramatic

metaphor of the *necessary* "Good Friday," or speculative "death" of absolute freedom, suggests quite a non-Schellingean, even non-romantic view of freedom. See *GW*, 414; *BK*, 190–1.

25. He does, at one point in the *DS*, remark that Kant's account of nature is, no matter apparently what Kant thought, a mechanistic account, not a dynamic one; the reasons he gives for this charge clearly refer to Schelling. *DS*, 69; *Diff*, 163–4.
26. There is also much evidence of collaborative work between Schelling and Hegel in the early (1801–3) period, and that Hegel's understanding of the issue greatly influenced Schelling. For a good discussion of this collaboration and of the relevance of this issue for understanding the problem of dialectic, see Düsing (1969).
27. See Locke, *Essay*, I, 124, the quotation from Locke in *GW*, 326; *BK*, 68–9; and the discussion in S. Rosen (1974a), 89–122.
28. Cf. also Harris (1983), 21ff.
29. On this issue, cf. Schelling's discussion of "Reflexion" as "Analysis" in *STI*, 173, and the use he makes of his account of reflection to criticize Fichte.
30. The strongest is at B679–A651, where Kant claims that without the "law of reason" there could be "no coherent use of the understanding" and even "no sufficient criterion of empirical truth." See the discussion in Pippin (1982), 201–15.
31. The decisive alteration in Hegel's understanding of such speculation appeared around the 1803–4 academic year, when Hegel began to call his "logic" itself an "idealism," although I believe that the passages cited in this chapter reveal that in Hegel's criticisms of his predecessors it is already clear that such a speculative logic could only be a "logic of subjectivity." *SS* already reveals how Hegel was reformulating the notions of dialectic and subjectivity and was formulating the goal of speculative philosophy in the idealist terms of an "identity" of intuition and concept. Cf. *SS*, 7; *Sys*, 99–100.
32. There is, though, an ambiguity in Hegel's early formulae about the Absolute and speculative knowledge that will return and ought to be noted. For the most part, Hegel appears to understand the content of speculative knowledge as a clarification of the *nature* of "Reason's self-producings," an account of the nature of the objectivity of such an activity, and an exploration of the general conceptual constraints any "thought" (truly non-empirical self-determination of Reason) must impose on itself and on what could be an object of experience, all for such a thinking to *be* such a rational producing. And sometimes Hegel appears to think that this (roughly) metalevel enterprise (with Reason as *its* object) is the first step in a deduction of, or even a rational comprehension of, *all* determinate content, from electricity to somnambulism. Needless to say, I am restricting myself to the former element in Hegel's thought, and I think that position is an identifiable and intended one in the texts under consideration. But the issue is a complicated one and will recur several times in later texts. For a helpful discussion of a particular aspect of this issue at this time, see Horstmann (1980) on the relation between the "logic" and the "metaphysics" of subjectivity, especially 189.
33. There are indications that Kant himself tended to think of the problem of apperception in terms of "intuition," once even describing apperception as an "indeterminate intuition." B422n. Cf. Pippin (1987a), 454–5.

34. For the practical version of this language, see *SS*, where Hegel claims that "Intellectual intuition is alone realized by and in ethical life" (*SS*, 53; *Sys*, 143). Cf. Rose (1981), 59–72.
35. *STI*, III, 369.
36. Kant, *AA*, vol. 5, 404; *CJ*, 252–3. For an extensive discussion of the connections between Kant's doctrine of reflective judgment and Hegel's speculative logic, see Wohlfart (1981), 1–65.
37. *AA*, vol. 5, 403; *CJ*, 251.
38. *AA*, vol. 5, 407; *CJ*, 255.
39. In *DS*, Hegel praises Fichte for not requiring, as Kant did, that Nature be "determined" by "another understanding" to account for those determinations not explained by the understanding's formal organization. Fichte realized that "Nature is determined immediately by and for intelligence" (*DS*, 54–5; *Diff*, 143). Although Hegel will disagree that nature is "immediately" so determined, this is one of the passages that makes it appear that Hegel believes he can be more successful than either Kant or Fichte in uniting concept and intuition by demonstrating the rational necessity of *all* the determinations of Nature. I shall try to show later that this is not a genuine implication of his idealism, that the issue at stake is only the "Notional" determinations of Nature, even though for Hegel such a domain is certainly considerably broader than it was for Kant's account of pure concepts.
40. Some of the characteristics of what Hegel will defend as Absolute Knowledge are present in *DS*, in the section on "The Relation of Philosophizing to a Philosophical System." On the one hand, Hegel's account of the "self-production of Reason" and "Reason's activity" as a "pure self-exposition" confirm the "concept idealism" direction I have attributed to him. On the other hand, it is not clear how much he wants to claim when he says that "philosophizing must aim to posit this [finite] manifold as internally connected . . . [in] . . . a system of science," and he is still partly relying on a Schellingean language of a "speculation/intuition–conscious/unconscious" schema he will soon abandon. See *DS*, 30–1; *Diff*, 133.
41. Harris (1983), 3–73; Görland (1966), 15.
42. *TJ*, 346. Cf. the helpful account given by Harris in his introduction to *Diff*, particularly 3–15.
43. *SuW*, I, 242. There is a wonderful presentiment of the German Idealist tendency to intermingle transcendental and theological issues in this passage from Herder (written in 1787): "Zwischen jedem Subjekt und Prädikat stehet ein Ist oder Ist nicht und dies Ist, diese Formel der Gleichung und Ubereinstimmung verschiedener Begriffe, das blosse Zeichen = ist meine Demonstration von Gott" (1967), 16, 516ff.
44. Görland (1966), 15.
45. Cf. the relation between "concept" (labor, *Bildung*) and "intuition" (love, need, feeling) in *SS*, 9ff.; *Sys*, 102ff.
46. I note that in the German, when Hegel writes "a priori," he includes the appositive *d.h. absolut*, and that later in *EL*, Hegel will explicitly gloss his own notion of the "freedom" of thought as the "apriority" of thought. (*EL*, section 12.) This equation of *absolut* and freedom and the a priori will be important in Chapter 10, this volume. See Sections 1 and 4.
47. See the claim in *GW* that "the In-Itself of *empirical* consciousness is Reason itself" (329; *BK*, 73) and the numerous a posteriori examples used in this section.

48. See Pippin (1978).
49. This is not to say that Hegel is not in this period committed to some kind of a claim about numerical identity, a claim that derives from the monistic implications of the account of the "totality of Absolute *Geist*," implications he was still working out. See Horstmann (1980), 187ff.
50. That Hegel regards the identity issue as this kind of truth claim is confirmed by a discussion of Kant and his "true idealism" in *GW*, 332; *BK*, 76. What is not clear in the passage is just what Hegel takes his criticism of the "mere formality" of Kant's view of the objective identity between subjective concept and objective world to entail.
51. Thus what I am claiming is that elements of Hegel's "logical" or idealist version of identity are already present in *GW*, even though he was still also under the influence of Schelling's romantic metaphysics. So I think Düsing goes too far in claiming that Hegel's early theory of subjectivity radicalizes Descartes against Kant and conceives of self-knowledge as indeed knowledge of substance. I have tried to show throughout the last two chapters the preservation of the transcendental theory of apperception. See Düsing (1976), 239. If I am right about this continuity, Kimmerle's central problem with Hegel's early and later idealism, its *Abgeschlossenheit*, or the "closedness" of thought upon itself, would also have to be rethought (1970), 51–85.
52. Although the text is far from clear, some evidence for this claim can be found in the 1804–5 Jena system "Metaphysics," in the section on "Cognition as System of First Principles," which begins with the claim that cognition is "self-equivalence that persists even in opposition" (*JS*, 128FF; *LM*, 133ff.). Cf. Horstmann (1980), 184ff. See also even earlier evidence in the 1803–4 *Philosophie des Geistes, PG*, 273, and Kimmerle's (1970) remarks about the passage, especially his claim that they represent a "Wendepunkt in der Entwicklung des Hegelschen Denkens in Jena" and that they signal the return to a Kantian–Fichtean "Transzendentalphilosophie" as the "Zentralbegriff der Philosophie" (259). (Cf. also Kimmerle's evaluation of this development, 263.)
53. *Ethics*, 2, prop. 7.
54. Rosenkranz (1963), 178ff., 201ff. Cf. Kimmerle (1969), 43, 44.

Chapter 5. Skepticism, knowledge, and truth in the Jena phenomenology

1. This recalls again the significance of Hegel's charge, at first glance tendentious and inaccurate, that Kant was an empirical psychologist. As we begin to see, he means to charge that although Kant correctly reformulated the problem of objective categories, of the fundamental structure of things, as the problem of transcendental subjectivity, he misunderstood his results by comprehending them in a quasi-empirical way. This meant that Kant was seduced into worrying that, since the phenomenal world was "conditioned" by our conceptual scheme, had we a different scheme, there would be a different (phenomenal) world; hence the thing-in-itself problem. Since Hegel *denies* that this could be so, many have taken him to mean that the world is as we (fundamentally) think it to be *because* it is the product of thought's positings or itself somehow mental. See Rorty (1972), 664. Things look different, I am trying to suggest, once we read Hegel's denial of Kant's skepticism as grounded not in such a monistic metaphysics but in a way of *demonstrating* what Rorty himself keeps suggesting but does not

demonstrate: that the thing-in-itself world is simply a "world well lost." (All Rorty basically has is a very abstract "Who cares?" response to the realist skeptic and his doubts.)

2. It is important to note especially that Hegel does not refer to the *Encyclopedia* as a whole here; only the *Science of Logic* is *Wissenschaft*.
3. Miller translates a "spontaneous" here. I agree with the sentiment, but it's not in the German.
4. Perhaps the best extended (i.e., book-length) argument showing, quite convincingly, why Hegel's theory of subjectivity cannot be understood in "substantialist" terms is that of Brockard (1970). See especially 59ff. I am in agreement with much of what Brockard concludes, but (predictably, I suppose) I do not think he deals in sufficient detail with the Kant and Fichte connections in Hegel, and so the self-consciousness theme, for him to be able to state clearly what such a "subjectivity" theory finally is.
5. The problem Hegel faces can be usefully compared with similar issues in Wittgenstein. Hegel too, speaking informally, is interested in showing that understanding what the Wittgensteinean would call a fundamental human "like-mindedness" is the way to understand and legitimate what would otherwise be considered ontological commitments, or what there is about "the world" that could not change. [Cf. Brockard's formulation (1970), 89.] And he is interested in showing that this like-mindedness is not a "fact" about us that might have been different, that it is pointless to wonder about a possible other-mindedness, or about the world as it "really" is. But Wittgenstein does not think there is much that can usefully be *said* about such like-mindedness, and so cannot raise Hegel's "Deduction" problem or Hegel's phenomenological account of how we come to be as like-minded as we are. (In essence, this is because there is no account of self-consciousness, at least as insisted on in the idealist tradition, in Wittgenstein.) For a discussion of similar topics, see the illuminating articles by Lear (1982, 1984). In Lamb (1980), an explicit attempt is made to connect the Wittgensteinean and Hegelian programs, with, I think, predictable results. Lamb throughout, with the Wittgensteinean influence, threatens to lose sight completely of the critical, deductive intention of much in Hegel, all in favor of a "descriptive" program. See 31–41. Much of this characterization stems, if I am right in what has been said so far, from an exaggerated emphasis on Hegel's "rejection of the critical method" (31). Findlay (1958) is probably the commentator best known for a Wittgenstein-influenced reading of Hegel. See also n. 13 in Chapter 6, this volume, on Taylor.
6. For initial support of such a reading, see also this remark in the *Vorlesungen über die Geschichte der Philosophie*:

> Es ist eine neue Epoche in der Welt entsprungen. Es scheint, dass es dem Weltgeiste jetzt gelungen ist, alles fremde gegenständliche Wesen sich abzutun, und endlich sich als absoluten Geist zu erfassen, und was ihm gegenständlich wird, aus sich zu erzeugen, und es, mit Ruhe dagegen, in seiner Gewalt zu behalten. Der Kampf des endlichen Selbstbewusstseins mit dem absoluten Selbtsbewusstsein, das jenem ausser ihm erschien, hört auf. Das endliche Selbstbewusstsein hat aufgehört, endliches zu sein; und dadurch anderseits das absolute Selbstbewusstein die Wirklichkeit erhalten, der es vorher entbehrte.
>
> (*JA*, 19, 689ff.)

7. It is true that Hegel claims, "But to want the nature of cognition clarified prior to the science is to demand that it be considered outside the science; outside the science this cannot be accomplished, at least not in a scientific manner and such a manner is alone here in place" (*WL*, I, 52; *SL*, 68). However, this is not inconsistent with Hegel's claims about the *PhG*'s deduction of "pure knowing," since he makes clear that in the *Logic* he is concerned with "the nature of cognition simply as such," that the problem of the "nature of cognition" is different from the issue of whether there *is* "absolute knowing." Cf. Aschenberg's discussion (1976), 225–47. In this context, I can see no justification for Maker's claim (1981a) that Hegel intends the *PhG* to be a wholly "negative" introduction, the "self-sublating" of "knowing" itself, so that the *SL* can be understood as radically presuppositionless. Hegel had abandoned the idea of a "negative" or wholly self-destructive introduction after 1804 and never returned to it. (Cf. *EL*, section 78.) Cf. also the much clearer statement of the *PhG–SL* relation in the original (1812) opening remarks, "Womit muss der Anfang der Wissenschaft gemacht werden?," which Miller, using Lasson's edition, does not translate. *GWe*, 11, 33.
8. I discuss subsequently the relevance of this association of realism with skepticism for Hegel. For a clear thematic statement of the issue itself, see Kupperman (1975).
9. What I am calling the "deductive" intention of the *PhG* has recently been characterized in a different way in an important book by Flay (1984). He understands the *PhG* as a "quest for certainty," or an attempt to "establish warranty for one's certainty of access" to an account of "the ultimate nature of reality," the Absolute Standpoint (1ff). Although I am in substantial agreement with many of Flay's conclusions about the *PhG*, I would disagree with two things. First, I think the emphasis on "certainty" is misleading; it suggests a kind of Cartesian completion to the Hegelian project and distorts the nature of the skepticism problem in the *PhG*. [One way of stating this problem is simply to note that Flay has provided us with a very well worked out version of Heidegger's interpretation of Hegel. See Heidegger (1970) and Flay, 271. This leaves Hegel open to a number of criticisms, especially Heidegger's own, but only if Heidegger's association of Hegel with the traditional history of ontology is correct. I do not think Heidegger is right, but obviously I cannot argue it here. See Flay's closing remarks (249–67).] Second, Flay's account of the *PhG*'s methodology makes use of the notion of a "praxical presupposition," an interpretive term Flay often explains by reference to problems of meaning and truth value (see 22). As I assume is already apparent, I think that the "presupposition" or "condition" question in Hegel is better articulated in terms of the post-Kantian apperception problem crucial to all German Idealism. So, when Flay says that his praxical presuppositions can be said to "form the a priori synthetic unity of the constituents of experience" (24), I am in complete agreement, but would argue that we need the *whole* story of the Hegelian transformation of this Kantian problematic before we can properly understand the *PhG*.
10. *GWe*, IV, 197–238.
11. *GWe*, IV, 202–3; *RPS*, 318–19.
12. This is roughly the accusation against the Kantian approach raised by Stroud (1984), 162.
13. Of course, as will be quickly apparent, "skepticism" will come to mean some-

thing quite specific to Hegel's project. He will be especially concerned with distancing himself from classic Enlightenment skepticism, which Hegel regards as wholly "negative" and ultimately inconsistent. (See *EL*, section 78.) The most famous and perhaps most influential example of this attempt to undermine completely, in his own way, "skeptically," the self-understanding of a "shape of spirit" while preserving its implicit expression of speculative truth is in his account of religion. Cf. Fulda (1965), 30. Cf. also Kortian (1980), 34–47, for a "critical theory" reading of the problem of skepticism (i.e., the critique of positivism).

14. Cf. again Lear (1982), especially his claim on 392 about the Wittgensteinean acceptance of "Only because we are minded as we are do we see the world as we do" and rejection (as "nonsense") of "If we were other minded, we would see the world differently." I am suggesting that the same strategy is at work in Hegel, but with a much different strategy for showing *why* the latter claim ought to be rejected.
15. There are so many contemporary versions of antirealism, ranging from Dummett's generalization of intuitionism in mathematics to Putnam's "internal realism" to van Fraasen's empiricism, that it is difficult and potentially confusing to introduce Hegel into the debate. But there are several classic problems faced by antirealists, such as the rejection of bivalence, the necessity for something like "degrees" (or "moments") of truth, counterintuitions about true propositions that can never be verified, and so on, that Hegel not only faces up to but enthusiastically embraces. Cf. the discussion in Chapter 4, Section 4, and Chapter 9, Section 3, on Hegelian "contradiction." For a useful summary of such antirealist problems (and an account of how they appear in British Objective Idealism), see Smart (1986).
16. What this approach suggests about reading the *PhG* is that the line of argument that begins with Hegel's appropriation of and criticism of Kant and Fichte now comes to a relative completion in the *PhG*, more particularly, that it is completed essentially in Chapter Four. This resolution will itself introduce a different topic and several different problems in the *PhG* (not to mention in European philosophy after Hegel), and it will, in effect, create a kind of skepticism problem different from the one considered here. This will mean that there will be a great deal left "to do" in the chapters on Spirit, Religion, and Absolute Knowledge, but, I shall suggest in the last section of Chapter 7 of this volume, these tasks are wholly subordinate to, are only worth pursuing, if the central idealism issue is successfully resolved in the first four chapters. To some extent, this means that I am siding with the reading given the *PhG* by Pöggeler (1973d), but for essentially thematic rather than historical reasons. See also Pöggeler (1973c) and his strong characterization there of the *PhG* itself as the "phenomenology of self-consciousness." Fulda (1965) is the most convincing opponent of such readings (117ff). But that is because Fulda lays so much stress on the "introduction" problem, sometimes to the neglect of the "deduction" issue, although he is clearly quite aware of the "double" issue (165ff). Cf. Aschenberg (1976), section V, 263ff., and Hegel's own rare remarks on the issue in *EL*, section 25.
17. I should stress again here how many different problems were introduced into the idealist tradition by the Kantian claim about the implicit self-consciousness of consciousness. In this context, there are at least two serious issues involved. One involves what some commentators call the "formal-logical" issue, the "logic" of this peculiar kind of self-relation. For many, the problems of such a

logic both generate and constitute the core of speculative logic itself. The other involves what we might call the "content" of such a transcendental self-relation, the content of, in a word, the Notion. On the former issue, see Cramer (1979), 219–21, and (1974), 594–601.

18. I should note that this "reconstructive" suggestion about Hegel's methodology is quite controversial, given the well-established views about Hegelian theodicy. I shall be suggesting that Hegel is pursuing such a reconstructive argument in demonstrating the truth of idealism in general (i.e., that he proceeds negatively, by showing the undeniability of such a position, its necessary presupposition in what first appear more straightforward, realist positions), in demonstrating the necessary moments of an idealist "logic," and finally, in accounting for the role of such a logic as constraining the knowledge of Nature and Spirit. For some Hegelians, this will raise the question of what originally grounds or accounts for such a reconstruction of Spirit's internal rationality; whence the originally constructive activity? (It is also the chief issue of contention in the rejection, by both the later Fichte and the later Schelling, of idealism.) And they point to Spirit's hidden hand again, or to some other teleological account of *why* this reconstruction would originally be possible. I am arguing that Hegel's account is a reconstruction of the possibility of self-conscious, objective judgment and action, and that his idealism *excludes* such a metaphysical ground. There is a brief explanation of the strategy of reconstruction (*Nachbildung*) in *EL*, section 12, although it is eliminated in the translation by Wallace's use of "copy." For a fuller use of such a reconstructive strategy, see the account of self-consciousness in Chapter 7 and my account of Hegel's rejection of "external teleology" in Chapter 10, section 3. Cf. also the important remarks by Hartmann (1976a), and Henrich (1982a).
19. The particular way in which Hegel is relying on such a putative "experience" to establish his results will be clearer in the next chapter. See also Aschenberg (1976), especially his remarks concluding section II on "transcendental experience," 247; Pippin (1975); and Dove (1971) for his useful survey of the literature and his own comments, especially 55–56.
20. Cf. Chapter 7, Section 3, this volume.
21. See Aschenberg's summary of the literature (1976), 263ff., and Fulda's *Vorwort* (1965), 1–13, for another overview. For similar arguments denying the dispensability of the *PhG*, see Fackenheim (1967), 31–74, especially 67–73; Rosen (1974a), 123–30; Labarriere (1968), 17–30; and Baillie's clear summary of the issues (1984), 195–217.
22. A well worked out recent example of such an interpretation is given by Solomon (1983).
23. See Fulda (1965), 9, for a concise Hegelian formulation of the problem: "does the sceptical self-destruction of consciousness precede the completion of science, or follow from it?" Even more broadly, the issue is how and why philosophy itself can be said to "begin," what calls for it, if anything, and what it "leads to."
24. Pöggeler (1973d), 170–230. For more on the Haering issue, see Fulda (1965), 131ff; Labarriere (1968), 21ff.; and Aschenberg (1976), 263–4. For the opposing view of the *PhG*'s structure see Fulda (1966), 75–101.
25. Briefly, Fulda's position (1965) is that the *PhG* is an introduction to Hegel's system, not part of the system, but not a mere propadeutic and itself "scientific." See 110 and especially his remarks about Hegel's 1816 alterations on 114. Ac-

cordingly, although Fulda often stresses both the introductory and justificatory dimensions of the *PhG*, he constantly focuses on the former and interprets the latter in terms that create problems with what Fulda recognizes as the *SL*'s own demonstration or justification of claims about the limitations of "finite thought." I am interpreting the latter problem as more prominent and am trying to understand it in terms more consistent with the original Kantian Deduction problem. This narrows my focus somewhat to issues relevant to the idealism problem (especially the realist skepticism problem). Fulda's approach makes possible a way of understanding the function of the chapters on Spirit and Religion, but only, I think, at the philosophic cost of slighting the problem of legitimating the idealist standpoint. (Or: *Why* introduce natural consciousness to an understanding of the Absolute Standpoint when there might be little reason to think it *is* "absolute"?) Cf. 132 ff. and n. 16, this chapter.

26. This problem also involves the complex, much discussed issue of the extent to which Hegel can be considered a genuinely "critical" philosopher, as that neo-Hegelian, neo-Marxist movement came to be known. The clearest "critical theory" attack on Hegel is Habermas's (1971). For a general summary of the Habermas–Hegel relation see Kortian (1980). Habermas claims, in sum, that "the assumptions of the philosophy of identity kept Hegel from reaping the real harvest of his critique of Kant" (43). He says this because although Hegel, according to Habermas, "sees through the absolutism of an epistemology based on unreflected presuppositions" (10), he "presumes as given" throughout the *PhG* a "knowledge of the Absolute," by which, at the very least, Habermas understands "absolute knowledge independent of the subjective conditions of possible knowledge" (11). Obviously, the key to Habermas's criticisms involves his understanding of this contrast between a "radicalized epistemology," committed to the "self-constitution of the species," and an "identity theory," committed to "Absolute Knowledge." Accordingly, this criticism (not to mention Adorno's) is weakened by the lack of precision in casually attributing such an "identity theory" to Hegel. (Habermas often simply makes use of the historically received, prominent understanding of that position, one forged in the early "left–right" Hegelian fights.) Where he does indicate what he takes such an attribution to consist in (24), Habermas reveals that he thinks Hegel is trying to "usurp" the "legitimacy of independent sciences by a philosophy claiming to retain its position as universal scientific knowledge." I have been arguing that such an interpretation of Hegel (1) seriously underestimates the extent of Hegel's *appropriation* of Kant, and so exaggerates the criticism of Kant; (2) can be made consistent with Hegel's own characterization of Absolute Knowledge as the "realization of the Notion" or Spirit's full "self-consciousness" only by saddling Hegel with a traditional understanding of real (numerical) "identity," and so a metaphysical monism he does not espouse; and (3) confuses the issue of "Absolute Knowledge," a knowledge *about* the proper understanding of Reason and Actuality, with Hegel's *Encyclopedia* animadversions about the implications of such a claim. In sum, much of Habermas's criticism is irrelevant if the "subject matter" of Absolute Knowledge, "the Notion," concerns the empirically undetermined and so historically "self-constituted" Notionality of any possible experience, if the core of Hegel's idealism in no way "usurps" the empirical investigations of various sciences, but continues in a different way the Kantian quest for the categorial conditions of all such knowledge. In a recent work, Habermas (1987) has restated his criticism of Hegel, and although he still relies

on an interpretation of Hegelian Spirit as a metaphysical "macro-subject," his main emphasis now is on Hegel's (and Marx's) reliance on the "philosophy of subjectivity" in general. This emphasis on, basically, Hegel's theory of reflective rationality (cf. 84) makes for a more powerful and more historically interesting assessment of Hegel and Hegel's place in the "modernity" problem. See n. 38 in Chapter 7, this volume. For more discussion of Hegel and the Frankfurt School, see Schmidt (1971) and Pippin (1985).

27. Cf. Fulda (1965), 29, 52ff. Fulda is certainly right to note that the fact that there is a nonphenomenological introduction to the *Encyclopedia* in no way demonstrates that Hegel thought he had eliminated the need for a separate introduction and justification of Science. See *EL*, sections 4, 25, and 78. For a clear statement of the opposing view (i.e., the denigration of the significance of the Jena *PhG*), see Petry's "Introduction" to the *BPhG* (1981), xiii–xciv.
28. Tugendhat (1979), 310. All the objections cited earlier are raised by Tugendhat.
29. For more discussion of the differences between the ordinary senses of *Wissen* and *Wahrheit* and the use to which Hegel puts these terms in the *PhG*, see the discussion by Cramer (1976), 77ff., especially his account of the general relation between *Bewusstsein* for Hegel and the *Gedanken der Wahrheit* and *Anspruch des Wissens* (91). Aschenberg's is one of the most comprehensive and interesting studies of the problem of truth in the *PhG* (1976). For a decisive rejection of Tugendhat's supposed "Last dance with Hegel," see Siep (1981).
30. Cf. Hegel's remarks in the Preface about how even factual claims, such as when Caesar was born, also require the "movement of self-consciousness" (*PhG*, 31; *PS*, 23) or the development of a criterion of truth. He makes the same sort of claim about how a mathematical proof also presupposes what he calls the "essentiality" of the proof, a philosophic understanding of the relation between such a proof and "truth" (*PhG*, 32; *PS*, 24).
31. This charge is typical of Tugendhat's approach in (1979) and in his extended statement of his own "analytic" program (1982). I discuss some problems with the latter in Pippin (forthcoming b). See also Theunissen's remarks on Tugendhat (1978b), 66, 434.

Chapter 6. Overcoming consciousness

1. On the manifold and sometimes quite subtle differences between Hegel's idealist theory of intentionality and later realist theories, especially those of Natorp, Husserl, Brentano, and Dilthey, see the fine study by Cramer (1974). He demonstrates well how the problems in such latter theories (focused, for Cramer, around the issue of *Erlebnis*) ought to prompt a return to Hegel's account of the necessary relation between conscious intending and self-consciousness. See especially 593–4.
2. It should be noted, though, that to view this chapter in this way, in terms of the justificatory function of the *PhG* within Hegel's idealist project, is also to introduce the concerns of the chapter in a relatively restricted way. That is, although Hegel has spoken of the *PhG* as the education of natural consciousness, this does not mean that he thinks he has here identified the "most natural" or intuitive understanding of consciousness's relation to its objects. The first sentence of the chapter refers only to what kind of knowledge must at the start be *our* object, for the tasks of the *PhG*, and Hegel does nothing throughout the chapter to alter the impression that the epistemological position described bears

little resemblance to a commonsense or philosophic theory. The theory supposedly at issue restricts itself to what would be an incomprehensible language of exclusively demonstratives (or perhaps, deictic expressions in general), and the proponent of the position is far more opposed to the mere mention of a universal term than any defender of common sense or empiricism need be. Accordingly, when Hegel speaks of natural consciousness as an assumed context for this beginning, I take him to be simply referring to the assumption that consciousness *can* intend objects. There is thus all the difference in the world between "beginning" with the natural consciousness assumption of intentionality and then, in a highly abstract, methodologically determined way, "beginning" with the first candidate reflective account of the possibility of this relation. The former could loosely be called a "natural" assumption. The latter is a product of reflective theory, and is as it is because of the proposed project of the *PhG*, not because this is the account the man in the street would think up first. Cf. Cramer (1976), 91ff.

3. "In apprehending (*Auffassen*) it [the object], we must refrain from trying to comprehend (*Begreifen*) it" (*PhG*, 63; *PS*, 58).
4. Although Hegel is trying to show that reference to a particular requires such a mediating, describing, and theorizing capacity, he is also trying to show that the "dependence" of such intentional reference on such capacities should *not* be understood as a simple subsumption of a particular under a description or of an intuition under a concept. Since conscious intending is originally a function of a subject's form of apperception, there is no such independent particularity in Hegel's full account. This creates, obviously, a vast complication, one that involves Hegel's basic claim, that "objects are, in truth, the Notion." Ultimately Hegel will claim that knowledge *can* be of "individuals" or "concrete universals," although it won't be clear for quite a while what this entails.

   Thus with respect to Soll's (1985) criticism of Taylor's (1975) position on just this point: I think Taylor is quite within his rights to state Hegel's argument from "within" the position of consciousness (in which there are external, determinate particulars to be "reached") and to restate Hegel's dialectical overcoming of such a position in terms of the assumptions about determinacy and selectivity inherent in that point of view. Soll is right to point out that Hegel is *ultimately* after the very Notion of particularity [something Taylor himself admitted in an earlier interpretation (1976, 166)], but Soll's point is premature without some detailed explanation of what such an ultimate attack on particularity is supposed to involve.
5. The classic account of the relevance of this section of the *PhG* to aporiai in Greek philosophy is that of Purpus (1908). See also Purpus (1904–5). Rosen (1974b), although relying much more on the *SL*, has also established the connection between such issues. Solomon (1983) has pointed out the relevance to Russell (321ff).
6. As we shall see in much greater detail, this "determinacy" (*Bestimmtheit*) issue, which plays so large a role in the *SL*, is the Hegelian successor to the Kantian problem of "unity" in experience and, I am arguing, will require a similar Hegelian account, a "dependence" on the "unity of apperception" and the "Notional moments" of such a unity. See Section 2.
7. This issue has been one of the most contentious in the literature: To what extent can the difficulty encountered by a "sense-certain experiencer" in "saying what it means" be said to be a problem inherent in such an experi-

ence, and to what extent is it an "external" philosophical problem, the lack of resolution of which has no bearing on whether such an experiencer can mean what he means? (The original formulation of this objection was made by Feuerbach.) For a clear counter to the objection, see Westphal (1978), 73ff. For one of the best accounts of how and why sense certainty can be said to be already "playing the philosophical game" in its intending, its *Meinen*, and so to be differentiating itself between a *Bekanntschaft mit der Sache* and the *Schein der Bekanntschaft*, see Wiehl (1966), especially 110–11.

8. Cf. Soll (1985), 63–4.
9. With respect to this issue of determinacy, it should be noted in anticipation that all Hegel is ultimately interested in is *qualitative determinacy*, the conditions required for an object to be picked out as to *kind* or "universal." This does *not* mean that Hegel thinks particulars do not exist, as I am reading him (contrary to the metaphysical-monist reading), but it does attribute to him the claim that such Notional determinacy is the "truth" or "essence" or, most properly, the "actuality" of what there is. Given that position, I see no reason to deny Hegel the full use of singular terms, demonstratives, and so on, as long as one keeps in mind that in his position the singularity presupposed by such subject terms is not an ontological ultimate, but dependent for its specifiability on "Notional determination" and the interconnections (and "history" properly understood) of such Notions.
10. It is characteristic of Hegel's idiosyncratic terminology that he wants us to understand universality as such a mediation of "this" and "not-this," in this case, a thing that stays the same (this) even as its sense qualities change (not-this). He uses this language at the beginning of the next chapter on perception. For some useful remarks on this mediation issue, as well as on what sense certainty "presupposes," see Wiehl (1966).
11. See Hume (1967), 2, and the problem Stroud poses for Hume on this issue, (1977), 20–1.
12. Hegel's position is, very roughly, that what makes an intellectual activity, like "judging," a *cognitive* activity, *and* a claim about this, or this set of objects, is its functioning within the conditions established by the "self-developing Notion," or Spirit's collective self-understanding, a practice, to use a non-Hegelian word, at once social and teleological. He does not spell out in detail why the possibility of something like reference should be a matter dependent on such institutional *functions*, but there is still much of relevance in his position to contemporary, especially post-Wittgensteinean, attempts.
13. Taylor (1976) has associated the argument of the first three chapters of the *PhG* with Wittgensteinean, anti-Cartesian, antiempiricist, transcendental arguments. As noted in Chapter 5 (see n. 5), there are indeed a number of important points of comparison between the two. However, in this case, Wittgenstein's anti-systematic, informalist methodology greatly complicates attempts to associate his later approach with Hegel. For example, Hegel is not trying to show that various candidate accounts of experience are individually impossible (as in the private language argument of the *Investigations*) or comparatively better or worse than others. His interest is developmental and systematic, a reconstructive account of the possibility of experience driven by the consciousness/self-consciousness problematic and the objectivity issue that it raises. Taylor's approach in this article does not, and given the Wittgenstein orientation, cannot, address

such an issue. In his book (1975), his narrative of Hegel's developmental case is determined by a metaphysical reading of Hegel's claim about "Spirit's knowledge of itself."

14. Thus, what is driving Hegel's argument forward here is not some simple assumption about the determinacy of possible objects of knowledge or a requirement for a capacity to "select out" relevant features of experience, but this kind of demonstration that such an indeterminate object, what sense certainty is Notionally committed to as the object, is internally incoherent, subject fatally to regular, old-fashioned "contradiction," and so not a possible object. However, as Hegel has also tried to show, the nature of this incoherence and the story of its generation reveal what is necessary to preserve consciousness's assumption about intending in a way directly responsive to such problems. There is a way, formulated by "Perception," to maintain that such an object must be both this and not-this, *this* instance of a universal, while *not* being such a universal.
15. Heidegger (1970). Much of the contemporary French attack on Hegel seems to me simply to reproduce the Heideggerean approach. I have in mind *inter alia* the work of Deleuze (1962) and Derrida (1978a, 1982b).
16. Wiehl (1966) has tried to make use of Kant's distinction between *Wahrnehmungsurteile* and *Erfahrungsurteile* to restate the claim being made in this section. This is not, I think, a particularly useful approach, since Kant's formulations of the distinction in the *Prolegomena* are imprecise and often inconsistent. A better example of the same kind of dilemma faced by Kant, one of relevance to the issue in this chapter, is what he calls the "paradox" of the apperception–inner sense relation. See Pippin (1982), 172–82.
17. For reference to some of the historical allusions here, many of which can be quite confusing, see Hyppolite (1974), 100–10. Solomon (1983) makes some useful remarks about the various possible historical addressees of Hegel's case: see 337–46. Cf. also Purpus (1908), 70–101, on the perception paradoxes.
18. Hegel makes clear the connection between his attack on the position of Perception and Kant in the *EL* addition to section 42.
19. Cf. Kant's "Anticipations of Perception," A167–B207ff.
20. Cf. Taylor's account (1976), 168–82. Taylor presents Chapter Two in a way that introduces the "resolution" of its "One/Also" paradox in "force" as the necessary reliance of consciousness on "causal powers" to explain the determinacy of the perceived object. Cf. the different account in Chapter 7, Section 1, this volume. Although he notes (174) that Hegel is thereby making a move similar to that in Book II of the *SL*, he does not note that this move is, there and here, a move to *reflection* and so an introduction of the problem of the "subject's determination of itself." Cf. Taylor's very brief, but I believe quite accurate, summary of this transition in his book (1975), 146–7. Note that Taylor here refers to the Hegelian Notion as "the structure of subjectivity."
21. For one of the clearest accounts of the relevance of this chapter to general problems in the philosophy of science, see Westphal (1978), 93–119. Lamb's comments on similar issues are also helpful, but brief (1980, 104–8).
22. Cf. *CJ*, 21; *AA*, vol. 5, 184–5; *KrV*, A644–B672 and especially A651–B679. Cf. also, in this regard, Kitcher (1986).
23. Gadamer (1976c) uses the Platonic *chorismos* as his central example of the inverted world issue (40ff). At several other points in his essay, Gadamer also alludes to what is quite an important point: that Hegel's claim here is paradigmatic for

much of what he wants to say about the limitations of traditional philosophical reflection, especially for his well-known attack on abstract or formal principles of practical rationality. Such principles either "invert" the real world, attempt to turn it into another, unreal world, or "pervert" it (another meaning of *verkehren*) by judging it to be permanently corrupt. However, Gadamer's essay, although beginning with a reference to the centrality of the consciousness/self-consciousness issue, concludes with no indication of how the specific problem of the inverted world is supposed to raise the issue of self-consciousness. He suggests that what we are now going to do is to think "of what is, as a self" and thereby "penetrate into the interior of nature, i.e., its life" (see 52–3). Hegel has already rejected this notion of "penetrating" into the interior of anything (that would be another *jenseits*) and, I shall argue in the first section of Chapter 7, this volume, Gadamer's romantic reading of the "life" issue is not supportable by anything in the text. For a clearer account of the "transition" issue, see Cramer (1979), 220–5.

Chapter 7. Satisfying self-consciousness

1. To be sure, this passage can also be read as much as a beginning, perhaps the true beginning of the *PhG*, rather than as the kind of closure I am suggesting. Cf. Kojeve (1969), 31ff., especially 36–7, or Habermas on Hegel's demonstration that epistemology must become "social theory" (1971), 43ff. However, it will not be difficult to show that the idealism issue I have been tracing through German Idealism, Hegel's early work, and the first two chapters of the *PhG* is, in Hegel's eyes, "resolved" in many important respects in this chapter, and if that is so, then, I shall suggest, the Marxist or social-theoretical approach to the rest of the *PhG* will prove difficult to maintain. Cf. Marx (1975) for a defense of the claim that the whole "idea" of the *PhG* is contained in the "principle of self-consciousness" (98), and Bernstein (1984a) for a decisive refutation of the materialist reading and criticism of this chapter.

   I note also the "architectonic" evidence for reading this chapter as a kind of culmination of the major work of the *PhG*: the correspondence between the Objective Logic of Being, and consciousness and Perception, between essence and the reflective, essence–appearance paradoxes of understanding, and between the Subjective Logic of the Notion – introduced by the reference to Kantian apperception and *Leben* – and self-consciousness. For a discussion of such a relation, see the important article by Pöggeler (1973c), 257ff. But cf. Fulda's influential contrary view in (1966) and his detailed position in (1965).
2. Pöggeler (1973c), 248. In the early sections of this article, Pöggeler stresses the metaphysical dimensions of Hegel's early account of life. Cf. 246: "Das einzelne stellt sich hinein in ein übergreifendes Ganzes." But by the end of the article, he is treating the introduction of the topics of life and self-consciousness in ways relevant to Descartes, Kant, and Fichte (and not, that is, Schelling). Cf. 293–7. I do not understand how Pöggeler interprets the relation between these two dimensions, as at the top of 293.
3. This language, of course, is reminiscent of Fichte's *doppelte Reihe* formulations. See Chapter 3, Section 2. And Cf. Wildt (1982) on the *Fichteanismus* of the *PhG*, 372–83.
4. I am stressing the link between Hegel's account of the "autonomous" "self-determining" and "infinite" nature of thought and Kant's original antiempiricist,

antinaturalist insistence on "spontaneity" in the first *Critique*. Cf. Pippin (1987a). I do not thereby mean to slight other influences that helped determine Hegel's position on such autonomy, especially the moral practical influences. Such a topic is simply complex enough to require a separate study. Cf. especially Henrich (1963) and the connection between the "foundation of ethics" problem and "speculative idealism" and Wohlfart (1981) on the links between Kant's aesthetic and teleology theory and Hegel's speculative position.

5. I should note that this notion of a self-limitation or constraint is only a preliminary way of understanding what Hegel is after. For Hegel it would be too Fichtean a formulation and would conflict with his own final version of the "absolute freedom" of thought's "self-determination." Cf. Siep (1974b), 391.
6. Cf. Siep (1979) on the relevance of a "genetic" account, an account of what he calls the process of *Bedeutungsentwicklung*, in establishing various principles, and his notes to Lorenzen and Schwemmer, 17.
7. Since Chapter Five often recapitulates much of the idealist argument of Chapters One through Four, the crucial point of dispute concerning the connection between the reconstructive deduction of Chapters One to Four and the references to "historical Spirit" centers on the roles of Chapters Six and Seven in the *PhG*. For one version of such a thematic connection, see Kimmerle (1978). Virtually all of what I am interested in with respect to the idealism problematic is contained in the first four chapters of the *PhG* and the *SL*, but I try to indicate briefly the nature of the link between that problem and Chapters Six and Seven in Section 3 of this chapter.
8. Cf. the first three chapters of Habermas (1971) and his interpretation of Hegel's early theory of self-consciousness in (1973b), 142–69. Cf. also Wildt's criticism of the latter (1982), 326–9, and Siep's discussion (1974b) of the relevance of Hegel's recognition theory for Habermas's communicative theory of intersubjectivity.
9. Heidegger, of course, prefers to accentuate his differences with Hegel. See (1962), 480ff, and (1970).
10. It is thus correct, I think, to state the *provisional* assumption of the chapter as Flay (1984), 82, does: that "desire governs the way things are and appear" and that "Warranty is to come from the satisfaction of desires in a world which is the arena of life for the desiring individual." But I state, somewhat differently than Flay, Hegel's reasons for introducing this topic and stress far more the provisional and soon "sublated" character of this claim about "interest as desire."
11. This chapter thus does not begin a case for the primacy of practical reason. In Kant and Fichte, this had meant that even though here was no theoretical deduction of freedom, we were nevertheless unconditionally obligated to the moral law, on the "practical assumption of freedom." In Hegel's view, most clearly presented in the last book of the *Logic*, there is no priority for either "theoretical" or "practical" reason. The central issue for him, Spirit's knowledge of itself, its determination for itself of the Notions required for the determinate thought of objects and for self-understanding in genuinely free action, represents the "unity of the theoretical and practical idea." See Chapter 10, Section 4. Thus, although Bernstein (1984a) is right to point out that Hegel is arguing that "self-consciousness presupposes recognition," I think it is ambiguous to state that this means that human freedom and self-consciousness are "grounded in community" and that Hegel is the "first systematic philosopher of praxis" (39). The claim that self-consciousness presupposes *recognition*, as I am interpreting it, means

that self-consciousness presupposes some development of the determinate forms of self-consciousness, forms that are genuinely *universal* forms, and so allow the genuine mutuality required for consistently free action. Although such an achievement does not, as Bernstein rightly notes, involve any "onto-theology," it does involve Hegel's case in the *Logic* (cf. his n. 4, 280), since achieving such genuine mutual satisfaction is clearly the work of Reason in its self-knowledge. Now Hegel clearly intends that this should not mean a reassertion of some view of a wholly "independent" Reason, to use the language of this chapter, either with respect to desire, or happiness (as in Kantian morality), or with respect to objects (as in Fichte's abstract antiempiricism), but how and why it does not is, it seems to me, the central task of any Hegel interpretation.

12. Cf. Siep's formulations (1974a), 196; (1974b); 390.
13. The immediate sentiment of self thus introduced by life as a "shape of Spirit" allows Hegel to begin to discuss a number of elements crucial for his full theory of subjectivity. Life also involves a kind of "separation" of the subject from itself; it not only lives but must continue to pursue or lead its life; it is in a relation of independence and dependence with respect to its "other." And it is not simply a living individual, but lives out the life of the species; its life reproduces in its general structure the life of the species, and even literally reproduces that "universal life." See Gadamer's remarks (1976b), 58. Marcuse (1987) demonstrates the importance of the life thematic for a number of idealist themes, particularly the problem of development, an issue central to Marcuse's account of Hegelian historicity. See 231ff. and especially his summary claim about Hegel's "greatest discovery," 246.
14. For a clear instance of how Hegel intends to make use of the results of his own idealist project to reinterpret the meaning and intention of traditional religion, there is this passage from the introduction to the lectures on the history of philosophy: "Der subjektive Geist, der den göttlichen Geist vernimmt, ist selber dieser göttliche Geist. Das ist die wahrhafte Grundbestimmung des Verhaltens des Geistes zu sich" (*EGPh*, 177).
15. "It is in fact in the life of a people or nation that the Notion of self-conscious Reason's actualization – of beholding, in the independence of the 'other,' complete unity with it, or having for my object the free thinghood of an 'other' which confronts me and is the negative of myself, as my own being-for-myself – that the Notion has its complete reality" (*PhG*, 194; *PS*, 212).
16. Cf. again the passage from the Heidelberg *EL*, quoted in Chapter 2, n. 8, where Hegel explicitly rejects a "Seelending" approach to subjectivity.
17. The "only within which" qualification in this sentence can be taken as one way of understanding what Hegel ultimately means by an "Absolute idealism." Viewed in this way, it can be considered one of the most important aspects of Hegel's contribution to contemporary discussions. With respect to current versions of naturalism and reductive and eliminativist strategies, Hegel can be seen as offering a (perhaps *the*) contrary, antinaturalist claim about the constitutive status of "Spirit" (or what may be demotically identified as "culture"). For one of the boldest statements of such a claim about the centrality of historical spirit or human activity, see Marcuse's "ontological" reading (1987), and compare Brockard's many references to Marcuse's attempt (1970).
18. Roughly, this means that for Hegel, acting well or rightly is acting freely and for the good, both of which he interprets in terms of self-knowledge. (He calls morality, for example, Spirit "certainty of itself.") See especially his references

to "knowledge" in his characterization of the overcoming of this moral point of view (*PhG*, 361–2; *PS*, 408–9).

19. The most extreme and influential example of such an emphasis is certainly Kojeve (1969), although there are legions of others who also construct a sociopolitical and/or anthropological interpretation of this section. [The simplest version of the "sudden shift to the social" view is Findlay's (1958), 95–103.] For a concise, extremely helpful survey of such attempts, with capsule summaries of or references to the views of some twenty-one commentators, see Flay's n. 2 (1984), 299–301. Aside from Flay's own account, 81–112, two of the best attempts to keep the Absolute Knowledge problematic in mind in reading the chapter are Siep (1974b) and Rosen (1974a), 151–82. Gadamer (1976b) notes that the idealist claim, the identity of Reason with all reality, must be kept in mind as a telos of this chapter, but he does not say much, apart from a brief remark on 72, about how such a goal is to result, and his own analysis concentrates heavily on the social dimensions of the issues.
20. Cf. the differing accounts of Wildt (1982) and Siep (1979) of Hegel's appropriation of Fichte's theory of recognition.
21. The original suggestion of a Hobbsian influence on Hegel is from Strauss (1963). It appears to based on the fact that the struggle for recognition concludes in a Master–Slave relation and is dominated by the fear of death. Siep has shown (1974a) that the differences between Hobbes and Hegel far outweigh any similarities. One difference Siep does not mention involves the implicit issue of rationality in the two accounts. Hobbes, like Hegel, begins by assuming that there is no possible appeal to a common interest, idea of the good, or objective fact that could resolve conflict in the state of nature (although Hobbes makes this assumption substantively, Hegel only provisionally). But whereas Hobbes tries to show why a covenant among warring parties would be rational, even in such a radically "skeptical" situation, Hegel's position is even more radical. He argues, in effect, that Hobbes begs his own question of rationality by not admitting that one of these warring parties could consistently *win*, that his courage and/or strength would make irrational *any* negotiation with warring parties inclined to "dependence." (Hobbes simply denies that this is a possibility because he assumes the possibility of concerted action by "the weaker," an assumption that simply raises his own covenant dilemma before it gets started.) It is in *this* situation, that of Master and Slave, and not a war of all against all, that the problem of "mutuality" arises.
22. This is Wildt's terminology (1982) and is used by him in his brief account of the *PhG* in ways that often raise questions inappropriate in that context. He argues, without much textual support, that Hegel's *PhG* account of recognition should be viewed as a theory about the "consequences which underdeveloped forms of Ego-identity have for relations to others" (340). Such an approach leads Wildt, I believe, to stress prematurely the Fichte/ethics and to discount the Kant/Deduction issue. See, e.g., 375. For a fuller, considerably more balanced statment of the Hegel–Fichte relation on this issue, see Siep (1979), 23ff.
23. Cf. Marcuse (1960), Lukacs (1975), and Adorno (1963). For a general summary of the Critical Theory transformation of epistemology into social theory see Kortian (1980). On the interpretation presented here, this transformation begins with an unacceptable characterization of Hegelian identity theory and ends up with no successful account of the relation between this chapter of the *PhG* and the problem of Hegelian rationality.

24. This passage introduces Hegel's account of Stoicism, the insufficiencies of which Hegel will soon explore. However, he never retracts his affirmation of this initial connection between the problem of recognition and "thought," and he certainly does not, as Kojeve maintains, treat Stoicism as a "slave ideology." In fact, such a connection, and the general "Absolute Knowledge" orientation in the *PhG*, dominate even those passages where Hegel explicitly discusses the problems of ethicality and "right." Cf. *PhG*, 260–2; *PS*, 290–3.
25. *PG*, 265–315, especially 307–15; *FPS*, 206–42, especially 235–42.
26. *PGII*, 222–52. Siep (1979) is quite right to note that in the *PhG* Hegel is not as interested in "interaction" forms of recognition as in his earlier writings, and that the issue of the "identity of particular and universal consciousness" is not an issue that concerns forms of acting, but "theoretical, religous and philosophical consciousness" (74–5). Thus, he claims, we get in effect "less" of Hegel's full theory of recognition rather than "more" in the *PhG* (75). See also similar claims in Siep (1974a), 193. Cf. also Harris (1980), especially on how the developments in Hegel's theory of recognition (and the differences between the Jean writings and the *PhG*) can be used to detect his growing break with Schelling.
27. Cf. Hegel's remarks in the *Encyclopedia* (section 433) on the relation between recognition and the state.
28. It is important to note that Hegel is not engaged in any account of the "origin" of self-consciousness, as if he were maintaining that human beings "become" self-conscious in interaction with others. What he wants in this section is an account of the determinate and objective forms of self-consciousness, an issue that is a problem for him because of his insistence on the "independence" of self-consciousness. On the issue of *why* Hegel is entitled to presuppose the "fact" of self-consciousness, I would cite the argument of the first three chapters and the goals of the project as a whole. Cf. Bernstein's use of Gricean communication conditions (1984a), 19ff., and Rosen's account (1974b), 125–6.
29. The familiar Hegelian language for this issue: After the phenomenological sublation of the subject–object relation as understood by consciousness, the subject is independent but "homeless," ultimately seeking satisfaction merely in its independence from sensibility (Stoicism), or in admitting its own inability to resolve the oppositions created by such subjects (Skepticism), or permanently dissatisfied (the unhappy consciousness). See Rosen's formulation of the issue (1974a), 154.
30. Part of the great difficulty here is that Hegel is simultaneously inventing and pursuing a new form of philosophical argument. He is attempting to replace a transcendental deduction of the conditions for the possibility of experience with a phenomenological account of the ideal development of constitutive forms of Spirit. And he is not making it clear how and why a number of restraining assumptions enter into this account, particularly the radically secular (again, Hobbes-like) assumptions about opposed subjects that dominate the beginning (though not the conclusion) of his account.

    Moreover, Hegel does not make clear exactly how much his idealized reconstruction is supposed to show. To say that a subject would be dissatisfied or self-negating if it "reduced" itself to its natural "life," or as a Master or a Slave, is certainly not a prediction about what such an existing subject would actually do. History is full of examples of brutal tyrants who can very well tolerate their "existential impasse," the contradictions in their attempt at recognition, for as long as they can. All Hegel can do is demonstrate that there is such a practical contradiction, do so in a way internal to the Master's own desires, and reconstruct what would be a potential resolution.

31. There is thus *some* similarity between Hegel's topic here and recent "dialogic" theories of rationality, particularly those inspired by Habermas. The similarity involves the common attempt to understand the "conditions" for the rational resolution of any disagreement, the conditions for a possible rational exchange, in terms of a free interaction among participants. The most challenging recent pursuit of such a possibility, including an attempt to interpret the *Logic*'s account of the Notion as "universal communication theory" is Theunissen (1978b), 433 ff., an account I discuss extensively in the notes to Part III of this volume.
32. Cf. Gadamer's note (1976b), 62, critical of Kojeve's importation of the issue of a "desire for another's desire" (or love) into this context. Gadamer points out rightly that this is a premature importation and that Kojeve confuses *Begierde* with "desire," that Hegel never uses the word that would justify Kojeve's view, *Verlangen*. In other respects, though, Gadamer's account seems to me heavily influenced by Kojeve on the issue of "the fear of death" and on the Master's impasse.
33. The paradox Hegel describes is similar to an old problem pointed to by Aristotle: that "respect" cannot be the highest human good, that the respect of others is of no intrinsic value unless it is linked to the value one is respected *for*. In Hegel this means that the struggle for recognition that must ensue in the situation he describes – opposed and wholly "self-determined" subjects – can be resolved only if such subjects come to understand themselves as capable of mutual recognition by being (and only by being) *rational* subjects.
34. Wildt (1982), 340, asks such a question, although, as I am attempting to show, it is completely inappropriate in the context of the *PhG*'s account of recognition.
35. Kojeve (1969), for all the faults of his interpretation, still contains the most compelling account of the Master's impasse, 45 ff. For the clearest statement of what is wrong with Kojeve's account, see Rosen (1974a), 161. For a very useful discussion of the significance of the Slave's attachment to life, particularly as this issue touches on the idealism/materialism theme, see Bernstein (1984a), 16–18. It is of the greatest importance for virtually every other aspect of Hegel's thought to keep in mind his rejection here of "abstract independence." Throughout the rest of his project, this will mean that he wants an account of "independence" within some recognition of "dependence," a desideratum as true of his social theory as of his epistemology and one that simply makes impossible the textbook view of Hegel's idealism.
36. For further discussion of the limitations of the self-consciousness discussion in the *PhG*, see Cramer (1974), 601–2.
37. Hegel appears to think that this answer must demonstrate a strict necessity in actual historical development in order for the skeptic to be answered. All he really needs is an account of the way his view of the problem of "independent self-consciousness" or "Spirit's self-certainty" does explain the conceptual problems inherent in the various positions he analyzes, a claim that his account is a *better* explanation of the motivation of conceptual change than any other (e.g., materialist, psycho-historical, sociological), and a challenge to any potential competitor.
38. Habermas, in a recent work (1987), notes that "Hegel conceived of reason as the reconciling self-knowledge of an absolute spirit" (84), and although he con-

tinues to interpret Hegel's theory of absolute spirit as the "infinite processing of the relation-to-self that swallows up everything finite within itself" (36) (cf. n. 38a, Chapter Five), he generalizes here his criticism of Hegel into a pointed attack on the aporiai of any "philosophy of subjectivity" or of reflective self-consciousness. He means to attack the "dialecticians of the Enlightenment," like Hegel and Marx, who attempt to make use of the principle of the Enlightenment – self-critical and ultimately self-grounding rationality – to overcome its central crisis – postivity, or the alienation of subject and object – as well as to attack the counter-Enlightenment, post-Nietzschean thinkers who reject the entire premodern and modern Enlightenment as fundamentally self-deceived. Much of this version of Habermas's attack is quite relevant to the Hegel interpretation proposed here since, in this account, Hegel *does* ultimately link the question of rationality with a kind of *complete* self-consciousness, and however post-Kantian one views that telos to be, Hegel is still strikingly optimistic about the degree of self-transparency and completion possible for his philosophically satisfied subject. However pertinent, though, Habermas's criticisms still suffer from the truncated and tendentious view of Hegel that he presents. In all of his writing on Hegel, he has a tendency simply to skip from the pre-*PhG* Hegel, whom he approves of, to the post-Heidelberg Hegel, whom he does not, leaving out Hegel's account of such things as the link between rationality and social recognition, discussed earlier, and the critique of metaphysical and scientific positivity presented throughout the *SL*, discussed subsequently. Moreover, Habermas's own version of a dialectic of Enlightenment, with his theory of intersubjective communication (rather than monologic self-reflection) is (1) more internally Hegelian and idealist in the sense defended here than is acknowledged; (2) with its reliance on merely "procedural rationality," it leaves intact so much of the substance of a liberal pluralism about ends and interests that it is destined to reproduce the modern dilemmas Habermas describes; (3) it has yet to show why his own version of the realization of self-consciousness – the recognition of the presuppositions of speech acts – represents an *internally* developing dimension of modernity, or indeed a *rational* dimension (his reliance on Piaget models of "development" often begs the relevant question); and (4) it could be said, with enough space and fair attention to the details of Habermas's case, to be subject to many of the self-contradictions outlined in Hegel's account of the fate of modern individualism in the section on the "Individuality which is real in and for itself" in the *PhG*, especially the subsection on the "spiritual zoo."

39. Cf. Harris's comment (1980) about the "self-recognition of the *Volk* in its God as the speculative self-knowledge of the philosopher" (247) and his citation there of a pertinent passage from the *PG*, II.
40. Again, as noted earlier (n. 31), the best-known recent attempt to illuminate the social dimensions of the *SL* is Theunissen's (1978b). Cf. also a preliminary discussion of such issues in Pippin (1979), Pippin (1981), and the account in Fulda (1968), especially Section III, "Die konservative Aufgabe der Philosophie: Recht auf Selbstgenügsamkeit," 24ff.
41. The modal version of this issue is Hegel's theory of contingency. Cf. Belaval's (1974) argument about the similarity between Kant and Hegel on the notion of a contingent *Wirklichkeit*. The issue for both is some sort of a priori determination of what is "possibly real" (in Kant as subscribing to the "conditions of actuality," especially causality; in Hegel as subscribing to the conditions of the "absolute relation"), all as opposed to a metaphysical account of the "really

possible." Cf. 126–7. This means that if the proper "Notional level" is kept in mind, Hegel's "conceptual determination" of the "essentially necessary" does not deny contingency but requires a contingent specification of such essential or categorial conditions. Cf. also Henrich (1971d), especially section 4.

Chapter 8. Objective logic

1. As Fulda has noted in his critique of Theunissen (1980), 40ff., Hegel's use of the counterfactual subjunctive here invites further interpretation of the relation between the Objective Logic and transcendental philosophy. I think Hegel means to say that they "*would* correspond – if Kant had not left so much of his own theory of subjectivity and categoriality unexplored. If he had not, then, Hegel is claiming, the limitations of various required but finite categories, and their relation to each other, and the general structure of Absolute Subjectivity, could all have been properly explored, as he presumes to be doing in *SL*." Transcendental philosophy would then lose its restricted quality (to "our conditions") but not its reliance on a theory of "self-determining" subjectivity, properly understood. Cf. Baillie's comments (1984), 240ff.

   Theunissen (1978b) has suggested that the structure of the *Logic* is best viewed in terms of Hegel's appropriation of the structure of *metaphysica specialis*, the world–soul–God, cosmology–psychology–theology structure. Cf. 39–41. This forms part of the basis of Theunissen's argument that Hegel successfully shows the "illusory" nature of the metaphysical notions inherent in the first two kinds of account giving, but also reveals Hegel's positive commitment to a theological metaphysics in Book III. See n. 8, this chapter.
2. Taylor (1975), 225–6. See also 110, 231, and Walsh (1983), 95. One of the clearest recent statements of the "ontological idealism" interpretation is Sarlemijn's oft-cited but quite unmotivated and so unconvincing study (1971). Cf. his programmatic statements, 17, 47ff., and his summary of the relation between logic and metaphysics, one very different from that presented here, 103ff.
3. Findlay (1958, 1976).
4. Hartmann calls his imaginative and quite promising interpretation an "Ontologie," or more precisely, an "Ontologie als Kategorienlehre" (1976a), 1. Technically, for him, a category is a concept that succeeds in expressing the unity of thought and being, although his account of "being" is not precritical but transcendental. (What is at stake is the possibility of *judgments* of experience or the possibility of the individual *sciences* of being, although Hartmann's use of transcendental terminology is more related to theorists like Wagner and Cramer than to my use of Kant.) This means, as he shows convincingly, that on such an interpretation Hegel's dialectical method is necessarily "reconstructive" and that the "Absolute" *is* "Categoriality." See also Pinkard (1985) and Bole (1987). See n. 7, this chapter.
5. For example, Henrich (1971a, 1982a) and Rohs (1969) have both demonstrated how much of Hegel's theory of categorial interrelations can be discussed and evaluated without any necessary reliance on realism or monism.
6. The same might be said for a somewhat similar approach suggested by Fulda (1978b). Instead of a category analysis, he reads the *Logic* as a "meaning theory" (*Bedeutungstheorie*), in particular, an attempt to disambiguate the uniquely "vague" general concepts of the speculative tradition. For him the entire dialectic involves the attempt to reduce or limit such vagueness (cf. 60). Much of what

Fulda says seems to me true and useful, in particular, his closing comments on the "contradiction" problem, but, like versions of the categorial approach, incomplete. Fulda's remarks in Section II of this article usefully distinguish the *Logic*'s enterprise from the commitments of traditional metaphysics, but they do not suggest a positive way to understand the "objective" significance of the ever less vague, more concrete, categories of the *Logic*.

7. Horstmann (1984) has claimed against Hartmann that Hegel's project cannot be successfully understood in terms of a traditional theory of categoriality, a concern with the necessary conceptual functions involved in the thought of "whatever is." Horstmann claims that Hegel is still committed to answering the question of "*what* really is," 45ff. [Cf. also Theunissen (1978a).] I have raised a similar objection in a different way, one connected with the Kantian problematic of the "logically" versus "really" possible. In this context, that comes down to an explanation of the "objective status" of these categories. [See (1972), 53, for Hartmann's clearest expression of the Kant/objectivity issue.] In (1976a), Hartmann tends to view the problem of "thought's other" as unproblematic (from the categorial-ontological point of view), that any such other is always already a "conceptualized" other. See 18. This seems to me to share some problems with Reinhold's unsuccessful "short argument" for idealism, where "thought" fulfills the same function as "representation" (see n. 32, Chapter 3, this volume). In (1976c) the issue is more explicit, as Hartmann talks about the "appropriation of the real by thought" (103), but this locution raises the Kantian-skepticism problem we have been discussing throughout. I do not see how, on Hartmann's view, Hegel's theory of categories can defend the claim that such categories represent "determinations of the real" (104) (rather than "of the real as thought" and so not necessarily *real*) or that they "*have* to coincide with what must be granted in view of experience, science and philosophy" (104; my emphasis). (See 107–8 for what is the initial move in the response to this issue. But it is only initial, and when the issue reappears in this essay on 119, it is discussed only in terms of Hegel's formal/material mode confusions.) All of this, of course, leads to a further disagreement about the *PhG*, since Hartmann reads it as a *partielle Kategorienlehre* (1976a), 24, a position best worked out by Heinrichs (1974).

8. An important recent nonmetaphysical approach to Hegel is Theunissen's (1978b). He assigns to the *Logic* a "critical" function, one that is opposed to all forms of "positive" metaphysics and that begins to free thought and rationality from their traditional positivity and to suggest a view of thinking and reasoning as "communicative freedom." Theunissen's interest is mainly in reconstructing from Hegel's *Logic* a left-Christian social theory, one in which the central metaphysical notions involved in conceptions of social relationality ("indifference" in Book I, "mastery" in Book II) are, through a complex process of "critique" and "presentation" (*Darstellung*), revealed to be *Schein*, illusory being, not yet the truth of the Notion. That truth is the claim that any form of "being a self" or an individual is inextricable from "being in an other." For Theunissen this is the truth contained in the Hegelian theory of the *Satz*, or speculative proposition. (At once the most concise summary and most extreme version of this thesis is his claim on 461 that the *copula*, of all things, represents the "logischen Vor-Schein der unendlichen Mitteilsamkeit sich verströmender Lieb.") This latter dimension of Theunissen's project attributes some sort of transcendental intention to the *Logic*, an account of the conditions necessary for understanding a *Satz*. (Cf. 58, 458, 469.)

I shall refer to aspects of Theunissen's account in subsequent notes. For the moment, I note these disagreements. In the account I am presenting, (1) Hegel does not need to be saved from himself in Book III; he does not attempt to restore some metaphysical version of Christian theology (Cf. 42, 137ff., 177); (2) there are many more dimensions to the "transcendental" problem that need to be explored and dealt with before the relation between the *Logic* and transcendental philosophy can be understood; (3) it is extremely unlikely that such a critical theory in Hegel is grounded on an account of the speculative proposition; and (4) Theunissen has not yet worked out (and it remains unclear how it could be worked out) the relation between his problem of a social relations ontology and the *general* problem of *Erkennen* in the *Logic*. Several aspects of such criticisms have been posed for Theunissen in Fulda (1980), and he has there responded to some of them.

9. Cf. this claim in *SL*: "The most important point for the nature of spirit is not only the relation of what it is in itself to what it is actually, but the relation of what it knows itself to be to what it actually is; because spirit is essentially consciousness, this self-knowing is a fundamental determination of its actuality" (*WL*, I, 16; *SL*, 37).
10. In *EL*, section 12, Hegel claimed that philosophy "owes its development to the empirical sciences," and in *PN*, Remark to section 246, he says directly that "Not only must philosophy be in agreement with our empirical knowledge of Nature, but the origin and formation of the Philosophy of Nature presupposes and is conditioned by empirical physics" (*E*, 200; *PN*, 8). Of central importance for this issue is also the *Zusatz* to section 381 in the Introduction to the *Philosophy of Spirit* (*PM*, 8). See also Buchdahl's illuminating discussion (1984).
11. How Hegel means us to understand his use of *wirklich* and *Wirklichkeit* is a separate and crucial issue. Cf. Chapter 9, Section 4, and Chapter 10, Section 4, this volume.
12. Schelling, in *Zur Geschichte der neueren Philosophie*, was one of the first to charge that Hegel's *Logic* represented a reversion to a pre-critical, dogmatic metaphysics (*SW*, 10, 128–9). Cf. White's summary discussion (1983a), 15–41. Schelling, of course, has his own reasons for characterizing Hegel's position in so tendentious and, as I am trying to show, inaccurate a fashion.
13. Cf. Löwith (1967), for more on the significance of Schelling's Hegel critique, and Schulz (1975).
14. Cf. also the recent charges that Hegel's *Logic* is committed to a form of "hyper-intuitionism" in M. Rosen (1982) or that Hegel inconsistently excludes a necessary intuitionism (essentially Platonic or noetic) in his own understanding of the *Logic* in S. Rosen (1974a). See also Harlander (1969), 106ff.
15. In the opening discussion of being in *EL*, Hegel says that "Das Sein ist der Begriff nur an sich," that "Being is the Notion, [but] only in itself" (*EL*, 181; *EnL*, 123).
16. Henrich (1971b). Henrich does not mention in his survey Schelling, who first made many of both kinds of criticism. For a survey of the contemporary literature, see Theunissen (1978b), 130ff.
17. This is what Hegel means when he says that the transition is to be understood without reflection, that is, that nothing is not "posited in being"; both are the same. Cf. Gadamer (1976d) on this passage. Much of what Gadamer says about the deceptiveness of the idea of an original "transition" is quite to the point, but since he does not introduce any view of the structure of the *Logic* as a

whole, he gives little indication of how the notion of logical "movement" later in the work *is* to be understood. Further, his reliance on the *symploke* model of Platonic metaphysics obscures the post-Kantian dimensions of Hegelian categoriality, and so "Platonizes" Hegel's project that Hegel is, in effect, "set up" for the Heideggerean criticisms leveled at him by Gadamer, 94–99. Cf. the account of Gadamer and of Schulz's critique (1973) in Theunissen (1978b), 83ff., and his remarks on 118.

18. Henrich (1971b), 80ff. Cf. Theunissen (1978b), 137; Fulda (1980), 28ff.
19. M. Rosen (1982), 149–50.
20. Taylor (1975), 233ff. Cf. also Theunissen's similar problems (1978b), 137, and Fulda's (1980) comments on the latter, 28.
21. Henrich (1971b), 82.
22. Henrich (1971b), 80. To be sure, Henrich has his own version of why Hegel's occasional remarks about the radical immediacy of the beginning, the pure transition to determinate being, and so on are illusions, that a great deal of methodological presupposing has already gone on. Basically he is not convinced that Hegel can justify the *eigentliche Dynamik des logischen Prozesses* without begging the question. Cf. his first "Reflexion" article (1971c), 102, and ns. 22 and 23, Chapter 9, this volume. Cf. also Fulda's comments on Flach and neo-Kantianism (1978b), 45; Theunissen (1978b), 80; Bubner (1976), 39; and Rohs (1969), 41–2.
23. Theunissen (1978b) is thus right to point out that there must still be a "separation" of subject and object in some logical sense if we are to explain logical movement at all in *SL*, Cf. 80ff. His account of the problem of *Schein* as a way to explain the problem of incompleteness or finitude in the *Logic* is an illuminating one, although, for a variety of reasons, still somewhat misleading. The central issue (i.e., the one I think Theunissen still leaves unresolved in his book and in his response to his critics) is how Theunissen understands the origin of the illusoriness of the Notions in the Being Logic and the Essence Logic, an issue that comes up frequently in questions Fulda and Horstmann pose for Theunissen in Fulda (1980). For my own version of the "internal negativity" issue, one linked to the telos of full self-consciousness in the *SL*, see Chapter 10.
24. Theunissen (1978b) is correct to insist that here and elsewhere in the *SL*, there is "direkt keine Analyse der ausserlogishen Wirklichkeit" (138). But Theunissen then faces the problem of what to do with what appear to be the *SL*'s claims about such "reality in itself." To explain them, he invokes his "restoration" of metaphysics thesis and complains that there is in the Objective Logic a *Zusammenspiel* of metaphysics and metaphysics-critique. This, though, is because Theunissen seems to regard his "constructive semantics" interpretation as the only plausible nonmetaphysical construal of the valuable aspects of the project. His own account of the metaphysical idealism inherent in the *Logic* omits any serious consideration of Hegel's appropriation of Kant and Fichte, and interprets instead Hegel's "positive" moment, for want of a better word, "Platonically." Cf. 139–41. Cf. Rohs's very different version of Hegel's "Restitution des Platonismus," an interpretation with which I am in sympathy (1969), 34, all in contrast to Sarlemijn's textbook version of Hegel's "monistic Platonism" (1971), 48.
25. Taylor (1975), 237.
26. No "now" can be determined or thought *as* now; it is immediately a "then,"

as in the dialectic "experienced" by consciousness in the *PhG*. Here the claim is that such Heraclitean flux is a Notional contradiction.

27. As I have suggested in earlier notes, it might be expected that, without a clear interpretation of the objectivity of thought's self-determination in the *Logic*, the "categorial" approach would often slip from formal to material modes of expression, even more frequently than Hegel appears to, and without justification. This in fact happens, I believe, in White (1983a), 37, and Pinkard (1979), 214. The latter states his position more clearly in (1985), but still seems to me to attribute to Hegel the very conflation so many commentators rightly worry about.
28. Cf. Brockard (1970), 40ff., and Horstmann's (1984) account of Hegel's "weak monism," 102. This sort of issue (i.e., in just *what* sense can Hegel's critical overcoming of inherent limitations of various Notions, like finitude, also be said to be an incipient "presentation" of the truth?) is at the heart of much of Theunissen's very valuable analysis of Hegel's use of *Schein*. In some of Theunissen's formulations, it would seem that the "unity" of *Kritik* and *Darstellung* involves the "presenting" critically of the one-sidedness and illusory incompleteness of some Notion or other, and that the "truth" emerging from such a critique is simply the final truth of the communicative freedom model. [See 84–6 and his responses to criticisms from Horstmann and Fulda on this point (1980), 50–8.] Although I can do no justice in notes to Theunissen's interpretation, I can note programatically that the line he takes makes it difficult to see how he can take account of Hegel's intention to "present critically" some aspect of *Schein* as a way of indicating *its* "truth," not merely its pointing toward "the" truth of the Notion Logic. See Horstmann's distinction between two senses of a "unity" of "critique" and "presentation," Fulda (1980), 18–22.
29. In *EL*, the discussion occurs in the Zusatz to section 92, where limit is introduced; in *SL*, it occurs after "Determination, Constitution, Limit" (*WL*, I, 116–17; *SL*, 129).
30. The corresponding phenomenological moment here, were we referring to how the determinations of finitude would be "experienced" by consciousness, would be the restriction to sensible, immediately apprehended qualities, sense properties, in the determination of a thing as a sensible this. Here the issue is the "concept" of a thing's immediate determinations, on the assumption that "being" is an immediate object of thought.
31. I note that, strictly speaking, Hegel wants to distinguish the Notion of something and its qualities from the Notion of a "thing" having "properties." For my purposes, so strict a distinction between qualities and properties is not important. Hegel himself makes the same point just stated in the Addition, where he rather vaguely tries to insist on the distinction. See *EL*, 256–7; *EnL*, 182.
32. Cf. Hegel's unusual use of the language of perishing, ceasing to be, beginning, and moving, even when discussing the relevance of limit for existentially nonperishing objects, geometric objects (*WL*, I, 115–16; *SL*, 127–8). See also Pinckard (1981).
33. Cf. Guyer's representative remarks (1979), 97, and Sarlemijn (1971), 110–11. Interpreting the issue this way also allows one to see the "idealist" dimensions of Hegel's general position on "otherness," an issue much in dispute. Cf. Rickert (1911–12) and, more recently, Flach (1959). The issue can be understood by recalling the Platonic critique of Parmenides or Plato's interpretation of nonbeing

as otherness. Difference could be explained, Y could *be* "not X," without a commitment to "non-being" (*a* not-X) if X and Y were simply "other" than each other. The question in Hegel has been whether he reverts to an assertion *of* non-being in his dialectical logic. In the interpretation I am presenting, the answer is "no," but Hegel is also undermining the possibility of explaining "otherness" in a Platonic or realist way. What is *fundamentally* (Notionally) other is a *result* of "thought's self-determination." Cf. Theunissen (1978b), 248ff., and, for a very different view, Rosen (1974a). The great difference between them stems from Theunissen's avoidance of and Rosen's embrace of the Fichtean dimension of thought's "self-positing." See also Rohs (1969) for a thorough discussion of the relation between Kantian Form and Hegelian Negation.

34. "External reflection" is a Hegelian term of art and requires an independent explanation. See Chapter 9, Section 2.
35. Cf. *EL*, Zusatz to section 136: "Etwas ist an sich das Andere seiner selbst."
36. Cf. Guyer (1979). For a considerably more detailed view of the relation between Hegel and Leibniz, see Belaval (1970, 1972, 1974). Belaval demonstrates how much of the structure of Book II is determined by Kant's "Amphibolies" chapter and by Hegel's disagreements with Kant's analysis of the concepts of reflection. He then notes that the criticisms by Hegel would seem, by a "negation of negation" process, to return Hegel to the position Kant was most out to criticize, Leibniz's. He notes correctly (1970) that one can see the similarity of Hegel and Leibniz if one compares their position on essence with their common stand against Aristotle, and one can see their differences if one compares both with Kant, 558. But in all three articles, Belaval accepts Russell's characterization of both as committed to a philosophy of "internal relations," a position I think Horstmann (1984) has called into serious question.
37. "Essential relation" does not here mean that objects are essentially related *by* being other. It means that the nature of any such relation is determined, made possible by, their essential properties and what relations those properties exclude or allow.
38. This programmatic statement obviously sums up the most significant single claim of Hegel's idealism. The promissory note issued so often in Hegel's early formulations begins to become a concrete issue, argued for directly by him, in the account of "determining reflection" in Book II. That section, although omitted in the *EL*, is the decisive point at which Hegel's positive idealist argument begins to succeed or fail.
39. Horstmann (1984). I note also that when Hegel is explaining the limitations of classical atomism as an example of the absolutization of finite existence, he points out that their principles were "thoughts, ideal entities, not things as they immediately present themselves to us." This "principle" must then be considered ideal ("and still more must the Notion, the Idea, spirit be so named"), just as, he goes on to say, the moments of concrete being are also ideal, since all "sublated" in this universal; or, in the reading I am suggesting, they can be determinately specified as such moments only if we presuppose the self-determining activity of thought (*WL*, I, 145; *SL*, 155).
40. This is, it should be noted, one of the many places where a presumably systematic architectonic breaks down for Hegel. A "bad" versus a "good" infinite is an absurdly un-Hegelian opposition and is perfectly typical of *Verstand*, not true

Denken. Theunissen is correct in noting that Hegel should be exploring ways to understand how this first appearance of the Notion of infinity "points beyond itself" toward true infinity. See Theunissen (1978), section 2.2.2, especially 282ff.

41. Cf. *EL*, 209–9; *EnL*, 145, for a clear formulation of this transition.

Chapter 9. Reflected being

1. I have substantially altered Wallace's translation. (It is even more grossly inaccurate here than usual.)
2. I am not trying to defend any claim about the necessity of transitions in the *Logic*. It should be noted that the inadequacy of the Being Logic cannot establish that this very problem of inadequacy (indeterminacy) can itself be comprehended and resolved *only* if the activity of reflection is presupposed. That would be true only if some grand disjunctive syllogism were simply already assumed as the "totality" of possible conditions of determinate objects of judgment. (So that, roughly, the denial of some disjunct does entail, necessarily, the truth of some other disjunct or set of disjuncts, all without intellectual intuition.) Cf. Seebohm (1974, 1976). As noted previously, at most, what such a transition can do is motivate the introduction of this topic and then defend it against competitors.
3. According to Henrich, the shift from the Notion of "immediacy" at work in the Being Logic to that introduced in the Essence Logic, a shift from *Vermittlungslosigkeit* to *Selbstvermittlung*, is a paradigmatic example of a dialectical "advance," and can be understood as a "meaning shift," as part of a Hegelian theory about alterations in meaning that provide some sort of continuity within radical conceptual change. See (1971c), 111, 115, 134 (on the relation to dialectic), and Section III, 136ff. and his (1978c) version, 210ff., 309ff. In this version of the problem, Henrich must deal with the issue of whether the "immediacy" of *Schein*, ultimately the self-relating immediacy of reflection, represents an alteration or shift (*Verscheibung*) in the meaning of immediacy, or whether it constitutes an alteration that eliminates all reference to immediacy in favor of a different, successor notion (reflected being). In the interpretation presented here, this amounts to the question of whether Hegel has provided any real alternative to the Kantian and Fichtean "imposition" and "self-positing" models of reflection. Henrich in the (1978c) version highlights prominently the connection between his "meaning shift" interpretation and the idealism issue. See 307.

   Cf. the account of Henrich given by Theunissen (1978b), 344, and Theunissen's own different version of this "immediacy" issue. As noted, my account links this *Schein/Sein* issue with the idealism issue and so with the "immediacy/mediation" issue. Theunissen had earlier noted (179) that Henrich's account of the Reflection Logic is determined by a post-Kantian theory of subjectivity, but Theunissen professes not to see "wie und inwieweit diese Einsicht im Kommentar selber fruchtbar wird." If I have been right throughout, it is an extremely fruitful approach.
4. Hegel very roughly seems to have in mind here something like the difference between the immediacy of particularity in Aristotle, where primary ousia just is the *tode ti*, and the Leibnizean, "reflected" account of individuality, where monads are the particulars they are as a *result* of their "representing" from a point of view. Cf. Belaval (1970), 558; (1972), 438; (1974), 119ff.
5. Although Kant was eager to avoid scholastic terminology in the presentation of

his own project, he was not averse to associating critical philosophy, and its unique notion of "form," with the problem of "essence." See his 1796 essay, "Von einem neuerdings erhobenen Ton in der Philosophie," where he appropriates in his own way the scholastic "forma dat esse rei" formula. *AA*, vol. 8, 404. Cf. Rohs on *cause formalis* as *Grund* in Hegel's *Logic* (1969), 15, and the connection he establishes between that notion and the Kantian problem of the a priori synthesis. Cf. 39 especially on the connection between the Hegelian problem of negation and the Kantian *Verbindung*. In general, Rohs tries to argue that German Idealism should not be understood as a "consciousness–metaphysics" but, taking full account of the post-Kantian subjectivity of form, a "metaphysics of form." His use of the notion of metaphysics is thus, for me at least, somewhat idiosyncratic in the critical context. See his remarks on transcendental philosophy, 44.

My approach here is thus quite different from Theunissen's (1978b), 301–32, whose focus explicitly remains Platonic-Aristotelian metaphysics. (He calls Aristotle the "Mutter aller Reflexionsphilosophie," 324.) There is clearly much a relevance here to Aristotle, particularly the section on external reflection (see n. 32, this chapter), but Hegel's own remarks on the relation between *Schein* and subjectivity, his frequent charge that the Greeks lacked a worked out-sense of subjectivity, and his references to Kant (not Aristotle) when discussing external reflection all demonstrate that Hegel is trying to assess "logically" the subjective turn in post-Cartesian philosophy. There is a note (335) where Theunissen admits this omission in his account, and there he seems to think it of no great consequence. But his lack of integration of the Fichtean dimension in Hegel's account of reflection is, it seems to me, what sets up Hegel for Theunissen's attack on the positivity of the Notion Logic.

6. *Allein der Schein ist das eigene Setzen des Wesens*. Theunissen (1978b) helpfully separates the interrelated claims Hegel is trying to make in this book: Being is its appearing; the truth of being is essence; essence is the showing of itself in itself; the showing of itself in itself is reflection. Cf. 301ff.
7. Cf. Rosen (1974a), 109, and Brockard (1970), 40ff.
8. Belaval's work has established that, whatever the problems of this section, Hegel is not making *this* precritical mistake. He shows clearly, in his discussions of the difference between Hegel and Leibniz on the modalities of necessity and contingency, that Hegel has taken into full account and accepted the differences between Kant's apperceptive subject and Leibniz's self-representing, monadic I. See (1970), 558ff., and (1974), 116ff. and 135–6. Belaval's position requires him to explain how, if Hegel is rejecting Leibniz's "intellectualism" as an inadequate ground for resolving the problem of "difference," and also rejecting Kant's reliance on a doctrine of pure forms of intuition, the crucial relation of form and matter, or, at a "reflected" level, identity and difference, *is* to be understood in Hegel. As far as I can see, the position he ends up ascribing to Hegel replaces Leibniz's multiplicity of monads with one monad (1974), 136, and deals with the problems caused by Leibniz's reliance on God's creation by replacing that notion with a Hegelian creation that is a "perpetuel jaillissement de l'"Etre hors de lui" (1972), 438. I do not understand the latter doctrine and have tried to argue that Hegel is not a metaphysical monist or an internal relations theorist.
9. Cf. Allison (1983), 173–98; cf. Pippin (1986), 369–70, and the discussion in Chapter 2, Section 2.

10. The most well-known reliance on such a formal determination is in Kant's "Analogies of Experience," where the argument to establish "necessary connection according to a rule" must make use of the "form of inner sense" doctrine.
11. For more on the relation between this section and Fichte, see Henrich (1978c), 210, 273, 307ff.
12. Cf. Rohs (1969) on the relation between Hegel's discussion of *Schein* and the German Idealist rejection of the Kantian *Ding an sich*, 60.
13. This is the Hegelian version of the Kantian charge that Berkeley and Hume, even though "idealists," were inconsistent realists in their acceptance of an immediate direct awareness of contents of inner sense ("in themselves").
14. Cf. Belaval's discussion (1974), 119ff.
15. Cf. the distinctions Theunissen makes in trying to follow the ambiguous use of *Schein* by Hegel (1978b), 337ff.
16. Cf. Rohs (1969), 69.
17. In Hegelese, the claim at stake, given the "negation" of *Sein* and so the collapse of *Sein* into *Schein*, involves the "negation of the negation" and so a kind of restoration of immediacy in a sublated form. In somewhat non-Hegelian terms, what is involved is a reconstruction of the grounds for the claim that what is "immediately given" in experience is "*immediately*" insufficient for a determinate experience of an object, and is so because of the immediately "self-related" character of experience. Cf. Henrich (1971c), 108.
18. McTaggart (1910), 99.
19. Cf. Henrich (1971c), 106, 123; Rohs (1969), 46ff.
20. Cf. Henrich (1978c), 210, 273; 307ff.
21. Henrich (1971c), 126; (1978c), 291.
22. That positing reflection is always a presupposing, and that external reflection is always a kind of imposing, thus reraises the idealism problem first raised by the new "immediacy" issue in the Essence Logic, the "self-relating" of reflection. See Henrich (1971c), 121, and, on the logic of presupposing, 122. Again the issue is whether what Hegel begins to discuss here as "determining reflection" is really a third alternative to Fichtean and Kantian idealism, whether there could possibly be any such thing as a self-mediated immediacy, or a determination of possible objects that is not a mediation (synthesis, thought) of some pregiven immediacy, with Kant's skepticism as a remainder, or a mediation that has eliminated any theoretical role for immediacy. Cf. the dense formulation of the position he would like to defend, at the beginning of the section on "Grund," *WL*, II, 64; *SL*, 445. A reflected immediacy is "being which has been restored by essence, the non-being of reflection through which essence mediates itself." Throughout I have suggested that Hegel does not so much intend a "third alternative" as he wants a way of undermining the assumptions that lead to the expectation that an alternative is what is called for, that thought's self-determining mediations (essence) can be said to be and not to be *Schein* (what there "immediately" is) without a blatant (standard) contradiction. The task for much of the rest of the *Logic* is to articulate this different self-consciousness by thought about itself. Cf. Rohs (1969), 64–6. It is a task only partly fulfilled, as I shall try to show in the next chapter. A different version of this issue is also recognized in Henrich's account. See (1971c), 129; (1978c), 242ff.
23. This is an aspect of Henrich's basic criticism of Hegel. Cf. (1971c), 152ff., 155. Here he also makes a point relevant to the issues raised in n. 24, this chapter. In his terms the issue is the difference, and potential tension between, an in-

dividual *Thema* in the *Logic* and its *Explicationsmittel.* See (1971c), 152–3. For Henrich, in this early version of the reflection article, this tension reflects a larger one in Hegel's *Logic*, which Henrich reads as "in between" a *Bedeutungstheorie* and a substantive, metaphysical idealism (an *Ontologie*). In (1978c), he formulates the reflection problem less polemically and in a way much more compatible with the approach taken throughout here. Cf. 205–7 and similar points made in his (1982a) article.

24. To put this point in a way of relevance to Theunissen's (1978b) account: This way of reading the structure of the *Logic* provides a different answer to Theunissen's questions about *Schein* and *Wahrheit*, *Kritik* and *Darstellung*, and their "unity." On this reading, the source of the illusory nature of various categorial determinations is an inadequate self-consciousness about the self-determining teleology of thought itself, the attempt to understand such categories realistically or "positively," either as metaphysical predicates or as judgmental functions of a "posited" or "given" transcendental subject. Thus the proper "unity" of *Darstellung* and *Kritik* involves a *speculative-idealist interpretation* of these "thought determinations," and so a "critical" presentation of their status and a continually more self-conscious account of their origin. This would avoid much of Theunissen's criticisms of Book III (and would provide the means, I hope to show, to take account of far more of the book than Theunissen can), but it also introduces equally difficult problems. Said all at once, it seems to commit Hegel to the view that thought's final self-understanding involves a realization of the necessity for thought's self-misunderstanding, a realization of the impossibility of thought's "free" self-determination except in finite and so "positive" forms. This extraordinary result, connected in various ways to later claims like Marx's on the "necessity" of alienation and capitalism in general, will be addressed, insofar as I know how to address it, in the next chapter. [The issue is similar to one raised by Fulda in his critique of Theunissen when he distinguishes between logical aspects of thought determinations themselves and the way they are presented. See (1980), 25ff., a problem Theunissen regards, mistakenly I think, as a "Husserlian" issue (58ff).]
25. Cf. Rohs's remarks (1969), 36–7.
26. Cf. the summary discussion by Belaval on the similarities and differences between Hegel's account of identity and difference and Leibniz's in sections 8 and 9 of the *Monadology* (1972), 436–40.
27. Cf. Pippin (1978).
28. Even though this notion requires more development, it is obvious how obscure it is at the start. Rohs offers a useful initial example of the kind of relation Hegel is interested in: In explaining what Hegel means by claiming that "otherness" is truly other only as sublated otherness, he suggested that we think of the case of a human "other" who can be truly *fremd*, strange, other to me, only if I know him well (1969), 82.
29. For a useful summary of the relativity problem, and one that echoes the end of Book I and the problem of "roving" about from quality to quality, here called *ein endloses Herumtreiben* for an adequate ground, see *SL*, 465–6; *WL*, II, 86–8. A similar discussion, in some respects clearer and more informally expressed, occurs in *EL*, 180; *EnL*, 255.
30. Cf. the discussion in Chapter 4, Section 4. As noted there, this is what one would expect from the "idealist" (i.e., anti-realist) view of logic developed thus far. Or, when Hegel seems to be saying that he is abandoning the "reflective"

principles of identity and contradiction, I am interpreting him to mean that he is rejecting the principle of bivalence for Notional determinations.

31. Rohs (1969), 79.
32. Some of Hegel's remarks certainly prompt a metaphysical, Aristotelian reading of this notion of activity, i.e., as *energeia*. But this is because Hegel has a completely idiosyncratic, Fichtean interpretation of *energeia* in Aristotle. See his remarks construing the principle of *Lebendigkeit* in Aristotle as the principle of *Subjektivität*, and that *energie* is "konkreter Subjektivität, Möglichkeit des Objektive" (JA, 19, 319ff). Cf. Rohs's discussion (1969), 28–9, and his contrast between Hegel and Aristotle on essence, 73ff.
33. Rohs (1969), 26–37.
34. So, in later discussions of ground, many of which repeat the original problem of positing and external reflection, Hegel's examples continue to reveal that the problem of ground remains conceptual, at a high level of abstraction. A good example occurs in his description of "real" ground, where he discusses what it would mean to call Nature the "ground" of everything; that is, he introduces the issue of the kind of explanation a full-blooded version of naturalism means to offer. Again he argues that such claims are always incomplete; they depend on the determinate understanding of Nature advanced, and *that* understanding itself has been derived from a concrete investigation already informed by a presupposed version of naturalism. See *WL*, II, 85ff; *SL*, 464ff.
35. The logical problem here clearly calls to mind Hegel's phenomenological discussion of similar issues in the "inverted world" section of the *PhG*. Cf. Chapter 6, Section 3.

Chapter 10. Hegel's idea

1. Hegel's account of the Notion is thus the final logical version of his theory of subjectivity, where subjectivity is understood as self-conscious thought, or reflection. Since, Hegel thinks he has shown, there cannot be any ground for such reflective activity in metaphysical substance (whether material or immaterial) or in "immediacy" (whether a Schellingean self-intuiting or a Kantian representation of the forms of immediacy), the central logical problem of reflection, presumably to be resolved in Book III, is the claim that determinate "moments" (Notions) of any such possible reflective activity can be reconstructed from a consideration of the necessary conditions for such a self-conscious judgment about determinate objects. The insufficiencies of various such possible Notions in the "Being Logic" and the "Essence Logic" thus introduce the problems of this book: an account of the teleology of this reconstruction, or what Hegel could mean by the "realization" of possible Notions *in* the Absolute Idea, and a final account of just what *reaching* this telos involves, what absolute reflection consists in. Cf. Düsing's useful account in (1986), 22–5. A more general statement of the problem of Book III, and of Hegel's project generally, can be found in Rosen (1974a). Cf. 233 and especially 239: "The Idea is the activity of forming 'things' (*res*), whether subjective or objective, and so it is the actuality (*energeia*) of what we ordinarily call the 'real world' (*realitas*)." The problem with this correct formulation of Hegel's position is what it means in the light of the idealist tradition and how it can be connected to the details of the text.
2. Sarlemijn is thus right to note that "All of Hegel's dialectic is teleological" (1971), 153, but the teleological explanation Hegel gives is, I have been arguing, logically

reconstructive; the telos is a kind of full self-consciousness about the conditions of one's claims to know (absolute reflection); and so, the dialectical "negation of finitude" that plays so large a metaphysical role in Sarlemijn's book is in reality a critical rejection of the possibility of empirical immediacy or metaphysical positivity, not the "vanishing" of finite particulars into the Absolute Subject. See n. 26, this chapter.

3. For the reasons one might attribute such a view to Hegel, and an attack on the philosophic consequences of such a view, see Becker (1969).
4. Henrich, in his (1982a) article, summarizes concisely the basic difficulty any reading of the *Logic* must face. See especially his remarks on 162, where he distinguishes between understanding Hegel's theory as an *Indikation des absoluten Prozesses* (what I am calling the metaphysical reading) and the *Konstruktion* of this *Prozess* (what I regard as an idealist reading). Henrich believes that the latter approach contradicts *Hegels Selbstverständnis*, and especially his monistic challenge to the traditional understanding of truth and thought, but I have tried to show that an idealist reading of Hegel's "mono-logic" does considerable justice to a wide variety of texts. (This article by Henrich is the best summary statement of the results of much of his work on Hegel's theoretical philosophy.)
5. Cf. Henrich (1971c), 98; Rohs (1969), 72.
6. I note that nothing in this view of Hegel's theory commits him to the claim that particularity as such is somehow determined by the Notion. On this view, only certain concepts are Notions in Hegel's technical sense, and their making possible the determinacy of particulars is their making possible the Notional determinacy of particulars. Such universals become "concrete" not by determining all their instances, whatever that could mean, but by being properly understood as required, presupposed, in any empirical determination of particularity. There is a valuable discussion of the concept–individual relation in Book III in Pinkard (1979), one that shows how Hegel's differences from traditional subject–predicate logic on just this issue make highly implausible the attribution to him of a traditional (individuals-as-bundles-of-concepts) idealism. See especially 222–3.
7. As noted frequently throughout, at the core of Hegel's attempt at a speculative logic is his account of the possibility of "thought's self-determination," the issue he most frequently discusses as the problem of "negation" or "thought's negativity." I have been suggesting that we understand this issue as part of an ideal attempt to reconstruct a "completely objective" ("Absolute") conceptual scheme without reliance on the instrumentalist or pragmatic strategies of most antirealisms and without Kant's use of pure intuitions. Within this project, I shall try to show, in Section 4 of this chapter, that Hegel understands thought's "negative relation to itself" (its dialectical self-negation and preservation) to be a result of an inadequate, and, in the reconstruction, progressively more adequate, "presentation" of the ideal status of these thought determinations. This will turn out to be a relatively minimalist reading of Hegel's theory and will include a denial that there is a unified theory of dialectical opposition in Hegel's Logic. (See esp. p. 253 and n. 26.)

   Such a project should, one last time, be compared with Theunissen's (1978b), who does try to construct a more ambitious theory of all dialectical opposition, one based everywhere on the opposition between the *Schein der Positivität* and the *Wahrheit des Negativen*, and so between *Kritik* and *Darstellung*. As noted earlier, Theunissen wants to identify Hegel's chief accomplishment as a critique of metaphysics. I have been suggesting that Hegel's post-Kantian strategies against empiricism, versions of naturalism, *and* traditional metaphysics should all be understood together as based on an idealist theory of thought's "autonomy." This difference is what leads to the differing accounts of negation (as stemming from the "thought's self-understanding" issue and not from a *chiffrierte politische Theorie* of communicative freedom). See 154ff. Theunissen recognizes the dimension I am stressing – see his remarks on *Negativität* as *Tätigkeit*, 173ff. – but without the history of idealism context, he can make no use of it. And without it, to succeed in his reconstruction, he is forced to account for much of the text in Book III as dependent on Hegel's "metaphysical" doctrine of God. Cf. 177ff. Cf. Rohs's discussion of Book III and the traditional Christian notion of God (1969), 31ff.

8. Cf. Rosen's (1974a) defense of Hegel from the Schellingean and Kierkegaardean charge that he attempted to "deduce" life from the Notion, 236, and his account of life as purposive and so self-conscious existence.
9. Cf. the accounts in Wohlfart (1981), 257–349; Lakebrink (1968), 382–524; and Trendelenburg (1964), 1–155.
10. Hegel again makes clear here, as he had throughout the *PhG*, his unique understanding of specificity and concreteness. A sensuous particular is an instance of *abstract universality*, a mere this, and is more and more concrete the more we are able to understand its Notionality, finally in terms of the "developed universality of the Notion." Cf. Pinkard's remarks on the differences between Hegel's position and the standard predication theory so compellingly criticized by Frege (1979), 222ff.
11. This emphasis on the centrality of judgment, together with Hegel's unusual denigration of the importance of "propositions," makes much more difficult an understanding of what Hegel elsewhere (in the Preface to the *PhG*) calls the "speculative proposition." A full interpretation of such an issue would have to involve an explanation of how Hegel understands a *Satz* to function as the "content" of the speculative identity asserted in a judgment. Although this would obviously be complicated, the passages discussed here already demonstrate that it is misleading to think that Hegel's account can be viewed as some sort of transcendental theory of language, and the conditions for understanding a *Satz*, as in Theunissen's account (1978b). The most one could say by analogy would be that Hegel is interested in the conditions, not for a *Satz* being a *Satz* but for a *Satz* being *asserted* as a cognitive claim, in the conditions of language use in acts of judgment. Wohlfart's study (1981), focused as it is on the specific problem of the "linguistic representation of the speculative," is a useful guide to the controversy.
12. One of the rare extended discussions of the nature of "Notional truth" and of the criteria for Notional conceptuality occurs in the Remark to section 24 in the *EL*. It is, however, a highly metaphorical and uneven discussion.
13. Theunissen (1978a), here as elsewhere much under the influence of Kahn's work on the Greek verb "to be," heavily stresses this Platonic element.
14. Stated extremely crudely, the grand Hegelian syllogism is thus: What there is in truth, a possible object of a cognitive judgment, can be such a possible object only if distinguishable according to the determinations of the interrelated logic of being and essence. The determinations of being and essence are themselves possible only as the result of the Notion's self-determination. Therefore what there is, a possible object of judgment, is itself a (Notional) result of such self-

determination. For indications of Hegel's speculative reading of syllogistic connections, see his Remark on "The Common View of the Syllogism," *WL*, II, 328; *SL*, 681; his account of the "disjunctive syllogism," *WL*, II, 349; *SL*, 701; and his later remarks in the "Absolute Idea" section, *WL*, II, 487ff.; *SL*, 827ff. Also helpful is Düsing's article (1986), 15–38.

15. The most important recent attempt to account for Hegel's systematic pretensions is Hösle's (1987) two-volume study.
16. *CJ*, 218–31; *AA*, vol. 5, 372–84.
17. *CJ*, 233; *AA*, vol. 5, 376.
18. Rosen (1974a) has mounted a compelling attack on Hegel's notion of Absolute Knowledge by focusing on the problem of intellectual intuition and on Hegel's rejection of that doctrine. See 266ff. The question I am raising is whether the text of Book III indicates that Hegel *wants* Absolute Knowledge to be understood as something like "the recollective comprehension of the moments of the Absolute formation process" of the whole, or whether his account is so metalogical, so concerned with the issue of establishing that there *is* such a formation process, that the "intuition criticism" cannot be said to concern Hegel's final resolution. Viewing the issue this way in a sense relocates the problem Rosen is raising to the "systematic" issue of the relation between Notional determinations and the specific sciences of Nature and Spirit. There, the problem of "seeing" the relation between the "method" and the moments of the whole is a serious though not necessarily fatal problem, as I shall argue later.
19. This emphasis on process and self-determination is precisely what is stressed in Hegel's initial discussion of the "immediate" idea – life. By life here, as in the *PhG*, Hegel means self-conscious, purposive life, although here he is interested in the concept of purposiveness rather than the experience of a living attempt at self-satisfaction. Throughout his account, he particularly stresses the "life process," the way in which the implicit Notionality of such self-direction "proceeds" to a greater explicitness and so greater actuality. Any self-directing being, in merely continuing and propagating his life, makes his own life an end self-consciously. He thus acts in terms of some Notion of life, a fact that quickly reveals both "life's" reliance on some knowledge of life, its true end, and the means to attain it. Or it reveals "the idea of cognition" and the purposiveness of cognition, or the reliance of all purposive inquiry on the "idea of the good."
20. And this is still more complex than stated because Hegel will also argue that any a priori attempt to determine whether a Notion is indeed a possible Notion, an attempt that will reveal the completion of that Notion in an other, is itself an extension or progression only because the original self-determining nature of Notionality is not fully understood, because some Notion is considered in the fixed and misleadingly isolated way characteristic, necessarily, of all reflective thought. This complicates even further the appropriation of the analytic/synthetic schema. Cf. Rosen (1974a), 244–8, on Hegel's "analysis of analysis," especially the comments on the relation between analysis and synthesis, 247.
21. This is all a "logically stated" version of an issue that arose in discussing Book II, that Hegel's speculative identity statements are "transcendental essence" claims, and that they "contain nonidentity," in this Book = "are synthetic." Cf. Belaval's discussion of identity and syntheticity (1970), 571ff.
22. In a recent article much influenced by the category–theory approach of Hartmann (and Hans Wagner), Bole (1987) also distinguishes the problem of con-

tradiction as it arises in Hegel's account of the "essentialities of reflection" and as it concerns Hegel's speculative system (as "determinate negation"). See especially his persuasive account of why Hegel is not "embracing" or celebrating contradiction in the former passages, 526 and 527. On the latter issue, I have the same problems with his version of an "intracategorial" reading of the *Logic* as with Hartmann's project. See n. 7, Chapter 8.

23. Cf. Lakebrink (1968), 1–39, 490–524.
24. Cf. Pinkard's (1979) account of the *Logic* as a systematic "redescription" of ordinary conceptual oppositions, all leading to a certain kind of compatibilist position. As noted in other remarks on such Hartmann-inspired positions, the project requires more of an account of the difference between conceptuality in general and "autonomous" Notions, a more thorough integration of the Fichtean elements of Hegel's theory of thought, and especially an encounter with the transcendental skepticism issue that claims for the "conceptuality of being" immediately raise, before such a promising proposal for a reconstruction can move on from its programmatic statements of intention.
25. Cf. the similar criticisms by Henrich (1971c, 1978c) (basically that the *Logic*'s justification of absolute reflection presupposes what it seeks to prove), and by Rosen (1974a), 273.
26. I can express this point about dialectic by agreeing with an insightful recent article by Taylor (1986). He too rejects any notion of a "dialectical science of reality," of nature itself, as well as of human life (as in Engels-influenced Marxism), but claims that we cannot dispense with the notion of a dialectical explanation. For him the key to such an explanation is the case for the indispensability of certain logical determinations, especially contradiction as a form of *self*-negation, in an account of goal-oriented individual and social activity. With such activities, we cannot simply offer "external" explanations of the body movements involved; understanding what the activity *is* essentially involves a consideration of the agent's (or group's) self-understanding, its "self-conceiving," if you will. Cf. 146–7. The activity is what it is only as so "taken," in the language used here. And in such situations, it is clearly possible that the agent has formulated contradictory goals, or goal–means relations, and that we cannot understand or explain his behavior unless we take account of such self-negation.

    As I have tried to show throughout, and especially in this category, I believe that this general argument is true not only of goal-oriented action but also of the teleological "practice" of *Erkennen*. The issue there too is not a "panlogicism" that attributes conceptual conflict to reality, but involves the self-negations involved in the *attempt* at "Notional determination," at the fully self-conscious articulation of the Notion. Although I also reject the idea of a dialectical science that can provide a universal explanation of the supposedly necessary resolutions of such self-negations, much of an assessment of Hegel on this issue comes down to the account he or anyone must give of the general "origin" or reasons for such self-negations (if there is one). The Marxist analog for such an origin (a putative human drive to produce efficiently, and so to sublate or determinately resolve such contradictions) may rely on a simplistic psychology (cf. 151), but in Hegel such an origin in the self-consciousness condition – and its violation in various ways – is not, I hope to have shown, so simplistic. This still means, as Taylor puts it, that we cannot have a complete picture of such a telos, that any self-negating part of the Text depends for its sense on a whole, or full Text that we never have (152), but the passages I am citing from Book III show how sensitive Hegel is to that point, that the telos he is describing, all he thinks he needs to make his extremely abstract point, is "textuality," not the text itself, to use the current jargon.

27. For a thorough study of the development and meaning of Hegel's notion of circularity, see the recent work by Rockmore (1986). Rockmore ends up (157–8) charging Hegel with much the same objection Hegel himself made against contemporary German philosophy in "Belief and Knowledge," but that is due, I believe, to an avoidance by Rockmore of the *PhG*'s argument in favor of a detailed account of such things as Hegel's early critique of Reinhold and his *Encyclopedia*.
28. Cf. Kimmerle's charge (1970) about the "closedness" of Hegel's view of "thought thinking itself," 35–8, 135–54, 292–5. This problem is a severe one in Kimmerle's account, given the extreme position he attributes to Hegel, one not supported, I believe, by the *SL*.
29. Kolb (1986) has recently proposed a "transcendental" reading of the *Logic* and has made some valuable suggestions about the relevance of Hegel's account of the "categories of modernity" and the post-Weberian "problem of modernity." For the most part, however, Kolb is interested in the Hegel–Heidegger contrast on the modernity issue (and not in a scholarly reconstruction of Hegel's texts), and so simply states a number of conclusions about what the *Logic* is or is not, without much attention to details or to alternative views. Although there is much of value in Kolb's approach, I am not sure Hegel can be of use in "overcoming modern formalism" unless the full dimensions of his account of self-consciousness as a condition of action as well as thought, and his claim about the inherent, rational teleology of such self-conscious action, are taken account of.

Bibliography

Adorno, T. (1963). *Drei Studien zu Hegel*. Frankfurt, Suhrkamp.

Albrecht, E. (1986). "Zu Fragen der methodologischen Funktion der Dialektik," in Henrich (1986), 154–63.

Allison, H. (1983). *Kant's Transcendental Idealism: An Interpretation and Defense*. New Haven, Conn., Yale University Press.

(1986). "Reflections on the B-Deduction," *The Southern Journal of Philosophy*, XXV, 1–15.

Ameriks, K. (1983). "Kant and Guyer on Apperception," *Archiv für die Geschichte der Philosophie*, 65, 174–86.

(1985). "Hegel's Critique of Kant's Theoretical Philosophy," *Philosophy and Phenomenological Research*, XLVI, 1–35.

(forthcoming). "Reinhold and the Short Argument to Idealism," *Proceedings of the Sixth International Kant Congress*.

Aquila, R. (1985). "Predication and Hegel's Metaphysics," in Inwood (1985), 67–84.

(1987). "Self-Consciousness, Self-Determination and Imagination in Kant," *Topoi*, 6, 63–77.

Aschenberg, R. (1976). "Der Wahrheitsbegriff in Hegels 'Phänomenologie des Geistes,' " in Hartmann (1976a), 211–304.

Baillie, J.B. (1984). *The Origin and Significance of Hegel's Logic*. New York, Garland.

Beck, L., ed. (1972). *Proceedings of the Third International Kant Congress*. Dordrecht, Reidel.

Becker, W. (1969). *Hegels Begriff der Dialektik und das Prinzip des Idealismus*. Stuttgart, Kohlhammer.

(1970). *Hegels Phänomenologie des Geistes. Eine Interpretation*. Stuttgart, Kohlhammer.

Belaval, Y. (1970). "La Doctrine de l'essence chez Hegel et chez Leibniz, I," *Archives de Philosophie*, 33, 579–604.

(1972). "La Doctrine de l'essence chez Hegel et chez Leibniz, II," *Kant-Studien*, 63, 436–62.

(1964). "La Doctrine de l'essence chez Hegel et chez Leibniz, III," *Studi Internazionali di Filosofia*, 108, 115–38.

(1978). "L'essence de la force dans la logique de Hegel," in Henrich (1978a), 329–39.

Bernstein, J. (1984a). "From Self-Consciousness to Community: Act and Recognition in the Master–Slave Relationship," in Pelczynski (1984), 14–39.

(1984b). *The Philosophy of the Novel: Lukacs, Marxism and the Dialectics of Form*. Minneapolis, University of Minnesota Press.

Beyer, W., ed. (1982). *Die Logik des Wissens und das Problem der Erziehung*. Hamburg, Felix Meiner.

Bird, G. (1987). "Hegel's Account of Kant's Epistemology in the *Lectures on the History of Philosophy*," in Priest (1987), 65–76.

Bole, T. (1974). "The Dialectic of Hegel's Logic as the Logic of Ontology," *Hegel-Jahrbuch*, 144–51.

(with J.M. Stevens) (1985). "Why Hegel at All?" *Philosophical Topics*, 13, 113–22.
(1987). "Contradiction in Hegel's *Science of Logic*," *Review of Metaphysics*, 40, 515–34.
Bonsiepen, W. (1977). "Phänomenologie des Geistes," in Pöggeler (1977), 59–74.
Breazeale, D. (1981). "Fichte's Aenesidemus Review and the Transformation of German Idealism," *Review of Metaphysics*, 34, 545–68.
Brockard, H. (1970). *Subjekt. Versuch zur Ontologie bei Hegel*. Munich, Pustet.
Bubner, R. (1974a). *Dialektik und Wissenschaft*. Frankfurt, Suhrkamp.
(1974b). "Dialektische Elemente einer Forschungslogik," in Bubner (1974a), 129–74.
(1974c). "Problemgeschichte und systematischer Sinn der 'Phänomenologie' Hegels," in Bubner (1974a), 9–43.
(1976). "Strukturprobleme dialektischer Logik," in Guzzoni et al. (1976), 36–52.
Buchdahl, G. (1984). "Conceptual Analysis and Scientific Theory in Hegel's Philosophy of Nature (with Special Reference to Hegel's Optics)," in Cohen and Wartofsky (1984), 13–36.
(1985). "Hegel's Philosophy of Nature and the Structure of Science," in Inwood (1985), 110–36.
Burbidge, J. (1981). *On Hegel's Logic. Fragments of a Commentary*. Atlantic Highlands, N.J., Humanities Press.
Butler, J.P. (1987). *Subjects of Desire: Hegelian Reflections in Twentieth Century France*. New York, Columbia University Press.
Butts, R., ed. (1986). *Kant's Philosophy of Physical Science*. Dordrecht, Reidel.
Claesges, U. (1974). *Geschichte des Selbstbewusstseins. Der Ursprung des spekulativen Problems in Fichtes Wissenschaftslehre von 1794–95*. The Hague, Nijhoff.
(1981). *Darstellung des erscheinenden Wissens. Systematische Einleitung in Hegels Phänomenologie des Geistes*. Bonn, Bouvier.
Cohen, R. and Wartofsky, M., eds. (1984). *Hegel and the Sciences*. Dordrecht, Reidel.
Cramer, K. (1974). "Erlebnis: These zu Hegels Theorie des Selbstbewusstseins mit Rucksicht auf die Aporien eines Grundbegriffs nachhegelscher Philosophie," *Hegel-Studien*, Beiheft 11, 537–603.
(1976). "Bemerkungen zu Hegels Begriff vom Bewusstsein," in Guzzoni et al. (1976), 75–100.
(1979) "Bewusstsein und Selbstbewusstsein," in Henrich (1979), 215–26.
(1983). "Kant oder Hegel – Entwurf einer Alternative," in Henrich (1983), 140–48.
Deleuze, G. (1962). *Nietzsche et la Philosophie*. Paris, P.U.F.
Derrida, J. (1978a). "From Restricted to General Economy: A Hegelianism without Reserve," in Derrida (1978c), 251–77.
(1978b). "Speech and Writing According to Hegel," *Man and World*, 11, 107–30.
(1978c). *Writing and Difference*, trans. A. Bass. Chicago, University of Chicago Press.
(1982a). *Margins of Philosophy*, trans. A. Bass. Chicago, University of Chicago Press.
(1982b). "The Pit and the Pyramid: An Introduction to Hegel's Semiology," in Derrida (1982c).
Dove, K.R. (1971). "Hegel's Phenomenological Method," in Steinkraus (1971), 34–56.
Düsing, K. (1969). "Spekulation und Reflexion. Zur Zusammenarbeit Schellings und Hegels in Jena," *Hegel-Studien*, V, 95–128.
(1976). *Das Problem der Subjektivität in Hegels Logik*. Bonn, Bouvier.
(1979). "Hegels Begriff der Subjektivität in der Logik und in der Philosophie des subjektiven Geistes," in Henrich (1979), 201–14.
(1983). "Constitution and Structure of Self-Identity: Kant's Theory of Apperception and Hegel's Criticism," *Midwest Studies*, VIII, 409–31.
(1986). "Syllogistik und Dialektik in Hegels spekulative Logik," in Henrich (1986), 15–38.

Engelhardt, P., ed. (1963). *Sein und Ethos. Untersuchungen zur Grundlegung der Ethik*. Mainz, Matthias-Grünewald.
Fackenhein, E. (1967). *The Religous Dimension in Hegel's Thought*. Chicago, University of Chicago Press.
Fahrenbach, H., ed. (1973). *Wirklichkeit und Reflexion*. Pfullingen, Neske.
Findlay, J. (1958). *Hegel: A Re-examination*. London, George Allen & Unwin.
(1974). "Reflexive Asymmentry: Hegel's Most Fundamental Methodological Ruse," in Weiss (1974), 154–73.
(1976). "The Contemporary Relevance of Hegel," in MacIntyre (1976), 1–20.
(1979). "Hegel's Conception of Subjectivity," in Henrich (1979), 13–26.
Flach, W. (1959). *Negation und Andersheit*. Munich, E. Reinhardt.
(1964). "Hegels dialektische Methode," *Hegel-Studien*, Beiheft 1, 1964.
Flay, J. (1984). *Hegel's Quest for Certainty*. Albany, SUNY Press.
Fleischmann, E. (1965). "Hegels Umgestaltung der kantischen Logik," *Hegel-Studien*, Beiheft 3, 181–208.
Fulda, H. (1965). *Das Problem einer Einleitung in Hegels Wissenschaft der Logik*. Frankfurt, Klostermann.
(1966). "Zur Logik der Phänomenologie des Geistes von 1807," in Gadamer (1966), 75–101.
(1968). *Das Recht der Philosophie in Hegels Philosophie des Rechts*. Frankfurt, Klostermann.
(1978a). "Hegels Dialektik als Begriffsbewegung und Darstellungsweise," in Horstmann (1978), 124–75.
(1978b). "Unzulängliche Bemerkungen zur Dialektik," in Horstmann (1978), 33–69.
(with R.-P. Horstmann and M. Theunissen) (1980). *Kritische Darstellung der Metaphysik. Eine Diskussion der Hegels Logik*. Frankfurt, Suhrkamp.
(1986). "Dialektik in Konfrontation mit Hegel," in Henrich (1986), 328–49.
(1973). *Materialen zu Hegels "Phänomenologie des Geistes."* Frankfurt, Suhrkamp.
Gadamer, H.-G., ed. (1966). *Beiträge zur Deutung der Phänomenologie des Geistes. Hegel-Studien*, Beiheft 3,
(1976a). *Hegel's Dialectic. Five Hermeneutical Studies*, trans. Christopher Smith. New Haven, Conn., Yale University Press.
(1976b). "Hegel's Dialectic of Self-Consciousness," in Gadamer (1976a), 54–74.
(1976c). "Hegel's 'Inverted World'," in Gadamer (1976a), 35–53.
(1976d). "The Idea of Hegel's Logic," in Gadamer (1976a), 75–99.
Girndt, H. (1965). *Die Differenz des Fichteschen und Hegelschen Systems in der Hegeleschen "Differenzschrift."* Bonn, Bouvier.
Görland, I. (1966). *Die Kant Kritik des jungen Hegel*. Frankfurt, Klostermann.
Guyer, P. (1979). "Hegel, Leibniz and the Contradiction in the Finite," *Philosophy and Phenomenological Research*, 40, 75–98.
(1980). "Kant on Apperception and a Priori Synthesis," *American Philosophical Quarterly*, 17, 205–12.
(1986). "Dialektik als Methodologie: Antwort auf. E. Albrecht," in Henrich (1986), 164–77.
Guzzoni, U., Rang, B., and Siep, L. (1976). *Der Idealismus und seine Gegenwart*. Hamburg, Felix Meiner.
Habermas, J. (1971). *Knowledge and Human Interests*, trans. J. Shapiro. Boston, Beacon Press.
(1973a). *Theory and Practice*, trans. John Viertel. Boston, Beacon Press.
(1973b). "Labor and Interaction: Remarks on Hegel's Jena *Philosophy of Mind*," in Habermas (1973a), 142–69.

(1987). *The Philosophical Discourse of Modernity: Twelve Lectures*, trans. Frederick Lawrence. Cambridge, Mass., MIT Press.

Harlander, K. (1969). *Absolute Subjektivität und kategoriale Anschauung. Eine Untersuchung der Systemstruktur bei Hegel*. Meisenheim an Glan, Hain.

Harris, H.S. (1972). *Hegel's Development: Toward the Sunlight, 1770–1801*. Oxford, Clarendon Press.

(1980). "The Concept of Recognition in Hegel's Jena Manuscripts," *Hegel-Studien*, Beiheft 20, 229–48.

(1981). "Religion as the Mythology of Reason," *Thought*, 56, 301–15.

(1983). *Hegel's Development: Night Thoughts (Jena 1801–1806)*. Oxford, Clarendon Press.

Hartmann, K. (1966). "On Taking the Transcendental Turn," *Review of Metaphysics*, 20, 223–49.

(1972). "The 'Analogies' and After," in Beck (1972), 47–62.

(1973) "Zur neuesten Dialektik-Kritik," *Archiv für die Geschichte der Philosophie*, 55, 220–42.

(1976a). "Die Ontologische Option," in Hartmann (1976b), 1–30.

(1976b). *Die ontologische Option. Studien zu Hegels Propädeutik, Schellings Hegel-Kritik und Hegels Phänomenologie des Geistes*. Berlin, de Gruyter.

(1976c). "Hegel: A Non-Metaphysical View," in MacIntyre (1976), 101–24.

Heidegger, M. (1962). *Being and Time*, trans. John Macquarrie and Edward Robinson. New York, Harper & Row.

(1970). *Hegel's Concept of Experience*. New York, Harper & Row.

Heinrichs, J. (1974). *Die Logik der Phänomenologie des Geistes*. Bonn, Bouvier.

Henrich, D. (1963). "Das Problem der Gundlegung der Ethik bei Kant und im spekulativen Idealismus," in Engelhardt (1963), 350–86.

(with Hans Wagner) (1966a). *Subjektivität und Metaphysik*. Frankfurt, Klostermann.

(1966b). "Fichtes ursprüngliche Einsicht," in Henrich (1966a), 188–232.

(1969). "The Proof Structure of Kant's Transcendental Deduction," *Review of Metaphysics*, 88, 640–59.

(1971a). *Hegel im Kontext*. Frankfurt, Suhrkamp.

(1971b). "Anfang und Methode der Logik," in Henrich (1971a), 73–94.

(1971c). "Hegels Logik der Reflexion," in Henrich (1971a), 95–156.

(1971d). "Hegel's Theorie über den Zufall," in Henrich (1971a), 157–86.

(1971e). "Hegel und Hölderlin," in Henrich (1971a), 9–40.

(1976a). "Hegels Grundoperation," in Guzzoni (1976), 208–30.

(1976b). *Identatät und Objektivität*. Heidelberg, Carl Winter.

(1978a). *Die Wissenschaft der Logik und die Logik der Reflexion*. Bonn, Bouvier.

(1978b). "Formen der Negation in Hegels Logik," in Horstmann (1978), 213–29.

(1978c). "Hegels Logik der Reflexion. Neue Fassung," in Henrich (1978a), 203–324.

(1979). *Hegels Philosophische Psychologie*. Bonn, Bouvier.

(1980). "Absoluter Geist und Logik des Endlichen," *Hegel-Studien*, Beiheft 20, 103–18.

(1982a). "Die Formationsbedingungen der Dialektik. Ueber die Untrennbarkeit der Methode Hegels von Hegels System," *Revue International de Philosophie*, 36, 139–62.

(1982b). *Fluchtlinien*. Frankfurt, Suhrkamp.

(1982c). "Selbstbewusstsein und spekulatives Denken," in Henrich (1982b), 125–81.

(1982d). *Selbstverhältnisse. Gedanken und Auslegungen zu den Grundlagen der klassischen deutschen Philosophie*. Stuttgart, Philipp Reclam.

(1983). *Kant oder Hegel: Ueber Formen der Begründung in der Philosophie*. Stuttgart, Klett-Cotta.

(1986). *Hegels Wissenschaft der Logik: Formation und Rekonstruktion*. Stuttgart, Klett-Cotta.

Herder, J. (1967). *Sämtliche Werke*, ed. B. Suphan. Hildesheim, Olms.

Hoppe, H.-G. (1983). *Synthesis bei Kant. Das Problem der Verbindung von Vorstellungen und ihrer Gegenstandbeziehung in der "Kritik der reinen Vernunft."* Berlin, de Gruyter.

Horstmann, R.-P. (1972). "Probleme der Wandlung in Hegels Jenaer Systemkonzeption," *Philosophischer Rundschau*, xix, 87–118. (Review of Kimmerle, 1970.)

(1977). "Jenaer Systemkonzeptionen," in Pöggeler (1977), 43–58.

(1978). *Seminar: Dialektik in der Philosophie Hegels*. Frankfurt, Suhrkamp.

(1980). "Uber das Verhältnis von Metaphysik der Subjektivität und Philosophie der Subjektivität in Hegels Jenaer Schriften," *Hegel-Studien*, Beiheft 20, 181–95.

(1982). "Preface," G.W.F. Hegel, *Jenaer Systementwürfe*. Hamburg, Felix Meiner.

(1984). *Ontologie und Relationen. Hegel, Bradley, Russell und die Kontroverse über interne und externe Beziehungen*. Königstein/Ts, Athenaum.

Hösle, V. (1987). *Hegels System. Der Idealismus der Subjektivität und das Problem der Intersubjektivität. Band 1: Systememtwicklung und Logik*. Hamburg, Felix Meiner.

Hossenfelder, M. (1978). *Kants Konstitutionslehre und die transzendentale Deduktion*. Berlin, de Gruyter.

Houlgate, S. (1986). *Hegel, Nietzsche and the Criticism of Metaphysics*. Cambridge, Cambridge University Press.

Hume, D. (1967). *A Treatise of Human Nature*, ed. L.A. Selby-Bigge. Oxford, Clarendon Press.

Hyppolite, J. (1974). *Genesis and Structure of Hegel's Phenomenology of Spirit*, trans. S. Cherniak and J. Heckman. Evanston, Ill., Northwestern University Press.

Inwood, M. (1983). *Hegel*. London, Routledge & Kegan Paul.

(1985). *Hegel*. Oxford, Oxford University Press.

Janke, W. (1970). *Fichte. Sein und Relexion: Grunlage der kritischen Vernunft*. Berlin, de Gruyter.

Kelly, G. (1978a). *Hegel's Retreat from Eleusis*. Princeton, N.J., Princeton University Press.

(1978b). "Hegel's 'Lordship and Bondage'," in Kelly (1978a), 29–54.

Kimmerle, G. (1978). *Sein und Selbst. Untersuchung zur kategorialen Einheit von Vernunft und Geist in Hegels "Phänomenologie des Geistes."* Bonn, Bouvier.

Kimmerle, H. (1969). "Zur Entwicklung des Hegelschen Denkens in Jena," *Hegel-Studien*, Beineft 4, 33–47.

(1970). *Das Problem der Abgeschlossenheit des Denkens. Hegels System der Philosophie in den Jahren 1800–04*. Bonn, Bouvier.

(1982). "Hegels *Wissenschaft der Logik* als Grundlegung seines Systems der Philosophie. Ueber das Verhältnis von *Logic* und *Realphilosophie*," in Beyer (1982), 52–60.

Kitcher, P. (1981). "How Kant Almost Wrote 'Two Dogmas of Empiricism' (and Why He Didn't)," *Philosophical Topics*, 12, 217–49.

(1986). "Projecting the Order of Nature," in Butts (1986), 201–35.

Kojeve, A. (1960). *Introduction to the Reading of Hegel*, trans. J.H. Nichols, Jr. New York, Basic Books.

Kolb, D. (1986). *The Critique of Pure Modernity*. Chicago, University of Chicago Press.

Kopper, J. (1967). "Reflexion und Identität in der Hegelschen Philosophie," *Kant-Studien*, 58, 33–53.

Kortian, G. (1980). *Metacritique. The Philosophical Argument of Jürgen Habermas*, trans. J. Raffan. Cambridge, Cambridge University Press.

Kroner, R. (1961). *Von Kant bis Hegel*. 2 vols. Tübingen, Mohr.

Kupperman, J. (1975). "Realism vs. Idealism," *American Philosophical Quarterly*, 12, 199–210.
Labarriere, P.-J. (1968). *Structures et Mouvement Dialectique dans la Phenomenologie de l'Espirit de Hegel.* Paris, Aubier-Montaigne.
Lakebrink, B. (1968). *Die Europäische Idee der Freiheit. 1. Teil. Hegels Logik und die Tradition der Selbstbestimmung.* Leiden, Brill.
Lamb, D. (1980). *Hegel: From Foundation to System.* The Hague, Nijhoff.
Lauth, R. (1963). "Die Bedeutung der Fichteschen Philosophie für die Gegenwart," *Philosophisches Jahrbuch*, 70, 252–70.
Lear, J. (1982). "Leaving the World Alone," *Journal of Philosophy*, LXXIX, 382–403.
(1984). "The Disappearing 'We'," *Proceedings of the Aristotelian Society*, Supplementary Volume LVIII, 219–42.
Löwith, K. (1967). *From Hegel to Nietzsche.* New York, Doubleday.
Lukacs, G. (1971). *History and Class Consciousness*, trans. R. Livingstone. London, Merlin Press.
(1975). *The Young Hegel*, trans. R. Livingstone. London, Merlin Press.
MacIntyre, A., ed. (1976). *Hegel: A Collection of Critical Essays.* Notre Dame, Notre Dame Press.
McTaggart, J. (1910). *A Commentary on Hegel's Logic.* Cambridge, Cambridge University Press.
Maker, W. (1981a). "Hegel's *Phenomenology* as Introduction to Science," *Clio*, 10, 382–97.
(1981b). "Understanding Hegel Today," *Journal of the History of Philosophy*, 19, 343–75.
Marcuse, H. (1960). *Reason and Revolution. Hegel and the Rise of Social Theory.* New York, Beacon Press.
(1987). *Hegel's Ontology and the Theory of Historicity*, trans. Seyla Benhabib. Cambridge, Mass., MIT Press.
Marx, W. (1975). *Hegel's Phenomenology of Spirit: Its Point and Purpose – A Commentary on the Preface and Introduction.* New York, Harper & Row.
Negt, O., ed. (1971). *Aktualität und Folgen der Philosophie Hegels.* Frankfurt, Suhrkamp.
Ogilvy, J. (1975). "Reflections on the Absolute," *Review of Metaphysics*, 28, 520–46.
Pelczynski, Z. (1984). *The State and Civil Society: Studies in Hegel's Political Philosophy.* Cambridge, Cambridge University Press.
Petry, M.J. (1981) "Introduction" to *G.W.F. Hegel: The Berlin Phenomenology (BPhG* in primary text list). Dordrecht, Reidel, xiii–cx.
Pinkard, T. (1979). "Hegel's Idealism and Hegel's Logic," *Zeitschrift für philosophische Forschung*, 23, 210–25.
(1981). "Hegel's Philosophy of Mathematics," *Philosophy and Phenomenological Research*, 41, 452–64.
(1985). "The Logic of Hegel's Logic," in Inwood (1985), 85–109.
Pippin, R. (1975). "Hegel's Phenomenological Criticism," *Man and World*, 8, 296–314.
(1978). "Hegel's Metaphysics and the Problem of Contradiction," *Journal of the History of Philosophy*, 16, 301–12.
(1979). "The Rose and the Owl: Some Remarks on the Theory–Practice Problem in Hegel," *Independent Journal of Philosophy*, 3, 7–16.
(1981). "Hegel's Political Argument and the Problem of *Verwirklichung*," *Political Theory*, 9, 509–32.
(1982). *Kant's Theory of Form.* New Haven, Conn., Yale University Press.
(1985). "Marcuse on Hegel and Historicity," *Philosophical Forum*, 25, 181–206.
(1986). "Kant's Transcendental Idealism, By Henry E. Allison" (review), *Kant-Studien*, 77, 365–71.

(1987a). "Kant on the Spontaneity of Mind," *Canadian Journal of Philosophy*, 17, 449–76.
(1987b). "The Philosophy of F.J. Schelling, by Werner Marx" (review), *The Philosophical Review*, 96, 620–3.
(forthcoming a). "The Idealism of Transcendental Arguments," *Idealistic Studies*.
(forthcoming b). "Traditional and Analytic Philosophy, by Ernst Tugendhat," a review, *Independent Journal for Philosophy*.
(forthcoming c). "Hösle, System, and Subject," *The Bulletin of the Hegel Society of Great Britain*.
Plant, R. (1973). *Hegel*. Bloomington, Indiana University Press.
Pöggeler, O. (1966). "Die Komposition der Phänomenologie des Geistes," in Gadamer (1966), 27–74.
(1973a). *Hegels Idee einer Phänomenologie des Geistes*. Freiburg/Munich, Karl Alber.
(1973b). "Hegels Jenaer Systemkonzeption," in Pöggeler (1973a), 110–69.
(1973c). "Hegels Phänomenologie des Selbstbewusstseins," in Pöggeler (1973a), 231–98.
(1973d). "Zur Deutung der Phänomenologie des Geistes," in Pöggeler (1973a), 170–230.
(1977) *Hegel*. Freiburg/Munich, Karl Alber.
Pothast, U. (1971). *Ueber einige Fragen der Selbtsbeziehungen*. Frankfurt, Klostermann.
Priest, S., ed. (1987). *Hegel's Critique of Kant*. Oxford, Clarendon Press.
Puntel, L. (1973). *Darstellung, Methode und Struktur. Untersuchungen zur Einheit der systematischen Philosophie G.W.F. Hegels*. Bonn, Bouvier.
(1982). "Was ist 'logisch' in Hegels *Wissenschaft der Logik*?" in Beyer (1982), 40–51.
(1983). "Transzendentaler und absoluter Idealismus," in Henrich (1983), 198–229.
Purpus, W. (1904–05). *Die Dialektik der sinnlichen Gewissheit bei Hegel, dargestellt in ihrem Zusammenhang mit der Logik und die antike Dialektic*. Nuremberg, Sebald.
(1908). *Zur Dialektik des Bewusstseins nach Hegel*. Berlin, Trowitzsch.
Rickert. H. (1911–12). "Das Eine, die Einheit und die Eins. Bemerkungen zur Logik des Zahlbegriffs," *Logos*, 2, 26–78.
Rockmore, T. (1986). *Hegel's Circular Epistemology*. Bloomington, Indiana University Press.
Rohs, P. (1969). *Form und Grund. Interpretation eines Kapitels der Hegelschen Wissenschaft der Logik*. Bonn, Bouvier.
(1978). "Der Grund der Bewegung des Begriffs," in Henrich (1978a), 43–62.
Rorty, R. (1972). "The World Well Lost," *Journal of Philosophy*, LXIX, 649–65.
Rose, G. (1981). *Hegel Contra Sociology*. London, Athlone.
Rosen, M. (1982). *Hegel's Dialectic and Its Criticism*. Cambridge, Cambridge University Press.
Rosen, S. (1973). "Sophrosyne and Selbstbewusstsein," *Review of Metaphysics*, 26, 617–42.
(1974a) *G.W.F. Hegel: An Introduction to the Science of Wisdom*. New Haven, Conn., Yale University Press.
(1974b). "Self-Consciousness and Self-Knowledge: The Relation between Plato and Hegel," *Hegel-Studien*, 9, 109–29.
(1987). *Hermeneutics as Politics*. New York, Oxford University Press.
Rosenkranz, K. (1963). *Hegels Leben*. Darmstadt, Wissenschaftliche Buchgesellschaft.
Sarlemijn, A. (1971). *Hegel's Dialectic*, trans. P. Kirschenmann. Dordrecht, Reidel.
Schmidt, F.W. (1971). "Hegel in der kritischen Theorie der 'Frankfurter Schule'," in Negt (1971), 21–61.
Schulz, W. (1975). *Die Vollendung des Deutschen Idealismus in der Spätphilosophie Schellings*. Pfullingen, Neske.
Schulz-Seitz, R.-E. (1973). " 'Sein' in Hegels Logik: 'Einfache Beziehung auf sich'," in Fahrenbach (1973), 365–84.
Seebohm, T. (1974). "Das Widerspruchprinzip in der Kantischen Logik und der Hegelschen Dialektik," *Akten des 4. internationalen Kant-Kongresses*, II, 2.

(1976). "The Grammar of Hegel's Dialectic," *Hegel-Studien*, Beiheft, 11, 149–80.
Siep, L. (1970). *Hegels Fichtekritik und die Wissenschaftslehre von 1804*. Freiburg/Munich, Karl Alber.
(1974a). "Der Kampf um Anerkennung. Zu Hegels Auseinandersetzung mit Hobbes in den Jenaer Schriften," *Hegel-Studien*, 9, 155–207.
(1974b). "Zur Dialektik der Anerkennung bei Hegel," *Hegel-Jahrbuch*, 388–95.
(1979). *Anerkennung als Prinzip der praktischen Philosophie. Untersuchungen zu Hegels Jenaer Philosophie des Geistes*. Freiburg/Munich, Karl Alber.
(1981). "Kehraus mit Hegel? Zu Ernst Tugendhats Hegel Kritik," *Zeitschrift für philosophische Forschung*, 35, 518–31.
Smart, J. (1986). "Realism v. Idealism," *Philosophy*, 61, 295–312.
Smith, J. (1973). "Hegel's Critique of Kant," *Review of Metaphysics*, 26, 438–60.
Soll, I. (1969). *An Introduction to Hegel's Metaphysics*. Chicago, University of Chicago Press.
(1985). "Charles Taylor's *Hegel*," in Inwood (1985), 54–66.
Solomon, R. (1983). *In the Spirit of Hegel*. Oxford, Oxford University Press.
Steinkraus, W. (1971). *New Studies in Hegel's Philosophy*. New York, Holt, Rinehart & Winston.
Strauss, L. (1963). *The Political Philosophy of Hobbes. Its Basis and Genesis*, trans. Else M. Sinclair. Chicago, University of Chicago Press.
Stroud, B. (1977). *Hume*. London, Routledge & Kegan Paul.
(1984). *The Significance of Philosophical Skepticism*. Oxford, Clarendon Press.
Sturma, D. (1985). *Kant über Selbstbewusstsein*. Hildeshein, Georg Olms.
Sussman, H. (1982). *The Hegelian Aftermath: Readings in Hegel, Kierkegaard, Freud, Proust, and James*. Baltimore, Johns Hopkins University Press.
Taylor, C. (1975). *Hegel*. Cambridge, Cambridge University Press.
(1976). "The Opening Arguments of the Phenomenology," in MacIntyre (1976), 151–87.
(1986). "Dialektik heute, oder: Strukturen der Selbstnegation," in Henrich (1986), 141–53.
Theunissen, M. (1978a). "Begriff und Realität. Aufhebung des metaphysischen Wahrheitsbegriff," in Horstmann (1978), 324–59.
(1978b). *Sein und Schein. Die kritische Funktion der Hegelschen Logik*. Frankfurt, Suhrkamp.
Trendelenburg, A. (1964). *Logische Untersuchungen*. Hildesheim, Olms.
Tugendhat, E. (1979). *Selbstbewusstsein und Selbstbestimmung: Sprachanalytische Interpretation*. Frankfurt, Suhrkamp.
(1982). *Traditional and Analytic Philosophy. Lectures on the Philosophy of Language*, trans. P.A. Gorner. Cambridge, Cambridge University Press.
Vesey, G., ed. (1982). *Idealism Past and Present*. Cambridge, Cambridge University Press.
Wahl, J. (1951). *La malheur de la conscience das la philosophie de Hegel*. Paris, P.U.F.
Walsh, W. (1946). "Hegel and Intellectual Intuition," *Mind*, LV, 49–63.
(1982). "Kant as Seen by Hegel," in Vesey (1982), 93–109.
(1983). "Subjective and Objective Idealism," in Henrich (1983), 83–98.
(1987). "The Idea of a Critique of Pure Reason: Kant and Hegel," in Priest (1987), 119–34.
Weiss, F., ed. (1974). *Beyond Epistemology. New Studies in the Philosophy of Hegel*. The Hague, Nijhoff.
Westphal, M. (1978). *History and Truth in Hegel's Phenomenology*. Atlantic Highlands, N.J., Humanities Press.
Wetzel, M. (1971). *Reflexion und Bestimmtheit in Hegels Wissenschaft der Logik*. Hamburg, Fundament-Verlag Dr. Sasse.
White, A. (1983a). *Absolute Knowledge. Hegel and the Problem of Metaphysics*. Athens, Ohio University Press.

(1983b). *Schelling. An Introduction to the System of Freedom.* New Haven, Conn., Yale University Press.

Wiehl, R. (1965). "Platos Ontologie in Hegels Logik des Seins," *Hegel-Studien*, 3, 157–80.

(1966). "Uber den Sinn der sinnlichen Gewissheit in Hegels Phänomenologie des Geistes," *Hegel-Studien*, Beiheft 3, 103–34.

(1986). "Das Gesetz als Kategorie in Hegels Philosophie des Geistes," in Henrich (1986), 291–319.

Wildt, A. (1982). *Autonomie und Anerkennung. Hegels Moralitätskritik im Lichte seiner Fichte-Rezeption.* Stuttgart, Klett-Cotta.

Winterhager, E. (1979). *Selbstbewusstsein: Eine Theorie zwischen Kant und Hegel.* Bonn, Bouvier.

Wohlfart, G. (1981). *Der spekulative Satz: Bemerkungen zum Begriff der Spekulation bei Hegel.* Berlin, de Gruyter.

Index

INDEX

Printed in the United Kingdom
by Lightning Source UK Ltd.
895